Economic
Value Management

T0271361

John Wiley & Sons

Founded in 1807, John Wiley & Sons is the oldest independent publishing company in the United States. With offices in North America, Europe, Australia, and Asia, Wiley is globally committed to developing and marketing print and electronic products and services for our customers' professional and personal knowledge and understanding.

The Wiley Finance series contains books written specifically for finance and investment professionals as well as sophisticated individual investors and their financial advisors. Book topics range from portfolio management to e-commerce, risk management, financial engineering, valuation and financial instrument analysis, as well as much more.

For a list of available titles, please visit our Web site at *www.WileyFinance.com*.

Additional Praise for
Economic Value Management

"In a era when EPS has been redefined as 'expecting prison sentence,' Eleanor Bloxham's call for back-to-value-basics is a breath of fresh air. Any CEO, director, or investor who wants to get a handle on the real numbers that show how companies perform should grab a hold of Economic Value Management. Viva EVM!"

—Patrick McGurn, Vice President & Special Counsel, Institutional Shareholder Services

"Bloxham has a clear, common-sense, practical approach that provides welcome guidance to managers and directors on how to measure, create, and reward value. She avoids the usual jargon with sharply drawn examples and illuminating illustrations and the result is well worth reading."

—Nell Minow, Editor, *The Corporate Library,* and co-author of several books including *Corporate Governance* and *Watching the Watchers*

"The word 'book' means many things ranging from any written communication that is securely bound, to the "total available knowledge and experience that can be brought to bear on a task or problem" (Webster's Ninth Collegiate). Eleanor Bloxham's Economic Value Management *fills the latter bill. The author has given her 'all'—rigorous scholarship, systematic thinking, and first-hand cases and the result is an authoritative guide for corporate leaders who want to break out of financial ratio boxes to build sustainable value."

—Alexandra R. Lajoux, Editor in Chief of *Director's Monthly* and co-author (with J. Fred Weston) of *The Art of M&A: Financing and Refinancing*

Economic Value Management

Applications and Techniques

ELEANOR BLOXHAM

John Wiley & Sons, Inc.

Library of Congress Cataloging-in-Publication Data:

Bloxham, Eleanor.
    Economic value management : applications and techniques /
Eleanor Bloxham.
        p. cm.
    Published simultaneously in Canada.
    Includes bibliographical references and index.
    ISBN 0-471-35426-0 (cloth : alk. paper)
    1. Economic value added—Management. I. Title.
HG4028.V3 B484 2003
658.15—dc21   2002011154

contents

list of exhibits

CHAPTER 6

CHAPTER 7

CHAPTER 8

CHAPTER 9

CHAPTER 10

acknowledgments

In writing this book, I am indebted to many people. First and foremost, I am indebted to my husband, Robert, who was my chief companion in this enterprise, my typist, and my skillful editor.

Writing a book for John Wiley and Sons is truly a pleasure. I am deeply grateful to John DeRemigis who read my proposal and gave me the opportunity to write this book. I am very appreciative of Sheck Cho who provided patient support and encouragement throughout the process, guiding it to a smooth conclusion. I am grateful to Stacey Rympa for all her help in review of the entire manuscript and for her many beneficial and supportive comments. I am also appreciative of the contributions of Louise Jacob in taking the manuscript and moving it through production.

I am deeply grateful to my brother, Robert Earle, for his review of the manuscript, his insightful comments and suggestions, and his acting as a sounding board when we were in the last throes of completing the work. I am also appreciative of the review and very useful suggestions provided by my father, John Earle. I thank my parents, Eleanor and John Earle, and my brothers, John and Robert Earle, for their ongoing support and encouragement.

This book includes specific references to people to whom I am indebted for helping me to develop and grow my understanding of these topics. In addition, there have been many colleagues and mentors who have helped shape my thinking and have been of great encouragement to me. I thank them for their wisdom and their support.

I am deeply appreciative of all the people, experiences, books, and conversations that have been a part of my life and that have encouraged me to dig and raise the bus shades to look outside.

Above all, I offer my humble thanks and praise to the Creator.

Eleanor Bloxham
ebloxham@thevaluealliance.com
May 2002

foreword

Given the current economic climate and recent accounting scandals impacting major U.S. corporations, this book, *Economic Value Management*, should be required reading for members of the board of directors of every U.S. corporation, especially for members who serve on audit committees.

In addition, the board of directors should mandate that all senior managers and line managers not only read and study the publication but be prepared to provide a report for the board of directors on how their individual company measures up with respect to the recommendations, applications, and techniques contained in *Economic Value Management*.

The board and management can do no more—no less if they want to build a bridge of trust between management, board, shareholders, and stakeholders, and establish their credibility in the capital and world markets.

John M. Nash
President Emeritus, National
  Association of Corporate Directors
Former Vice Chairman,
  Center for Board Leadership
Principal, Board Governance Advisors

introduction

"**H**ow do I become rich?" J. Paul Getty was once asked. His famous reply? "Rise early, work hard, strike oil." Most of us can relate to the rise early and working hard part. What about striking oil? To strike oil, one must dig deep and dig in many places. One must use the intelligence one gathers in the digging process to determine where to drill next. Organizations must do this, and individuals must do this. They must dig inside themselves to find the treasures that are buried there, and they must be open to the new insights they discover. If there is no oil in Smithtown, even if that is where they thought it would be, they must let go and move on. These truths apply to CEOs and executive management teams, to boards that monitor their work, and to all constituents (employees, suppliers, customers, investors, lenders, and you and me).

In the long run, there is no substitute for digging—although it may mean working very hard. As accounting is under increasing fire and fixes are made, investors, to do well over the long run, must dig deep and dig intelligently in many places. Lenders must do it. Suppliers choosing their customers must do the same. Customers who care about who their suppliers are must do it. Similarly, employees in choosing their employers must dig deeply. Regulators, analysts, and other critics are recognized to have those responsibilities.

The advice of J. Paul Getty is written across the pages of this book. It is a book that encourages stewardship and care, courage and leadership by all constituents.

Rise early, work hard, dig deep, and dig intelligently in many places. The result will be striking oil—new insights, innovation, and creativity and the ability to execute based on superior information.

This book is about where to dig and how to dig. It is about the roles of you, me, and everyone. And when oil is struck it is a result of a shared effort, the bounty of which belongs to all of the participants.

My early working career included, among other things, exposure to and work on major technology systems, reengineering efforts, budgets, marketing, underwriting processes, research for legislative lobbying efforts on the Hill, community and social responsiveness, strategic planning, activity based costing, and training executives to use personal computers. I was fortunate. This eclectic series of experiences fostered a big picture perspective and an interest in the personalities of organizations. When I attended New York

University's Stern School of Business for my MBA, I majored in finance and became interested in the decision sciences, particularly corporate finance, which intrigued me. Richard Brealey and Stewart Myers's book on corporate finance is my favorite text from those years.[1]

When I became manager of Prudential's equity investment operations, my interest in performance attribution began to bloom. My understanding of fiduciary duty and SEC law also grew, and I managed a project to build an expert system for investment compliance in the early 1990s.

Soon after, I was hired away to build a balanced scorecard. After it was in place, I was asked to work in the areas of risk capital attribution and capital resource planning.

It was at this time that I was introduced to *The Quest for Value.*[2] This book, written by Bennett Stewart, spoke to me. It held the promise of practices that could link corporate finance, investor models, and organizational change.

As I began the work of implementation at Bank One, I became a believer. I could see the power of these ideas to transform, a power that went beyond a numbers exercise, a way of managing that could address both the decision and anthropological issues of organizations. Since then, I have worked with many organizations. When open to the insights and prepared to do the digging, organizations can reap benefits in the millions of dollars in the first year alone.

My contribution in this area, I believe, is to recognize its potential, to see how deeply the transformation can go and how the insights that are provided can be used in multiple settings in multiple ways. Economic Value Management, an integrated management approach using sound governance principles, is based on seven years of personal in-depth research and work with organizations, including some of the largest financial institutions in the world. My other specific contribution is in the area of financial services which, on a stand-alone basis, represents about a fifth of the S&P's market capitalization, and much more if financial subsidiaries are included. The work I have done from this perspective illumines new ways in which firms outside the financial sector can leverage their efforts as well.

Why do some organizations experience this transformative power and not others? One key reason—and what this book addresses—is the level of the dig. How often is the organization willing to dig deeply to get the insights, to try multiple approaches, and then once uncovered, to throw off preconceived notions about their meaning?

As I have worked with more and more organizations, I came to see this fundamental distinction: Those that benefited—that had a new vantage point and a new view—were those willing to dig. In a time of quick fixes, shortcuts, and busyness, time is not always allocated to these necessary tasks:

- "We don't have time to do it right."
- "We already believe this or have started that."
- "We can't make a change now—we have to be consistent."

"A foolish consistency is the hobgoblin of little minds, adored by little statesmen and philosophers and divines," wrote Emerson.[3] These are the echoes in some organizations.

In other organizations, however, there is a different conversation. It is a conversation of "Mmmm . . . I didn't realize that. Mmmm . . . that puts a new light on it. Mmmm . . . I wonder how soon we can take advantage of what we now know."

Organizations I have worked with that have taken the latter approach have reaped huge gains. Thirty percent growth in net income and economic value in the first year alone has been achieved in some organizations. Others have seen strategic shifts and hundreds of millions of dollars in value creation.

As this book outlines, the process is not that difficult. Any organization can do it. Any individual can do it. Just rise early, work hard, and *dig*—and eventually *you will* strike oil.

NOTES

1. Richard A. Brealey and Stewart C. Myers, *Principles of Corporate Finance, Third Edition,* New York: McGraw-Hill, 1988.

2. G. Bennett Stewart III, *The Quest For Value,* New York: HarperCollins, 1991.

3. Ralph Waldo Emerson, "Self-Reliance" Essays, First Series (1841, repr. 1847).

What Is Economic Value Management and How Does It Relate to Organizations Today?

What Is Economic Value Management?

When he gets out of bed on Monday morning and gets ready for the long commute to work, John thinks about the morning staff meeting, the presentation he'll be making, the reports he'll need to review, and the people he'll have to placate and cajole that day. His day is structured by the tasks in front of him, the tasks he is asked to perform, and those he feels compelled to address. Some time during the course of the year he may reflect on it all, but then again he may not, especially as long as he is well paid, likes his colleagues, and finds his job tasks acceptable.

John's life, the life of everyone, brings to mind the story about human nature that Anthony de Mello, a Jesuit priest, tells in a chapter titled "Profit and Loss":

> And here is a parable of life for you to ponder on: A group of tourists sits in a bus that is passing through gorgeously beautiful country; lakes and mountains and green fields and rivers. But the shades of the bus are pulled down. They do not have the slightest idea of what lies beyond the windows of the bus. And all the time of their journey is spent in squabbling over who will have the seat of honor in the bus, who will be applauded, who will be well considered. And so they remain till the journey's end.[1]

Does de Mello mean by this story that the most important issue related to human nature is work/life balance and "stopping to smell the roses"? I think he means much more. He speaks of everyone's habitual actions and desires. His story asks us to consider our intention and awareness: What is the intent of our work life's bus trip? How clearly do we wish to see?

John and his colleagues are like travelers on that bus, scrabbling with their fellow travelers to sit in certain seats. And it keeps them busy and occupied, so much so that John, like his fellow travelers, never thinks to pull up the shades and look outside. And, in fact, they travel along, never pulling up the shades, never looking out, and never really knowing what lies beyond.

As with this tale of everyone, many organizations go about their daily routines, their daily *busy-ness,* without stopping to look outside—to see beyond what *appears* in front of them. Similarly, constituents of organizations also develop narrow views of what their relationship to the organization means, narrow definitions that often do not serve them.

To truly see, to really understand, the bus shades must be pulled up and a wide-angle view taken. The viewer must see broadly and be able to zoom in as well. What is this Economic Value Management that can pull the bus shades up, revealing the view outside?

DEFINITION

In broad terms, *Economic Value Management* can be defined as *an integrated approach to managing any organization, one that is based on the principle of stewardship (and the inexorable consequences of failed stewardship; see* Exhibit 1.1).

This description, which is really quite simple, embodies two key concepts:

1. Economic Value Management is a management approach
2. The foundation for the approach is a set of principles or beliefs

These concepts are important in understanding the true power of Economic Value Management and sorting out whether an organization is using the management approach, and if so, how far along it is.

Many people are already familiar with "economic value added," although they often mean different things by it and their understanding of the concept varies widely. On an ongoing basis, popular business periodicals or news sources refer to corporate organizations and the concept of shareholder value. Ostensibly, *Managing for Shareholder Value* (a phrase often emblazoned on a company's annual report) reflects a management approach focused on the enhancement of shareholder value (i.e., earning returns for the shareholder). Managing for Shareholder Value embodies the concept of stewardship by clearly and explicitly recognizing the importance of the obligation to the shareholder (the capital provider) in the management of the business.

Recently, the Securities and Exchange Commission (SEC), analysts, and institutional investors (who invest mutual funds and retirement savings) have expressed concerns over the numbers reported to investors about company results. Unfortunately, as the SEC has recently pointed out, it is not always easy to judge a company's performance by its annual report disclosures. At the same time, individuals' retirement and savings are tied increasingly to the fortunes or misfortunes of the companies in which investments are made. The cost of the ink to say Managing for Shareholder Value is cheap. The real question is: Is the company *really* doing it and, if so, how?

Fortunately or unfortunately, Economic Value Management impacts people beyond their roles as investors. The fate of a company and its management

> **"Economic Value Management is an integrated approach to managing any organization, one that is based on the principle of stewardship (and the inexorable consequences of failed stewardship)."**
>
> Economic Value Management is a *management* approach, a series of practices, that are based on *stewardship*, and that yield *economic, value-creating* results.
>
> All three words, *economic, value,* and *management,* speak to the concept of *stewardship* and to its consequences. (Definitions come from *Webster's Collegiate* and the *Oxford English Dictionary.*)
>
> *Stewardship* is defined as the "conducting, supervising or managing of something, especially the careful and responsible management of something entrusted to one's care," or "the responsible use of resources, especially money, time, and talents."
>
> *Economic* implies not accounting or record keeping, but rather means a process "marked by careful, prudent use of resources," "yielding advantageous returns or results."
>
> *Value* is defined as something "held in high esteem or appreciation," "having worth," something that is "valid, sound." It is a "measurement of relative worth," "the estimate in which something is held related to principles or standards of what is valuable in life," and "the quality of a thing considered in respect of its power and validity for a specified purpose or effect."
>
> *Management* is defined as the "judicious use of means to accomplish an end," "the application of skill or care in the conduct of an enterprise," "the exercise of executive, administrative and supervisory direction," and "the taking of control of the course of affairs by one's direction." It is "the fulfillment of duties," "handled or directed with a degree of skill," "treated with care," "carried on successfully" "to achieve one's purpose."
>
> Source: *www.thevaluealliance.com* website

EXHIBIT 1.1 Economic Value Management

approach can impact everyone: employees, customers, suppliers, and the like. To be empowered, *all individuals* must actively manage their own participation.

In that sense, and in others, Economic Value Management is much larger than simply "shareholder value" or what is generally referred to as "economic value added." This book describes these distinctions. As the pages that follow show, Economic Value Management is more encompassing and significantly more powerful.

This book examines Economic Value Management from the perspective of people's various roles and the organizations to which Economic Value Management may be applied. The book will also highlight the area of financial services organizations—banks, insurance companies, brokers, and investment advisers—which, for a variety of reasons, are often neglected. This is one key class of organization with which everyone interacts as customers and on whom everyone depends as the direct custodians and managers of their wealth.

To clearly understand the impact of Economic Value Management concepts, it is important to reach a common understanding and provide a definition of the potential constituents of an organization and their roles in more depth.

IMPORTANCE OF ALL CONSTITUENTS

Is Economic Value Management only about the investor? The question may *seem* simple, but it was not so simple to "The Raleigh Organization."[2] With headquarters located in the United States at a beautiful campus situated among tall trees and lush green lawns, Raleigh is a large global association and a household name in almost every country in the world. For many years, Raleigh has had a large paid management team and has been able to attract bright talent, yet it faced an issue not uncommon in large organizations. Sally, the head of strategic planning, had been asked to spearhead the annual (yes, annual) development of performance measures. These performance measures were used to monitor performance and to pay incentives to the management team. Sally outlined the measurement process that the organization was currently using and some of the difficulties Raleigh was having with it:

> *Raleigh has historically struggled with the issue of performance measures and has tried a number of approaches over the last four to five years. We have had a goal of trying to use capital wisely but didn't know if it made sense or how to translate this into an overall way to manage the association's business. Unsure of how to proceed, we currently plan to use a new set of measures that have been recommended to us by one of our most powerful members.*

As Raleigh's history unfolded, the concepts of Economic Value Management entered the discussion. One of the staff in the strategic planning department, Fred, who was somewhat familiar with the concept of "economic value added," said: "This cannot apply to us! We don't have shareholders; we have members—and they are more like customers than shareholders. So Economic Value Management can't apply." Was he right? Is Economic Value Management only about the investor?

The answer is *no!* Unlike other approaches, Economic Value Management is an approach to managing any organization and can be useful to everyone who interacts with the organization.

Lack of clarity on this point, however, can result in difficulty in understanding the larger benefits and applications of Economic Value Management. To make the relationships clearer, the diagrams in Exhibits 1.2 through 1.8 outline the constituent groups for different types of organizations.

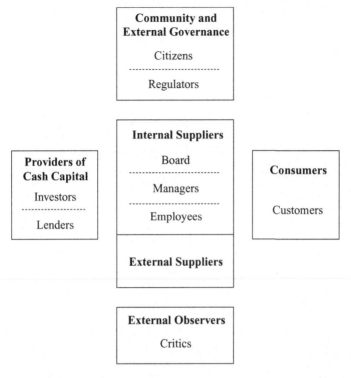

EXHIBIT 1.2 Stock Company

Community and External Governance

In each of these exhibits, the uppermost box in the diagram represents the community and external governance for the entity.

The *citizen* role belongs to every individual in the community, whether the community is the individual's town or country, or the world as a whole. Of course, citizens can take on other, more specific roles as outlined elsewhere on these charts.

The role of *regulator* concerns established frameworks such as the government, agencies, or other associations charged with regulating the organization and ensuring its own, as well as the greater community's well being. In some industries, such as financial services, these entities establish a required level of capital or regulatory capital requirement.

Providers of Cash Capital[3]

The leftmost box in each diagram represents the providers of cash capital for the organization. In the case of publicly traded companies, the providers of cash capital include investors and lenders. For private companies, this

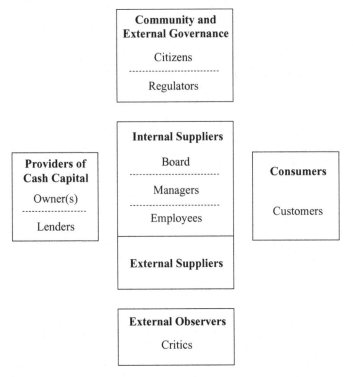

EXHIBIT 1.3   Private Company

constituency comprises owners and lenders. Mutual companies and membership organizations, including religious organizations, receive capital from their policyholders or members. For government, citizens and taxpayers have this role.

The *investor* role deals with investors who buy stakes in companies and share in the results of the company's activities. They are providers of cash capital through their purchase of the company's stock.

Lenders provide cash capital through loans to the company or by the purchase of debt securities but do not share in the results of the activities of the company (or organization or government). Their only concern is with the organization's ability to generate cash to service its debt.

The *owner* role belongs to private company investors or owners who hold the stakes in a company and share in its results. They are providers of cash capital in a very direct manner.

The role of *member* comprises individuals who support an organization by paying dues. Members often share in the benefits of the organization, while their dues provide the cash capital for its operations. Members also have another role as well. They are generally the individuals for whom the

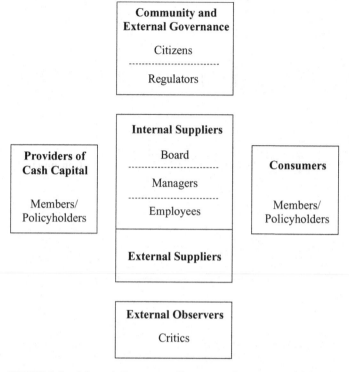

EXHIBIT 1.4 Mutual Company (for example, a mutual life insurance company) or Membership Organization

organization runs its activities, and in this role, they are the customers of the organization.

Policyholders are individuals who hold insurance policies that have been issued by a mutual company. They share in the results of the company through dividends and provide cash capital through the purchase of insurance policies. Policyholders also have another role as customers of the insurance company.

Taxpayers are the individuals who support their government by paying taxes and, generally speaking, share in the benefits that the government provides. (One may say this relationship is not optional. However, as numerous examples show, one may choose one's jurisdiction. To wit, in the United States, not only are businesses choosing where to locate, but individuals are using location as an element of financial planning as well.) The payment of taxes provides the cash capital for the operation of government.

For social service organizations, *contributors* perform the role of cash capital provider. These individuals usually do not share in the tangible, direct monetary benefits of the efforts of the organization but rather share in the general intangible good through the gift of contribution.

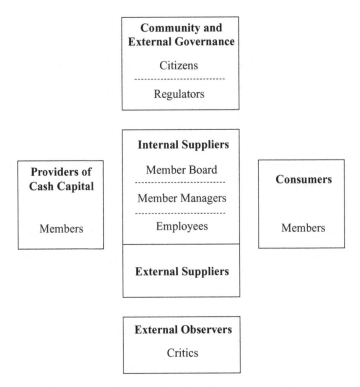

EXHIBIT 1.5   Another Membership Organizational Form

Suppliers

The middle box in each diagram represents the suppliers of intellectual capital and other inputs that are necessary for the governance and the day-to-day operations of the organization. (This use of the term *supplier* is broader than that in general usage.)

The *Board of Directors* deals with the governing body of an organization. In their oversight role, these individuals supply intellectual capital and assess the use of capital in the organization, including cash, regulatory, intellectual, and risk capital.

Managers are responsible for the day-to-day management of the organization. They supply intellectual capital and manage the daily transactions, including the conversion of cash capital to other goods and services. In the management of the conversion process, they make the decisions required to take nonrisky assets and put them at risk to generate returns for the investors while maintaining the ability to pay the lender. In this process, they manage the risk capital of the business and monitor any regulatory capital requirements.

Employees are responsible for the day-to-day conversion of cash capital to other goods and services. They are suppliers of intellectual capital.

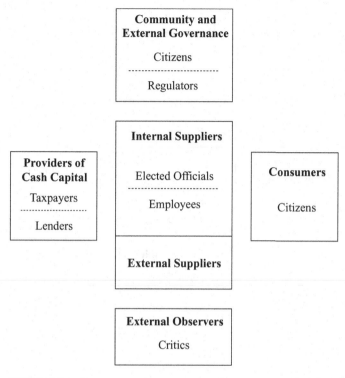

EXHIBIT 1.6 Government

The role of *external suppliers* deals with individuals external to the organization who supply materials in exchange for cash capital or directly supply intellectual capital not provided internally. Today, more and more organizations are working in partnership. These partners are a special case of a supplier relationship.

External Observers

The bottom box in each diagram is for the external observers of the organization. They may or may not have influence over the outcomes of the organization. At times, they may act in a quasi-regulatory fashion. Generically defined here as *critics,* these outside observers comment on and rate the activities of an organization. They use their intellectual capital to benefit the organization's internal and external constituents. Some evaluate the firm's cash and risk capital. Examples of critics include:

- Analysts who comment on and give buy, hold, or sell recommendations for a company's stock
- Rating agencies that assess the safety of the organization's bonds

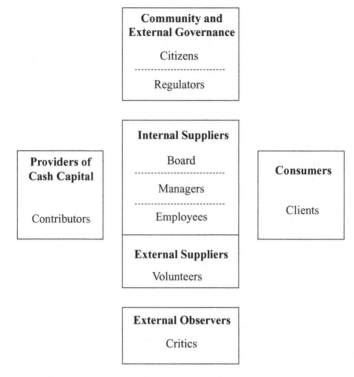

EXHIBIT 1.7   Social Services Organization

- Consumer groups who rate the safety and effectiveness of the organization's products
- Surveyors who rank the company's employee friendliness
- Journalists who provide critiques of the business
- Special interest groups who rate the organization's environmental policies or its ethics

Consumers of the Organization's Efforts

The right-hand box represents the consumers of the organization's efforts.

The *customer* role is filled by the customers or clients who act as consumers of the products or services of the organization. Often this consumption is in exchange for some form of cash. Members, policyholders, and citizens represent special cases of customer. Depending on the structure of the organization, members may or may not pay for these services in addition to their dues. Clients of social service organizations or recipients of government services often do not pay cash in exchange for the services that they receive, although they generally do give up their time in this exchange. The

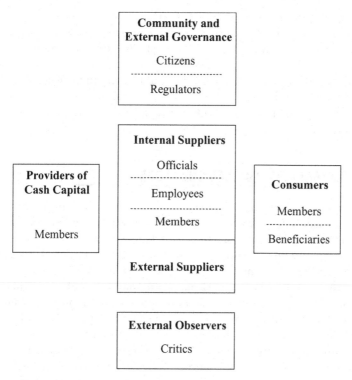

EXHIBIT 1.8   Religious Organization

customer relationship with a financial services firm is particularly sensitive, because these firms act as custodians and managers of the customer's wealth.

As we all know, one individual may, and often does, fulfill multiple roles. An employee of one organization is a customer of another, and may be both a customer and employee of the same organization. Many managers are also investors in the firm, holding a portion of their net worth as stock in the company. Members are often both investors/contributors and customers of an organization. To make it easier, throughout this book the term *investor* will be used to represent everyone who provides paid-in capital and has the right to share in the benefits that the capital provides. In other words, *investor*, depending on the organization, will mean policyholder, member, taxpayer, or contributor, as appropriate. Likewise, *customer* will be used generically, although specifically, the terms policyholder, member, citizen, or client might apply. *Critic* is already a generic term and will be used to describe the constituents described earlier.

Although there were no shareholders at The Raleigh Organization, the members contributed cash capital to pay for the operations of the organization. They were both consumers of the services and suppliers of the upfront cash required to run the association. As such, they were concerned not only with the price for services and the nature of those services, but also that the organization was running effectively in order to minimize the need for dues (i.e., additional cash infusions). The members acted as shareholders; however, the open question still is, could Economic Value Management apply? To answer this question, an exploration of the concept of Economic Value Management is in order. However, an even larger question looms: Why bother?

WHY EVERYONE SHOULD READ THIS BOOK

When large organizations fail, fingers start to point. Was it the fault of the auditor (an example of an external supplier)? Was it the fault of the board or the managers? Although blame is usually assigned to one or two parties, all of the constituents (as shown in Exhibits 1.2 through 1.8) have the ability to impact the outcomes of the organizations with whom they interact.

Yes, the auditors, board, and managers may be to blame. What about regulators? Did they perform the required oversight? Employees? Did they continue to work for a firm that was dishonest? Did they alert their managers or the board and, failing that, the media or regulators to potential issues? How about investors? Did they perform due diligence? External observers? Did the press report accurately and dig into the story? Did analysts do their job? Did rating agencies accurately reflect the state of the company's risk? Did customers seek alternative suppliers if they were being gouged and make their issues known to regulators, the media, and others? When fingers are pointing the blame, usually both hands and all fingers are needed.

Economic Value Management supplies solutions that can help constituents do their job better, remain alert, and see out of the bus window. In addition, the use of Economic Value Management can dramatically impact the outcomes for all constituents. Used by an organization to its full potential, it *will* have the following effects:

- For investors, Economic Value Management will positively influence the stock price of a company, directly and indirectly. For nonpublicly traded organizations, Economic Value Management will ensure that the capital of the firm is used wisely, thus stretching the value for each dollar of dues, taxes, or contributions.

- For lenders, Economic Value Management will positively impact an organization's ability to repay loans and obtain additional capital when needed.

- For the Board of Directors, Economic Value Management embodies the concepts of corporate governance and reflects what boards most need to know to do a good job and, selfishly, to limit their liability. For audit committees, Economic Value Management includes processes to challenge the accounting numbers, and for incentive compensation committees, practices that ensure fair incentives based on true pay for performance.

- For managers, Economic Value Management will mean less waste and more focus. It will unleash the possibility of actually running the business, rather than fighting fires. It will also generate the opportunity to share in the economic gains achieved for investors.

- For employees, organizations that use Economic Value Management practices will be more stable, both financially and strategically. The decision-making processes of the organization will be clearer. In addition, the organization will be more inclusive and provide better opportunities and better environments in which to work.

- For external suppliers, Economic Value Management organizations will be more financially stable and make better partners.

- For customers of financial institutions, Economic Value Management companies provide a stable, long-term relationship. The underlying financial stability and management approach of financial institutions is of critical importance to their customers. (This is also true of other organizations where long-term relationships provide important benefits to the customer.) In practice, Economic Value Management organizations continually reassess service offerings to determine those that are most beneficial (and for corporations, to provide those for which customers are willing to pay). The generally longer-term focus of Economic Value Management companies (compared to many U.S. companies) extends to the view of the organization toward its customers.

- For citizens, regulators, and critics, Economic Value Management organizations are better governed and more financially stable. They are also better able to communicate their true results than other organizations because, in fact, they understand them and recognize disclosure as an important element of stewardship.

WHY ECONOMIC VALUE MANAGEMENT?

Economic Value Management is an integrated approach to running any organization. Although the concept seems simple and is based on sound business stewardship practices, the fact is that many organizations do not know if they are being good stewards. The government misplaces battleships. A Big 5 consulting firm loses 40% of its intelligent, hard-working employees every year. Major banks collapse due to the activities of one "lone ranger" trader. Why does this happen? Why aren't they good stewards?

One reason is that organizations tend to be very inwardly focused. One of the largest social organizations in the United States, "The Magnificence Society" (MS), has volunteer members who serve as regional directors and who set budgets and recruit members for their local areas. Although MS manages millions of dollars in cash and properties, the regional directors lack understanding of their roles and responsibilities. For example, although membership had fallen off considerably in their local areas, their recommendations in terms of programs and budgets remained unchanged. To address this, MS called a special meeting of the regional directors to discuss membership issues. When asked what they were going to do to prop up membership, many of the regional directors did not understand how this related to their roles of providing programs and setting budgets. "We are responsible for budgets and programs, not membership," they said. "This may technically be true," Caroline, a board member, explained, "but unless you have a sizable membership, you won't be able to get the budget to carry on the programs you want." While this may sound obvious, many of the regional directors were stunned by this revelation and objected vehemently. This is not uncommon, however. This relationship between organizational functions and the capital providers is often missed in social organizations and elsewhere.

A similar issue occurred at "Rural City Bank." The bank was new and growing in its marketplace. It had attracted capital from individuals across the United States, including a retired president of a major banking institution. There was just one problem. Bill, the CEO of Rural City, believed that capital was free. When a major shareholder suggested that a return to the investors be considered in making decisions, Bill rejected the idea out of hand. He considered the proceeds from issuing stock to be free money. Whenever he wanted to expand, he sought to gain board approval to issue additional stock. To Bill, it seemed, stock was indeed free.

While these examples represent cautionary tales, it is very easy for companies to become systems that are no longer appropriately addressing their constituents' needs. To become internally focused is natural. The de Mello story of the bus illustrates these natural tendencies—life as a bus where the shades are pulled down and all of the passengers spend their time fighting over where to sit, never seeing the beautiful views outside the bus windows.

What Economic Value Management asks an organization to do is lift the shades, look outside, and then set its goals and objectives. Simple as it sounds or looks, it is not often done. So how is it sparked?

Many processes other than Economic Value Management have attempted to address this. Total Quality Management (TQM), for example, attempts to move organizations outward by focusing some of the business processes more closely on the quality of the product, in the hope that the organization will be rewarded in the marketplace. This focus on the customer and the product is very important, and it is also very beneficial. It just needs the broader context, which Economic Value Management provides.

Companies preparing for an initial public offering (IPO), for example, often recognize quite suddenly the need to look out the bus window. "Petry Meyers," for example, which had been privately held for many years, decided that the time was right to become publicly traded. Before its decision, Petry had a convoluted and complex strategy that was unclear to the employees. Petry's organizational structure was dysfunctional, and the reporting relationships were needlessly complex and confusing. Prior to the IPO, reporting relationships were established to ensure that each of the executive partners had their own turf. These "turfdoms," however, overlapped and crisscrossed to the extent that a strategy to target one customer impacted five to six different line managers, and it was never clear who was responsible for what. This caused issues both inside and outside the firm. Another issue at Petry Meyers was that managers almost never came together to discuss strategy. Each turf was separately maintained (and if the manager were politically astute, enhanced).

As Petry Meyers began to formulate its IPO plans, it suddenly occurred to the executive team that its structure and strategy could be problematic. People inside and outside the company would want to understand its strategy before investing in it. The fact that the IPO would create interest in the company's business practices caused Petry executives to see their own organization in a new light and made them realize that these problems were not going to be fixed overnight. As a result, the executive team decided, in their words, to "simplify their strategy" so that they could attempt to "explain it to the analysts."

In another IPO, a mutual insurance company, "The Member's Group," went overboard in this regard. After its IPO, the managers, constantly worried about meeting net income goals, were encouraged to spend their time in radically different ways: They were expected to provide very detailed updates of projected revenues and expenses and an explanation of variances on a *weekly* basis. The Member's Group forecasting process became so detailed and underwent so much scrutiny by top executives that it was seriously detracting from the ongoing business of the firm. "We don't have time for our customers or our operations," Martha, an executive at the Member's Group, stated. Economic Value Management takes a middle ground. It requires a discipline of sustainable value creation, a focus on the fundamentals, but not a minutiae projection focus!

Economic Value Management encompasses not only stewardship but also consistent stewardship. How is an Economic Value Management organization different from other well-managed organizations? An organization can be well managed while not consciously a value organization. An organization can be well managed but not consistently so. The idea behind Economic Value Management is that it allows good management to be replicated. The change in thought process engendered by Economic Value Management can be replicated and is not based solely on the charisma of a leader. In that way,

Economic Value Management, through its practices, creates a sustained and replicable model of good management; it encompasses a move from super-hero involvement to *all* involvement. If organizations want internal suppliers (i.e., managers and employees) to act like owners (and reward them as such), internal suppliers will expect to have a voice. Economic Value Management provides an integration of the processes of the organization into an explainable and meaningful framework. This integration is soulful in its stewardship of the various pieces while creating a whole greater than the individual parts.

As an idea, Economic Value Management is simple. In fact, it properly introduces the right level of complexity and eliminates unnecessary complications. These are the complications that take up the bus rider's time. One example of unnecessary complications was discussed at a winter tax conference held in Boca Raton, Florida. In a morning panel discussion, directors of tax at several major companies discussed how their roles had expanded and how their jobs were more consultative than they used to be. "What are the consultations spent on?" called out an audience member. Gary, one of the tax directors, replied, "I have more conversations with the CEO today than ever before. In most of these discussions, I spend most of the time explaining the accounting rules, book versus tax differences, and how to make things look OK from a book perspective. Although I know we care about paying the least amount in taxes, we also seem to care a great deal about the optics or appearance of book accounting even though these conversations do not impact value creation one bit." The other panel members nodded in agreement. "Can this be fixed?" another audience member inquired. "Not really," Gary answered. "This confusion over the accounting measures seems inevitable. I don't think there is anything to be done."

While the tax managers felt resigned to spending more and more of their time with CEOs, going over issues that ultimately did not impact the creation of value, the case is not hopeless. Economic Value Management provides the solution and, in time, more organizations and those involved with them will seize the potential it offers.

It is, unfortunately, true that the time from academic thought to wide-spread implementation can be quite long. As information and technology moves forward, changing the minds and hearts of people is a slower process. Even as late as the 1970s, major, well-regarded U.S. corporations were using financial measures like payback to make decisions, although the science of finance had moved ahead much further. Similarly, it is taking time for organizations to understand that Economic Value Management is a management approach, one that is robust enough to yield significant benefits.

While many organization management teams say they would like to be "value based" or "increase shareholder value," Economic Value Management is not for amateurs. Anyone can do it; it does, however, require study and experience. As the car ads say, it is a closed road with a professional driver. Jeff Bezos, CEO of Amazon.com, says his life strategy is *Regret Minimization*. Economic Value Management provides a framework to minimize regrets by providing the information and the best preconditions for success. The driving is then up to the organization and to everyone who interacts with it.

NOTES

1. Anthony de Mello, *The Way to Love: The Last Meditations of Anthony de Mello*, New York: Doubleday, 1992.

2. The organizational examples throughout this book are based on real cases. The names of the organizations, the people, and some of the other details presented, however, have been changed to respect confidentiality and make the example clearer. In addition, one organization may appear under different pseudonyms.

3. The term *cash capital* is used here to distinguish providers of cash capital from providers of intellectual or other forms of capital. Later in this book, for simplicity, they will be more generally referred to as capital providers.

CHAPTER 2

The Value Management Wheel™

OVERVIEW

Alex, the CFO of "Smartway Bank," believes Value Management is a finance program. Mary, the head of human resources at "James & Smith," believes it is a performance-measurement and compensation program. Sam, the CEO of "Mockingbird Corp.," sees it as a management program. To Max, the hedge fund manager at "The Orange Group," it is a better way to assess the fundamentals of organizations for investment decision making. To Sally, at the "AllWorld" pension plan, the sophistication of its implementation at a company is a way to assess the effectiveness of their corporate governance. The views of Economic Value Management's functions are often based on the perspective of the person doing the viewing, the facet of the prism through which they look.

So, what are the facets of Economic Value Management? The Economic Value Management Wheel™, shown in Exhibit 2.1, displays the different components of Economic Value Management in a single diagram. This wheel has six major sectors:

1. Performance assessment
2. Value-based strategy
3. Process and technology
4. Organizational structure
5. Rewards process
6. Training and communication

PERFORMANCE ASSESSMENT

Fourteen Key Questions

Performance assessment is a topic that has been surrounded by a great deal of controversy. The chapters that follow discuss the areas of controversy

EXHIBIT 2.1   The Value Management Wheel™

in detail. The point here is that, without Economic Value Management performance assessment, organizations cannot measure value creation systematically. The following 14 key questions should be addressed by any Economic Value Management performance-assessment system. The questions are separated into two groups: those that look at the history to understand what has happened and those that predict the value to be created in the future:

Evaluative:

1. Has the organization added value? How much?
2. How does this compare to the organization's peers and competitors?
3. Has the organization been managed such that each sector has added value?
4. Has the organization been managed such that each product, service, distribution channel, or process has added value?
5. Has the organization been managed such that each customer relationship has added value?
6. What are the major drivers of value creation for the organization?
7. For all of the above, how has this changed over time?

Predictive:

8. How much value does the organization expect to create?

9. How much value do capital providers (shareholders, if publicly traded) expect the organization to create?

10. How much value does the organization expect to create by sector, product, service, distribution channel, process, and customer?

11. What are the expectations related to the major drivers of value creation over time?

12. What are the capital provider's expectations for the organization's peers? What are the peer's expectations for itself by sector, product, service, distribution channel, process, customer, and major drivers of value creation?

13. How do internal, peer, and capital provider expectations differ from current steady-state value creations?

14. For all of the above, how will this change over time?

There are an astounding number of organizations that have failed to address the answers to these 14 important questions. However, as basic as these questions may appear on the surface, without Economic Value Management performance-assessment tools, organizations are powerless to answer them. How are individuals influenced by the answers to these questions?

Evaluative Measures

While past results are not necessarily indicative of future performance, evaluative measures, unlike predictive measures, are not educated guesses. Rather, they represent what has actually happened. And to understand that in value terms is to understand more about an organization than just its earnings or cost ratios and much more than anyone, on the surface, would imagine.

Question 1: *How much, if any, value has been added to the organization?* All constituents care about the answer to this question. For some, change in market value represents one answer, but change in market value is really a change in prediction. A change in market value is a change in a prediction of value into the future (see Question 9).

With the answer to this question, we are looking for an evaluation of what has been done, of the value that has already been created. As organizations evolve, this issue becomes increasingly important to capital providers, whether they be shareholders, debt holders, dues providers, or taxpayers. These interested parties rationally want to know whether their capital contributions are currently producing adequate and acceptable returns.

Although current buyers' estimates of future value imbedded in the stock price are of interest, existing capital providers need to understand whether value is being created now, during their holding tenure.

Taxpayers want to understand how an agency, legislature, or judicial body is performing and how the results may compare with the spending required of a private effort. Dues providers want to understand whether the benefits are clearly worth the cost and whether costs are accelerating while benefits are stagnating. Using traditional measurement systems, many capital providers are unsure about robust answers to these questions.

This question is also important to both internal and external suppliers. As employees, or potential employees, the question is very important as a backdrop to understanding the viability of the company as an employer. Similarly, this is also important to other suppliers as well, because they need to determine the financial stability and future potential of the organization as a customer of their products and services.

While traditional earnings measures may be useful for a quick review, value measures provide a bigger picture and a better measure of value creation. For high-growth firms that have not yet turned a profit, value measures are key to better understanding the organization's past and future. While no, or low, earnings are an indicator, value measures allow investors to assess the level of current value creation and compare those results with the future value implied in the current stock price. During the high-tech bubble of the late 1990s, these analyses would have clearly shown investors how far the stock prices diverged from any possible estimation of value creation. For suppliers and external observers, understanding the value answer gives important insights into the management of the organization and its effectiveness. This is particularly important to the Board of Directors, management team, analysts, and others who wish to ensure that the organization is effectively run and well governed. While earnings can be manipulated, properly designed value metrics are much less subject to manipulation.

From the customer's point of view, both the viability of the organization and its ability to innovate are important. If, as a consumer, you are obtaining good value, what potential exists for these services to continue to be well managed? If this relationship is important, to what extent is the history of the supplier organization known? Where has this organization been? Especially in today's partnering environment, changing suppliers can be expensive. While suppliers are using technology to provide better services and more information to the customer, it is also used to "lock in" a customer. Where changing suppliers is difficult, understanding one's supplier partner in value terms becomes extremely important.

From a community and external governance perspective, review of the organization's historical value creation can help determine whether value has been added to, or subtracted from, the community by the organization's efforts and the extent to which actions should be taken to boost or modify those efforts.

Question 2: *How does this compare to the organization's peers and competitors?* For capital providers, creation of value is important in terms of the alternatives. In this context, the value creation of peers, competitors, and other benchmarks is important to understand so that the results of the organization can be put in perspective and alternatives found in terms of funding more beneficial enterprises. Again, the answer to this question is important to capital providers not only in terms of market estimates of future value, but also as a measure of how well, in similar economic climates, an organization *has done* compared to its peers.

For taxpayers or members of a nonprofit, the question is whether alternatives exist that would represent a better route for their objectives or provide areas of study to improve the performance of the organization or governmental body. For equity or debt holders, one of the questions is whether more lucrative investments exist.

For suppliers, including employees, managers, and board members, this performance assessment represents value-based benchmarks of performance that can demonstrate whether the company is measuring up. For external observers, it serves as a way to rank the results versus the competition and provides a comparison mechanism for customers and the community as well.

Question 3: *Has each key sector added value?* While management is responsible for ensuring that each sector adds value, the answer to this question is important to everyone else as well. It is important for capital providers to understand more than the total organization's results. In understanding whether value has been created during their holding period, capital providers need to also determine which parts of the organization may be adding or eroding value. For example, are new businesses or old businesses creating the most value? If the organization has areas that are not adding value, is there a focus on fixing them? While traditional measures do not take into account the amount of capital used or give a true picture of operating results, value metrics provide a much better picture of sector results by reflecting these issues.

Employees, customers, and suppliers want to understand whether value has been created at their level of interaction. While it is interesting to understand the overall dynamic of the organization as outlined in Question 1, existing employees, customers, and suppliers also want to understand value creation dynamics in terms of the specific division or unit with which they interact. For employees, this measurement can be made for both line and staff functions, and taken to the next level, ranked among peers.

The information provided by answering this question is critical to portfolio decision making for top executives and the Board of Directors. Without it, they cannot determine which units to keep and grow and which to divest.

The information on value creation at the business segment level will help external observers better understand the organization's results. Financial Accounting Standard (FAS) No.131 requires this information, at least at a high level, for traditional accounting earnings results. Taken to the level of value measurement, it provides useful analytical information. Detailed information on the viability of components of the organization provides the community as well with a better perspective on the organization as a whole and its overall viability.

Question 4: *Do individual products, services, distribution channels, and processes add value?* In most organizations, even basic accounting information for this level of their operation is considered confidential and is available only to certain internal suppliers. As a result, peer or competitive information is often not available nor is this information generally provided to capital providers, external suppliers or observers, customers, or the community. For internal suppliers, this information is important in understanding how the business has been performing at the product, service, distribution channel, and process level and what areas may require focus or attention. From a top executive viewpoint, as with the business segment analysis, this question must be answered to form the context for decisions regarding which products, services, distribution channels, and processes should be expanded and which should be eliminated.

Question 5: *Which customer relationships have added value?* Organizations today continue to restructure to better meet customer needs and address areas of customer focus. Many organizations, however, do not know which customers create value for the organization and which destroy value. As with question 4, the answer to this question is generally either not available at all or is only available to internal suppliers. For them, this information is critical to understanding how best to address customer needs and how to shape the organization's processes going forward.

Question 6: *What are the drivers of value?* At a high level, the answers to this question can apply not only to the company itself, but also to peers and competitors. For the organization itself, these answers can be extensive. The value drivers of the organization may encompass not only its financial drivers (like revenues or costs), but also the underlying strategies and competencies required to produce those results. These competencies may involve, for example, employee, operational, or customer service components. Drivers may include widgets produced per hour or customer complaints successfully resolved. This question also involves understanding what drives value from a customer perspective (i.e., what they are willing to pay for and what they are not). At a high level, this information is likely to be shared in various forms and be of interest to all constituencies. At a lower level of detail, this information is likely to be private and used only by internal suppliers.

Some organizations build an initial performance-measurement system by selecting several of these value drivers for the organization's focus. When selected from a well-rounded list of categories, the results are placed in what has become known as a *balanced scorecard*.[1] This performance-measurement approach will be discussed in more detail in Chapters 3 and 9.

Economic Value Management uses an understanding of a broad set of value drivers to drive organizational results. Although traditional balanced scorecards are generally developed through a selection process based on top management's intuition, Economic Value Management uses a fact base to modify any initial hypotheses and prioritize the appropriate value drivers. The value drivers that receive focus are those that have a significant historical and predicted impact on value creation.

Question 7: *For all of the above, how has this changed over time?* The answers to this question get at the heart of value creation trends in the organization as a whole, with peers and competitors, and with particular lines of business or divisions. These answers can help in understanding cyclical trends often masked by traditional metrics and newer structural changes that may impact an organization's business proposition. The same, of course, can be said for the value information on products, services, distribution channels, processes, customers, and the value drivers themselves.

Although so-called *backward-looking* (i.e., evaluative) measures are often disparaged, the right kind of evaluative measures—value-based ones—can provide extremely useful insights. For one thing, the seeds of the future are often hidden in the past. For another, the past is what has been. The future involves projection, speculation, and estimation. Evaluative measures represent what has happened, and that can be very important indeed in building an accountability system.

Predictive Measures

Question 8: *How much value does the organization expect to create?* Although earnings estimates for companies are often shared with external observers, value estimates are generally not. Given past observations and trends and an understanding of the value drivers of an organization, however, it is possible to construct potential value creation scenarios.

Unlike earnings, value creation is not easy to manipulate. The "Alphonse Finance Company" implemented value metrics and was astounded by this aspect. "You mean we have to generate new business to create value?" remarked Peter, the surprised CFO. "This means we can't overcome operational losses as quickly!"

As a result of this inability to manipulate well-designed value metrics, an organization's trend in value creation will not be artificially up each period with no breaks. Rather, for most organizations, it is quite usual to witness several positive years followed by a negative one.

Question 9: *How much value do the capital providers expect will be created?* Rather than taking the organization's view, this question asks what capital providers expect in terms of value creation. Obviously, because capital providers each have their own perspectives—for publicly traded companies, they buy in at different prices and anticipate different valuations—this question is multipronged.

1. What return do capital providers demand on their capital? (What is the minimum threshold?)
2. What value creation is anticipated?

The answers to these questions for publicly traded companies can be estimated. For private companies, quantitative algorithms can be used to answer this question. For other organizations, the task is more complex but doable.

Understanding the answers to these questions helps any one capital provider to understand the perspectives of the others. Suppliers, including employees and managers, can use the answers to understand the expectations and the context in which they will run the company. Prospective internal and external suppliers, as well as customers and external observers, can use the answer to provide an excellent indication of others' views of the health of the organization.

Question 10: *How much value does the organization expect to create by sector, product or service, distribution channel, process, and customer?* Obviously, capital providers, prospective suppliers, customers, and external observers would want to assess this. Again, however, some information will not be available at this level but may be inferred. For example, a press release may state: "Our internet channel is important for our future success." If it goes beyond this brief indication, it is possible that information can be gleaned that could be useful in answering this question. Nonetheless, internally, this information is critical for all suppliers to understand. This level of information, along with detailed historical information, will form the basis for future decision making, inform strategy, shape it, and be shaped by it. Answering this question is an iterative and ongoing process. Critics will also want this information. For rating agencies and analysts, the changes in these numbers can be important over time (Question 7) and important indications of the organization's health.

Question 11: *What are the expectations related to major drivers of value creation over time?* Drilling down to competencies and other value drivers, this question addresses the issue of critical success factors and critical attributes at a detailed level. Ultimately, results at this level will drive the organization's performance. While important to all constituents, this information will be most readily available to internal suppliers and may have to be sought via inference from compilations of industry information for all others.

Question 12: *What are the capital provider's expectations for peers? What are a peer's expectations for itself by sector, product, service, distribution channel, process, customer, and major drivers of value creation?* Obviously, this kind of information at any level is helpful to internal suppliers in understanding the competitive landscape in value terms. For capital providers, external customers, suppliers, and critics, this information can help benchmark prospects of the organization and its expected incremental value creation over and above the competition.

Question 13: *How do these internal peer and capital provider expectations differ from current steady-state value creation?* The answers to this question outline the gap between the organization's current state and future expectations. The answers are critical to understanding the work required to meet expectations and the benefit of intellectual capital to the firm. Arguably, these answers are some of the most important insights in the Economic Value Management framework.

Question 14: *For all of the above, how will this change over time?* Key to developing true perspective linking the past to the future, the answers to this question complete the picture of value creation in the organization under review.

VALUE-BASED STRATEGY

The Importance of Value Metrics to Value-Based Strategy

Ever notice how some companies eliminate divisions without ever knowing the value they create or the value that could be created if internal suppliers were asked to focus on value maximization? Or organizations eliminate or add programs without this crucial information? Without a blink or hesitation, companies and organizations around the world today formulate major strategies within their organizations without any idea of the value to be created. It is like spending money for a "mystery bag" at the elementary school fair with the hope that it will contain something of value. Or, like starting out on a road trip without a map.

But is this true? Is it really that grim? Don't companies or organizations know the earnings or other impacts they hope to derive from a strategy? By way of an answer, a company example may be of help.

"Twilight Industries," like many others, is focused on "shareholder value" according to its annual report. Like others, a key to its strategy to create earnings and meet budget objectives involves "cost reduction initiatives." Unfortunately, at Twilight, as in many other cases, these initiatives are not subjected to the fact-based rigor of their impact on value. The metrics in place in the organization do not take value into account. While some Twilight employees involved in these initiatives intuitively understand value impacts, including increased risk, future impact on revenues, and so on, they are not in a position to articulate their intuitions in a clear, quantifiable manner. Economic Value Management provides a more inclusive and better way to make these strategy decisions, taking these factors into the fact basis of decisions. In Economic Value Management, strategic choices include only those strategies that enhance value, regardless of whether costs are reduced or additional money is spent.

Many organizations do not have a clear picture of value, and this incomplete picture can adversely impact strategic decision making. For example, many organizations do not know how much value is being created from period to period by existing strategies or by other possible alternatives.

Why is that important? Well, how important is it to know the advantages of taking the current highway or an alternate route?

Building Blocks of Economic Value Management Strategy and Some Remarkable Advantages

While this all may sound simple, performance assessment is a key building block to Economic Value Management strategy. Value-based strategy requires not only honest assessments of the organization and its peers, but also capital provider expectations. It involves quantification of the benefits of human capital expenditures. It weighs the advantages of risk and returns and optionality. If these metrics are not incorporated with a view to both the past and future, the management approach is not an Economic Value Management discipline.

Does this mean that there is no room for intuition in value-based strategic planning? No; however, the intuition in an Economic Value Management approach will be regulated with a fact-based governor. Both intuition *and* facts in value-based strategic planning will be used with a common goal of increasing value.

Many popular strategic processes have recently emphasized free-form thought generation (so-called out-of-the-box thinking), encouraging creative thought processes with a clear emphasis on intuition. And yet, interestingly enough, the creative process is often enhanced by the Economic Value Management framework. Why is this?

A Remarkable Advantage — Better Ideas. This is actually a curious result and one that has recently been explained in part by new science in this area.

Recently, physicists and computer scientists have studied problems to understand which seem solvable and which seem to be impossible to solve. The research, which looks at the transition of problems from solvable to impossible, points out what intuitively might be expected. The more constraints in an equation, the more it will tend to move from solvable to difficult to unsolvable.[2]

How does this relate to Economic Value Management? This phenomenon explains something about Economic Value Management that those who have experienced it might describe but do not have a name for. That is, Economic Value Management provides a structure that allows for a better flow of solutions, rather than a constriction of ideas. Unlike environments where an organization might be operating under many conflicting measures and approaches to solving problems, Economic Value Management eliminates multiple, conflicting constraints and imposes only one — value creation. This makes problems simpler and easier to solve. Rather than constricting the flow of ideas, Economic Value Management actually opens the floodgates because, consciously or unconsciously, internal suppliers are not mentally wrestling with multiple (balanced or otherwise) constraints.

What makes this all the more remarkable, of course, is that Economic Value Management asserts a much more rigorous selection process (using a value-based financial discipline). Because, however, the conflicts are resolved within the value metric, constituents attempting to *generate* value ideas are not wrestling with multiple constraints. Thus problems are more solvable, and potential ideas and strategies are not screened prematurely.

Exhibits 2.2, 2.3, 2.4, and 2.5 illustrate the differences in idea generation and selection between traditional and Economic Value Management strategic processes. In traditional approaches, worthwhile ideas may not be generated because of confusion about constraints and related issues. Exhibit 2.3 outlines five key reasons why the idea pool in Economic Value Management is larger.

In traditional approaches, there are issues in the selection process as well. Because of inadequate screening, some ideas will be eliminated that could create value (false negatives). Furthermore, the ideas that will be used will fall into two categories:

1. Those that will destroy value (false positives — because of inadequate screening) and

2. Those that will happen to be coincidental with value creation (lucky breaks). See Exhibits 2.4 and 2.5.

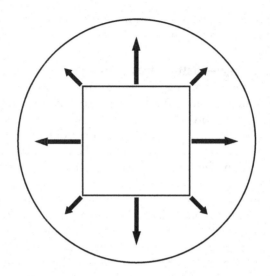

Notes:

The box encompasses ideas generated in a traditional framework (in the box).

The arrows represent the enlargement of the box, the generation of new ideas that occurs as a result of Economic Value Management insights.

The larger circle encompasses the ideas generated in an Economic Value Management framework. (To understand why, see Exhibit 2.3.)

EXHIBIT 2.2   Idea Pool

Why is the idea pool larger in an Economic Value Management framework?

Five key reasons Economic Value Management sparks innovation:

1. The revitalization and continual renewal of the management system invigorate the development of new ideas.

2. The Economic Value Management process provides new insights that trigger new ideas.

3. Lack of conflicting constraints allows better flow of solutions.

4. Clear understanding of the criteria and processes for decision making allow participants to "save face" and avoid the pain associated with the immediate rejection of ideas.

5. In Economic Value Management, personal risk and return are tied to the generation of good ideas; this incentive is supplemented by confidence that the evaluation and monitoring processes that will be used to select ideas and monitor their execution are sound.

EXHIBIT 2.3   Five Key Reasons

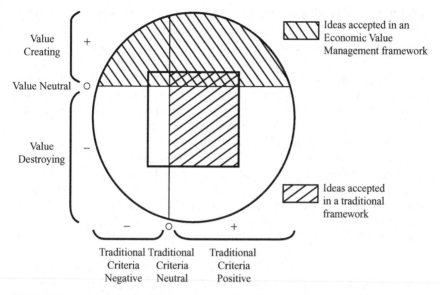

EXHIBIT 2.4 Idea Selection: Ideas Accepted under Each Framework

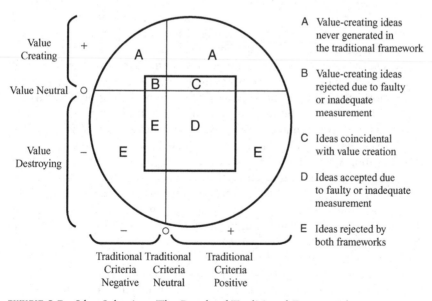

EXHIBIT 2.5 Idea Selection: The Result of Traditional Frameworks

Budgeting and Planning—Time Horizon and an Instant Winner Advantage.

Today, the rate of change has increased. Because of technology and the spread of information, the time between significant strategic events for an organization has become shorter. For this reason, most well-run entrepreneurial companies seriously assess their mission and strategies at least quarterly; some firms do this even more frequently than that. Today, however, many organizations run planning processes in conjunction with annual budgeting processes. Many large organizations have a budgeting process that lasts over three months in the summer or fall months. "Strategic planning" occurs sometime at the start of this process. Typically, in these organizations, no matter what, the budget process rules. What does this mean? In these organizations, no matter the value creation potential of a given strategy, if it requires more than an acceptable budget in any given year (of head count, dollars, etc.) it is often rejected in favor of a slow incremental increase in that unit's investment. Quite frankly, there are good reasons for this protective mechanism. Many organizations do not know what creates value and do not hold internal suppliers accountable for value creation, just parts of the equation or current returns. In addition, a perception exists that there is less risk involved in small incremental growth than in major initiatives. This is because incremental growth is a known quantity and thus deemed "less likely" to destroy value (using the philosophy: if it is working, and it must be since we have not been shot yet, we should not fix it). Budget represents the major control.

In an Economic Value Management world, budget is no longer king. Rather, it takes a back seat to the notion of value-based strategy. It may sit there and from time to time alert the driver of turns, but it is not the road map for the organization's future. Unlike the fixed annual process, value-based strategic processes generally have a different time horizon, pegged to the nature of the business and sculpted to maximize the time horizon look and reassessment of the business itself. The formulation of value-based strategies removes the blinders concerning which current and proposed activities will create the most value. In addition, processes are instituted to reassess strategies on a more frequent than annual basis. Does this disconnect strategy from the annual budget? To a rigid annual budget, yes. To a flexible budget and plan, no. And in addition to other advantages, this ensures something more important—midcourse corrections as needed.

For those who have worked in budget-intensive organizations, you may already see the advantage of putting budget in the back seat where it belongs. The cost of formulating budgets—a process that can be useful to those requiring a backseat navigator (those who do not have the value-based road guides)—is extremely high for the organization.

But because the organization does not know where value is being created, what is the alternative? Top management and the board need some yardstick—is the organization on track or not?—and since they have not invested in value metrics, budget will have to do. But the cost to companies is staggering. In some organizations, as much as 50% or more of executive and middle-management time is spent on this exercise for one-quarter of the year. As a result, as much as 20% or more of the annual compensation of the firm is not focused on customers, product innovation, or operations but on an annual budget—which may or may not create value! So by adopting Economic Value Management, organizations can be instant winners by eliminating an inordinate concentration on budgeting.

PROCESS AND TECHNOLOGY

Exhibit 2.6 shows the relationship among performance assessment, strategy, process, and technology in an uncomplicated manner. The metrics of Economic Value Management support performance assessment. In turn, this performance-assessment information is used to formulate strategy. And the strategies themselves result in new organizational processes. As noted in the description of value-based strategic planning, even the processes of strategic planning and budgeting are restructured in an Economic Value Management world.

The impact of strategy on process, however, extends further than that. To implement new strategies, even cost initiatives that are value based, requires changes to organizational processes. In an Economic Value Management approach, not only the strategies will be value based, but the processes required to effect these initiatives will be implemented in a way that is consistent with the principles of stewardship and Economic Value Management core competencies. From this standpoint, it is clear that not

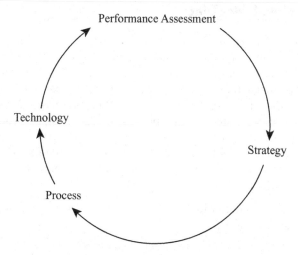

EXHIBIT 2.6 Elemental Relationship Diagram

only do strategy idea generation and selection matter, but so does facilitating the *how* of the changed processes in a value-based way.

As an example, one key process that will change under Economic Value Management is metrics reporting. Metrics may need to be reported more frequently. Multiple value measures will need to be reported. The time horizon of the metrics will need to be examined in light of supporting midcourse corrections and long-term views. And key metrics related to new processes, that is, their success factors and value creation, will need to be implemented and produced.

Often, the metrics reporting processes will require the implementation of technology solutions. Other processes required by value-based initiatives may require technology solutions as well. The choice of technology and how this technology is implemented will now be done in an Economic Value Management framework, considering not only future benefits and costs, but also the risks associated with internal versus external supplier solutions and a clear understanding of the value impacts of a smaller (scaled down) versus a broader solution to the technology issues.

From a constituent perspective, of course, this all sounds reasonable. The real issues for internal suppliers are the implementation and the maintenance mindset required to adhere to the process. As the changes unfold, Economic Value Management creates more questions to be answered and more areas of performance to be assessed, measured, and adjusted.

What else happens? As the processes and technologies evolve, changes will be required in the way in which organizations work together, which leads us to organizational structure.

ORGANIZATIONAL STRUCTURE

Of all corporate strategies, organizational structure and technology probably represent the most immediate intuitive decisions made in corporations. It is an area where internal suppliers often move quickly or thoughtlessly, looking for the magic bullet. Why, then, is organizational structure listed as a critical (separate) piece of Economic Value Management? Organizational structure deserves separate attention because it clearly impacts the organization's operations by impacting its staff. Organizational structure has evolved as kind of an odd issue. For some organizations, if a vacuum exists in terms of strategy, organizational structure changes can be counted on to step in and fill the void:

- "We don't have a better idea to make our mark than to redesign or reorganize—so let's do it."
- "It will hide problems in the underlying business if we do."
- "At least it will look like we are doing something."

For Economic Value Management organizations, of course, this is anathema. Denise, a long-term employee of the large "Mendel Corporation," was relating what seemed to be Mendel's corporate strategy. "Every three years we change our organizational structure. We centralize to improve profits and customer service. Then three years later we decentralize for the very same reason."

Value-based organizational structure changes are instead a result of either

1. The requirements of the Economic Value Management discipline itself, or
2. The strategies and initiatives that come out of the Economic Value Management discipline

Requirements

In Economic Value Management–centered organizations, what gets attention changes. Fewer staff will be devoted to certain functions. As noted in the section on strategy, excessive budget emphasis is out. Earnings management is out. Performance assessment on a value basis and risk assessment and reward/risk trade-off is in. And training and communication is in (see the sections that follow on these topics).

Understanding these issues can be important to everyone. The dedication of resources to the right activities can be an important indicator of the organization's commitment to the principles of stewardship. The time commitment to certain activities translates into use of capital. It signals focus (or lack thereof) on the customer, regulations, or other constituent issues. The requirements of the Economic Value Management discipline will not permit squandering of the organization's resources. The need to restructure then arises out of the requirements of the discipline itself.

Strategies and Initiatives

Organizational structure may also change as a result of the strategies and initiatives of Economic Value Management. Typical changes include an organizational shift to interdisciplinary cooperation *to achieve desired results* (line functions working with the back office, finance with human resources, etc.). Some organizations hang up signs that proclaim, "Together Everyone Achieves More." While the slogan may be true, together everyone achieves more only if there is a common understanding of goals, strategies, and directions. In some organizations, there is no common yardstick and no common philosophy about corporate governance. If executives want to say TEAM, they can say it, but what does it mean?

With Economic Value Management, there is a common yardstick for all entities of the organization. That means that even staff functions use the disciplines of the performance-assessment processes and work with other line and staff functions in new ways to support the overall value-based goals of the organizations.

As functions in organizations become more complex, and separation of duties increases, Economic Value Management also provides an integrating approach that balances the need for entrepreneurship and common objectives. The common objectives come out of the specific philosophy of stewardship and entrepreneurship, from the principle that internal suppliers should think, feel, and act like capital providers.[3]

To ensure that the new organizational structure has legs, two other areas are key in Economic Value Management:

1. Rewards processes
2. Training and communications

REWARDS PROCESS

The rewards process in Economic Value Management is designed to enforce a consistent message about value creation. The intention of this process is to give internal suppliers and, for that matter, external suppliers and customers, rewards based on the value created for the capital providers. For external supplier relationships, that may mean establishing relationships with stakes in the outcomes of the business; for customers, rebates or other incentives that add value benefits to the relationship.

For internal suppliers, this reward system can encompass the basis for base pay, variable compensation (short or long term), 401-k matching, benefits, and stock-based incentives. While pay is clearly not the only criterion for motivation, it does make a huge difference in many cultures to align aspects of pay with the benefits of stewardship.

Frankly, too many organizations with quasi-value-performance measures and processes have not yet aligned pay with value-based performance. Whatever the basis for pay in these organizations—whether it be (a) subjective (i.e., whatever the boss thinks) or (b) other performance measures not linked to value—these bases are huge motivational forces in the organizations. How does this impact the organization? For subjective processes, biases commonly exist to meet the intuition and ego needs of the bosses. For other, non-value-based performance-measure processes, this means managing the numbers to achieve the desired result, which is usually a preset or determined budget level. Whether subjective or otherwise, non-value-based reward systems tend to destroy value. Internal suppliers often rationally devote energy to non-value-producing activities, and the processes often have the potentially damaging impact of motivating for the wrong results.

"Manacle," a large company, is a telling example. Jane, the head of human resources, was discussing the issue of pay for performance with a small internal group of Manacle employees: "We have been talking about the possibility of moving toward performance-based pay. We haven't really decided yet, but we think it is something we might want to move toward."

As people at the table nodded, she continued: "It won't be an easy transition, though. The whole idea is so new to our company. Managers are worried that if they get paid based on performance, their pay may be less. Plus the whole process seems like it could take a long time," she said. "But we hope to begin discussions next year."

Even organizations today that have a *stated* focus on performance criteria may still operate on the basis of boss determination. At "The Nile Company" there is a bonus pay structure for sales reps. According to the plan, the variable compensation of the reps is based on "sales and relationship management criteria." In effect, however, since sales managers determine the bonus pay for each sales rep in their unit, pay is subjectively determined. As a result of this practice, despite superior performance, women sales reps consistently receive lower bonuses than their male counterparts. Installing the financial disciplines of Economic Value Management and value-based pay would reward all sales reps for their value creation and thus would eliminate the inequities.

Although Economic Value Management offers hope, the practices in many organizations lag far behind. Even the basic issue of performance-based reward systems is problematic in many organizations. This can be witnessed in an issue that is beginning to receive attention in the press: the level of pay in certain jobs. From the early 1980s to the turn of the century, there has been a substantial increase in the gap between the lowest-paid worker and the highest-paid executives. In addition to institutional investor involvement and increasing press coverage, activist groups like Responsible Wealth are sounding the alarm on the relationship between capital provider rewards and the high level of executive pay. (In some organizations, the reverse situation is also causing problems. In these organizations, low pay scales inhibit the ability to hire the personnel necessary to generate the greatest benefits for capital providers.)

The dialogue in the press concerning pay for performance continues to highlight instances where pay is not based on performance; where capital providers, lower level internal suppliers, the community, or customers are damaged while executive level internal suppliers are well rewarded. However, the simple analyses found in some press reports does not sufficiently explain the issues surrounding this problem. For example, if executive performance is judged based on measures that are not relevant or are outside the executives' control, then how can it be said that there has been pay for no performance?

To dig deeper, sometimes the press compares pay to the earnings of the firm. If earnings is the measure, and earnings are raised via selling off parts of the business, has the capital provider benefited? Maybe, or maybe not. If earnings have been manipulated, does that mean high pay is justified?

Often the press reports review the executive's pay in light of the stock price of the company. Sometimes annual changes in pay are linked to annual changes in stock price. (For example, has pay risen dramatically with a small increase in stock price?) Is this a valid comparison? It can be argued that if the stock price only rises by a small amount, pay should as well. On the surface, this argument appears plausible. But what does the stock price actually represent? Has the market reacted to good news for the industry as a whole? How much has this to do with the efforts of the executive?

The stock price, of course, is forward looking. It represents the market's beliefs about what the company will be able to achieve in the future. If the stock price rises dramatically in a year, should the executives be compensated for the increase? Will the executive stay and implement the proposed vision? Suppose they do and their plan is great, but the implementation is weak? Should they be rewarded in the year the stock price goes up because they created hope? And if the price comes down because of unrealistic views of the sector should they suffer?

Should the market determine pay in publicly traded firms? There are several problems, of course, with tying pay to stock price. One problem is period mismatching—lack of alignment between effort and measurement. Consider recent discussions about IPOs or demutualization. Should current management get credit and be rewarded for all the value created in the past to build the franchise to what it is today and for the market's view, on that basis, of what it will become in the future?

Second, what will be the motivation of executives if stock price increases are rewarded? To prop up the stock price? To disclose just enough to gain in the short-term and leave the real issues to everyone else? Consider recent bankruptcies that have involved just such practices.

The use of stock options can also create what is sometimes called the "Silicon Valley problem." This problem occurs when a company awards stock options and the stock value later declines, prompting one of two events:

1. The knowledge capital walks out the door when it is needed most.
2. More stock options are issued, or changes are made to the strike price, so that employees face no real decline, thereby breaking the link between stock price and compensation.

In Economic Value Management, internal suppliers are rewarded for the value they create. Sometimes this means being very creative and careful in the design of plans to achieve proper alignment. Economic Value Management addresses this by ensuring that the rewards are tied to value creation and matched to the appropriate time horizon.

The area of compensation can be very delicate. Some jobs that may have been considered "glamour jobs" using traditional measures do not necessarily look as value-enhancing when placed under the microscope of Economic Value Management. Because of cultural issues, organizations are often slow to incorporate this new information about value creation in their reward systems. When implemented, the changes can be dramatic, however.

Successful Economic Value Management companies extend the concepts and rewards through the organization. When shortcuts are taken in implementing plans, this can have a dramatic impact on the effectiveness of the program as well as the pay individuals receive in any given year. When top executives will not relinquish control and insist on making subjective decisions, several things are likely to be happening. First, one should be alerted to the strong likelihood that the environment for the top ranks is highly political—and that relationship may be valued over competence or results. Second, the command and control philosophy can cause issues in other aspects of Economic Value Management, as illustrated in the following example.

"Candymaker Company" had a very strong CEO, Marvin, whose vision and views on operating tactics dominated the company. He was so controlling, in fact, that he only hired and promoted people with whom he had a prior relationship. Marvin led a group of relatively smart people who wanted to use an Economic Value Management approach to run the business and compensate managers. Because of Marvin's excessive control and desire to use his own intuition, unchecked by other views and analyses, the staff reporting to him could only move very slowly in the Economic Value Management implementation process. Marvin's hindrance of their progress resulted in too many delays. Candymaker became exposed because they did not have all the performance-assessment tools in place to understand the true risks in their business. Unable to react, the business began to suffer losses, the stock declined, and the company was taken over in a matter of months.

Greed and manipulation of results are other key issues in unfair compensation. Because consistent stewardship is Economic Value Management's goal, a true value-based management compensation plan will address these issues. Greed is placed in the context of sustainable value creation, value that has been created, and the long-term benefits for all constituents that make value creation sustainable. Manipulation of results in a true value-based plan is controlled through the structure and design of the plan. Shortcuts taken in the compensation design process have caused companies to either throw out the baby with the bath water or not achieve the full benefits of the system. One common issue for organizations occurs when they attempt to base pay on a *budgeted* value number. Budgeted numbers, however, as a basis of pay *encourage* manipulation, even if the metrics are value based.

The "TipTop" company, which was often cited as a "value-based" company, publicly stated that "shareholder value" was key to its strategic processes. Although value was the mantra, the mechanics and tactics at TipTop were little understood throughout the organization, and metrics were available only at the highest level. TipTop, which has since been gobbled up by a larger international firm, might have moved forward to improve its implementation had its compensation process not been so flawed. To wit, the compensation process did not include several key design elements and features of value-based plans. Accountability and integrity (i.e., nonmanipulation) were lacking. Related to accountability, unfortunately, TipTop's plan reflected a preconception that some new initiates tend to take. This preconception is that Economic Value Management is not really an operating approach to managing the organization but merely a financing one. That is, it has no need to influence day-to-day operations; rather, its major "recommendation" is balance sheet manipulation. While, of course, certain moves to restructure the balance sheet can benefit an organization and its capital providers, these actions do not ensure that operating managers will be good stewards working to improve the firm's value. At TipTop, using the flawed compensation plan, managers (both staff and line) received compensation based on achieving (through manipulation of the results) a set of budgeted, so-called value-based, numbers. Because of the plan's structure, TipTop's management team always received high bonuses; it was almost impossible not to. While the metric might have been "economic profit" or "economic value added," the plan was certainly not focused on rewarding management appropriately for value creation.

At the "Marshswamp" organization, the basis for pay had been related to meeting or exceeding certain budgeted earnings targets. As a result of this, the financial staff at Marshswamp consistently spent time, not only reporting numbers, but also working with the organization to ensure that the numbers goals were met. Sam, Marshswamp's CFO, explained it this way: "When things were going well from an earnings numbers perspective, we would approve making investments in the business such as advertising and marketing expenditures, which are important for our growth. When things were not doing as well, we would help the operating units sell off pieces of the business to generate earnings. We knew it would reduce earnings in future periods, but we needed to hit earnings targets now. During down cyclical times, these sell-offs often helped us to continue to generate consistent earnings growth."

Of course, everyone at Marshswamp was rewarded when the earnings targets were achieved, and the staff was lauded for both growth and the "ability to deliver." The problem was that even in the best of times it became difficult for Marshswamp to sustain the kind of results that could be achieved through even minor sell-offs. As the earnings and budget focus in the compensation process caused noneconomic motivation and wasted the talents of the finance staff, Marshswamp's finance staff became more attuned to *timing* than to *economics*. (Although the issues at Marshswamp were problematic, they were not as intense as those in a similar firm, "Desert

Hollywood," whose dependence on trading had become so great that the analyst community was able to pierce the veil and expressed concern about the company's future prospects.)

Marshswamp, in search of a better way, moved forward to implement an Economic Value Management compensation program. The compensation design process focused the management team on the changes in behavior that would be required. Sam remarks, "Certain quick fixes were no longer the best solution. Instead of meeting the old numbers, long-term value creation was now the order of the day."

Demographically, while those entering the workforce today may care less about dollar compensation, for many of them, time is valuable. They expect to be well compensated and seek more balance between work and nonwork. For this group, the flexibility of the organization is key. This means organizations need to rethink how to motivate Economic Value Management behavior and what the range of potential incentives might be.

Economic Value Management is a matter of eliminating bad habits and replacing them with more healthy ones. Like quitting smoking, not all organizations will accomplish it successfully on the first attempt. Some organizations find, for example, that they need to rework their reward systems several times to eliminate manipulation and create the right behaviors. Others find they need to strengthen training and communication programs to fully achieve the results.

TRAINING AND COMMUNICATIONS

Economic Value Management is a discipline and a series of practices. Although the linkage to compensation is very powerful, this does guarantee that the organization will understand the discipline or what is required to create value. The "RightCenter" organization, although relatively small, had created a national reputation for themselves in part because of their strong implementation of "shareholder value." They had instituted measures, a reporting system and two compensation plans: one for executives and one for their sales force. Their annual reports and web site discussed their commitment to "economic value," and their executives frequently spoke on the subject. Because of their implementation, their stock return exceeded that of both the S&P 500 and other comparable firms in the same industry. This was a model implementer! And yet, RightCenter exemplifies how much the process of Economic Value Management implementation is a long-term one, a process that belongs, as Stephen Covey would say, in the critical but not urgent quadrant. (Economic Value Management is never urgent until it is too late.)

At RightCenter, even though the executives were rewarded based on value creation, and it produced powerful results, particularly because of the sales compensation plan, most of the top executives did not really understand it. "We aren't really sure how it works," executive team members confessed. Because of this, although RightCenter created a more cohesive process, a pride in the focus, and a better sales process, it did not really drive day-to-day executive decision making or intuitions. What was missing? This organization had been communicating to external analysts and even sharing its value creation metrics from time to time with analysts and investors. And some members of middle management had received training in the value metrics and management. Executive management, however, had not stopped long enough to focus and really understand the *implications* of value strategy on decision making or compensation. Without this focus and training, RightCenter was able to take the benefits only so far.

The message? As organizations learn to achieve the full benefit of Economic Value Management, a learning attitude and appropriate programs are a requirement. Without them, the full value of Economic Value Management will not be achieved. What does this involve? At a minimum, this involves three distinct elements:

1. Appropriate training, learning systems, and programs

2. Appropriate internal communications

3. Appropriate external communications

Appropriate Training, Learning Systems, and Programs

Sometimes Economic Value Management seems so simple, why would anyone need training? But much of the power of the process is lost without this important step. For one, and this is especially true for the finance staff, the old ways are so ingrained that reinforcement and intervention are often needed to be truly successful. For another, knowledge assets are some of the most important assets that an organization has. Therefore, if the employees better understand how to drive value, the return in value creation is demonstrably there.

The real question, however, is whether the organization wants to just hack at "shareholder value" or invest the effort to do Economic Value Management well. To achieve the latter, the training program instituted should include one or more of the components outlined in Exhibit 2.7.

Appropriate Internal Communications

Appropriate reporting of the metrics on performance and strategy implementation is just one aspect of internal communications. During initial implementation, and then as new communication vehicles are created, all communications in the organization need to reflect the new world view. They should emphasize, inform, and stimulate continuous improvement around the value drivers and key mindsets necessary to truly become an

Using various media, the components of the training program should include:

▓ General financial education training, which teaches the basics of Economic Value Management business and metrics principles.

▓ A performance diagnostic program, which helps managers and employees identify issues to be addressed within their own organizations.

▓ A strategy skills course that is value based.

▓ A course for the board of directors explaining corporate governance and how Economic Value Management can help them to fulfill their duties.

▓ A detailed performance assessment course, which includes the key issues in building the metrics and effective reporting.

▓ An executive communications course, for both internal and external communications.

▓ Learning programs needed for the new technology and process initiatives and to support the new organizational structure and other value-based processes.

EXHIBIT 2.7 Components of the Training Program

Economic Value Management organization. Forms of communication may include those outlined in Exhibit 2.8.

As in advertising, the messages ideally will communicate emotionally, as well as logically, and stimulate the creativity required for success. To achieve the cohesive benefits, this messaging must be ever present and repetitive.

Stanley, a well-known CEO at "Largesse," one of the world's largest companies, understood the value of both internal and external communications to reinforce the mantra of value. Despite weaknesses in other parts of the

- Newsletters

- Electronic Brochures

- Reports

- Documents in Various Formats

- Videos

- Websites

- Discussion Forums

EXHIBIT 2.8 Forms of Communication

management system, the efforts at the company during his reign were highly successful because Stanley's communications' emphasis was so clear.

The communications efforts benefit everyone. In *Rules for Revolutionaries,* Guy Kawasaki states "The higher you go in a company, the less oxygen there is, so supporting intelligent life becomes difficult . . . people high within the hierarchy . . . only have the brainpower to contemplate the status quo."[4] While obviously not always true, or confined to those high in the hierarchy, certainly requiring that the leadership repeat over and over the mechanisms for decision making not only reinforces it for the staff but for themselves as well. Practicing the fundamentals is key to winning in any endeavor. Outlining the value creation goal and reinforcing its message is one way organizations can practice the fundamentals to win.

Appropriate External Communications

This is a scary area for many companies. It is the way, however, for external constituents to understand whether the organization's so-called value-based program is pure bluster or has truly transformed the company. For external constituents to benefit, however, they must be knowledgeable regarding Economic Value Management and be able to discern the difference between the organization's words and deeds. That, in part, is one of the purposes of this book.

Recent articles have pointed to the increasing influence of analysts and investors on the way in which companies are managed. Many organizations have felt the pressure of external critics—analysts, (institutional) investors, and rating agencies—to disclose real information on value creation, the drivers of value, and value-based management, including corporate governance and compensation.

As pension and retirement systems have changed, individuals' decisions have had more influence on the economics of their retirement. Investors' financial savvy has grown, supported by do-it-yourself investing tools, including periodicals like *Money Magazine* and *Worth,* internet advice like The Motley Fool, and the emergence of inexpensive online trading. Today, capital providers want the tools to make their own decisions about the organizations they aid and hope to benefit from. The experience at one particular hedge fund shows that you cannot necessarily trust so-called experts. In addition, analysts' poor records on tech stocks and other spectacular bankruptcies have reinforced this caution.

If one of the top reasons CEOs fail is that they believe their own annual reports, then clearly external critics and capital providers have the same issue as well. Beyond earnings manipulation, which is getting some attention from the SEC, the accounting numbers as stated just *do not* provide the picture required to make an intelligent judgement about the organization and its future prospects.

So, value-based external communication may require a radical rewrite of the existing process in the firm. As we discussed earlier, the first step in Economic Value Management is *to not fool oneself* internally in the organization, but rather to make an honest self-assessment. The step of external communication requires that one not fool others as well. But to do this requires a dynamic of listening and also being listened to. From a tactical perspective, it means changing the language of discussion to value terms; discussing strategies, long-term bets, and what they mean; and holding one's ground that earnings volatility (i.e., not managing earnings) is ok.

It also includes having a conversation to *educate* external critics, including the press, on why accounting changes (i.e., FASB rule changes) do not matter and do not impact the nature of the business. They are simply a reporting convention, nothing more, nothing less. It is an easy concept but often a matter of confusion, and even internal managers are often confused. For example, "GARP Inc." was trying to develop value-based calculations after the FASBs had recently been changed. For GARP's CEO, David, who had lived by the earnings results, this FASB change was devastating. "This has literally changed my business proposition," he said. "What once was profitable no longer is; what wasn't, now seems so. I am going to have to change the nature and focus of my business. I cannot go on as I have. My strategies must change." After having paid a consulting firm several million dollars to confirm his belief, David sold the supposedly now unprofitable segment of the business. Unfortunately, value intervention at this point was too late. The damage had been done. How so? Because from a value perspective, *nothing changed when the FASB did*—except for the reported numbers. These FASBs did not affect any value drivers. They did not change the marketplace or the views of customers. They did not change sales or pricing. They did not change the cost of capital or the firm's financing options. Nothing changed. Except, as it turned out, GARP had sold their *most* profitable segment from a value perspective and was losing money hand over fist on the segment they kept.

The point of the GARP example is that if we tell others the wrong thing too often, we may begin to believe it ourselves. So what is needed is external communication consistent with Economic Value Management principles and lived internally. If we talk about earnings, we will come to believe that a change in rules-based accounting matters—when it really does not. What matters is how the company is run and what it is doing to create value. This means having an honest discussion about strategies and value drivers, once the efforts can be communicated publicly, and about the continuous improvement work in the areas of corporate governance, compensation, financial education, and so on, happening within the organization. The education of external critics and others is key to this effort. The reward will include enhanced trust, access to the capital markets, and better reputation over the long term.

ORGANIZATIONS TODAY AND WHY EVERYONE SHOULD GET INVOLVED

The picture of organizations today has bright spots. As organizations face new challenges, they look to examples of both success and failure to understand the lessons to be learned. Dilbert cartoons strike a resonant chord for a reason. Many organizations are struggling and desperately need what Economic Value Management has to offer.

"Honeydo Stores" is a retailer that has recently gone through a series of transitions. Honeydo began as a local company in its area. It had a reputation for selling high-quality merchandise and had the unique practice of extending interest-free credit to customers, who were only required to pay a certain percentage on their bill each month. Oddly enough, because of the interest-free policy, customers tended to pay this bill first to maintain their good credit standing. The sales staff on the floor of Honeydo's store was responsible only for selling. Sales associates at Honeydo were encouraged to build customer relationships and focus on sales. Buying and stocking of merchandise were handled by other staff. Commissions were paid to the sales associates based on their sales. To grow customer loyalty, associates would often attend, on their own time, some of the important events in the lives of their customers such as funerals, christenings, and the like. Honeydo's business proposition was working well, and the firm was profitable. However, rather than continue to march to its own drummer, Honeydo decided to follow the crowd. A corporate decision was made to change to a more typical customer-financing scheme for the business, with interest now being charged on unpaid balances. As a result, sales immediately began to plummet, while accounts receivables increased.

Rather than reverse its policy change in response to the decline, Honeydo sold out to a larger regional franchise, "The Melon Group," which had its own business philosophy. The rules for the sales associates immediately changed. Sales associates at Melon were responsible for more than just sales; they were now required to stock shelves as well. Base pay for the associates was increased but there were no incentives, quotas, or commissions. Sales fell even further, and eventually the company sold out again, this time to a larger national franchise, "The Cantaloupe Corporation."

Unsurprisingly, Cantaloupe had its own philosophy on retailing. As with Melon, stocking shelves has remained part of the sales job. To boost sales, however, the company decided against sales commissions but rather adopted the "stick" approach to motivate their sales staff. Each associate is given a very high and strict sales quota based on expected or required sales dollars per hour. Missing a quota quickly results in probation, fines, or dismissal. One impact of this new method has been to create a conflict of interest between the full-time and part-time associates at Cantaloupe. Full-time associates are given the same per hour quotas as the part-timers who are hired to work only during the busy lunch hour and on weekends. Full-time associates have to share sales with their part-time counterparts at the busiest times and then stick around to stock the shelves while still being held to the same per hour quotas. From the perspective of the full-timers, the so-called benefit of full-time status is that you get to stock shelves and then get fined for not meeting your sales quota. As of this writing, to avoid being fined, some of the full-time staff are trying to convince management that part-time help is not needed. The others are trying to determine how they can become part-time employees since they would make the same money, work fewer hours, and enjoy greatly reduced stress! Motivated workforce? Concern for the customer? Pushing product? Motivated to create value? Three companies—three views—same business.

The caricatures of the incompetent pointy-haired boss and his lethargic staff are popular because they are real. While Economic Value Management is not a panacea, there is work to be done and Economic Value Management can help. The Economic Value Management approach provides a way to improve organizational performance in a repeatable way, using an integrated approach to manage the organization based on the principles of stewardship.

But Economic Value Management is not for everyone. It is for professional drivers only. To build the cohesion through Economic Value Management requires effort. To build the metrics requires patience. To monitor and continually enhance the process requires persistence.

The next chapters will discuss some of the hows and some of the cutting edge applications of Economic Value Management. Join the ride.

NOTES

1. Robert S. Kaplan and David P. Norton, *The Balanced Scorecard: Translating Strategy Into Action,* Boston: Harvard Business School Press, 1996.

2. George Johnson, "Separating the Unsolvable and the Merely Difficult," *The New York Times,* July 13, 1999.

3. For more information on this topic, see especially Chapter 9, Value Drivers—Application of Metrics-Organizational Structure.

4. Guy Kawasaki and Michele Moreno, *Rules for Revolutionaries,* New York: Harper Business, 1999.

CHAPTER 3

The Performance Measurement and Management Context

OVERVIEW

Financial measures are the starting point for most organizations' performance-measurement systems. Whether it is donations raised, net income earned, or retained net profit, most organizations start with monetary numerics as the initial measures for success. For corporations, these financial measures come directly from (or are calculated using) accounting information from the regulatory financial statements (see Exhibit 3.1).

IMPACT OF ACCOUNTING ON MEASURES AND ACCOUNTING PRACTICE ON MANAGEMENT

Accounting rules specify which measures must be provided in the regulatory financial statements and the calculation framework for those measures. For example, accounting rules govern the calculation of net income (revenues less expenses, including taxes) on the income statement. Accounting rules also govern the derivation of assets, liabilities, and equity on the balance sheet. Because the accounting measures are often used as primary measures for the corporation, the impact of the accounting rules on managers' thought processes is pervasive.

Income Statement	Balance Sheet
• Revenues	• Assets
• Expenses	• Liabilities
• Net Income	• Equity

EXHIBIT 3.1 Traditional Accounting Statements

Principle of Conservatism

One of the key concepts of accounting is what many textbooks refer to as the *principle of conservatism*. In effect, this accounting principle describes that an organization's bias in calculating the amount of income or assets of the firm should be to understate rather than overstate these amounts. For example, many assets are generally recorded on the balance sheet at cost and then assumed to lose value over time (reflected in accounting depreciation or amortization). Exceptions to this rule exist for certain assets where market values may be more readily available. These assets may be recorded at the lower of cost or market; that is, the assets cannot be marked up in value, only down. Other assets are never recorded at all, including certain intangible assets or investments that the firm makes. Using this conservatism principle as well, the rules specify requirements that the calculation of income is to err on the side of understatement versus overstatement. The result of this principle is that, in some cases, items flow through on a cash basis (as cash is received) and in others, on an accrual basis. For example, rather than *overstate* income, revenues would not be recorded on the income statement when received if the time period for receipt occurs before the resources associated with that revenue have been employed.

One key result of the conservatism principle is that, at times, to be conservative, certain activities may be accrued or amortized while others must be expensed. For example, some assets must be depreciated over their normal life. This depreciation or amortization expense must be done to recognize the imputed economic loss of the assets. Sometimes this loss is real. At other times, however, there is no loss; in fact, the organization may actually experience a gain in market value of the asset. For example, an office building would be depreciated, although its value might be rising. While the rules require a stated loss even if there is a market value gain, in other instances they require investments to be immediately expensed. For example, rather than amortizing the marketing costs over the life of the sales revenues, unless data are available to exactly match these expenses with their associated sales revenues, all the expense must be taken in the initial period.

Principle of Materiality

Materiality is another key concept in accounting. The materiality concept states that disclosures must be made by public corporations for material information, and appropriately reflected in the corporation's financial statements. Materiality is a good example of the fact that although the rules of accounting attempt to be specific, at times at least the interpretation of them misses the mark. Citing materiality, for example, some corporations and their accounting auditors have interpreted this rule to mean (or used this rule to justify) that a misstatement need not be corrected—as long as the misstatement is so small that it does not meet the materiality threshold.

While this may seem reasonable, in some instances this level of materiality has been interpreted to be as high as 5% of net income. Because of these kinds of interpretations, the SEC has started to question so-called earnings management techniques in organizations. These techniques are characterized as manipulative, but nonetheless they meet the requirements of many external accountant auditors, because of the legalistic interpretation of the accounting principles of conservatism and materiality.

Using Rules to Manage or Manipulate

One of the issues the SEC has pinpointed related to accounting and annual report numbers has to do with the latitude some firms and their external accountant auditors have taken on the issue of conservatism. Some external auditors, for example, have taken the position that as long as the organization in any given period is employing conservatism, they will approve the bookkeeping as being in line with generally accepted accounting principles (GAAP).

For example, an organization might have an expenditure that could potentially be accrued and charged over two years, rather than expensed. The organization might, with the external auditor's approval, however, expense the entire amount in the first year. The auditors might agree to the difference by citing the principle of conservatism.

This very issue was faced by the "Cowboy Bank." They were having an extremely good year. Marvin, the CFO, lunched with the auditor. "We need to take advantage of this good year," Marvin said. "We plan to front load as many expenses as possible. No point spreading them over the next year . . . I'm just not sure we can continue the great year we're having. This will help take some of the pressure off."

"Sounds logical and it won't overstate this year's results," said Sally, the auditor, munching on her salad. "The economy is less stable. Let us know what you want to do."

Exhibit 3.2 shows the kind of decision Marvin and Sally were discussing. Marvin could charge expenses that would normally result in a volatile earnings picture or take advantage of the revenue benefits in year 1 to charge more expenses in that year as well.

Tax reasons aside, there could be several reasons an organization might pursue this course of action. As Exhibit 3.2 shows, from the organization's perspective, one reason to take this action could be related to the impact it would have on the organizations' income statement (also known as profit and loss statement). The impact of taking the expenses in the first year rather than charging them normally over two years would be to lower the income in the first year and raise it in the second. This impact might prove beneficial to the organization if the first year results were turning out better than anticipated and the second year results were less certain. The advantages in

"Managed" Earnings Display Steady Increase:
Net Income Increases Year 1 to Year 2

	Year 0	Year 1	Year 2	Year 0, 1, 2
Revenue (A)	800	1,200	1,000	3,000
Expense (B)	200	500	200	900
Net Income (A – B)	600	700	800	2,100

"Volatile" Earnings:
Net Income Declines from Year 1 to Year 2

	Year 0	Year 1	Year 2	Year 0, 1, 2
Revenue (A)	800	1,200	1,000	3,000
Expense (B)	200	300	400	900
Net Income (A – B)	600	900	600	2,100

EXHIBIT 3.2   Cowboy Bank: Year 1 Decision

this instance to the organization could take several forms. By placing all the expense in the first year, the organization's increase from the prior year would look less dramatic. Ordinarily an increase from the prior year is welcomed, but too dramatic an increase can be problematic. The advantage of the lower number is that it could help to set up lower expectations on the part of critics and capital providers for the following year. If the results in the first year were higher, capital providers might wrongly anticipate higher results in the second year. Lower expectations could make it more likely that the company would please rather than displease critics and capital providers with less than anticipated results in the second year when returns will be less certain. From the organization's perspective, if the earnings were not managed, it might increase the organization's public relations cost by having to explain why this level will be unlikely in the future or create needless undue internal pressure that might not be able to be fulfilled (i.e., following the mantra, *our profits must increase every year*). In addition to keeping expectations in check, placing all the expense on the first year would also make the organization's second year look better. The chances would improve that the second year would show an increase over the first year, an attribute unsophisticated capital providers often value. And following this logic, not only might this be valued for the current period but the value might then be projected in the organization's valuation and stock price as an upward trend. From an internal viewpoint, this valuation might not only look good on paper but also could improve the value of the executives' stock options, which might be an important source of their personal wealth. While focusing on earnings management may not be an ideal thought process, understanding the rationality of this focus can be an important first step to making changes.

A similar example that has been experienced in many corporations uses conservatism to recognize potential future losses. As a matter of practice, when a company anticipates future losses, it often creates reserves for these losses by setting up or adding to a liability account on the balance sheet. This increase in the liability account occurs in conjunction with an expense for the future loss (an accrued expense) on the income statement. For example, if the company management believes that customers will not pay their bills, it might establish a reserve for the bad debt (i.e., for the losses it anticipates in the future). In conjunction with the setup of or addition to the bad debt reserve on the balance sheet, the income statement will reflect a bad debt expense (although no actual loss may have yet occurred). Using the conservatism principle, the company might (conservatively) project the amount of future losses. If year 1 looks like a particularly good year but year 2 less certain, the company might use the conservatism principle and increase its reserve and expenses in year 1. In year 2, if the (extreme) losses did not develop, this reserve could be lowered. In conjunction with the lower reserve, there would be a lowered expense, thus resulting in higher income in year 2.

Exhibit 3.3 shows an example of how (and why) an organization might find reserves a useful earnings management tool. "Reservoir" is a firm with a fairly steady business proposition. When Reservoir increases the reserve for bad debts, it creates an expense on the income statement. As shown, if

"Conservative Managed Reserving": Increase in Net Income

	Year 1	Year 2	Years 1 and 2
Revenue (A)	1,000	900	1,900
Bad Debt Expense (B)	300	100	400
All Other Expenses (C)	500	500	1,000
Net Income (A − B − C)	200	300	500

"Unmanaged Reserving": Decrease in Net Income

	Year 1	Year 2	Years 1 and 2
Revenue (A)	1,000	900	1,900
Bad Debt Expense (B)	200	200	400
All Other Expenses (C)	500	500	1,000
Net Income (A − B − C)	300	200	500

EXHIBIT 3.3   Reservoir Firm

the reserving process were *nonmanaged,* the bad debt expense each year would be $200.

In year one, Reservoir's revenues are up considerably from previous years. Unsure if they can sustain it, Reservoir conservatively increases its reserve and thus its bad debt expense in year one. When year two comes around, the CFO, Ronald, breathes a sigh of relief. "I guess we were too conservative. We can lower our reserve this year." As shown, Reservoir does lower its reserve and thus its expense in year two. As a result, a nice increase in net income is posted year over year.

One association has used the reserving process extensively. The "Markham" association is not publicly traded and is not required to follow GAAP. Some of their reserves are legitimate, and others are, by their admission, somewhat less so. "We put on reserves when we need to," says Bill, with a wry smile. For the association, the benefit of extra reserves has been to show low retained profit to its members. (As liabilities, reserves reduce retained profits.) This makes it easier for the association to continue to charge relatively high dues to its members, who might otherwise balk at the amounts if higher retained profits were shown. Reserves also allow the association's management group the flexibility to make certain investments or to cover losses they would prefer to hide from their members.

This is made possible because a general reserve can be set aside in an earlier period and expensed at that time. Later, Bill and his team can use that reserve, without creating any entry to the income statement, as needs arise.

Public companies also use reserves to their best advantage. The "Golden Egg Corporation," for example, was going through the process of selling one of its businesses to "Chickpea Limited." The way this sale was structured, the entire business including employees, plant, and equipment were taken over by Chickpea. However, a clause in the agreement allowed Chickpea to return any employees to Golden Egg if they were no longer needed. (In essence, Chickpea held a significant put option exercisable over a period of time. It had the right, but not the obligation, to put the employees back to Golden Egg.) In accounting terms, this represented a liability for Golden Egg and conservative accounting required that the potential liability be recorded on the Golden Egg's books. This potential liability was sizable, and the reserve was recorded as required. (Because of the accounting principle of conservatism, companies are allowed—and often encouraged—to book the full amount of potential liability although the probability for a large portion of it may be very low.) Fortunately, for Golden Egg, Chickpea never exercised the put so none of the reserve was needed. While uncertain at the beginning, this fact became clear over time, as Chickpea continued to use the human resources and, in fact, expand its hiring. Golden Egg, however, did not release all of its reserves at one time. Instead, it acted conservatively and incrementally, in its own best reporting interests (see Exhibit 3.4). As Jim, the plant manager at Golden Egg remarked, "When Golden Egg needed

Gradual Reserve Release*

	Year 1	Year 2	Year 3	Year 4	Year 5
Proceeds from Sale of Business (A)	1,000	—	—	—	—
Reserve Expense for Employee Put (B)	800	—	(200)	—	(400)
Net Income Impact (A − B = C)	200	—	200	—	400
Other Net Income (D)	500	600	500	800	500
Total Net Income (C + D)	700	600	700	800	900

If Reserves Released Immediately in Year 3:

	Year 1	Year 2	Year 3	Year 4	Year 5
Proceeds from Sale of Business (A)	1,000	—	—	—	—
Reserve Expense for Employee Put (B)	800	—	(800)	—	—
Net Income Impact (A − B = C)	200	—	800	—	—
Other Net Income (D)	500	600	500	800	500
Total Net Income (C + D)	700	600	1,300	800	500

*Golden Egg continues to have reserves that can be released beyond year 5.

EXHIBIT 3.4   Golden Egg Reserves

to boost earnings, release of this reserve became a convenient mechanism." In this way, accounting conservatism and earnings management went hand in hand.

Impact of Earnings Management in Real Terms

The process of earnings management is prevalent. Whether accounting principles such as conservatism or materiality are cited or other rationales are used, the impact is the same. Just as with budgeting, excess time and energy are often spent by finance staffs in organizations delivering a *certain earnings number.* Some organizations have even had separate sections in their finance divisions informally titled the "The Earnings Management Group." For "Bellwealthier Bank" in the late 1990s, this unit became the most important unit in the bank's finance and accounting divisions. Mark, the CFO, conferred on a monthly and quarterly basis with this unit, which was charged with predicting and producing the necessary earnings per share.

Aside from the informational effects, the potential cost of earnings management from a salary standpoint usually includes not only finance but also the top-line managers as well. Depending on the intensity of the efforts, for some organizations it leaves executives with less time for running the business, often when the business needs their attention most.

The issues related to earnings management are not simply issues related to a few bad apples. The issues are more systemic that that. Over time, the controller and CFO functions have come to know that their job security is tied to "no surprises." It is drilled into young accountants and young financial analysts that, if nothing else, this concept is key to their survival. They understand that the CEO wants "no surprises," and that they must do whatever they can to deliver the projected numbers. (These projected numbers are usually numbers that grow smoothly over time. If the projected numbers cannot be delivered, the only other possibility for the controllers and CFOs is to predict deviations from the projections well in advance so that some action can be taken. Line managers, of course, are also held accountable for surprises.) One example of the impact of this thinking occurred at "Favorite Financial Services Corp." when they hired Peter to run a brokerage business, which was a new line of business for the corporation. This business was less stable than the older mature entities headed by the CEOs of other lines of business at Favorite. Despite this, the corporation entered the brokerage business because it knew that to retain customers in the future and be viewed as a full-service provider, this was strategically important. The organization had not been in brokerage before and so, because they wanted to be viewed as cutting edge and a market leader, they moved into the business rapidly expecting Peter and Sam, the CFO, to provide the necessary infrastructure for financial reporting. As luck would have it, Favorite launched into this business in the very year that the brokerage industry began to experience a downturn. Because the business was new and had not predicted an immediate market downturn (although a typical cyclical event, the market as a whole had not predicted it), Peter and Sam were treated harshly by the organization's executive management. Within one year of startup, Peter and one of his presidents were fired and Sam was demoted. More than anything, the reason was they had violated the inviolate rule of no surprises. Unlike mature businesses, since the line of business was new, they did not have any reserves or other cushions to ease the blow. In addition, they had not been able to fully develop the infrastructure to monitor, manage, and report the results. They had not predicted the result properly, as a budget-focused organization requires, and so the organization was surprised. Worse than the loss itself were the issues around the last-minute surprise.

Although often a career-ending move for several individuals, how do large organizations ultimately handle surprises they would rather not disclose? One common strategy is to time certain actions around the same time period as the surprise, actions that are explainable, seem inevitable, or represent significant investments or *wise moves,* all of which will overshadow the surprise in the numbers. Such moves are made in the year when the surprise is occurring and serve to mask the impact and causes of the loss. Because of this phenomenon, it is often common practice of many CEOs to turn a bad year into a *really* bad year. The CEO may even announce his (praiseworthy) efforts to ensure that all the major costs should be put behind the organization at one time. Such series of actions may, in fact, have the impact of making the original cause immaterial.

Sometimes when there is a change of CEO in an organization, this phenomenon can also be witnessed. Tony was appointed CEO of "Alliance Enterprise," an organization that had been experiencing lackluster performance. During his first year Tony *restructured* the entire organization and took huge charges to income. From then on, the organization has witnessed "tremendous, steady growth." (This growth, however, is actually modest compared to the results obtained before the restructuring. Of course, in its discussions, Alliance Enterprise does not necessarily highlight this information.) Tony's record appears stellar, and he is touted by Alliance and the media as having taken the steps necessary to turn the company around. Because of cases like these, the SEC has been cracking down on the definition of *restructuring charges* as a special category of earnings manipulation. This term can be used to cover a multitude of sins and make it difficult to discern what has really happened in the organization.

Accounting and Traditional Financial Metrics

Despite the issues just discussed, accounting numbers are valued by organizations (and rightly so) for certain reasons. One major reason is that the rules of accounting are highly developed. In addition, the rules, while inconsistent, are extensive. Although open to interpretation, these rules are in many cases quite specific, and they apply to all publicly traded corporations. In other words, maybe it is not right . . . but at least it is specified! (And, based on personality typology, for 75% to 80% of all personalities, the presence of highly developed rules in and of itself provides a comfort.)[1]

For these reasons, despite weaknesses, confidence has grown in the accounting numbers, particularly in developed countries with developed accounting rules. For most organizations in these countries, performance measurement has evolved (see Exhibit 3.5). Organizations have used numbers on accounting statements and ratios based on these numbers as the primary performance-measurement tools, later adding to them in a variety of ways.

Accounting measures, however, have remained core. They are not only important to organizations but also are heavily relied on by capital providers and external critics. Exhibit 3.6 illustrates some of the typical accounting numbers and ratios used by organizations and other constituents in evaluating an organization's performance. Most accounting measures and ratios in use today include no adjustments to the accounting results in calculating the measures, although that trend has been changing in recent years.

While capital providers and external critics rely on accounting metrics, external suppliers, customers, and employees tend to use them sporadically.

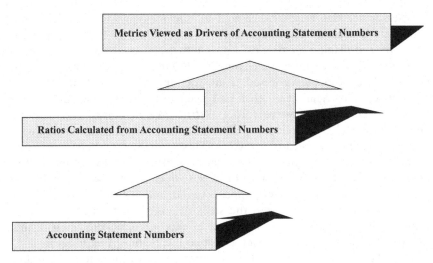

EXHIBIT 3.5   Evolution of Performance Measurement

The discussion of value metrics in the chapters that follow will highlight approaches these constituents can use to gain greater leverage in their negotiations and decision-making processes with the organizations they interact with.

In summary, there has traditionally been a strong pull toward the use of accounting-based measures and ratios for a number of reasons:

- They are readily calculated.
- The calculations are based on a set of rules.
- They come from or are calculated from numbers on the *audited* financial statements.
- The accounting numbers on which they are based are presumed to be readily understood and respected.
- The results are ostensibly calculated in a similar way for all organizations.

TRADITIONAL ACCOUNTING-BASED PERFORMANCE MEASUREMENT: THE MANAGEMENT IMPACTS

Overview

Similar to accounting information, many performance measures use a set of rules, although the interpretation of these rules leaves them open to manipulation.

Measure	Formula
Net Income	Revenues – Expenses
Return on Assets	$$\dfrac{\text{Net Income}}{\text{Average Total Assets}}$$
Return on Equity	$$\dfrac{\text{Net Income}}{\text{Average Shareholders' Equity}}$$
Efficiency Ratio	$$\dfrac{\text{Total Expenses} - \text{Interest Expense}}{\text{Total Revenue} - \text{Interest Expense}}$$ **OR** $$\dfrac{\text{Total Expenses} - \text{Interest Expense}}{\text{Net Interest Income before Provision for Loan Losses}}$$ **OR** $$\dfrac{\text{Revenue}}{\text{Total Expenses} - \text{Interest Expense}}$$ **OR** $$\dfrac{\text{Operating Expenses}}{\text{Fee Income} + \text{Tax Equivalent Net Interest Income}}$$
Earnings per Share	$$\dfrac{\text{Net Income}}{\text{Weighted Average Shares of Common Stock Outstanding}}$$
Price/Earnings Ratio	$$\dfrac{\text{Market Value per Share}}{\text{Earnings per Share}}$$
Total Shareholder Return	The Internal Rate of Return Provided by Dividends and the Appreciation in Share Price

EXHIBIT 3.6 Examples of Typical Accounting Measures

The story, however, is more interesting than rules and numbers. It is behavioral. An examination of the natural behavior we can expect if a particular performance measure is emphasized and maximized will help us understand the impact of the use of typical performance measures. For constituents, this knowledge can help them see the natural bias of an organization and issues to be considered.

Net Income

A focus on net income can create behaviors and emphases that include:

* Short-term thinking
* Sales volume
* Balance between revenue and costs
* Lack of consideration of capital efficiency or risk
* Maximization of capital
* Manipulation of the numeric results

A net income focus (often viewed for the current or next period) can create an overemphasis on the short-term rather then the long-term horizon. One outcome of this thought process can be witnessed in ineffective expense management. Two forms that this can take include:

1. An organization not spending appropriately to manage risks or institute effective controls

2. Cutting costs when these expenditures will need to be rebuilt again or will create the need for offsetting or higher costs in the future

For example, laws against discrimination of older workers occurred, in part, because some organizations would fire or lay off older workers and replace them with younger workers to achieve an immediate reduction in wages and other related costs. In organizations where the perspectives and integrative thinking skills of older workers are important, this kind of action may produce short-term gains and long-term losses. One organization, "Pacified Investments," which is suffering from this short-term thinking, recently underwent a change in top management. The new top managers, called "Gainer's Team," came on board amid headlines of their roles in other organizations as efficiency experts and cost cutters. Six months into their tenure they went into virtually every line of business and laid off or fired nearly all vice presidents and above. Some of the VPs were replaced by previous colleagues of the Gainer team. Others were replaced by younger workers who were not yet VPs at the time. As a result, Pacified Investments today faces a great potential threat of litigation. In this case, the threat does not come from the displaced workers, although Pacified has had to deal with that situation in a number of ways. The real threat today is potential litigation from clients. That is because, particularly in certain lines of business, the products sold are rather complex. Not only has Pacified lost its competence related to its products' contractual obligations, it has also lost the client relationship bases to deal with concerns as they arise. Because of the changes in products in this particular area, it is especially important for Pacified to have integrative thinkers who can bridge past, present, and future. This bridge was removed with the layoffs and firings. Because Gainer's Team does not understand the business that well, this lack of understanding of the contractual obligations poses serious risks to the institution in terms of customer litigation and regulatory enforcement. While the mantra of many, an overfocus on short-term net income can cause long-range problems for Pacified or any organization.

A net income focus can also cause an organization to focus on sales volume. On the surface, this sounds worthwhile. In some organizations, for example, more sales volume can be generated with little impact on cost or additional investment. If not tempered, however, a focus on volume and earnings can cause the organization to lose sight of the other factors required for long-term success. One of these factors can be the infrastructure needed to handle the increased volume, including appropriate customer support. Another factor can be the controls required to meet audit committee standards, regulatory compliance, or other legal guidelines.

An overemphasis on volume can cause other problems as well. For growth, some firms focus on acquiring volume and market share by acquiring other firms who are in a similar business and have their own customer and distribution bases. This focus on earnings and volume has led to larger organizations with higher earnings. Some, however, undergo severe problems and incur major costs during the merger process. In some instances, the risk and control structures of the organization, as well as the stability of its workforce, are severely undermined in the process. "Catfish Bank," which regularly used this approach to grow earnings and volume, recently completed a merger with another, larger firm. Although initially the merger was touted as a success, today it is undergoing a great deal of scrutiny because it is not successfully managing the larger entity. While Catfish Bank's earnings are higher than before the merger, the combined firm's earnings have declined. The focus on volume and earnings has had a negative effect on the company, resulting in an entity that is nearly unmanageable. Another company, "The Velcome Group," employed a similar strategy, and made headline splashes when it encountered severe operational issues in the merger process. Velcome has now been gobbled up itself, perhaps successfully.

Sometimes a net income focus will result in an organization trying to maintain a balance between revenues and costs. On the surface, this seems like a wise idea. Don't we do the same thing with our own household budgets? Often, however, this can mean that an organization will not invest during times of low current revenues, although that investment could be beneficial. For example, an organization may delay important product enhancement or marketing expenses to hit target earnings rates. In addition, companies may tend to hire people in times of revenue growth because earnings are growing as well. In fact, they may overhire because the focus is so narrow; later this precipitates a layoff when revenues temporarily decline or new management determines the organization can be run more efficiently. Just as with the household budget, when there is a leak in the roof, sometimes investments must be made today to prevent regret down the road. A narrow focus on revenue versus cost balance can put an organization at a disadvantage in this regard.

A net income focus can also cause an organization to want to maximize its capital—particularly equity—rather than use it efficiently. Alex, CEO of "NewBank," has believed enough in the accounting numbers to conclude that equity is free. After about two years in business, Alex is attempting to get the board of directors to issue more shares. Additional equity, whether he needs it or not, helps him in a number of ways. From an accounting perspective, there is no cost to be reflected on the income statement. In fact, from an accounting perspective, the reverse is true. Equity can be invested in stocks, bonds, savings accounts, or other investments. Thus, it can generate a *free* return for accounting purposes. In some organizations, because of this accounting net income focus, equity has been stockpiled to generate so-called free investment returns.

Sometimes this focus on net income can also lead to riskier behaviors. It can include going after higher-risk, more lucrative business in lieu of the apparently less lucrative. To the extent that it does not immediately impact net income, it may not be on the radar screen of internal suppliers.

A focus on net income, unfortunately, can also lead to a focus on manipulation. Net income, as discussed earlier, is easy to manipulate, and this training begins early for many. This is an almost inevitable result of the complicated hodgepodge of accounting rules, the tenets of conservatism and materiality, the ease of manipulation, and the focus on numbers rather than principles.

What do these behavioral results mean to the various constituent groups? A focus on net income leads to a short-term viewpoint that hurts most constituents, though in different ways. For internal suppliers whose compensation is tied to short-term results (as most are today, either explicitly or in practice), this focus can yield benefits in the short term. However, it does not create a stable workplace. And it can create an organization that chases the short-term result and may find, as a result, that it must constantly make short-term decisions to keep the momentum. Does this imply that a focus on net income is all bad? No it does not, because a focus on increasing revenues and managing expenses can be helpful. The emphasis, however, also results in the behaviors discussed. For this reason, net income is not necessarily the *best* metric. Net income can create false comfort. Deciding on the principles for the business and understanding that the rest is merely a distraction help to clarify what, for many, is generally a murky path.

Return on Assets (ROA)

A focus on ROA tends to create behaviors and emphases that include:

- Increasing net income (see net income issues)
- Reducing assets
- Reducing inventory
- Moving assets off balance sheet
- Shrinking the business to maximize the ratio

Like net income, a focus on ROA can similarly impact the behaviors of the organization. In using ROA, organizations strive to increase their return on assets. This can be accomplished within the organization by either increasing net income or by lowering assets. Increasing net income has been discussed and the behaviors discussed apply here as well. Decreasing assets is the other side of the coin. This focus can create some helpful and not so helpful behaviors as well. One helpful behavior may be to reduce excess inventory and eliminate unnecessary costs associated with warehousing and holding inventory. Materials requirements planning (MRP) and just-in-time (JIT) management systems have been instituted in organizations to meet these objectives. Other behaviors associated with decreasing assets include moving assets off balance sheet through sales of assets or businesses not usually for sale. Sales of these assets may or may not be the best choice in the long term.

From an ROA perspective, these sales can provide two immediate benefits:

1. An immediate popup in earnings
2. A decline in end-of-period assets

For financial institutions, these may also be accomplished through securitizations in which the institution moves its assets off balance sheet. Only if structured appropriately do they make any economic sense for the institution, and unfortunately in many instances, they enrich only the investment banks that help structure the transaction.

Another tactic used wittingly or unwittingly to raise ROA is to keep the business performed by the organization narrowly circumscribed to business that can maintain a high ROA. "RedFish, Inc." unwittingly used ROA as its primary measure of performance. Because of this emphasis, RedFish only took on business that would maintain its high ROA. When the company was shown the impact on what it would do or might have done had other metrics been used, the result was a source of amazement. Given a net income measure, its business volume would have doubled; given a value metric, its business volume would have at least increased by one-third. The ROA focus was causing it to needlessly constrain its business.

Return on Equity (ROE)

A focus on ROE tends to create behavior and emphases that include:

- Increasing net income (see net income issues)
- Reducing equity
- Increasing debt
- Shrinking the business to maximize the ratio

Like ROA, the focus on ROE can also result in suboptimal behavior. For one large institution, "Salmon Brothers," this focus constrained the introduction of new products and was seriously hampering its business growth and ability to leverage its franchise. New products that could be introduced simply did not meet the hurdle rate of the existing ROE, that is, the ROE generated by its premier product. ROE focus can not only hamper business growth but also encourage shrinking of the business focus to only those with the very best ROEs. At "Carp & Co." this was so extensive that bragging rights were held by CEOs of lines of business with the highest ROEs, not those generating the highest net income increases or value creation.

Like ROA, where the focus is to increase net income and decrease assets, an ROE focus creates a double focus, also: to increase net income and decrease equity. The behavioral issues associated with an increase in net income focus apply, and reducing equity, the other focus, can result in financial decisions to increase debt and use it to replace equity on the balance sheet. A bonus to this approach is the potential tax benefit of debt (because interest payments are tax deductible), so increasing debt can often be a sound economic decision. It can also result in inadequate equity capitalization, however, which will be discussed as it relates to risk capital in Chapters 6 and 8.

Efficiency Ratio

A focus on efficiency ratio tends to create behavior and emphases that include:

- Reducing expenses
- Sometimes increasing revenues, but not often, because it is more difficult than cutting costs

An efficiency ratio focus tends to instill a cost-cutting, penny-pinching environment. Because revenues are often more difficult to grow than expenses, the focus tends to be on expense reduction (no matter the ultimate cost). (See Chapter 2 for information on strategic planning, specifically, cost-reduction strategies.) As with net income, this ratio also tends to promote a balance between income and expenses with the concomitant issues explained in the net income section.

Earnings per Share

A focus on earnings per share can tend to create behavior and emphases that include:

* Increasing net income (see net income issues)
* Decreasing number of shares

An earnings per share focus will create a focus on net income and the related behaviors, as discussed earlier. Sporadically, attempts may be made to lower the number of shares outstanding. Doing so through share buybacks, where the capital is not needed, can be beneficial to the equity holders. In some industries the focus on share buybacks has been so prevalent that investors are often relieved (and surprised) to learn of an organization's strategies beyond the share buybacks.

Price/Earnings Ratio

A focus on the price/earnings (PE) ratio tends to create behavior and emphases that include:

* Increasing price through excellent communications, increasing net income (see net income issues), and running the business well
* Usually not a focus, but an action that improves the PE: decreasing net income (see net income issues, especially in reverse)

Paradoxically, a coveted high PE ratio may be associated with low earnings (relative to price). For example, during the high-tech boom, firms with low current earnings commanded relatively high share prices. This meant extremely high PEs because prices as a multiple of earnings were very high. If earnings declined with no change in stock price, the PE would increase. To some extent, this kind of focus can be like a roller-coaster ride. During one quarter the "Sturgeon Savings Bank" had a charge to earnings with no or little change in the stock price. Sturgeon's executives crowed, "Our valuation is increasing; our PE is up for the quarter." The same quarter, "Swordfish Savings Bank" had a huge boost in earnings. Its EPS went up, but because of little or no change in the stock price, Swordfish's executives lamented that their PE was down.

Total Shareholder Return

A focus on total shareholder return tends to create behaviors and emphases that include:

* Increasing net income (because of the believed close linkage to stock price—see net income discussion)
* Increasing dividends
* Increasing share price (see price/earnings ratio)

The use of total shareholder return exemplifies the constituent issues discussed in Chapters 1 and 2. While total shareholder return may be a good measure as a proxy of the return to a shareholder, it is less useful as a performance guide to internal suppliers in the organization.

Because the argument is often made that internal suppliers should be acting as fiduciaries for shareholders, there is general confusion on this issue. After all, shouldn't internal suppliers use the same measures as shareholders? The discussions on value metrics will examine, in more detail, why this is not the case. However, it is important here to note that a key to Economic Value Management is not only finding the right measure for the right behavior, but also tailoring the measure to the constituent.

As we have seen in the discussion of accounting numbers, the numbers are not to be faulted because they serve one purpose well but do not serve all purposes. Managers, and more broadly constituents, are to be faulted for falling into the mental trap that if the number works well in one instance, it should work well in all. It is a common human frailty to attempt to simplify through assumption of one model instead of focusing on a set of principles and allowing the number of models that are required to become evident.

MEASUREMENT AND MANAGEMENT PRACTICES: MOVEMENTS BEYOND ACCOUNTING

Overview

In addition to the accounting measures, in recent years most organizations including the U.S. government have added other measures of performance to their arsenal. These measures have generally been added under the headline of several kinds of organizational projects:

* Costing projects
* Reengineering projects
* Total Quality Management projects
* Human resource leadership projects
* Balanced scorecard projects

Costing Projects

Costs are an important element in running an organization. While accounting reports provide costs by line item (salaries, benefits, rent, etc.), in recent years costing projects in the organization have moved from measuring costs at the division level and product level to measuring the cost of discrete activities (known as *activity-based costing,* or ABC).[2] This costing is based on the activities engaged in by the organization to produce its products or services. Of course, these costs can change somewhat frequently and thus need to be measured from time to time so that they do not go stale. Often these costs are compared to benchmark costs of other organizations. Some organizations implement very detailed systems; others implement at a high level.

"Spawning Financial" implemented a cost-accounting process at a fairly detailed level but failed to update the process on a regular basis. In truth, the system was so complex that no one person could explain it or how cost bundling was accomplished.

Unfortunately, in addition to cost bundling, there was also cost bungling. For example, Spawning had a number of units involved with one of its major products. In fact, one unit's activities were devoted *entirely* to that one product area. The cost system at Spawning, however, was so complex that the unit's costs had been allocated for years to every product *except* the one with which they were exclusively involved. The trees had become so thick that there was no forest to be seen.

While this may seem ho-hum, the issue can have more impact than first recognized. Since product costs often influence a company's price for that product, this kind of oversight can affect not only the strategic decisions and profits of organizations but also the wallets of customers.

Cost projects can also be expensive to implement. Some organizations, without a view to future strategic changes, spend aggressively on rigid systems that quickly become obsolete. Clearly understanding cost structures is important for assessing strategy and improving process efficiencies. All too often the structures employed are rigid and fail to inform strategy— or be informed by it.

Sometimes the results change too often. "The Berryfield Group" was growing by merger and acquisition and had numerous cost studies performed by in-house staff and outside consultants, with very different results. Each time the metrics were redone (and it was not long between each study), the choice of activities and the resultant product costs differed from the previous study. This created needless confusion and a lack of trust in the results.

One consulting firm, "Gaytem Partners" has been very confused. This firm is so imbedded in doing so-called cost-related projects that some of their practitioners argue that cost is paramount and cost accounting is the primary management tool. (In fact, in the case of Gaytem, they even argue that Economic Value Management is a subset of cost accounting!) While costing is an important, useful tool, it is certainly not always primary, as one of their clients discovered.

"Myrtle Bank," which did the kind of project advocated by Gaytem, faced a huge drop in stock price. Why? Instead of concentrating on cost measurement and management, this organization needed to be focusing on the fundamentals of running its business: its revenue generation, stewardship, strategy, and capital efficiency.

So while cutting out unnecessary cost and eliminating waste are important, as most analysts know, a company's value will be determined by its ideas and plans and its ability to execute them. Costs represent a necessary evil in the implementation of those goals.

From a broader viewpoint, in terms of cost, what organizations need is additional cost flexibility. Although cost efficiency is important, cost flexibility is equally important, and this fact represents a significant insight for organizations. In fact, to be able to flexibly adjust cost structures to changing plans may be more significant to the organization than simply installing soon-to-be-obsolete cost initiatives such as reducing paperclip orders or, more generally, reducing rather than eliminating the costs of processes that will not be needed because the business has changed. Technology and changes in intellectual capital have created this need for cost flexibility, and the old kinds of cost projects must be reexamined in this light.

From a measurement perspective, there is some confusion in costing circles concerning the need for different cost measures for different purposes. As we will discuss in more depth later, this need is clear and rational. Cost measures, like all measures, invite different behavioral responses, and cost metrics must be constructed with this fundamental idea in mind. In the end, all of this argues for the most flexible of systems.

Cost metrics, if executed well, cause an organization to focus on efficiencies, streamline processes, eliminate waste, and deliver more value at lower cost. As noted in Chapter 2, all cost analyses and metrics should be done within the context of value to ensure that no cost reductions are made that would impair the organization's ability to create real value in the future. The benefits of well-reasoned costing efforts help support the measurement efforts of Economic Value Management. These benefits are discussed in greater detail in Chapter 4.

TQM

Overview. Total Quality Management (TQM) has been very important in heightening management awareness of the decisions that are made in business operations.[3] TQM can involve important management as well as metric changes. In many instances, practice lags behind the thought process, and many organizations could benefit by pushing these initiatives further.

The objective of TQM is to better meet customer requirements by continuously improving the quality, efficiency, timeliness, convenience, and other important attributes of the product or service. Like Economic Value Management, TQM has been implemented by many organizations in very different ways. Some organizations emphasize the monitoring and metrics implementation of TQM. Others focus on clear definition of customer needs/wants/desires. Others focus on the management processes of TQM.

Monitoring and Metrics Implementation. As discussed earlier, many organizations develop financial measures of performance. Without a TQM initiative, however, many organizations' measures of performance tend to be underdeveloped in the areas of:

* Customer requirements or specifications

* Operations, product quality, and service efficiency

With TQM, many organizations have made vast improvements in understanding the key aspects of measuring customer satisfaction (the results) as well as instituted simple to sophisticated process monitoring and measuring systems. Some of the statistical work performed in this area in terms of measuring process volatility has also been utilized in risk analyses, which will be discussed in Chapter 8. From a broader perspective, the contributions in the area of volatility measurement have been key to many businesses' ability to get early warning signals of changes and risks in both its own business processes and external impacts on them.

Clear Definition of Customer Needs/Wants/Desires. TQM instills a customer-first attitude. Its aim is not simply to reduce costs but to improve and focus on all aspects important to the customer. TQM provides an important framework to aid organizations in this process.

To obtain the insights into customer needs, ideally organizations will have consulted customers directly, reviewed their opinions, and witnessed their behavior to make the requirements determination. In addition to this input, they will have considered customers' future needs and the trends likely to impact the customer. Without a TQM process, however, many organizations make these assessments in a vacuum.

Management Processes. The implementation focus for some organizations is on the management processes of TQM. These include:

* Continuous improvement

* Team-based decision making

* TQM-based reward systems

The basis for the continuous improvement philosophy of TQM is that no matter how good a process may be, there is a need to continually get new feedback and to rethink, reshape, and adjust processes to meet (or exceed) current customer requirements.

TQM team-based techniques call upon the organization to utilize the minds, energy, and talents of everyone. It teaches the organization ways to elicit ideas and gives control of the organization to teams. Indeed, these techniques can be very powerful and can empower individuals to feel real ownership for the processes for which they are responsible. "Peakco" chose to focus on this aspect in their TQM implementation. Rather than use top-down direction, managers and employees were taught facilitation skills to create team environments. During this implementation, Mary Beth, a Peakco manager, embraced the new process and used the brainstorming techniques for all meetings with staff. Significant decisions were also made using the team-based processes. Over a four-month period, these techniques became so instilled that when Mary Beth announced she was leaving for another company, the team members reporting to her felt empowered to consider who their new boss might be. They asked Mary Beth for her advice and met to determine who their next boss should be!

"Producto," a large manufacturing company, decided to implement TQM within its maintenance organization. The maintenance group reorganized into teams and began to put the principles of process measurement and continuous improvement into place. The results for one particular team were astounding. Its managers were so pleased they decided to make an example of the team's leader, Tom, by presenting him with a plaque and a bonus at a company-wide meeting. Tom was shocked. "They don't get it!" he exclaimed. "This will undo everything we have gained. I didn't earn this award, *the team* did." Tom's refusal to accept the reward did, however, get management's attention. The situation was resolved by awarding the plaque to the entire team and presenting all of the team members with a share of the bonus.

TQM reward systems and human resource structures promote empowerment. Although fewer companies have adopted these processes, TQM advocates team-based rather than individual reward systems. In some cases, individual reviews of performance and employee terminations are discouraged. Instead, it is recommended that teams become self-regulating. Teams using this approach can simply eliminate members by providing no work and thus no pay to those who cannot or do not deliver. While intriguing, some of these ideas may be unworkable unless teams are given a clear vision of their role, have experienced the benefits of diversity, and learned to respect its value. This is key to avoiding the pitfall of *groupthink*.

Both the continuous improvement and empowerment methodologies of TQM overlap with Economic Value Management. Drawing on the tradition of TQM makes Economic Value Management processes even stronger.

Experienced Drivers Required. As with all initiatives in organizations, TQM has sometimes been misunderstood. Some U.S. executives, first hearing about it, went to Japan to see what it was all about and came back thinking that TQM meant implementing a morning calisthenics program that would dramatically improve the business. While this may be helpful, it misses the breadth and depth of TQM and what it has to offer. TQM encourages managers to focus on the customer and work cross-functionally to improve corporate processes. It does this through the institution of metrics, new processes, and a management system.

Reengineering

Reengineering projects may be started in companies for cost, territorial, and/or improvement reasons. No matter the motivation, these projects often result in new metrics of before and after the project performance, either related to cost reductions, quality, or other improvements. When reengineering projects create an ongoing search for continuous improvement, they provide valuable support to the efforts of an Economic Value Management framework.[4]

Human Resource Leadership Programs

Human resource leadership programs often focus on the core competencies needed by the organization's human capital to succeed. These may include the metrics on a performance review or a series of competencies for promotion. Examples might include specific technical knowledge competencies, interpersonal skills, conflict management attributes, and the like. Often, when developing these attributes, organizations use qualitative judgments to develop the measurements.

Sometimes, in addition to performance-review tools, employee opinion surveys are used to judge the management effectiveness of a unit or of the company as a whole. Generally, the individual division and corporation measurements will be developed through the use of human-resource disciplined research or, as is often the case, through the intuition of individuals in human resources or management. Generally, these measures are not changed frequently or tested internally to determine if they are in fact the best measures of managerial performance.

Human-resource-based measures can have a profound impact on the culture of the organization or no impact at all. For those with impact, often the world view represented is that of *existing* human-resource and management practices. In these cases, the measures can become cultural reinforcers. One view is that this focus can be a good thing. The measures clearly enforce the expectations and make the rules of the game known and understandable. Another viewpoint, however, would wonder if cultural reinforcement might lead to minority adaptation or assimilation that will stymie organizational growth and change.

For example, "Barkey Corp." has had a strong history of cultural rein-forcement through these processes. The upside at Barkey is that there is a focus on attributes for success. The downside, however, is that it has rein-forced certain personal ties and certain viewpoints, consensus, groupthink, and a reluctance to confront tough issues or disputes. Because of the sys-tematic reinforcement, when fresh perspectives were needed at Barkey, unfortunately, they had been pruned out.

In other organizations, the human-resource initiatives are isolated from the ebb and flow of the business and do not represent top executives' beliefs. In this case, although these programs may exist, money may be spent on them, and time may be spent going through the motions, the initiatives have no impact. Many of us are familiar with similar initiatives when a kind of schizophrenia exists within organizations related to the priorities associated with issues in which we are involved.

Balanced Scorecard

The Benefits of Implementation. The balanced scorecard is another process undertaken by many organizations today that provides a broad set of met-rics.[5] There are four common classifications of metrics on a balanced score-card:

1. Financial
2. Process or operational
3. Customer
4. Employee or learning

It is clear that the scorecard measures encompass the sets of measures we have been discussing. Accounting and accounting-related measures fall into the financial category. Cost, and some TQM and reengineering metrics, fall into the process or operational category. TQM metrics fall into the customer category, and human-resource leadership measures fall into the learning or employee category.

Many balanced-scorecard processes are conducted using facilitated sessions similar to those used in TQM. In these sessions, however, top man-agement is generally involved, and they intuit the measures that the orga-nization or specific divisions should focus on. The choice of these measures is often informed by not only the view of the current but also the future strategic keys to success.

The advantages to this approach are many. The balanced scorecard reminds the organization of the multiple constituents that must be satisfied if the organization is to succeed. The measures point to management's view of the value drivers of the organization. Thus, those farther away from strategic decision making gain insight into top management views across a wide spectrum of corporate issues.

Implementation Issues. Another impact of the balanced-scorecard approach, however, can be the development of an insular view. Although the measures are supposed to be wide ranging, ultimately they are often chosen based on the existing mindset. For example, at "Cypress Savings," employee and learning measures were being considered for its new balanced scorecard. When employee satisfaction or, for that matter, any employee or learning measures were suggested, the existing mindset was reinforced—no employee measures were needed. While the results are not always this dramatic, the process by which many scorecards are put in place tends to echo the views of top management and thus the current mindset.

In some instances, a primary issue in the implementation is the cost. For example, top management usually choose what they consider to be the best measures in each category. Often, for at least some of the measures, there has been no prior calculation or tracking of those measures. In some cases, the cost to establish these processes for one or two of the scorecard's measures can be extensive and requires a large organizational effort. Sometimes the processes can be so costly or complex that, in fact, they never are implemented, or if they are, they are never measured accurately. Because financial and accounting measures are more readily available, this most often occurs with one or more of the customer, operational, or employee/learning measures.

Another issue in terms of behavioral impact is that a balanced scorecard rightly provides a multiple focus or view of the business. As with the other kinds of processes, issues arise when measures conflict with one another. For example, customer satisfaction and a cost per customer transaction may be in conflict. To raise customer satisfaction may require an increase in cost per customer transaction. Or decreasing the cost per customer transaction may lower customer satisfaction. Which measure should employees focus on? How should this be resolved? The scorecard does not provide a mechanism to *balance* the measure on the balanced scorecard.

In some instances, for organizations where objectives are based on pre-determined goals, as described in Chapter 2, the goals intuited at the beginning of the year may be used by the organization to decide which measure to maximize (see Exhibit 3.7).

For example, under Scenario A, the organization might set goals for (1) a customer satisfaction rating of 3.5, on a scale where a higher number is better, and (2) a cost per transaction goal of $5.00, where a lower cost is the objective. If these are the goals as shown in Scenario A, and if the current customer satisfaction rating is 3.7 and the cost per transaction is $7.00, the organization may take steps to lower the cost per transaction, even though the customer satisfaction may worsen as a result. Suppose instead, with the same goals, the current customer satisfaction rating is 3.4 and the current cost per transaction is $4.00. In this case, the organization may spend, if needed, to increase customer satisfaction. If, however, the customer satisfaction is 3.5 and the current cost is $8.00, the organization

		Goals		Current State	
			1	2	3
(A)	Customer Satisfaction	3.5	3.7 W	3.4 I	3.5 ▷
	Cost per Transaction	$5	$7 I	$4 W	$8 ?
(B)	Customer Satisfaction	3.8	3.7 I	3.4 I	3.5 ?
	Cost per Transaction	$8	$7 W	$4 W	$8 ▷
(C)	Customer Satisfaction	3.2	3.7 W	3.4 W	3.5 W
	Cost per Transaction	$3	$7 I	$4 I	$8 I

Legend:

I — Organization will take actions to improve measure

W — In balancing measures, organization may take actions that worsen measure

▷ — Organization may view result and goal as acceptable

? — Organization may question goal rather than result

EXHIBIT 3.7   Impact of Goals on Behavior

may not make any changes. This is because the organization may rationalize that the first goal is being met and a large decline in cost may seriously hurt the one goal of customer satisfaction score that the organization is currently meeting. In fact, the organization may extrapolate from this experience further and may intuit that while 3.5 was a good stretch goal, since $5.00 was not possible (by a long shot), perhaps the source of the problem is in the goal setting. Management should be rewarded for the 3.5 and be more realistic about the cost goal, they may conclude.

What would happen if different goals were set? What if instead the organization had set a goal of customer satisfaction of 3.8 and a cost of $8.00? Exhibit 3.7 shows the likely impact on the organization's behavior under this scenario as well—Scenario B. Scenario C provides a contrasting response; in the three cases, behaviors are not changed because of differences in reality but because of arbitrary goals—or perceptions of reality. These examples demonstrate how different behaviors may be encouraged as a result of any management system. The point is that goals that are arbitrarily set may determine the balancing of conflicts and the organization's resulting behavior. What is critical is the intelligence brought to the processes that shape behavior.

While on the surface it may seem worthwhile, organizations face similar issues when they utilize very directed and specific measures. At "The Sheeply Company," for example, behavioral complications associated with sales quotas made it very difficult for the sales force to maximize value. Sheeply's retail stores were given monthly and annual sales quotas for each product. These quotas were set based on a broad product mix. The quotas for the retail stores would be outlined as $100,000 in revenues for Product

A, and $200,000 in revenues for Product B, $150,000 for Product C, and so forth. If a retail store exceeded the quotas, the manager would receive a high bonus. *All* quotas had to be met, however, for the bonus to be achieved.

These quotas drove the sales behavior in the Sheeply stores, all of which were located in Northburg. Once a quota was reached, store managers would push sales in the other products to meet the quota. Rather than basing sales on customer needs and value added, sales behavior caused the managers to seek particular kinds of customers at various times to fulfill the requirements of the arbitrary quotas.

Sometimes the focus on the sales quotas was so strong that good sales opportunities were missed. One summer, Sheeply established a new retail location in Southville. This new location served a real need in the community by providing Product A. Product B, however, was not needed by the Southville customers. The sales quotas caused behavioral implications. Dan, the manager of the Southville store remarked, "It would have been so much better if we had focused on Product A and not wasted our efforts on Product B. But we were not rewarded for selling more of Product A, and selling Product B was mandatory!" Multiple objectives and separate goals for Products A and B made it difficult for the store manager to make the best value-based decision.

NOTES

1. Myers-Briggs personality typing is based on Jungian psychology. For more information, see Otto Kroeger and Janet M. Thuesen, *Type Talk at Work/How the 16 Personality Types Determine Your Success on the Job,* New York: Dell, 1992.

2. Some books related to ABC that may be helpful include: Gary Cokins, *Activity-Based Cost Management: Making It Work: A Manager's Guide to Implementing and Sustaining an Effective ABC System,* New York: McGraw-Hill Professional Publishing, 1996; Gary Cokins, *Activity-Based Cost Management: An Executive's Guide,* New York: John Wiley & Sons, 2001; Steve Player, *Activity-Based Management: Arthur Anderson's Lessons from the ABM Battlefield, 2nd Edition,* New York: John Wiley & Sons, 1999; Peter B. Turney, *Common Cents: The ABC Performance Breakthrough,* Portland, OR: Cost Technology, 1991; and James A. Brimson, John Antos, R. Steven Player, and Jay Collins, *Driving Value Using Activity-Based Budgeting,* New York: John Wiley & Sons, 1998.

3. For more information, see Mary Walton with W. Edwards Deming, *The Deming Management Method,* New York: Putnam, 1986.

4. See Michael Hammer and James A. Champy, *Reengineering the Corporation: A Manifesto for Business Revolution,* New York: HarperBusiness 2001.

5. See Robert S. Kaplan and David P. Norton, *The Balanced Scorecard: Translating Strategy into Action.* Cambridge, MA: Harvard Business School Press, 1996.

CHAPTER 4

Economic Value Management: The Measurement and Management Impacts

SOLUTIONS TO COMMON PERFORMANCE MEASUREMENT ISSUES

When properly implemented, Economic Value Management addresses the behavioral issues encountered in other metrics processes. It does this by providing an approach and a *set of metrics*

- Which are cost or benefit justified
- Which provide better decision making
- And provide more streamlined decision making.

Cost Benefit Justified

In many measurement systems, the appropriate measures of performance are intuited (see Chapter 3). What this means in practice is that the measures that are used are measures that the organization *believes* on an ongoing basis are the appropriate measures of performance. In many cases, these measures can provide a needed focus on the operational, customer, or employee aspects of the business. Unfortunately, however, in many cases no fact base is used to determine the real importance of the measures to the organization, and, in larger organizations in particular, no assessment is made of the cost of gathering the information to develop the measure. Both are critical process issues that a well-designed Economic Value Management program addresses.

In an Economic Value Management system, the kinds of metrics that address the wide spectrum of issues within an organization are called value drivers. The term *value drivers* is not accidental and signals the role of these measures in the management framework. The value drivers metrics represent those building blocks of the organization's processes, interactions with constituents, and individual performance objectives required to drive value within the organization. In an Economic Value Management system, the kinds of metrics produced are based on the degree to which the metrics have or will impact value. In understanding this impact on value, the context of their benefit in terms of value creation is weighed vis-à-vis the cost of producing them.

In practice, sorting out the degree to which the metrics have, will, or could impact value is answered by two key questions. One question is the degree to which the activity or outcome being measured impacts value creation. If the item has a relatively low impact on value creation today or it has a relatively low impact given future strategy, then it is not a good candidate and will be discarded. Although sometimes overlooked, the potential to impact value in the future can be as important as—if not more important than—the current impact. For example, as we will discuss in Chapters 6 and 8, monitoring risk issues provides excellent early warning signals that can have a huge impact on value, even though currently the organization may be experiencing no issues. Different businesses, of course, will tend to dictate different measures. For example, in a service business, a measure of inventory may not be critical to its success.

A second key question in sorting out the important value drivers is the degree to which the measure will influence behavior and thus future value creation. If the measure will not be used to influence future value-creating behavior, it is not as good a measure, obviously, as one that will. This is an area where management must be very aware: the choice of the measure to be cost justified must be meaningful. To make this determination, management, or any constituent using the measure, needs to understand

- Whether they will take action if the measure declines
- Whether they are willing to provide (or obtain) training to improve the measure's outcome
- Whether the measure is better than others for guiding the organization or constituents to ask the right questions and take the proper steps to improve the measure

Once these criteria have been satisfied, the measure needs to be selected in the context of the cost of developing the measure vis-à-vis the impact of the measure on value creation. Some organizations today only measure net income or one of a few other high-level metrics, while other organizations spend millions trying to measure far too much detail and minutiae.

If the organization is measuring so many items that no action will be taken on many of them, this is a waste of organizational resources. One example of inaction occurred at the "Paramour Trust Company." Quarterly surveys with standard questions were solicited of customers to measure 30 to

40 issues related to customer satisfaction. Raw data in the form of answers to multiple choice questions as well as general comments were solicited. The surveys provided potentially useful data and important strategic input. If Paramour executives had studied the trends in the surveys and carefully analyzed the results, they would have identified important strategic information. For example, Paramour would have recognized the need for different business models in different locations: high touch in certain areas, low cost in others. The information, however, was not effectively used by management. Although monthly reports were generated compiling the measures and trends in the measures, no strategy initiatives and no adoption of flexible business models were made.

Paramour's complete lack of attention to the results was evident over the course of one year in the survey results of one customer, Bob. In the surveys conducted early in the year, Bob commented on poor service that had been received and for which he would like to be contacted. Over the course of the year, as Bob filled out subsequent surveys, his tone became angrier and angrier. Not only was Paramour ignoring and mishandling his service issues, they had the audacity to continue to waste his time by asking that he complete a survey.

"Starling & Sons" experienced a similar situation in surveying employees. Rather than simply a broad survey of the entire organization, one division decided to perform its own more detailed survey as well. When the results came in, the survey indicated employees' desire for significant improvements in a number of areas. For some reason, Starling's management had not expected that reaction and was unprepared to take action. Morale decreased significantly in that division when employees realized that areas that they considered important on the survey would not be addressed.

Economic Value Management embodies a commitment to take action to create value. Marginal items that will not impact value are not included because those are the areas where focus will not yield long-term results. Similarly, items that will not bring about action should also be excluded. A measure of an organization's adoption of Economic Value Management is the degree to which the organization makes the commitment to take the necessary action to create value. The creation of value is measured in the context of the cost of the action vis-à-vis its impact on value creation.

In this way, Economic Value Management is not unique. Those organizations that choose to define who they are and live by it also must implement the decision processes to support it. Choices will define the character of the organization. These will be governed by good or bad stewardship, or something in between. Organizations that embark on this choice process consciously, with good stewardship as the choice, seem to choose certain ways of changing. And they look to new information to inform their choices. It is to this that the future chapters will be devoted.

Better Decisions

Making decisions in organizations involves weighing alternatives. Some of the issues encountered in weighing alternatives were discussed from an organizational perspective in Chapter 3. For customers as well, weighing alternatives is critical. Customers must define their needs and what they are willing to pay for. They need to determine whose advice and information they can believe: Can they trust what the Internet says, or is a local sales representative or an expert in a given area a better source of information?

Internally, within an organization, similar questions are asked. Whose information should we trust in making decisions—is this based on hierarchy or expertise? How will decisions be made? Depending on the culture of the organization, different answers may be given.

As outlined in a 1999 article by the author of this book to assess the decision-making culture of an organization, it can be helpful to understand the cultures' leanings in the following areas:[1]

- *Achievement or affiliation*
  - ☐ Is the achievement of dollars or certain goals valued?
  - ☐ Are certain attributes or experiences valued?
  - ☐ Is relationship or affiliation valued?
  - ☐ To what extent is achievement versus affiliation the path to success, and is this real or simply a stated phenomenon?

- *Quantification or qualification*
  - ☐ Must something be measurable to be valued?

- *Results or process*
  - ☐ Are decisions based on a review of results or process or both?
  - ☐ Are there multiple routes to a goal as long as the same result is achieved?
  - ☐ Is success determined based on a certain process without regard to the near-term outcome?

- *Consensus or mandate*
  - ☐ Are decisions made by consensus, and if so, which groups are involved in this process?

- *General principles or context*
  - ☐ To what extent are decisions based on general principles (*truths*) or based on a particular context?

- *Multiple truths or single truth*
  - ☐ To what extent does the culture allow multiple truths (views), or is a single view encouraged?
  - ☐ To what extent is it acceptable to articulate multiple views?

▓ *Egalitarian or hierarchical*

  ☐ Are decisions based on position in hierarchy?

  ☐ Are ideas judged on *merit?*

▓ *Practical or theoretical*

  ☐ To what extent is the culture concerned with the tangible result versus the quality of the ideas?

As with Economic Value Management, it is important to separate the difference in culture between *want to be* and *reality.* Often, these are not the same. Reality can be viewed by looking at the actions of the organization instead of what it claims its processes are.

Of course, another large issue is what filter to use in making the decisions. Peter Koestenbaum has rightly said that decision making necessarily includes polarity and guilt: polarity because one must weigh alternative goods, and guilt because making decisions means a choice and an exercise of *no.* He emphasizes that the process by which decisions are made and the motivation behind the decisions are critical.[2]

In Economic Value Management, the filter of stewardship is used to make the decisions of the organization. This means dealing with different constituent concerns and balancing them appropriately. To do a good job from a process standpoint, key focuses must include:

▓ A clearly articulated objective (in this case stewardship and the creation of value)

▓ A robust process that uses this objective as the filter

Organizations often not only lack a good or clearly articulated objective, they also lack a robust process for decision making. For some organizations this lack of a robust process is reflected in as simple a form as a preconceived idea of the correct decisions and a lack of review of all appropriate alternatives.

As an example, "SparrowCorp" wanted to assess the benefit of replacing a piece of equipment to make workers more productive. A couple of vendors were analyzed, but the search was not extensive. As was standard practice, one or two choices were presented and a cost justification submitted. Other alternatives were not studied. No one at SparrowCorp considered possibilities such as training to improve productivity instead of adding new equipment. Process change to eliminate the need for the function entirely may have solved SparrowCorp's problem, but this was never considered either. The location of the equipment may have impacted the outcome, but we will never know. Perhaps a communication device linked to equipment at another location would have solved the problem, or perhaps the old equipment could have been upgraded. Who's to say? It was never considered. The proposals submitted for new equipment did not review the extent to which the old equipment should be eliminated or whether a second shift could solve the problem more cheaply and flexibly. In considering the overall solution, SparrowCorp did review the economic consequences of rent versus purchase and explored whether one vendor versus another provided more flexibility in this regard. Although it would have been helpful, SparrowCorp only considered meeting the organization's current needs; the needs of the future or strategic planning of needs two to five years in the future were never considered. And the risks as well as the return benefits of the various scenarios were not articulated in the scenarios presented for review.

One organization, "FinchCo," well known for its financial discipline, had this problem related to retail store locations. Often proposals would be submitted to the corporate office with recommendations concerning store locations. These proposals would explain and quantify the benefits of the new locations. Unfortunately, most of these proposals contained little thought and even less documentation on, for example:

- Potential alternative locations for the new store
- Potential alternatives in terms of projected revenues or costs
- Potential alternatives in terms of the store size
- Potential impacts on existing stores
- Potential impact of closing or replacing existing stores

This lack of information caused FinchCo to make bad decisions. As a result, after many of the locations had been established, a larger project had to be undertaken to rationalize these decisions and determine which stores to keep and which to eliminate.

This study was advisable. It was just unfortunate that it was undertaken after the stores had been built and staffed, rather than before expenditures, with long-term obligations in many cases, had been made. For the employees of these rationalized locations, it was unfortunate as well.

When alternatives are weighed, it is advantageous to use the proper scale. Frequently, organizational decisions are made based on short-term results rather than long-term value creation. Or they are based on hitting arbitrary future targets (some percentage of market share in five years, for example, or lowest cost decile). Better decisions will result by using value metrics as the filter, and often the decisions will be very different from those based on other metrics.

As our cultural discussion noted, there may be reasons that explain the cultural or political context influencing decision making. Unless we are smart about these issues, it is not clear that we can expect much in terms of change, either in terms of the filter or the process.

Chief executives can often forget the need to monitor the political issues within their organizations and the resulting impact on the quality of decisions. Typically, though not always, politics are played *to* them rather than with or against them. And the politics played to them are often played to their egos. Unless the CEO has done some serious soul searching and ego work, this can create an environment where decisions are made not on their merit but based on who articulated the idea and how they articulated it. For Economic Value Management to work, a focus on stewardship, which minimizes the impact of egos, is required. Making decisions must be based on the proper filters. *This is radical.*

If good stewardship is ignored, no matter what the stated performance measurement and management mechanisms, decisions will be predetermined. They will be made to achieve a given result or accommodate a certain feeling. In the latter case, it is most likely that the decision makers in the organization will first determine the approach and how they feel about it, and then the case will be made to support it. In one organization, "Pendark, Ltd.," this happened so routinely that when the executive management team decided to relocate most of the corporate headquarters, no alternatives were examined, and no performance or financial based analyses were performed. In fact, only after construction began were staff involved in pulling together the numbers to be used for planning purposes. This example may seem unusual, but it is not as unique as one might hope. Often alternatives are never considered in this regard—and if they are, they are usually limited by the thought processes of only the very top managers.

While one may say this is just human nature and there is nothing to be done, the impact of politics on decision making leaks through ultimately in the numbers posted by the organization. Further than that, internal constituents who are unaware can often be hurt in the process.

Recently, CEOs of major entities have lost or left their positions following major mergers because they have forgotten the political and cultural elements that impact the decision making, harm the organization, and ultimately damage their own careers. Following a recent merger, David, the departing CEO of "Farm & Country Bank," made the comment that he could not understand why such highly paid executives could behave in such political and territorial ways. Some human insights and inner work might have made David less incredulous. The organizational system by which these executives had been rewarded and coerced at Farm & Country had created what he now saw as personality flaws. Fear of loss was a dominant mindset. Attention to ego needs was paramount. Within this context, it is not surprising that adaptation to change would not be easy for the executives. And they continued to ride the de Mello bus (referred to in Chapter 1).

Economic Value Management provides a better way to make decisions through the filter of stewardship. Most organizations that do so come to new insights. The insights generate new questions and an ongoing discovery process.

One can spend years reading annual reports, looking at the year over year earnings increases and know very little about what has happened in the company. However, by taking the time to go through the process of developing the value metrics, like unwrapping a present, a surprise awaits—it may be good or it may contain switches—but it is likely unanticipated.

One large organization, "BrightTrust," uses economic value to understand its customers better and has been surprised by new insights about their customers and the industries they serve. "The earnings don't tell the story at all," commented one senior product analyst. "When the value metric is applied, it gives a very different result."

"The Banker's Friend," a large membership organization, developed metrics of value that pointed to its previous ineffective use of capital. The information stunned management, and the trend was so clear in the numbers that management did not want anyone to know, including the board membership.

"TinyTech," a small organization that is not publicly traded, developed the metrics for the first time and found surprises. While it was recording a positive net income, which had grown significantly over the last three to four years, it discovered that it had not generated a positive economic profit in any of those years.

"Megacorp International," a large conglomerate, went through the process of metric development for each of its businesses. One of its businesses, which Megacorp thought was its star performer, looked different under a value microscope. Megacorp was surprised to learn that this business's economic profit had been declining over the last few years. The metrics revealed that the acquisition and pricing decisions of the past few years had eroded value. While it did not happen at Megacorp, at this point in some organizations, top executives, unchecked, move to eliminate the business or fire the managers. The issue, however, is that without the right metrics, the managers couldn't have known. At Megacorp, management took steps to get the business back on track and created significant value going forward.

In addition to better decisions, Economic Value Management creates the ability to make more streamlined decisions as well.

Streamlined Decisions

Multiple alternatives, which must be examined, make any decision difficult enough. Multiple measures can create complex issues for decision making. This is particularly true, as is often the case when multiple measures conflict. A hierarchy related to the measures used is necessary to make the appropriate decisions and to streamline decision-making processes.

Even EPS and PE, favorite accounting-related measures, give conflicting signals. CEOs often say they want both a high EPS and a high PE. A high EPS means high earnings per share. A high PE can be obtained two ways: higher price or, paradoxically, lower earnings.

The example of two conflicting measures shown in Exhibit 3.7 is simple. For many organizations, however, the number of conflicting measures is much greater. In fact, in many organizations there can be 20 or more measures headlined under four or five categories. Because of this, some problems, which need not be so complex, start to appear unsolvable. (See science discussion in Chapter 2's "Value-Based Strategy—Building Blocks of Economic Value Management Strategy and Some Remarkable Advantages" section.) Taking Exhibit 3.7 as a starting point, the constraints in the equation may become customer satisfaction ≥ 3.5, cost per transaction $\leq \$5$, phone response time < 1 minute, time per call < 6 minutes, number of products sold per call > 1, and so forth, for the multiple measures.

And this is exacerbated if, as is often the case in many organizations, different divisions have different sets of these measures that may compete. Operational efficiency measures for one division, risk minimization measures for another, and gross sales for another are just a few examples. With this as a back drop, how is it possible to have the divisions come to agreement on the best course of action? Some might say these different areas provide different perspectives, which are then balanced by the organization. In the real world, however, the questions are: How will this agreement be reached? Will political clout break the tie? In many real-world situations, the basis for breaking the tie is left to political mechanisms, chance, or arbitrary processes. In some cases, no one approach seems to work and arm wrestling for the advantage occurs with every decision. Many companies waste energy because they have not resolved this issue in terms of process. Insurance companies, for example, often complain about the competing energies focused on attempting, and not succeeding, to resolve the needs of the claims area for operational efficiency, the underwriting unit for risk minimization, and the sales organization for gross sales. Similarly in manufacturing firms, the production staff may be focused on operational efficiency; internal audit and safety, on risk minimization; and sales, on sales. The lack of process to guide the resolution has caused numerous conflicts in many organizations and heartburn for internal suppliers.

The process is streamlined in Economic Value Management. This does not mean that conflicts do not happen or that competing issues do not have to be factored in. The difference is that there is a process sorter: Long-term value creation and true stewardship are the goals. As with any value-based activity, whether in business or in personal life, the overriding objective helps to guide the process.

DIFFERENT MEASURES OF VALUE FOR DIFFERENT PURPOSES

There is much confusion about so-called "shareholder value" metrics. This is probably because of the way in which they are often described and the simplifications that are used. Unlike other approaches, the fact that Economic

Value Management can encompass multiple measures of performance can be confusing. In part, this is because when some writers or speakers discuss "shareholder value" or "economic value added," they talk about presenting one measure of performance to replace multiple measures. Although Economic Value Management *does* reconcile conflicting multiple measures, it is not confined to one calculation or measure alone. It establishes multiple measures of value for different purposes.

The simplification in discussing "shareholder value" or "economic value added" metrics is used to distinguish it from typical financial systems where net income competes with market share; market share, with direct costs; direct costs, with PE; PE, with ROE; and so forth. And Economic Value Management certainly does eliminate this discord. There is an important distinction, however, that is particular to Economic Value Management. Although Economic Value Management may reconcile multiple measures, it does not replace them per se. While in any given circumstance there may be a central value-based measure or measures applicable to a given purpose, multiple measures are used that provide many benefits, including those that provide a way to:

▓ Address the measurement needs of various constituents

▓ Bring the focus on value to a level at which it is actionable

▓ More concretely understand where value is being created and where value is being destroyed

Value driver measures can be very important to an organization, and the value driver focus of an organization will be a reflection of the impact of an organization's strategy. For example, for certain lodging establishments, the ability to deliver top-level customer satisfaction impacts sales. For others, this is somewhat important, but what is more important is to deliver customer service in an operationally efficient manner and a lower cost. Both kinds of business might have similar scorecards. In Economic Value Management, however, it is important to discern which measures can or will most influence value creation. In each case, the key value drivers are significantly different.

Economic Value Management balances conflicting demands. A common example in companies is the different goals of line versus audit and legal functions. While the line may be focused on returns and sales, audit and legal may be concerned with operational and legal risk. The organization must then determine how much to spend on risk mitigation. Economic Value Management metrics balance those issues within the context of the return-versus-risk framework, balancing the level of risk to be tolerated in the organization against the reward or potential reward achieved.

"Innovest," a company that had a customized investment product set, came to a new understanding in this regard when implementing Economic

Value Management. As a result, the line area shifted its thinking away from just returns to balance legal requirements in a more holistic way. This was not done by enforcing a set of arbitrary goals or metrics, but through an understanding of how each component drives value.

Value drivers play a key role in the process. The right balance is achieved by the value-based hierarchy, a relationship that is often changing, so monitoring is critical of the potential contributions of each value driver to overall value creation. Economic Value Management simply reconciles the value drivers with each other. And it is at this juncture that value choices can be made.

Beyond the value driver concept, what makes Economic Value Management distinctive is that it has other multiple sets of measures. While this may seem confusing, in fact it reflects a needed reality. What Economic Value Management provides is an overreaching principle and an overarching prioritization, which is stewardship and value creation. It provides one view, that is, a unified perspective. Within that singular perspective, different measures are required under different circumstances.

Unlike rules-based accounting earnings or even many standard "shareholder value metrics," Economic Value Management metrics are not built through a rules-based process. They are not "hand-me-down" measures like the accounting ones discussed in Chapter 3 nor are they based on intuition, as are many scorecard measures. There are many reasons why this is so.

Rules that specify the calculation of a measure are designed to fit *one* particular purpose. As with games, the rules fit the *particular game* very well and do not fit other games. Rules are not open to selection for a given purpose. They apply no matter what; that is their nature. Rules, at least in the play of competitive games (which is encouraged as a prerequisite to understanding the business world), are meant to be pushed to their limits. Rules represent the limit, the crossing line. Skirting the edges of a rule is how the game is won. In tennis, for example, placing the ball in the opponent's court just at the serve line is often a winning strategy. So, rules are part of a particular psyche, and in many instances that psyche is win-lose.

Economic value management metrics are about a different kind of psyche entirely. Value is "the quality of a thing considered in respect of its power and validity for a specified purpose or effect" (see Exhibit 1.1). Rules are not flexible. They either apply or they do not. Rules-based approaches do not work because rules are not open to selection to serve an agreed-on purpose. If selection were possible, they could not be called *rules*. Rules do not work because stewardship is the goal; stewardship has nothing to do with meeting the result of some rule or competitively trying to skirt the edges of one. Unlike with accounting, one set of rules is not applied to perform the Economic Value Management metrics calculations. A very different process is used. It is more like a word problem in a math class. You must figure out the formula that best fits the problem. Information is explored and the best measure to explain any particular circumstance or describe any particular situation is developed and used. Simply knowing *why* a particular Economic Value Management metric applies creates insights. Economic Value Management asks, in the spirit of stewardship, that we awaken, that we see beyond the rules, beyond games and win-lose scenarios, that we take the step of lifting the shades (the green eye shades or the bus shades— whichever analogy you prefer) to really see.

So what are the different circumstances that drive different formulations? To understand this more fully, see Exhibit 4.1, The Value Metrics Circle™, which illustrates the different circumstances, purposes, or contexts that may impact the calculation of value:

- Different types of decisions
- Different behavioral impacts
- Different constituents
- Different kinds of organizations

Different Kinds of Decisions

Decisions and analyses in an organization can include a wide spectrum of issues:

- Which divisions have created value
- What distribution channels to use
- What organization structure to use
- How to price products
- Which services to enter, exit, or expand

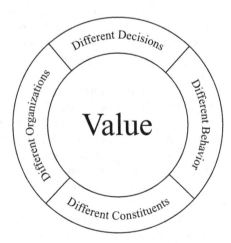

EXHIBIT 4.1   Value Metrics Circle™

* Where to allocate resources
* How to operate
* What risks to mitigate
* With whom to merge
* Which costs to eliminate
* How much to reward internal suppliers

Some issues are historical in nature, best answered by what was; some take the view of an ongoing concern; and some take the view of a merger or breakup candidate. For each of these major types of questions, different value metrics are required to achieve the best answer to "What shall we do next?" Often the historical reviews provide answers to instruct future strategy. For example, such analyses may provide important information about changes in constituent or marketplace behavior that will inform strategy. Historical reviews may also provide the information needed to reward internal suppliers for what they have done in terms of value creation. Historical reviews tell us what has been—not what it is believed will be.

Decisions about how to run the organization going forward are instructed by historical reviews and determined by analyses that examine what value will be created under different scenarios. The focus here is to choose strategies and make operational decisions based on the organization's mission and the creation of value.

Decisions about merger and breakup, while informed by historical and ongoing concern analyses, are answered by analyses that address organizational synergies, overall mission, and objectives. In these analyses, the value outside of current operations must be considered.

Economic Value Management is more than a metrics system, it is a management system, so conscious choices must be made to use the proper value metrics to make the best decision and to create and enforce the right balance.

Although there is one perspective,

* Analyses and reward systems
* Ongoing decisions
* Major strategic decisions

all require different metrics.

While the purpose of all decisions or analyses is to move us from where we are to where we want to be (that is, create the right behavior), different metrics are required for different kinds of decisions. By distinguishing among the kinds of analyses, we hope to clear up needless confusion. There are two major kinds of analyses requiring different kinds of metrics:

1. Evaluative metrics
2. Predictive metrics

Evaluative metrics may include what are generally referred to as financial and nonfinancial measures. Within predictive metrics there are two major types:

1. Fixed boundary
2. Changing boundary

Evaluative Metrics

Let's define what we mean by these terms. Evaluative analyses that use evaluative metrics assess how an organization has performed in a number of dimensions. Most performance measurement discussions focus on these analyses in the context of the performance measurement systems, as discussed in Chapter 3. Economic Value Management evaluative measures, discussed in Chapter 2's "An Overview" section, belong in this category.

There is confusion in the terms used by practitioners that can cause confusion about evaluative measures. Often, so-called financial evaluative measures are referred to as *backward looking,* and so-called nonfinancial evaluative measures, such as customer satisfaction, are considered *forward looking.* While it is true that current or past customer satisfaction will be a factor that *may* determine future financial results, this is true for every type of measure, including those labeled *financial.* The net income earned today or the cash flow for the month will influence how we will be able to run the business, what investments we will make, and our future cost of capital. In that sense, all measures, even financial ones, have a forward impact.

Similarly, the term *nonfinancial* can be confusing. If customer satisfaction is *forward looking* in any sense, it is so called because it will be a factor that will determine future *financial* results. In that sense, customer satisfaction *is* a financial measure (although it is clearly not an accounting one).

To be clear, when we say evaluative, what we are measuring is not an expectation but rather what has been done and what has been achieved. In Economic Value Management our primary focus in terms of evaluative measures is on what value has been created in the past and what has driven that value creation. Again, see Chapter 2's "Performance Assessment—Evaluative Measures" for a discussion of the seven evaluative analyses.

In Economic Value Management, evaluative analyses are used for many purposes. Since they provide information about:

- Where value has been created
- Where value has been destroyed
- Where value drivers have increased or decreased

In Economic Value Management they can be used to:

1. Provide feedback on past efforts
2. Evaluate past behaviors to appropriately reward and enforce value creation behavior

3. Evaluate the past as a springboard for the future and provide input for decisions to enhance value creation going forward

Predictive Metrics

Decisions to enhance value going forward use evaluative measures as the springboard and to that add predictive measures of two types: fixed boundary and changing boundary. By fixed boundary, we mean predictive measures of performance used to evaluate an organization on a going concern basis. These measures, in the best firms, are undertaken on an as-needed basis, with a fair degree of frequency. This frequency (where measures are appropriately used) represent the level of change or consideration of change in an organization. The analyses, using these measures, reflect potential shifts in the way the organization will be operated. However, they are not as radical as those in changing boundary analyses. For example, *fixed boundary analyses* include:

※ What distribution channels to use

※ What organizational structure is best

※ What work environment to have

※ How to price products

※ What marketing efforts to use

※ Where to allocate resources (within current operation)

※ How to operate

※ What risks to mitigate

※ Which costs to eliminate

※ What work to outsource (on a specific basis)

Changing boundary analyses include:

※ What activities represent core work of the organization and on the broadest level, what work should be done elsewhere

※ The impact on current operations of expansion or exit, purchase, or sale.

Generally, operations management will be concerned with fixed boundary analyses while top management will focus primarily on the more broadly strategic changing boundary analyses.

Some of the traditional financial metrics used by organizations for predictive decisions are explained below. Many corporate finance textbooks discuss these various metrics in detail and the merits of them.

Briefly, payback measures the amount of time until one recoups an investment. It is calculated as the amount of the investment divided by the annual cash flow from the investment. The measure creates a behavior that looks for a return in the shortest period of time, not the highest return. Although payback's shortcomings have long been recognized in academia, even in large corporations this measure is still used.

Internal rate of return (IRR) measures the percent return of a project. The behavior encouraged by IRR is similar to ROE or ROA (see Chapter 3). Organizations may be tempted to take on only the highest IRR projects rather than those that create the most value. This may limit an organization's profitable growth.

Discounted cash flow/net present value (DCF/NPV) measures do a good job of measuring value creation. DCF/NPV is calculated by measuring the cash flow of the project in current dollar terms. The results of these analyses are to move the organization to an understanding of value creation over several periods.

Where value metrics improve on the DCF/NPV process is in the explicit linkage they provide between the evaluative and predictive measures. Unfortunately, although DCF/NPV provide the right answers, it is not easy to link them to typical evaluative measures. This issue, in fact, creates the disconnect in non-value-based systems between the typical performance measures and the basis for decisions! It is quite common for organizations to make decisions on one basis but never use those metrics to evaluate whether or not their predictions actually came to be.

Options analyses recently have been used to supplement DCF/NPV's power by also taking into consideration not only the value implications of a particular decision, but also its timing (i.e., the value of waiting versus the value of moving forward). Economic Value Management uses these techniques as well and these will be discussed in more detail beginning in Chapter 6.

Valuation analyses used for mergers, acquisitions, and major sales will also usually include analytic metrics that involve not only inherent values, but also marketplace values. The marketplace values may include sales prices of the assets themselves (break-up value) or of the sales price for the organization, including the benefits of any synergies with another organization.

As with other decisions, value metrics provide a benefit in linking the evaluative metrics of the organization, its fixed boundary predictive metrics, and the changing boundary predictive metrics in one package. Before we describe the metrics and how Economic Value Management does this, let's discuss the other parts of the Value Metrics Circle™.

Different Kinds of Behavior

Even within the same kind of organization, the same metrics do not necessarily result in the same behavior. This may not be self evident. It would be fairly reasonable to suppose that given a certain metric, certain motivations or behaviors could be expected. Up until now, we have described the general impacts of different metrics on behavior. Economic Value Management takes this a step further by recognizing the need for different kinds of metrics in different circumstances to elicit or help foster the intended result. How can it be that a given metric would not produce identical behavior? The answer has to do with the current awareness of the organization and the awareness it needs to move to. Since the purpose of the metrics is to produce the behavior of stewardship, for each organization the set of metrics may be somewhat different. And for each organization to exercise greater stewardship, to create more value, may mean a need for different behaviors.

We discussed this when we discussed the balance scorecard. Intrinsically, it is why organizations have a scorecard process. Buying a balanced scorecard off the shelf is not the answer. In working with organizations, the process of its development itself can help the organization determine what it wants to do, be, become. Economic Value Management provides a similar process for the value drivers and metrics it uses as well.

Some organizations need to invest more for the future and their value metrics must reflect this. Time horizon is often a big issue for many organizations. Some organizations need information technology thinking and their value metrics must reflect this. Some organizations need a sense of urgency and their value metrics must reflect this. From the perspective of internal suppliers, then, Economic Value Management and metrics is not a blind rote fill-in-the-box process. It involves a determination of:

- What the organization wants to be,
- How best to be stewards in doing that, and
- The metrics involved to make it happen.

In Chapter 2 (the "Rewards Process" section) we discussed the "Marshswamp" organization that was selling off pieces of the business to meet earnings targets. Metrics in this organization might be designed to discourage sell-offs. These metrics, however, might not be required in a similar organization without such sell-off intentions.

Some organizations today are faced with the issue that the capital markets have bundled their products into marketable, tradable securities. This changes the nature of operations of the business. In fact, by our definitions, it moves operations managers from going concern, fixed boundary product producers to market players in which boundaries are changing on an ongoing basis.

In some organizations, the time between decision and impact can be very short, in others quite long. This fact can impact the nature of the metrics chosen.

In some organizations, inflation/deflation or currency fluctuations can impact value creation. Advocating, however, that all constituents or all internal suppliers should monitor and be concerned with inflation can cause value destroying rather than value creating behavior. The recommendation that, in all circumstances, inflation be accounted for in the value metrics can have unintended consequences. Although such a measure can be useful, the unintended result in some instances is to cause an organization to accelerate prices, thus continuing to fuel inflation, or to determine it is more profitable to sell off the assets rather than be in business.

When we think about metrics as behavior evaluators and motivators, a quick reference to change and motivation theory provides some clues to the process. Change theory indicates that individuals tend to be motivated in two ways: *away from* and *toward*.[3] "Away from motivation" is based on the desire to move away from a condition, and "toward motivation" is based on the desire to move toward a vision. Both can be very effective, although sometimes "away from motivation" does not last as we forget about the pain we are moving from. Economic Value Management tends to focus on "toward motivation" and change for the better. It is also a regret minimizer and thus encompasses "away from motivation" as well.

Another major influence that creates a need for different metrics in the organization is its culture. Organizations operate like a collective personality. Cultures in organizations influence how organizations will:

* Adopt change
* Adapt to change
* Create change.

Cultures can have a large impact on an organization's behaviors. Understanding the culture is key to developing the Economic Value Management metrics.

Perhaps a contrast between three organizational profiles will illustrate. "Forerunner, Inc." has a culture that creates a profile of itself as "on the forefront." This organization is often first to initiate in its industry. Some of what the organization tries works and some fails. Internally, the organization has a few leaders who are change agents. The vast majority of people within the organization are followers who operate successfully and are motivated by having clear rules and procedures to follow. For the few change agents in the ranks, change can be difficult to implement because, according to the organizational myths, consensus is sought prior to implementation. It is not until the new processes are proven, however, that most of the workforce will adopt them. They may speak acceptance, but really simply stand back and dissociate with the change process until it is proven successful. In addition, this organization tends to define success as short term economic success.

Another organization, "Integrative Technologies," is a monolith in its industry. This organization makes few changes, but when they are made, they tend to be implemented swiftly and everyone is expected to be on board. There is resistance to considering change in this organization. And the plans that are implemented must be adhered to strongly from a scheduling standpoint. Once planned, however, all hands are on deck to ensure accomplishment.

"DarkStar, Inc." has changed so rapidly on the surface, and yet not changed at all substantively, that members of the organization really just wait for the revolving door of management to change and to be told that they are doing poorly, then well, then poorly again by turns. Herb, a midlevel manager at DarkStar puts it this way, "Due to the lack of stability, nothing ever *really* changes at DarkStar. People are constantly pointing to other departments and each other so they don't catch the heat. Most of us don't try to be promoted to an executive level. We simply bide our time until the next series of bosses appear."

To create greater stewardship—more value creation—will have different focuses for each organization.

For Forerunner to create value effectively, the organization will need to focus metrics on the value created by change initiatives, the benefits in efficiency, improvements in the bottom line, and each division's and individual's positive or negative contribution to the efforts. The Forerunner organization will need to emphasize value metrics tied to cooperative efforts.

For Integrative Technologies to improve its value creation, metrics that would identify needs for change could help open the organization to more change efforts. This would include appropriate value-based trend metrics for processes, customer requirements, competition, and marketplace issues.

For the DarkStar organization, value metrics that emphasize retention and learning, change impact and long term value creation could provide valuable focuses.

Depending on the dominant personalities of the organization, behavior changes are best achieved by providing value metrics that reinforce stewardship of (alternatively, with emphasis on):

* Processes
* Relationship
* Choices.

Using personality information about the organization can help an organization self-assess what the personality of the organization will respond to.[4]

Different Constituents

Economic Value Management metrics, of course, must also be different for different constituents. Perspectives on Economic Value Management can be used in fact by all constituents inside and outside of the organization. In the most empowering sense, constituents shape the nature of the organization itself. For example, if employees want to work in a learning organization, what the employees do to ensure that training and related efforts create value rather than simply cost money can impact decisions that influence whether the organization becomes a learning one. If customers want certain requirements, the level of commitment to that position may be represented in their communication in the broadest forms. Do they speak or write to the organization or even make choices on this basis? If capital providers only want to invest in certain kinds of enterprises, the question is whether their actions match their values, because values will drive value creation.

If money is the only concern of all constituents, then the institution will reflect this. Economic Value Management will ensure proper stewardship of all resources to achieve the economic returns for the long term.

If other values come into play, these will be reflected in what is required to achieve value creation. As our discussion on streamlined decision making noted, the balancing in Economic Value Management occurs through a process that is less arbitrary than other performance measurement systems. If customers are not price sensitive and capital providers' only concern is economic return, the organization will structure around this. If customers, however, become price sensitive, it is imperative that the organization be alert and adjust to their new value proposition.

While the purpose of Economic Value Management is to ensure the appropriate stewardship for the benefit of all constituent resources, individual constituents will have different views on value creation. While this may seem obvious, this is often a large source of confusion caused by the often heard statement that the benefit of "economic value added" is that "it causes managers to think like owners" (i.e., causes internal suppliers to think like capital providers). Based on this statement, it is often then assumed that since it causes internal suppliers to think like capital providers, internal suppliers will use the same metrics as capital providers would. This, however, is not the case. This does not mean that one constituent group will not have an interest in the other constituent's metrics. Quite the contrary. That was part of the need to clearly delineate the constituent concepts in Chapter 1. It just means that the group of metrics they will usually focus on will be different. (As we discuss the specific metrics in the upcoming chapters, we will discuss this further.)

Ultimately, each organization must decide who it is and what it will do.

It is then the job of the constituents—shareholders, customers, employees—to also choose whom they will be in relationship with in these processes. That is why honest communications internally and externally are so important.

Different Organizations

Each organization must define for itself its purpose and all constituents must honestly understand its mission and how they will choose to respond to it.

Different organizations with different purposes will have different value metrics, including different value driver metrics. So the value metrics for a retail organization may differ from that of a financial services firm that might differ from a manufacturer. There will be basic similarities, but there will also be differences. Again, however, the principle of stewardship would be applied in all cases. For many organizations, economic returns (vis-à-vis risk) represent an appropriate measure of value. For other organizations, while a measure of economic returns may be an important component that they currently ignore, the purpose of their organization may otherwise direct the definition of stewardship and the appropriate value metric.

However, let us not confuse the points here. An economic model can, and has been, successfully applied to member and public service organizations. Once the goals of the membership or public service organization have been satisfied, anything leftover (sometimes called "excess value creation" from a relative standpoint) represents real resources that can be returned to the membership or used to fund additional programs. To wit, governments with excess in their coffers need these kinds of measurement devices precisely to determine whether or not the excess should be returned. They need to assess if the services were performed, what impacts were obtained, or has the organization simply gathered dollars and failed at the job. As the U.S. Results Act and other initiatives make clear, evaluative metrics, properly implemented, can help to shed light on the subject.

THE QUESTION OF STANDARDIZATION

With multiple measures for many different reasons, one question that is often raised is whether or not standardization is possible. The short answer is yes, but it requires a tradeoff. (See the earlier discussion of rules-based processes at the beginning of the "Different Measures of Value for Different Purposes" section.)

The matter up for debate related to value metrics is when, if ever, standardized measures should be used. Those who like accounting measures because there are strict rules argue that, yes, to the degree possible, all metrics should be standardized. So-called standardization creates problems, however.

Often, it is not possible or best to have standard measures. While so-called standard value measures are reported today in major business magazines or by stock analysts, like accounting measures, these measures, although consistent, may not represent the best measure of performance. The often cited advantage of consistency is comparison. However, major flaws in assumptions can be made if the information behind the metrics are not clearly understood. That is the problem with net income and this same issue can be a problem with standard value metrics as well. Standard measures or standard models are useful to internal suppliers and to others by providing the benefit of allowing benchmark or comparison. However, because internal suppliers have access to better information, particularly about their own operations, metrics developed in a standardized form tend to give up informational value if utilized in every instance. Unfortunately, some organizations where the accounting group has led the process have experienced this issue.

One large organization, "WhaleTrust," has used what it calls a value metric for a number of years. Unfortunately, the metric is standardized. It has had little impact on the organization for a variety of reasons, one of which is the metric itself. It is so *standardized* that it has not been adapted to the variety of decisions, behavioral contexts, constituents, and organizations within the larger bank. When organizations do not reap the benefits of using value metrics, this can be a reason why.

Not only are the right metrics important. In Economic Value Management, the learning process, the getting to the right metric, is important as well. In and of itself the process is transformative. It is like setting up the math problem on the test. The setting up of the problem correctly represents a large part of the student's learning. In Economic Value Management, this process is not only beneficial the first time, but also serves as a foundation of learning and knowledge that is applicable to more than the organization's current circumstance. By not just understanding the numbers but also learning the process, the organization can use the process to more readily and appropriately adjust the metrics as the organization changes. And each time it is used, the uncovering process of value metrics discovery makes the learning more meaningful.

Any organization can take some rules and apply them—that is rote. To truly understand how to apply them, their purpose and benefits, one needs to understand the why of their development and the contexts of their application. To do this simply and easily, the *experience* of choosing provides the easiest and best means. If a bank moves to become a financial services organization and then an electronic retailer and consultant, these choices and decisions will need to be made in the context of Economic Value Management. If the organization is using a rote process, the development of changing measures of performance will be difficult.

Becoming an Economic Value Management organization necessarily involves change. Process and technology changes are one aspect of this. Static organizations will not continue to serve any constituent group well. As we discussed in Chapter 2's "Process and Technology" section, changing metrics are a necessary result. The project mentality of "let's get these in" and "leave them to run" is insufficient to provide the information to make the right choices in the future.

One organization, "The Quibbling Group," understood this issue when it planned an expansion of its business lines. Quibbling had used metrics that were based on value concepts. When Quibbling had installed the original metrics, much of the process had involved procedures and analytics created by an outside source. As Ben, the CFO said, "The installation was rote, relying on this expert. When the importance of the new business unit increased, we needed to examine the existing metrics and enhance them to better reflect the new business strategy. Because we had not really been through the process phases of establishing some of the basic financial metrics, a new education process was required—and the need for new processes became evident—in response to the change." Quibbling would likely not have reached this awareness had the organization not begun the Economic Value Management adoption process. What Quibbling learned was the importance of owning both the metrics and the process.

In contrast, "BetaCorp" developed sophisticated measures of performance. Unfortunately, however, once having developed them, Beta wanted the metrics to last. Because of this, Beta did not establish processes to monitor the metrics themselves and update them as needed. A year or so after an installation, which was considered very avant-garde, the organization was caught short when unexpected marketplace issues began to influence their profit dynamics. Given the sophisticated system, one could ask, "How could this happen?" In fact, it happened because the organization had not changed some of the metrics, because the processes were not established to do so on a frequent basis.

Change: Its Impact on Multiple Measures

Banking is an example of changing models. For years, the job of banks was to provide safety and soundness for financial assets and extend credit not provided by the underdeveloped capital markets. It has only been in the last couple of decades that the job of banks has changed. Banks now aim to provide competitive returns on financial assets and competitive extension of credit facilities. Banks have shifted from marble lobbies with as many years in business as possible to institutions of varying age with multiple distribution channels.

For this reason, value-based metrics must be both backward and forward looking, evaluative and predictive. "LoanSource" did not pay attention to shifting customer requirements. LoanSource used standard measures and did not attempt to adjust them for changing circumstances. They also assumed that customers would accept or overlook differences between offerings of LoanSource and its competitors. While in the past customers may have made no changes, current customers were more knowledgeable and simply yanked their business. This caused the stock price of LoanSource to fall dramatically.

So the answer to standardization or not is contextual. In some contexts, it is the best one can do. In others, it will create a situation where less than optimal information is produced.

What are the basics of calculating value? The next chapter will describe the issues and calculation of value measures.

NOTES

1. Eleanor Bloxham, "Performance Measurement through U.S. Binoculars," *Journal of Strategic Performance Measurement,* October/November 1999, pp. 5–13.

2. See Polly Labarre, "Do You Have the Will to Lead," *Fast Company,* March 2000, pp. 222–230; and Peter Koestenbaum, *Leadership: The Inner Side of Greatness: A Philosophy for Leaders,* San Francisco: Jossey-Bass 1991.

3. Neurolinguistic Programming (NLP) provides insights into these human motivations. A recommended text on the subject is "NLP Comprehensive Training Team," in Steve Andreas and Charles Faulkner (Editors), *NLP: The New Technology of Achievement,* New York: Quill, 1996.

4. The Myers-Briggs Type Indicator is one example of personality typing that can be used in organizations.

CHAPTER 5

Economic Value Management: Demonstrating and Assessing Value Measurement Approaches

INTRODUCTION

When Tammy, the COO of "Millers Bank," thinks about the calculation of value metrics, the explanation and examples presented seem very simple and elementary. For others at Millers, the calculations seem more difficult to understand and implement. By making the examples and presentation in this chapter as simple as possible, perhaps everyone can understand the basic steps in measuring value creation.

For the undaunted, there are quite a few sources on the general topic of value measurement.[1] This book will not repeat all that is found in these resources but rather provide the Economic Value Management framework for understanding the logic behind the calculations and the arguments made about them.

Value metrics integrate the best corporate finance thinking with value-based period-to-period measures. Corporate finance provides a number of metric disciplines used in value measurement. One discipline is net present value (NPV) analysis or discounted cash flow (DCF). NPV or DCF analysis takes a series of cash flows (inflows and outflows of funds) and calculates the value in present terms. This allows an organization to compare, on a like basis, a number of different potential actions and the value of the cash flows that will result. If one series of cash flows *A* provides a higher NPV than another series *B*, then cash flow *A* creates more value than *B*. The concept of NPV can be used to understand the relative value of future cash flows on a like basis. It can also be used to evaluate past activities and their value contribution.

A similar concept is future value (FV) analysis. Here one takes a series of cash flows and calculates their value at some point in the future. This allows an organization to evaluate a number of different actions and their values on a like basis as well, comparing the values at a given point in time in the future.

Although in Economic Value Management, there are many calculations of economic value, one fundamental concept behind economic value metrics is that they take the NPV and FV valuation processes a step further. Rather than view capital expenditures as outflows in the period incurred, economic value metrics use a matching concept. This matching concept amortizes the cost of capital over time rather than charging it at a point in time. In essence, it calculates a rental cost for the use of capital.

Exhibit 5.1 provides an example. The first section shows the inputs in the example. Capital investments are made in periods 0 and 2. Capital employed at the beginning of the period is shown in periods 1 through 4. The capital rental charge, or capital cost, is calculated for each period as the amount of capital multiplied by a 10% cost of capital. The cash flows in each period are also shown.

	Period 0	Period 1	Period 2	Period 3	Period 4	Period 5 and Beyond	Total NPV
Inputs to Example:							
Capital (A) Invested	(1,500)		(500)				
Capital Employed Beginning of Period		1,500	1,500	2,000	2,000	2,000	
Capital Cost (B)		(150)	(150)	(200)	(200)	(200)	
Cash Flow (C)		400	500	750	1,000	1,000	
Calculated Net Cash Flow and Economic Values:							
Net Cash Flow (A + C)	(1,500)	400	0	750	1,000	1,000	
Economic Value (B + C)	0	250	350	550	800	800	
Net Present Value Calculations:							
NPV of Net Cash Flow	(1,500)	364	0	564	683	6,830	6,940
NPV of Economic Value	0	227	289	413	546	5,464	6,940
(PV discount factors used in NPV calculation)	1.0000	0.9091	0.8264	0.7513	0.6830	6.8300	

Assumptions:
Cost of capital = 10%.
Capital is invested at end of period.
Cash flows are equal to adjusted net income.
Period 5 and beyond assume perpetuity.

EXHIBIT 5.1 Simple Net Cash Flow and Economic Value

Using these inputs, net cash flows are calculated in the second section as the net of capital investment and cash flow. Economic value is calculated as the cash flow less the capital rental cost.

The third section of Exhibit 5.1 shows the NPV calculations on both a cash flow and an economic value basis. As this example demonstrates, net cash flow varies significantly from period to period because of capital changes. Economic value, however, amortizes the cost of capital over time, charging a cost for using that capital in each period based on the capital employed. In other words, a *capital rental* cost is employed. This allows an organization to understand, *in each period,* the amount of value that has been or will be created. It provides a way for the organization to witness progress or decline in a clear fashion, and with that understanding, it allows an organization to better forecast whether value will be created over time.

As demonstrated in Exhibit 5.1, the economic value information provides a clearer picture of the value created than does net cash flow. This is particularly true as capital is added at the end of period 2. The economic value calculation eliminates the distortion of a one-time full charge for the capital. This value model of charging a capital rental cost is very useful because organizations and their constituents prefer periodic guides and measures. (In fact, debt costs are charged in just this periodic fashion on the income statement.) The value model as shown in Exhibit 5.1 can be used for backward-looking purposes to measure results and for forward-looking purposes to forecast potential scenarios.

Exhibit 5.2 also demonstrates another reason that the economic value information is superior. In this example, the organization began with a capital infusion of $1 million. Because the capital rental cost is reflected in each period, the economic value calculation prevents the results in each period

	Period 0	Period 1	Period 2	Period 3	Period 4	Period 5 and Beyond
Capital (A)	(1,000,000)					
Capital Cost (B)		(100,000)	(100,000)	(100,000)	(100,000)	(100,000)
Cash Flow (C)		80,000	120,000	160,000	140,000	150,000
Net Cash Flow (A + C)	(1,000,000)	80,000	120,000	160,000	140,000	150,000
Economic Value (B + C)		(20,000)	20,000	60,000	40,000	50,000

Assumptions:
Cost of capital = 10%.
Cash flows are equal to adjusted net income.

EXHIBIT 5.2 Simple Organization Example/Analogy

from being overstated. The matching process better reflects the economics and makes the information much more useful. Clearly, traditional corporate finance models of DCF and NPV provide the underpinnings for economic value models. A value framework provides distinct information advantages on a period-to-period basis. This, however, is just one aspect of economic value calculations.

SAMPLE VALUE CALCULATION

Economic Value Management models are more complicated than the two examples just discussed. To better understand the models, it makes sense to begin where most economic value calculations do—not with cash flow data, but with accounting earnings. The reason accounting numbers are the usual starting point is simple: generally, they are more available than other sets of numbers. Given the troubles with accounting, the question might be posed: Why start there? Actually, using accounting as the starting point is beneficial because, despite the issues found in the presentation of accounting numbers, one highly desirable attribute of them is that in many parts of the world, their construction is highly regulated, and this regulation is increasing. This creates the ability to place some reliance on what is contained within them. Further, the value metrics process itself provides the opportunity to vet what they contain. In fact, the Economic Value Management process is designed to challenge the accounting numbers in order to develop the specific measures of value for the particular decisions and circumstances the firm faces. This establishes a process that allows boards and CEOs to vet the accounting information. By not using a rules-based process and challenging the accounting process itself, Economic Value Management helps boards, audit committees, and CEOs determine if, in fact, the accounting information is misleading. Any distortions of the true picture are understood by developing the variety of Economic Value Management metrics for the decisions of the firm.

How is this done? Calculating Economic Value Management metrics from accounting numbers involves locating the numbers, breaking them down, and repackaging them in useful ways to answer the questions:

- What value has been created?
- What value is forecasted to be created in the future?
- What may be expected in terms of value creation?

An example of how economic value metrics look from this perspective will help explain how the repackaging process works. The example in Exhibit 5.3 is taken from "RealBank."

As a shareholder, board member, employee, supplier, customer, or regulator, it would be natural to be dismayed by the earnings results of Real-Bank. The larger question, however, is what do the results mean for value

(in $ millions)	1st Quarter 2000	2nd Quarter 2000	3rd Quarter 2000	4th Quarter 2000	Full Year 2000
Net Income Attributable to Common (A)	500	(1,000)	500	(500)	(500)
Increase in Allowance (B)	0	400	100	800	1,300
Net Income after Allowance Adjustment (A + B)	500	(600)	600	300	800
Asset Write-Downs (C)		1,000			1,000
Net Income after Both Adjustments (A + B + C)	500	400	600	300	1,800
Cost of Equity/Equity Equivalents (D)	(1,000)	(1,000)	(1,000)	(1,000)	(4,000)
Economic Value (A + B + C + D)	(500)	(600)	(400)	(700)	(2,200)

EXHIBIT 5.3 RealBank

creation in the future? Will the losses continue to mount? What does the volatility in results from quarter to quarter mean in terms of sustainable value creation? In the first quarter, RealBank generates $500 million in earnings. The following quarter it suffers a $1 billion loss. RealBank rebounds in the third quarter with a $500 million gain, only to relapse again in the fourth quarter by losing the $500 million it had just earned. In addition to sorting out what happened, what are the earnings results saying about the future prospects for this company? What should be examined as future results are announced?

By applying an Economic Value Management analysis, the answers to these questions become clearer. One area to examine is the increase in the RealBank's allowance for loan loss reserves. (This allowance account is similar to a bad debt reserve account in nonfinancial services firms.) Firms hold these reserves as estimates of future losses that will be incurred. In banks, the reserve is a provision for loans that will not be repaid. In the case of bad debt in nonfinancial services firms, it represents payments that customers owe but are not expected to pay. Lowering the reserve estimate of future losses increases the earnings of the company in the current period. On the flip side, additions to the reserves decrease the earnings of the company in the current period. If the firm overestimates future losses, not only will current returns be understated, but future returns will be overstated when the reserves are subsequently decreased. Companies may increase or decrease reserves for a number of different reasons. (When a company increases its reserves dramatically, and it is not associated with a concomitant increase in business, it may have to do with a reevaluation of reserve requirements.) RealBank, in this example, has increased its reserves substantially, and this so-called fortification of the balance sheet could overstate future economic requirements. To get a clearer picture of the results, an adjustment is made to remove the increases in the loss estimates reflected in the income and capital accounts. In this way, only current period activities (i.e., current net charge-offs) rather than future estimates are reflected. After this adjustment to the results is taken, the net income after adjustment is much less volatile. In fact, a review of the quarterly results after this adjustment suggests a relatively stable set of returns with first, third, and fourth quarters of $500, $600, and $300 million, respectively. The second quarter continues to raise questions, however. Why is there a $600 million loss? Does this represent an ongoing issue for RealBank, or is it the result of a one-time event?

As it turns out, RealBank took asset write-downs in the second quarter of $1 billion, after tax. One way to reflect these write-downs on an economic basis, is to make an adjustment to spread the impact of the write-downs over the economic life of the assets. (That is, rather than show up as a one-time charge, as we demonstrated with capital investments in the NPV calculation, the write-down could be matched over time with the assets held.) This is something that employees or the Board of Directors could do to get a better sense of the true economics of the company.

For shareholders or other outsiders, however, it may be more difficult to assess how the unusual write-downs should be handled. A simple way to adjust is to remove the write-downs from the results to gain a clearer perspective on the firm's trends. To accomplish this, the amount of the write-down is reversed and added back to capital. When this is done, the result in the second quarter more closely resembles the other three quarters as reflected by the net income after both adjustments, as shown in Exhibit 5.3.

The next economic adjustment is to include the opportunity cost of capital for all equity and equity equivalents, since a charge is not already reflected in the adjusted net income.[2] With the other adjustments included, equity and equity equivalents are relatively stable in all years and amount to a cost of $1 billion in each time period. As Exhibit 5.2 demonstrates, excluding the cost of capital would create a distortion in our understanding of whether value has been created.

Once this adjustment is made, the result shows that the company *destroyed* value *in every quarter.* Specifically, $2.2 billion in value was destroyed for the year—much greater than the loss in originally reported net income of $500 million. What were the reasons for the difference? To recap, the charge for the cost of capital that was not included already in the income statement was $4 billion. For some companies, this charge for capital may not be a large component. In most companies, however, it is, and for this firm it was significant. This $4 billion charge was then offset by the two other adjustments of a $1.3 billion addition to net income (full year) for the increase in reserves and $1 billion for the asset write-downs (also full year). All together, they increased the actual loss by $1.7 billion, from $500 million on an earnings basis to $2.2 billion on an economic basis.

What does this mean for the company and its constituents going forward? For investors and others, continuing to adjust future results for changes in the allowance makes sense. If it turns out that the allowance is reduced in future periods because of an overestimate in 2000, the company's accounting earnings may indicate a turnaround that is not real. If there is a belief in management's prediction that losses will increase in the future, this view will be reflected in higher forecasted net charge-offs. (Net charge-offs are simply the write-offs or charge-offs of loans that went bad during the period offset by loan recoveries.) Making the adjustments and consciously monitoring the results allows all constituents to determine for themselves the legitimacy of a so-called earnings turnaround. It equips all constituents to judge more accurately a change in analysts' viewpoints. Similarly, if the assets that have been written down are later sold at higher values, this too will not represent true economic gains for the company. Shareholders, board members, employees, suppliers, customers, and regulators should monitor and adjust their estimations of the firm based on these realities. For anyone doing business with the company, getting clear signals is important. Understanding what is behind the numbers helps provide that clearer picture.

While RealBank's performance in 2000 was not stellar, by creating an economic statement of results, shareholders, board members, employees, suppliers, customers, and regulators have better information with which to hold the company's management accountable. For example, if the assets that are written down are later sold for a large gain, should management be rewarded for the accounting mis-estimate? What would represent a comparable year for RealBank in 2001? A comparable year for RealBank in 2001 (with no change in allowance or major one-time events) would be nearly $2 billion in earnings, not a loss of $500 million. How so? After adjustments, RealBank actually earned $1.8 billion, before a charge for equity capital (see net income after adjustments—full year 2000 in Exhibit 5.3) rather than incurring a $500 million loss in 2000. And clearly, with no significant capital changes, RealBank must earn at least $4 billion to create value and just cover its opportunity cost of capital. And that information should give the board pause. With the potential shenanigans removed, these hurdles are much higher than at first glance might be expected. The board, investors, and employees of the firm now have the information to discount any headline that reads: "2001 Is a Great Year for RealBank. Earnings Rise from $500 Million Loss to $1 Billion Profit." The first questions these informed constituents will ask are: How did RealBank slip by $800 million from the previous year, and when is RealBank going to create value, rather than destroy it?

Value is created when there is improvement in value creation. As the RealBank example indicates, to show improvement, it is important that the company and its constituents understand the real starting point. Economic Value Management metrics create transparency that the accounting numbers do not. These metrics integrate the best corporate finance thinking with period-to-period measures. Everyone benefits from an understanding of the true economic results.

CALCULATING VALUE METRICS

Earnings for RealBank in 2000 were extremely volatile. This is actually unusual, because generally corporate earnings show a steady, upward climb. (Chapter 7 contains many examples that follow those patterns.) Questions concerning the validity of accounting information stems largely from the ability of corporations to manipulate the timing of results and to create this steady picture.

A November 8, 2001, CBS MarketWatch.com story, "Earnings Debacle," reported that in a recent Broadgate survey of fund managers, 95% of all managers "would like more consistency in how EBITDA—earnings before interest, taxes, depreciation, and amortization—is calculated."[3] Economic Value Management provides a way for anyone calculating value to understand and adjust for differences in the way organizations present their numbers.

Here are some simple ways to apply the basics of economic value metrics to enhance understanding of what is happening within an organization. The objective is a pragmatic approach that can be communicated. It is not a memorized set of gymnastic calculations. What is most important is a conceptual understanding and an ability to discern whether the Economic Value Management metric, whatever it may be, is serving its intended purpose. Rather than letting the computer write the software, the idea here is to make the numbers do your bidding.

All the calculations described below are relatively simple. They can be performed by everyone considering investment in, employment with, or commerce involving an organization for which financial statements are available. The *key points* to consider are summarized in Exhibit 5.4. All adjustments can be summarized in these two categories. The process of evaluating the accounting information that is used can alert everyone to potential issues in the accounting and in the organization. If information is not available to make these assessments, that in itself is important to know.[4]

To perform a calculation, consider the following five steps as an approach:

1. Begin with net income available to common shareholders.
2. Adjust for nonrecurring or nonoperational items.
3. Adjust for reserves that are distorting the economic picture.

4. Adjust for the timing of revenues, investments, or expenses.

5. Charge for equity and equity equivalents[5] and any other charges missing from the earnings statement.

Accounting numbers, our starting point, form the basis for repackaging. The development of the Economic Value Management metric, using accounting numbers as the starting point, allows the practitioner to determine whether, and to what extent, the accounting information is "hocus pocus." This is certainly a critical issue today for all CEOs and boards.

One aspect of accounting that must be understood at the outset is that accounting treats different kinds of capital very differently (see Exhibit 5.5). Only borrowing or debt has its cost reflected on the income statement. This cost is reflected as interest expense. Traditional accounting does not, however, include a cost if the form of capital is equity. Therefore, the cost of equity capital is not reflected. As mentioned earlier, Economic Value Management metric concepts include the notions that capital is not free, stewardship of capital is expected, and capital providers should earn a return on the capital they invest. Consequently, an adjustment to net income is made to reflect the costs of equity capital (and remove the distortion that equity is free).[6] Step 1 handles the adjustment for preferred stock. Step 5 handles the adjustment for all remaining equity and equity equivalents. For purposes of discussion in this chapter, the term *equity* (and equity equivalents) will refer to all of the accounts related to stockholder equity with the exception of preferred stock.

---

1. Is there a *timing difference on a revenue or cost* that is distorting or may distort the picture we want to understand or the behavior we want to motivate?

For example:

- Asset write-downs or sales, nonrecurring charges, unusual gains or losses
- Investment sales, mark to market, or pension funding impacts
- Changes in reserves
- R&D, marketing, training, depreciation, and amortization costs.
- Revenue recognition

2. Is there an *economic cost not accounted for?*

For example:

- Cost of equity (and equity equivalents) (Equity equivalents are non-interest-bearing, long-term liabilities that represent an equity "carve out" such as reserves.)
- Cost of stock option compensation

EXHIBIT 5.4 Timing Differences and Missing Charges

Type of Capital	Reflected on Income Statement	Comment
Debt	Yes	Cost of debt and tax benefit of debt flows through income statement.
Preferred Equity	No	Dividends are not reflected on income statement.
Common Equity	No	Charge for use of common equity is not reflected on income statement.

EXHIBIT 5.5   Different Types of Capital

Net income available to common shareholders is needed to perform step 1. The easiest method of acquiring this number is to find "net income available to common shareholders" as opposed to "net income" on the income statement. The net income available to common will already include the cost of preferred dividends and minority interest. (If "net income available to common" cannot be found, then subtract preferred dividends and earnings attributed to minority interest from net income.)

Steps 2 through 4 require making adjustments that lend greater clarity to what is happening within the organization based on the purpose of the numbers. The benefits in making the adjustments are found in what is often referred to as *transparency* of the organization. Organizations that do not make these adjustments weaken the power of the value process. The adjustments made, of course, depend on the particular circumstance and purpose of the measure.

To better understand the benefits, suppose that instead of making the adjustments to RealBank in Exhibit 5.3, we had only made the adjustment for the capital charge (as shown in Exhibit 5.6).[7] While this one adjustment shows that value has been significantly destroyed, it certainly does not provide the explanatory power achieved by making a couple of additional

	1st Quarter 2000	2nd Quarter 2000	3rd Quarter 2000	4th Quarter 2000	Full Year 2000
Net Income Attributable to Common	500	(1,000)	500	(500)	(500)
Cost of Equity/Equity Equivalents	(1,000)	(1,000)	(1,000)	(1,000)	(4,000)
Net Income after Capital Charge (NIACC)	(500)	(2,000)	(500)	(1,500)	(4,500)

EXHIBIT 5.6   RealBank

adjustments. What does the pattern of results mean quarter to quarter, and what should the expectation be next year? Without the adjustments, the answer is unknown.

Given the benefits, let's proceed with a calculation that includes adjustments for:

1. Reversing or spreading the impact of nonrecurring items or investment returns that may not be a part of ongoing operations

2. Removing or spreading changes in reserves such as tax and bad debt reserves

3. Spreading the cost and benefits of R & D and other investment-related expenses

The removal of nonrecurring items is an attempt to determine whether value has been created excluding the impact of nonrecurring events. This information provides insight into the sustainability of the numbers. Since nonrecurring items are not expected to reoccur, they distort the picture of what profits should look like going forward. In addition, as discussed earlier, the organization, believe it or not, may have purposely set out to hit a certain accounting earnings target. To achieve this aim, it may have taken any number of actions, including the sale of parts of its business. Understanding the fact that the proceeds of the sale will not reoccur is important. For projection purposes, it is also important to understand the nature of the nonrecurring item since the sale of a business may have income impacts in future periods (either positive or negative). These impacts may increase future net income if the business was losing money or cause a decrease in net income if it had positive earnings.

To remove nonrecurring items, four steps are taken:

1. Add back nonrecurring losses (after tax) to net income. If the loss amounts are provided before tax, they may need to be converted to an after-tax basis. Using a pretax number can overstate the impact of the loss on net income. For example, if the corporate tax rate is 40% and the nonrecurring loss before tax is 1,000, then the organization may have originally incurred a loss of 1,000, resulting in reduced taxes of 400 (1,000 × 40%). So after taxes, the nonrecurring loss would have reduced net income by 600 (1,000 − 400), instead of the full 1,000. In that case, 600 then is the appropriate amount to add back.

2. Subtract nonrecurring gains (after tax) from net income. Again, the after-tax amount is used.

3. Add to retained earnings (an equity account) the accumulated amount of the nonrecurring losses (after tax).

4. Subtract from retained earnings the accumulated amount of the nonrecurring gains (after tax).

Exhibit 5.7 demonstrates the adjustment process to the equity accounts. Since the equity accounts are cumulative amounts, the adjustments for nonrecurring items need to be made on a cumulative basis. From the example, the year 1 nonrecurring loss of five (after tax) is added back to net income and the year 2 nonrecurring gain of two is subtracted from net income. Retained earnings will then need to be increased by five in year 1 and increased by three in year two (five from year 1 minus two from year 2). Depending on the purpose of the analysis, rather than reversed, the amounts could instead be spread over several periods.

Adjustment may also be desired in the area of reserves. As noted earlier, accounting reserves are conservative in allowing organizations to forecast future bad events and include potential future impacts in net income that otherwise purports to represent what has happened. While it can provide important information for forecasting purposes, it may negatively bias the numbers for an organization that is employing more conservative accounting policies than its peers. In addition, reserves can be manipulated to smooth earnings by increasing reserves (and thus lowering net income) in good years and using that reserve when needed (and thus increasing net income) when times are more difficult. It can also be used by CEOs beginning their tenure to clear the decks and then draw from, as needed, when they move forward. By eliminating the effects of reserves, one can better see what has happened in the period being measured. With this adjustment, as with other calculations, however, there are trade-offs that must be weighed dependent upon

	Year One	Year One Adjusted	Year Two	Year Two Adjusted
Net Income	100	105	150	148
Equity and Equity Equivalents	1,000	1,005	1,150	1,153
Nonrecurring Loss after Tax	5			
Nonrecurring Gain after Tax			2	

For Year One:
Net income plus nonrecurring loss = 100 + 5 = 105
Equity plus accumulated nonrecurring loss = 1000 + 5 = 1005

For Year Two:
(This example shows how the calculations are made if one wishes to view year two as if the year one and year two nonrecurring events had not occurred.)
Net income minus nonrecurring gain = 150 − 2 = 148
Equity plus accumulated nonrecurring losses and minus accumulated nonrecurring gains = 1150 + 5 − 2 = 1153

EXHIBIT 5.7 Nonrecurring Items

the purpose of the numbers to be used. By adjusting reserves, a much clearer picture of the reality of the period is formed. From this picture, however, one does not see (or it does not include) the potential negative impact of current actions on future periods.

To remove the impact of changes in reserves (a potential source of earnings manipulation), two steps are required:

1. Add back the net increase in reserves to net income (as if the increase had not been taken).

2. Add the accumulated net increase in reserves (i.e., the amount of the reserve) to retained earnings (equity).

The impact of this adjustment in the Economic Value Management calculation is shown in Exhibit 5.8. As with all adjustments, depending on the context and purpose of the calculation, the adjustment may be made to remove all impacts or simply to adjust the results to better reflect economic reality.

Another large category of adjustments is related to investments by the organization and is often made for a variety of reasons. One reason is the desire to understand a period's results on a basis that matches costs with the benefits when traditional accounting does not. With conservative accounting, the costs of R&D or of marketing, for example, may not be matched with the benefits of those efforts.

Another reason to make these adjustments relates to the behavioral impact. In some organizations, an immediate hit is taken to net income for certain R&D and market investments. Then in tough times when this investment might be needed most, the organization may discourage the expenditure. To encourage longer-term thinking and investment in these areas, the calculation is often used within an organization to adjust this thinking by making an estimation of the matched costs and benefits of R&D and other unmatched expense items.

	Year Two	Year Two Adjusted
Net Income	200	215
Equity	1,000	1,035

Reserve for bad debts (after tax):
  Year One: 20
  Year Two: 35
Increase in reserve for bad debt (after tax) = 35 − 20 = 15

EXHIBIT 5.8 Reserve Adjustment

To execute this adjustment, add back the expensed item to net income and retained earnings as appropriate. Then, if appropriate, spread the amounts as expenses and reduce retained earnings backward or forward in time as may be appropriate.

Revenue recognition has become an important issue related to earnings management. As with investments, an assessment of revenue recognition practices should be performed. How are revenues recorded? What are they for? Is recognition more aggressive than it should be? Is recognition postponed in any way, and if so, for what reasons? Answers to these questions will provide the input required to determine the timing differences that should be reflected in the value calculation.

Step 5, in calculating value metrics, is to calculate a charge for equity and equity equivalents and any other charges that have an economic cost and are missing from the income statement. Although the need to adjust for a charge for equity is widely recognized and accepted, some CEOs still do not understand it. They argue that, if no company includes the charge for equity, then all are on a like basis. There are several arguments, however, for adjustment to improve understanding and comparison of company information. For one, the amounts of equity used by companies as a form of capital vary widely on both absolute and relative bases. As Exhibit 5.9 shows, not only may the size of the firms differ in terms of capital utilization, but their capital structures may also differ in terms of reliance on common equity capital. In the exhibit, Company A uses debt while B, C, and D do not. Company C is much larger in terms of capitalization as well. Another area of difference can come from investors' expectations of returns from one company versus another. In other words, the costs of capital may differ from firm to firm. For example, a technology firm's cost of capital may be significantly different from that of an automobile manufacturer. In Exhibit 5.9, Company D is shown with a higher cost of capital than the other three. Therefore, to compare these companies, the adjustment for equity capital cost is necessary. Because these variables may be significantly different from company to company, a provision for the return required on equity capital cannot be assumed to be constant.

As an aside, those familiar with "shareholder value" may know that some approaches involve a more complicated formulation in handling capital—taking the charge for debt out of net income—and adding an average debt cost to the cost of capital. The issues (aside from its simplicity) of using an equity-only approach will be presented later in this chapter.[8]

As Exhibit 5.9 shows, although the operating profits or adjusted net incomes of Companies A, B, and C differ, the value created by the three firms is identical. For Company A, the value calculation is 210 less 10% of 2,000 or 10. Companies B and C also have economic value of 10. Company D demonstrates the impact of cost of capital. Although its adjusted net income and equity capital are identical to Company B, the cost of capital is higher. This results in an equity capital cost of 420 and value *destruction* of 130.

	Company A	Company B	Company C	Company D
Cost of Equity Capital (A)	10%	10%	10%	15%
Adjusted Net Income (B)	210	290	2,010	290
Debt (C)	800	0	0	0
Equity/Equity Equivalents (D)	2,000	2,800	20,000	2,800
Charge for Cost of Equity/ Equity Equivalents (E = A × D)	200	280	2,000	420
Economic Value (B − E)	**10**	**10**	**10**	**(130)**

Notes:

(A) Companys A, B, and C have a cost of equity capital of 10%; Company D's is 15%.

(B) Adjusted net income already includes the cost of debt as an interest expense. Only Company A has debt.

(C) Only Company A has debt on balance sheet; after-tax interest expense for debt is included in A's net income.

(E) Company C has a significantly larger adjusted net income and capital base. Companys A, B, and D have similar total capital amounts of 2,800, although 800 of the 2,800 is debt capital in the case of Company A.

EXHIBIT 5.9 Cost Equity/Equity Equivalents

While the calculation of a charge for equity and equity equivalents is fairly simple, determining the cost of equity is controversial. There are a number of ways the calculation can be done. Some consultants will simply recommend a flat rate anywhere from 10% to 15% to move forward and avoid controversy. Others use a calculation performed by a securities analyst. Others simply use their intuition in terms of what return they would require for holding the stock.

A more disciplined approach is to calculate the cost of equity using a capital asset pricing model (CAPM) calculation. This calculation involves three components: the risk-free rate, the market premium over the risk-free rate, and the beta of the stock. The issue with this formula is that it is a precise calculation involving components whose values are highly controversial. One typical example is to use the long-term U.S. Treasury bond yield for the risk-free rate, 5% for the market risk premium (for example), and to use the beta obtained from ValueLine® or other beta sources. The CAPM is then applied by multiplying the stock's beta times the market premium and adding the result to the risk-free rate of return. Assuming the stock's beta is 1.2 and the risk-free rate is 7%, the calculation would be:

$$(1.2 \times .05) + .07 = .06 + .07 = .13 \text{ or } 13\%.$$

While it is popular to talk about the problems with CAPM, a more rational approach is to discuss the quality of inputs and to choose those that make the most sense for the application being performed. Some practitioners use historical betas. Others use forward-looking betas. (Forward-looking betas may be more industry-like, including company differential for size and leverage.) Using more complicated and sophisticated risk arbitrage formulas are also a possible way to derive the cost of equity.[9]

Again, Exhibit 5.4 provides a simple way to think about the adjustments to use in Economic Value Management calculations. The simple calculations shown earlier use an equity-only approach. In other words, the cost of all equity not included as a charge to net income is reflected as a cost in the calculations. No adjustment is made for the cost of debt since debt cost is reflected already in the net income calculation.

While the equity-only approach has advantages, there are instances when special care is required. One such example can occur when the organization retires a large piece of debt (a nonrecurring blip). In this instance, value calculations may have to be adjusted for timing issues.

TO WACC OR NOT TO WACC AND THE USE OF APV

The examples in Exhibits 5.3 and 5.9 calculate Economic Value Management metrics by beginning with (a) net income available to common (which includes after-tax debt costs and the costs of preferred stock), (b) making adjustments as needed, and (c) including a charge for common equity capital since that charge is not already included in the income statement. While straightforward, a common calculation of "economic value added" or "shareholder value" does not use this approach. Instead, it uses a more complex formula. The more common approach begins with (a) net income available to common, (b) makes adjustments as needed, then (c) *adds back the after-tax cost of debt and preferred dividends,* and (d) *includes a weighted average capital charge for all debt and equity.* In the standard formulation, rather than a cost of equity, the cost of capital used in this calculation is a weighted average after-tax cost of debt and equity capital combined (i.e., weighted average cost of capital, or simply *WACC*).

Many organizations use WACC for discounted cash flow. For some organizations, one reason to use WACC for "shareholder value" calculations is the difficulty some organizations have in determining cost of equity versus the after-tax cost of debt capital at sector, division, and product levels. In other instances, such as the use of percentage calculators of "shareholder value," there can be an advantage in using a capital approach that includes debt.

Does that mean WACC is better? Calculations using WACC can have drawbacks, as Timothy Luehrman discussed in a series of articles in the *Harvard Business Review.*[10] Exhibit 5.10 provides several reasons to *not* use

WACC. One reason is that, in some cases, it is just an unnecessary step. Exhibit 5.11 demonstrates an example where it *is* unnecessary, comparing two calculations—one with WACC and one without. In instances like this, removing debt cost from adjusted net income and using debt as a component

---

- It may be an unnecessary step (see Exhibit 5.11).
- A separate after-tax cost of debt calculation, rather than a WACC, works *just as well* and in *some cases better* to handle situations where:
  (a) An organization wishes to use a current cost of debt rather than the actual cost the company is incurring.
  (b) A percentage value metric is used and the best comparison includes all capital.
  (c) Different units have different tax structures and a generic WACC will distort the results.
  (d) An APV analysis is advantageous.

EXHIBIT 5.10   Why Not Use WACC?

An example where there is no difference—just extra steps.

Net Income Available to Common	70
Adjustments	30
Debt—20% of Total Capital	200
Preferred Equity	0
Common Equity—80% of Total Capital	800
After-tax Cost of Debt	5%
Cost of Equity	10%
WACC (20% × 5%) + (80% × 10%)	9%

	WACC	Not to WACC
Net Income Available to Common	70	70
Adjustments (excluding debt expense)	30	30
After-tax Cost of Debt (5% × 200)*	10	
Adjusted Net Income	110	100
Capital Charge (9% × 1,000)	90	
Cost of Equity (10% × 800)		80
Economic Value	**20**	**20**

*Equivalent to after-tax interest expense.

EXHIBIT 5.11   To WACC or Not to WACC?

of capital represent additional steps. The more important issue is not with using debt as a component of capital but with using WACC as the cost of capital.

The most important reasons to not use a weighted average WACC approach are that it provides no distinct advantage and has several drawbacks versus separate calculations of equity, tax, and other financing effects. One issue of particular note is that WACC can distort the results at a subunit level. The issue of having good numbers at the subunit level is important because one of the significant benefits of Economic Value Management is the ability to measure value creation for an organization's component parts with enough precision that appropriate actions can be taken as a result. Certain subunit results may be distorted using a weighted average approach that employs a generic capital structure and a generic tax rate.

One example of a complex tax situation where a generic application of marginal tax rates to debt cost would cause a distortion are leasing operations found in financial institutions. From a value perspective, the taxes can make or break this business. It is important that the tax impacts are addressed separately for each unit rather than using a blended after-tax debt and equity cost, particularly in units like these.

Organizations in different locations can also benefit from specific financing and tax reviews. In global organizations, the tax issues and financing requirements of subsidiaries may vary considerably and should be addressed separately. Greater diversity in product lines can drive differential funding requirements. With more organizations moving to centralized treasuries, differential funding needs and financing effects as well as hedging costs are better understood and can be measured. An approach that removes the option of *one size fits all* found in WACC and forces these analyses is beneficial in better understanding and managing the organization's results.

In corporate finance valuation, there is a term called *adjusted present value* (APV) that is worth mentioning. APV consists of a way of breaking down a valuation for anything (although it is often used in the context of an acquisition or major project) into its component parts—the operating and financing pieces. It starts by creating an equity-only model and then adds in debt, tax shield, and financing and issue costs associated with the acquisition or project. This allows for specific delineation of these charges and the creation of appropriate scenario analyses to address potential financing alternatives.[11]

With Economic Value Management, APV (which provides benefits over NPV) can provide even greater benefits because the techniques of APV can be applied in a way that allows decisions to be easily tracked as part of the *normal* management reporting system. This is *important* because the efficacy of an acquisition or investment is rarely tracked in most organizations. At a recent conference of corporate finance experts, this was outlined in clear terms by Stanley, one of the speakers: "In our study of firms, in almost no organization are the results of acquisitions and strategic actions tracked." And for good reason. APV represents a step forward from NPV from a management perspective in providing a way of breaking down the valuation into component pieces. However, as the *Harvard Business Review* articles indicate, not all organizations take advantage of these attributes, possibly, in part, because of the common use of WACC.

Beyond APV alone, the step forward is to *use Economic Value Management in combination with APV*. Understanding the components of the value metrics on a period-to-period basis is incredibly powerful. It creates an ability to provide better information internally, to understand the value created and expected in each period, and to provide all constituents with useful information as well.

Because of the benefits of APV and the ability to establish better analyses for individual units, there is good reason to relinquish a WACC mind-set. Being able to clearly separate the operational aspects of an organization, while providing the ability to assess the financing issues, is very important. With Economic Value Management, the organization can understand these aspects on a period-to-period basis that accurately addresses each component.

Financial institutions today generally do not use WACC for the reasons cited earlier. Today, more and more large organizations have financial subsidiaries as well. A common example is a large retailer with a credit card unit. In addition, many large organizations have some financial operations that require special measurement processes. In these cases as well, it is necessary to develop measurement mechanisms that appropriately attribute costs of debt and equity financing and recognize the differential duration, funding, tax, and hedging needs of the subunits. Here again, separate analyses are not only useful, but de rigueur for the financial pieces of the organization. Adopting similar processes for the nonfinancial operations provides a bonus, that is, a greater level of information for these units as well. Economic Value Management gives organizations access to the possibility of a more dynamic capital model. By establishing the calculations more flexibly, a review of the financing assumptions of each suborganizational unit is accomplished and the distortions of a generic WACC are avoided.

DOES THE METRIC FIT?

The explanation of ways to calculate an organization's past value creation described earlier does *not* suggest that this calculation is a rote process. To function at its best, the Economic Value Management calculations must be customized for each organization and the user of the information. Economic Value Management is a discovery process, which transcends a rote calculation and provides new ways of thinking based on stewardship. Understanding the underlying concepts creates the best chance for success.

Are there strict rules for something this contextual? *No,* but guidance is possible. And guidance can come from asking the right questions. As in all areas of stewardship, it can be helpful to ask: *What is the likely outcome, and will the result be beneficial?* These and other questions in Economic Value Management provide guidance for the metrics (and, for that matter, the other aspects) of the value-based management system. This guidance provides reinforcement to the ways in which the organization thinks, relates, and ultimately takes action.

Are there questions that produce better thinking about the metrics? In the Economic Value Management decision process, the first set of questions refers to purpose. Related to the metrics, the questions include:

- What problems or issues should the organization address to be good stewards? These issues should be broken down as specifically as possible.
- What is the metric intended to do?
- What behavior is desired as a result of the metric?

Once a metric has been developed, a second set of questions involves a review of this "first draft metric."

- Does this metric fully answer what it is intended to do—its purpose? Is more than one metric needed?
- What potential behavior (thinking, relating, and actions) will the metric produce? (This was discussed earlier in the context of accounting numbers—a very important question.)
- To what extent and in what manner will long-term value creation and stewardship be served?
- Is the metric as complex as it needs to be? Is the metric as simple as it needs to be? What is lost or gained by this level of complexity?

Value-led organizations will make changes to the metric(s) to maximize its effectiveness, support value creation, and generate value-creating behaviors. Not only in the choice of metrics themselves, but also in the process of the choosing them, value-led organizations will gain the most benefit by engaging in this process openly and creatively using the process itself as a way to achieve the results of value creation.

More specifically, Chapter 2 outlined a set of 14 questions that most organizations will want to answer in the spirit of good stewardship. These questions are:

1. Has the organization added value? How much?
2. How does this compare to the organization's peers and competitors?
3. Has the organization been managed such that each sector has added value?

4. Has the organization been managed such that each product, service, distribution channel, and process added value?

5. Has the organization been managed such that each customer relationship added value?

6. What are the major drivers of value creation for the organization?

7. For all of the above, how has this changed over time?

8. How much value does the organization expect to create?

9. How much value do capital providers (shareholders, if publicly traded) expect the organization to create?

10. How much value does the organization expect to create by sector, product, service, distribution channel, process, and customer?

11. What are the expectations related to the major drivers of value creation over time?

12. What are the capital provider's expectations for the organization's peers? What are the peer's expectations for itself by sector, product, service, distribution channel, customer, process, and major drivers of value creation?

13. How do internal, peer, and capital provider expectations differ from current steady state value creations?

14. For all of the above, how will this change over time?

NEED FOR MULTIPLE MEASURES

Organizations on the value path recognize that for each of the questions the metrics each organization or subunit chooses may well vary. And, for any given question, the organization may wish to perform different calculations in different circumstances.

In the development of the approach, the issue for any organization or constituent is often not only what is the best calculation or model to use in a given context, but also what is the best business calculation or model to use given the data available.

"Shipboard Savings and Loan" found this to be the case when it came to four of the 14 questions, specifically:

- Has the organization added value? How much?

- How does this compare to the organization's peers and competitors?

- How much value does the organization expect to create?

- How much value do capital providers (shareholders, if publicly traded) expect the organization to create?

Shipboard developed a calculation for how much it had added value. Although it acted as a very good indicator, when it came to calculating the metric for peers and competitors, less data were available to perform the calculation than had been available internally. To put Shipboard's number on a comparable basis, a universal calculation was developed that was "dummied down" to the lowest common denominator of information.

It is important to discern when the calculation should be weakened and when a more robust approach is better. For example, when reviewing its own results on a periodic basis, Shipboard used the most detailed formula. This model created the best impact on behavior and provided the best guidance internally. For comparison of a few institutions for which data were readily available, Shipboard used another formula. And for a broader set of institutions where data availability was an issue, a still less refined analysis was performed. Susan, who ran the project explained, "It was not easy at first for the managers to embrace these different calculations. In fact, many personality types innately struggle with issues of ambiguity and multiplicity in general. When the purposes and consequences were understood, however, it was recognized that the tiered approach was clearly the best choice."

The issue of multiple calculations is one that organizations and analysts continue to confront. Although electronic data and standardized value calculation techniques are more readily available today, many organizations, and those analyzing them, *dummy down* their reviews to just using accounting earnings. Economic Value Management organizations, however, develop value calculations of various types and multiple answers to questions depending on the intended use of the data.

At "TalisTrust," a general model was adopted to describe the value of the entire organization, one that incorporated issues at the corporate level, including corporate expenditures. At the division level, however, all of these adjustments did not apply, and for behavioral and incentive reasons, it was important to consider separately the calculations for each division. That meant that TalisTrust had several calculations of value—a division might be represented as its piece of the total calculation—so that each division and the corporate office added to the total. It also had individual division calculations at greater levels of detail to promote value maximization at the division level. Although it was more complicated, TalisTrust created multiple calculations because each calculation best served the decision-making purpose and made the information simpler to use. Bob, TalisTrust's CFO, explained, "At the total corporate level, we needed a calculation of value that was clear, simple, and explainable. Because of the requirements (legally) to report earnings results and the need to be able to explain the relationship between earnings and value, a simple calculation of value made sense at the corporate level. If all the adjustments had been made at the corporate level that were not material at that level, but were material at the division level, the corporate calculation would have been needlessly complicated and much more difficult to explain to internal and external constituents with no added benefit for the additional precision. At the division level, however, failure to reexamine the calculation would have meant failure to address key issues that could influence that division's behavior in terms of value creation." The story of TalisTrust recalls Emerson's quote: "A foolish consistency is the hobgoblin of little minds."[12]

Not only may the number of adjustments or level of their complexity differ when developing calculations for different purposes, but in different decision-making circumstances other dimensions may also change. For example, depending on the nature of the question, expenses might be attributed to subunits of the organization. This attribution might allow the subunit to monitor and control their drivers of those costs. In other cases, however, the organization may want to understand the impact on value of incremental revenue. In that event, rather than attribute a slice of the overhead costs (which would not change), the organization would want to view the incremental value creation by looking at incremental revenue, cost, and capital requirements. While to some organizations this is obvious, others continue to battle a *one model* for all questions mindset. This prevents the organization from understanding the real impact of a decision from a value perspective. Some organizations have found this particularly problematic when they attempt to develop customer relationship profitability models that are not robust enough to answer the important questions using different approaches.

"Capland Consolidated" has not reaped significant benefits because of the *one model* approach they have adopted. Data availability and simplicity drive the calculations at Capland. Unfortunately, this has been done so much that the results of Capland's internal calculations of value look more like Exhibit 5.6 than 5.3: The explanatory power is missing.

Another example of the need for different models can occur at the product level. Even within a single product, value creation may be calculated on several bases:

* Measure value creation for a product on a full cost basis including the cost of the capital acquired to produce the product (perhaps by purchasing another company). This model would include the market value costs of the acquisition and most closely represent value creation from a shareholder's perspective.

* Value created for a product on a full cost basis excluding acquisition premiums. This value creation model might be used to understand the impact of acquisition costs on value creation results.

* Value created for a product on an incremental (variable / marginal) cost basis. This model would exclude other than incremental costs, revenues, or capital.

Beyond these different calculations, time horizons can also be an important factor impacting calculations for various purposes. In the author's article, "Finding Value Solutions: It's About Time,"[13] the issues of time in making calculations useful to the purpose are discussed. The organization may wish to understand value creation of the overall organization and of subunits on a monthly, annual, five-year, or longer basis. Its understanding of value creation at the customer level, however, may require different time period snapshots—perhaps of longer duration when customer relationships are of longer duration—that operate more on an ongoing basis rather than one-time events. The decision-making process must include careful selection of appropriate time horizons and include the options value of time (see Chapter 6).

CHOOSING THE MEASURES: DOLLARS AND PERCENTS

So far, the discussion of value metrics has centered on dollar measures. Some organizations, however, prefer to use percentage measures. One popular percentage that can be useful to investors is cash flow return on investment (CFROI). Before discussing the nuances, a generic review of percentage and dollar measures may be useful in understanding the benefits and issues. The numbers shown for 1998 and 1999 in Exhibit 5.12 were included as part of a table of operating profits in the October 8, 1999, edition of *The Wall Street Journal,* with the table headline, "Generating Power," and the article headline, "GE Earnings Gain 16% to Record, Led by Power Systems and NBC."[14]

The article states that "two units particularly stood out: GE Power Systems and NBC." Assuming these numbers tell the story about GE (i.e., that earnings or operating profits alone provide good information), what does an emphasis on Power Systems and NBC say? Is there information to know

| ($ millions) | Third Quarter | | Percent | Dollar |
	1999	1998	Change	Increase
Aircraft Engines	535	417	+28%	118
GE Capital[1]	1,262	1,082	+17%	180
NBC	265	202	+31%	63
Power Systems	383	254	+51%	129

[1]Net income

Source: Partial list of units results in *Wall Street Journal* October 8, 1999

EXHIBIT 5.12   GE Results in *Wall Street Journal*

in addition to what is immediately provided in the headlines to understand the factors driving GE's record performance? As Exhibit 5.12 shows, Power Systems, followed by NBC, showed the greatest percentage of gains over the time period. Power Systems reported a 51% increase, whereas NBC profits rose 31%; Aircraft Engines, 28%; and GE Capital, just 17%. On a dollar basis, however, for the units shown in Exhibit 5.12, GE Capital produced the most earnings at $1,262 million (three times that of Power Systems and five times that of NBC). Next in earnings was Aircraft Engines with $535 million, followed by Power Systems and NBC. Where was the increase in earnings coming from? A closer examination is required. Reviewing the dollar increases, GE Capital's earnings increased by $180 million; Power Systems, $129 million; Aircraft Engines, $118 million; and NBC, $63 million.

In fact, GE Capital's earnings increased in the third quarter 40% more than Power Systems ($180 versus $129 million) and 285% more than NBC ($180 versus $63 million). Although the percentage increases for Power Systems and NBC were greater than the others, the dollar amount and dollar increases were significantly lower. In this example, did the percentage increases at Power Systems and NBC drive GE's 16% gain? Not really. Alone, GE Capital contributed $180 million of the increase, compared to $193 million for Power Systems and NBC combined. Certainly the percentage increase can help represent potential momentum in the future. In the following year (also the third quarter), 2000, Power Systems was up 69%, but NBC was only up 10%. Aircraft Engines' increase dropped to 15%, and GE Capital again was up 17%.

GE Capital obviously contributed more to GE's record earnings than Power Systems or NBC. The example highlights the fact that the relevance of percentages is contextual. An extreme example, of course, is a new startup. If a new company earns only one dollar in its first year, doubling its earnings to two dollars represents 100% growth. It sounds great, but does it mean much?

Percentages are a quick way to look at returns and are often popular with financial managers. Although the issues may seem obvious, it is very common for there to be confusion in their use. One example that occurs often in banking is risk adjusted return on capital (RAROC). It is a percentage measure similar to return on net assets (RONA) or return on equity (ROE) measures.

Demonstrated in Exhibit 5.13 is an issue that banks confront everyday. In looking at this exhibit, only the options and the effects presented will be considered. For purposes of this discussion, any follow-on effects of the alternatives will be excluded. The example shows a choice that a loan officer has to make. Should the bank make the $3 million loan (column A) to a customer who wants the loan or the $750,000 loan (column B)? This issue was raised by Steve, a financial manager at "Athens Bank." Steve described

	(A)	(B)	Difference (A − B)
Loan Value	$3,000,000	$750,000	$2,250,000
Equity Capital	180,000	45,000	135,000
Economic Value	30,000	12,000	18,000
RAROC	27%	37%	−10%

Assumptions:
   Can make a loan of $3 million or $750,000 (mutually exclusive).
   Can raise capital needed to make loans.
   Both economic value and RAROC fully reflect the differential risk in both scenarios.
   Cost of capital is 10%.
   No follow-on impacts.

EXHIBIT 5.13   Athens Bank Loan Example: Part 1

the issue this way: "Although the $3 million loan requiring $180,000 in equity capital creates more value, the smaller loan, requiring $45,000 in equity capital, has the higher RAROC and is, therefore, the winner. It doesn't create as much economic value but it leaves $135,000 in equity capital available to make more loans. If three more loans could be made that are identical to the first $750,000 loan, economic value would be $48,000, which is higher than the $30,000 from one large loan. On this basis, RAROC is the measure to answer the question. Economic value has no bearing on the decision and, in fact, would lead to the wrong conclusion if used." Is Steve correct in this analysis?

To arrive at the correct conclusion, the problem must be broken down (see Exhibit 5.14). In this example, Athens bank can make one loan or four loans, using the same amount of capital, as Steve argues.[15] In this case, both economic value and RAROC produce the same answer. No discernment of metrics is required! The answer is clear: Make four loans to maximize value. However, returning to the example in Exhibit 5.13, if Athens Bank has a customer and can make *either* the $3 million loan or the $750,000 loan,

	(A) 1 Loan	(B) 4 Loans	Difference
Loan Value	$3,000,000	$3,000,000	$0
Capital	180,000	180,000	0
Economic Value	30,000	48,000	(18,000)
RAROC	27%	37%	−10%

EXHIBIT 5.14   Athens Bank Loan Example: Part 2

Athens would want to maximize economic value and make the $3 million loan for a number of reasons:

1. Maximum value is created.
2. Given the same economic inputs, a competitor of Athens will provide the $2.25 million in loans to the customer, creating value for that bank and improving its competitive position.
3. Athens may not be able to find three customers to make up for the $2.25 million in loans. If it cannot, the result is a significant decrease in RAROC and economic value.
4. Even if the bank can find three more customers, it is not necessarily better off having made a loan of only $750,000 as shown in Exhibit 5.13. Exhibit 5.15 outlines the outcomes of several scenarios. Scenario 1 shows making the $750,000 loan upfront plus three additional $750,000 loans. This creates $48,000 in value. If, instead, the $3 million loan is made initially and then the three $750,000 loans are made (Scenario 2), this results in $66,000 in value. If, however, four loans to four customers can each be made for $3 million, the result is $120,000 in value creation. Because the equity capital requirements differ in each case, this example also shows the importance of capital planning and understanding capital needs of the organization.

Why, in this instance, does a dollar measure provide better information? As in our example of the startup, the percentage measures in these cases represent a relative measure of return but do not account for the significance of the return or the magnitude of the value created.

When it comes to business lines and deciding among different investment opportunities, similar issues can arise. For Calvin, CFO of "Bedford Bank," the discussions around value caused him concern in terms of the impact on ROE. As shown, maximizing value may potentially produce a lower ROE (a percentage measure analogous to RAROC). If the ROE is

	1 Loan of $3 Million	1 Loan of $750K	3 Loans of $3 Million	3 Loans of $750K	Scenario 1 1 Loan of $750K + 3 Loans of $750K	Scenario 2 1 Loan of $3 Million + 3 of $750K	Scenario 3 1 Loan of $3 Million + 3 of $3 Million
Loan Value	3,000,000	750,000	9,000,000	2,250,000	3,000,000	5,250,000	12,000,000
Capital	180,000	45,000	540,000	135,000	180,000	315,000	720,000
Economic Value	30,000	12,000	90,000	36,000	48,000	66,000	120,000
RAROC	27%	37%	27%	37%	37%	31%	27%

EXHIBIT 5.15 Athens Bank Loan Example: Part 3

37%, for example, it may drop if 27% activity becomes the norm. (Although there is often concern, the reality is that without clear measures and reviews it is likely that there are many value-destroying decisions being made and implemented continually. With the ability to eliminate them comes the potential to raise ROE.) The goal, however, should *not* be to increase the value of the *favorite acronym* but to maximize value creation with each decision.

It is also very important in decision making to maximize value over the range of possibilities and to view these decisions in context. For example, returning to Exhibit 5.13, to look forward and understand the sources of value creation in the future, it may make sense to take into account the current *stage* of the business line. Perhaps the bank is the only one to offer this $750,000 loan product. For forecasting purposes, the extent to which this value can continue must be considered. For example, will the RAROC for $750,000 loans remain at 37% or can they be expected to decrease? In strategy and decision making, these contextual elements are important.

One final note: dollar measures of value can also be misleading. Popular magazines sometimes show a measure called market value added (MVA), which is calculated as market value less invested capital. The magazines often rank organizations on this basis. Obviously, firms destroying value now and those expected to do so in the future rank low. Firms, however, are ranked on a pure dollar basis so that, all else being equal, the smaller the firm, the lower it will appear in the rankings. Investors may want to understand instead what their dollar has returned (see "Total Shareholder Return," a percentage measure in Exhibit 3.6) or what, more importantly, their dollar has returned over and above a similar (benchmark) investment. In any case, the *meaning* is more important than the *measure*. The right measures help us discern meaning! They are not a goal unto themselves.

ALPHABET SOUP

In choosing the right metric, the first step is to clearly define the question (just as in math problems in high school). The big three components of the question should include information about the purpose, the desired impacts, and which constituents needs will be addressed by the measure. Each of these will have a major impact on the metric to be used.

Today, within the field called "shareholder value" or "economic value added," there is an "alphabet soup" of measures used by practitioners. Novices often believe that these acronyms represent the sum total of value measurement choices. As noted earlier, however, Economic Value Management recognizes that different calculations are required for different purposes. The acronyms do *not* cover the totality of possibilities. At times, it may make sense to use one of these measures versus another. To illustrate these points, Exhibit 5.16 is an open letter in response to an article in the *Financial Times*.[16]

Dear Sir:

Value measures can indeed provide better yardsticks than traditional ratios (New Benchmark for Investors—June 18). In fact, the criticisms that the June 18 article cites for particular measures often arise because different measures have different purposes and offsetting benefits. For example, while it is useful to compare performance yardsticks, the performance measures discussed (TSR, EVA®, CFROI, MVA) are not mutually exclusive; rather, each is properly designed for a specific purpose.

In discussing the criticisms of the measures, in one instance, the article states that critics may say that EVA can be distorted by inflation. EVA, although it accounts for inflation in the cost of capital, would be less simple to use if it always reflected inflation for every ongoing operation. Simplicity is a trade off that must be made with any of the metrics. (CFROI uses this adjustment, making it useful in certain valuation scenarios and in entities where mark to market of assets is more readily accomplished.)

Second, the article states that EVA may make adjustments for research and development costs and critics argue that EVA may discourage executives from making big investments. In fact, it is precisely the adjustments for research and development, when properly implemented, that avoid the potential for lack of investment described.

Third, the article states that both EVA and CFROI can be criticized for making potentially arbitrary adjustments to companies' reported profits. But in one sense, how could these adjustments be other than arbitrary when the accounting systems on which they are based are arbitrary (including the interpretations by various companies as well)? One day, pooling accounting for goodwill—the next day, no pooling accounting. From a management motivation standpoint, it would be a disservice to not make adjustments. And when the reasons for the adjustments are understood, the reasoning negates the "arbitrariness."

Lastly, TSR, while exactly useful for the purpose to which it is used in the report of sector performance, like the other criticized measures is a backward looking measure from the shareholder's perspective. And although we know past performance is no guarantee of future results, these value measures can tell us something traditional measures never could: in fact, how well have we done?

EXHIBIT 5.16   Open Letter to the *Financial Times*

MARKET VALUE FOR DECISION MAKING?

Another way to illustrate the importance of clarity around the purpose and constituent issue is to relay an example of confusion that occurred related to market value metrics. Marvin, a financial executive, in reading an early book on "shareholder value" became very confused about the right measure to use to decide whether to do a project or take an action. The source of confusion was the book's contention that *managers deciding what to do* should not calculate an economic value measure based on the historical capital, but should use the market value of the firm at any point in time (i.e., the stock price times the number of shares outstanding). "Shouldn't we be basing these analyses on market value?" Marvin asked. Looking at an example can help determine the response.

Exhibit 5.17 shows a company that has adjusted net income of 200 using capital of 1,000 with a market value of 2,000. Using a 10% cost of capital and capital of 1,000 produces a value creation metric of 100 (as shown in column 1). Using market value or market capital, it produces a value creation metric of 0 (as shown in column 2).

Now suppose the manager can re-deploy the 1,000 in capital and generate 500 in operating profit in the first year and that this one-year increase and future growth potential would cause the market value to go to 6,000.[17] What would each measure suggest or advise the company to do?

In Exhibit 5.17, columns 3 and 4 show the impacts on the economic capital and market value metrics respectively. If the manager used the economic value metric, the action would be taken. The action would increase value from 100 to 400. If the market value metric were used, the action would *not* be taken because it would drop value on a market value basis to negative 100. In fact, the perverse relationship would exist that the better the idea, the higher the market value would rise and the lower the value metric, on a market value basis, would become. Exhibit 5.18 shows the potential impacts.

Under Scenario 1 of Exhibit 5.18, the action, using the market value metric, appears to destroy value. Now assume that the stock market is thrilled by the prospects for the company's new actions and subsequently runs the stock price to a level that creates a market value of 10,000, as shown in

| | Today | | Immediately After Action | |
	(1)	(2)	(3)	(4)
Adjusted Net Income	200	200	500	500
Capital	1,000		1,000	
Market Value		2,000		6,000
Value Metric	100	0	400	(100)

Capital Metric: Columns 1 and 3
Market Value Metric: Columns 2 and 4
Assumptions:
  Cost of capital: 10%
  (No change in cost of capital after action is taken)
  Adjusted net income today: 200
  Potential future adjusted net income: 500

EXHIBIT 5.17 Market Value Example

	Today	Scenario One	Scenario Two	Scenario Three
Adjusted Net Income	200	500	500	500
Market Value	2,000	6,000	10,000	5,000
Value Metric	0	(100)	(500)	0

EXHIBIT 5.18   Market Value Metric

Scenario 2. Now, the poor manager will like it even less to the tune of a negative 500. However, if the market is less enthusiastic and the market value is 5,000 (as shown in Scenario 3), the manager is now much more likely to accept it—because in this case it is neutral to the current state.

This example clearly illustrates how the perspective, the constituent, and the purpose of the metric matter in choosing an evaluation process. If the manager uses as the basis for decision the market value that the market decides, a reduction in market value actually improves the market value creation metric.

Market value reflects an expectation of the future. It is precisely by taking actions that return more than the cost of the capital that expectations of the future are raised. To *require* a return on an expectation value, such as market value, as an assessment of whether to take action, however, creates a desire to lower the expectation (the market value), as was shown in Exhibit 5.18. If a manager uses market value as the basis of measure *in this way,* the shareholder is *doomed* because the manager may not take the very actions that drive the increases in market value the shareholder requires.

What's an organization to do? Avoid the trap. Being clear about means and ends is absolutely critical to being able to effectively use these principles and concepts. For this reason, it is necessary to understand the most important uses for these tools and then pick the tools that work best. Many would like to argue that all that is needed in our tool chest is a hammer. As discussed earlier, this is not the case. In Chapters 6 through 10, we will discuss some of the best implements in our Economic Value Management toolkit, how to use them, and when the use of market capital might, in fact, apply.

NOTES

1. For anyone interested in earlier work and views on the topics, *The Quest for Value,* by Bennett Stewart, and *Valuation,* by Tom Copeland, Tim Koller, and Jack Murrin, are both recommended reading. More recent books recommended for those wishing to delve further include *EVA® and Value Based Management,* by David Young and Stephen O'Byrne, and *CFROI Valuation,* by Bartley J. Madden. All four of these books have helped shape some of the ideas and insights in the pages that follow.

G. Bennett Stewart III, *The Quest For Value,* New York: HarperCollins, 1991.

Tom Copeland, Tim Koller, and Jack Murrin, *Valuation: Measuring and Managing the Value of Companies,* New York: John Wiley & Sons, 1995.

David Young and Stephen O'Byrne, *EVA® and Value Based Management: A Practical Guide to Implementation,* New York: McGraw-Hill, 2001.

Bartley J. Madden, *CFROI Valuation: A Total System Approach to Valuing the Firm,* Oxford: Butterworth-Heinemann, 1999.

2. For more information on the use of the equity charge versus an adjustment to net income for after-tax debt costs and an inclusion of debt in capital, see Exhibit 5.5 and the section in this chapter on "To WACC or Not to WACC and the Use of APV."

3. Craig Tolliner, "Earnings Debacle," CBS MarketWatch.com, November 8, 2001.

4. *The Quest for Value* provides an easy-to-follow description of potential adjustments (pp. 112–117, 742, and 744). For longer analyses, refer to Chapter 3 in *The Quest for Value,* Chapters 2 and 6 in *EVA® and Value Based Management,* and Chapter 5 in *CFROI Valuation.* In Economic Value Management, the idea is not to make adjustments using a rote, rules basis but rather to select the adjustments based on the need of the problem to be solved or situation being described (see also Chapter 4). See Note 1.

5. See note 2.

6. See note 2.

7. See note 2.

8. See note 2.

9. For worthwhile discussions on the issues of cost of capital in general and CAPM specifically, see *The Quests for Value, EVA® and Value Based Management,* and *CFROI Valuation.* An interesting international discussion is also presented in *Valuation: Measuring and Managing the Value of Companies.* More discussion is also presented in Chapter 6's "Types of Capital" section. See note 1.

10. Of special note is this article: Timothy Luehrman, "What's it Worth: A General Manager's Guide to Valuation," *Harvard Business Review,* May–June, 1997.

11. My favorite corporate finance text is *Principles of Corporate Finance,* by Brealey and Myers, which I recommend on this and any other corporate finance topic. Also, as noted earlier, Luehrman has explained APV lucidly in a series of articles in the *Harvard Business Review.* Richard A. Brealey and Stewart C. Myers, *Principles of Corporate Finance, Third Edition,* New York: McGraw-Hill, 1988.

12. Ralph Waldo Emerson, "Self-Reliance" Essays, First Series (1841, repr. 1847).

13. Eleanor Bloxham, "Finding Value Solutions: It's About Time," *Journal of Cost Management,* July–August 2001.

14. "GE Earnings Gain 16% to Record, Led by Power Systems and NBC," *The Wall Street Journal,* October 8, 1999.

15. In reality, the capital required for four loans of like risk might be lower than one loan since four loans would likely not be perfectly correlated. This might be offset by additional set-up costs for the loans and additional monitoring costs.

16. "New Benchmark for Investors," *Financial Times,* June 18, 1999.

17. Exhibit 5.18 shows other possible market value scenarios.

two

Applications and Techniques

CHAPTER 6

Has Value Been Created?
How Much?

USING VALUE METRICS

As Harold Bloom says, change happens to individuals when they overhear themselves.[1] Similarly, change happens in organizations when they can literally see themselves. That's what Economic Value Management metrics do. That is the potentiality they bring.

What are the most useful ways to use value metrics to gain the insights and increase the number and velocity of "aha moments"? This chapter will introduce ways that everyone can use value metrics to:

* See what is happening within an organization
* Understand their relationship to the organization
* Better understand the other constituents of the organization

Some of this material was first presented as an Economic Value Management toolset in a talk at the Bank Administration Institute's Performance and Profitability Conference.[2] The point of value metrics is not simply to have better measures; it is to use the better measures for clearer insights, that is, for insights that will fundamentally change the way organizations shape their future.

Seeing—really seeing—for the first time can be startling. When the insight is truly there, creating change and defining the future naturally follow.

One of the remarkable aspects of the Economic Value Management tools described in this chapter is that they are useful to people with very different predispositions and attitudes toward life and business. For those with a predisposition to predictability, better forecasts, and no surprises, this toolset enhances capabilities to do just that: to better anticipate and create valuation scenarios with deeper understanding.

Conversely, for those who want to shake up the status quo: for the organization to "overhear itself" and thus evoke deep recognition and change, this toolset provides a mechanism that can be the catalyst for just such profound

137

change and discoveries. And it can continue to provide this impetus over time as new insights are gained.

To achieve the results with either predisposition, the exercise must be addressed in a spirit of stewardship. Awareness is sometimes painful, or at least startling. The techniques will help achieve the benefits described only when those benefits are desired. This means any addiction to not knowing must be released, and the new awareness must be embraced.

THE ECONOMIC VALUE MANAGEMENT DIFFERENCE

As Exhibit 6.1 shows, Economic Value Management represents a sea change. These changes shape and improve the usefulness of value metrics. The changes reflect increased sophistication and greater applicability. They represent a movement from one approach to many, and they include better discernment and more choices in decision making and understanding. This is indeed a fascinating time for Economic Value Management leadership as the ability to enhance understanding and create better possibilities continues to expand.

The elements identified in the left-hand column of Exhibit 6.1 reflect characteristics of the metrics themselves and ways for the metrics to be used. Using the elements of time, type of capital, form of metric, and types of adjustments provides a way to examine the characteristics of the metrics. The latter portion of this chapter will include discussions of constituent focus, integration of metrics and techniques, and applications of the metrics

Metric Characteristics:	From (Traditional Implementation)	To (Economic Value Management)
Time	Evaluative, Primarily Annual	Evaluative and Predictive, Variable Time Periods
Type of Capital	Debt and Equity	Multiple Types of Capital
Form of Metric	Dollars or Percents	Dollars, Percents, Standard Deviation, i.e., Multiple Forms
Types of Adjustments	Simple	Simple and Complex
Measurement and Management Perspectives:		
Constituent Focus	Shareholder	Alliance of Constituents
Integrating Metrics	None or Few	Multiple—Optimal Number
Integrating Techniques	None	Multiple
Applications of Metrics	Strategic, Valuation	Broad Applications

EXHIBIT 6.1 How Economic Value Management Differs: Evolution of Value Practices

themselves that represent the measurement and management perspectives of Economic Value Management.

Exhibit 6.2 outlines some of the areas to be explored related to each element. The constituent focus will broadly include those shown in Exhibit 6.3.

Metric Characteristics:

Time	Types of Capital	Form of Metric	Types of Adjustments
※ Evaluative and/or predictive ※ Time horizon	※ Debt or equity ※ Equity ※ Special case equity equivalents – Human – Customer – Product ※ Regulatory ※ Risk ※ Cost of capital ※ Market value/ purchase price ※ Taxes, dues	※ Dollar ※ Percentage ※ Standard deviation	※ Availability ※ Complexity ※ Fixed/changed boundaries ※ Options value

Measurement and Management Perspectives:

Constituent Focus	Integration of Metrics	Integration of Techniques	Applications of Metrics
※ Community and external governance ※ Providers of capital ※ Suppliers ※ Consumers ※ Observers/ critics (see Exhibit 6.3)	※ Value drivers (the value-based balanced scorecard) – Relationship – Process – Choices ※ Activity-based information – Cost, revenue, capital ※ TQM process measures	※ Patterns of value creation – Trend and regression analysis ※ Volatility analyses ※ Information Gap Analyses™ ※ Statistical prediction rules ※ Market value analysis ※ Pictures ※ Scenario planning ※ Monte Carlo simulations ※ ValueMap™	The Wheel™: ※ Performance assessment ※ Strategy ※ Process and technology ※ Organizational structure ※ Rewards process ※ Training and communication (see Exhibit 6.4)

EXHIBIT 6.2 Economic Value Management: Metric Choices and Uses

```
                        ┌─────────────────────┐
                        │     Community        │
                        │        and           │
                        │ External Governance  │
                        │                      │
                        │  • Citizen           │
                        │  • Regulator         │
                        └─────────────────────┘
```

Providers of Capital	Suppliers	Consumers

• Investors
• Lenders
• Owners
• Members
• Policyholders
• Taxpayers
	• Board
	• Managers
	• Employees
	• Suppliers
	• Elected
	  government
	  officials
	• Members
	• Volunteers
		• Customers
		• Members
		• Policyholders
		• Citizens
		• Clients

```
                        ┌─────────────────────┐
                        │  Critics / Observers │
                        │                      │
                        │  • Analysts          │
                        │  • Rating agencies   │
                        │  • Consumer groups   │
                        │  • Surveyors         │
                        │  • Journalists       │
                        │  • Special Interest  │
                        └─────────────────────┘
```

EXHIBIT 6.3   Constituents

(For more detail on constituents, see Chapter 1.) Constituent focus will act as a lens through which these issues will be viewed. Exhibit 6.4 shows the primary areas where the metrics are applied.

Chapter 2 outlined a set of 14 questions (recreated in Exhibit 6.5) that most organizations will want to answer in the spirit of good stewardship. These will form the basis for in-depth understanding of these issues and the techniques for creating the "aha" phenomena.

Because of the numerous areas to explore, this chapter will focus only on a review of the elements in Exhibit 6.2 in the context of the first evaluative question in Exhibit 6.5: Has the organization created value? How much? (The remainder of Part 2, Chapters 7 through 10, will review the elements in Exhibit 6.2 in the context of the remaining 13 questions.)

EXHIBIT 6.4 The Value Management Wheel™

Evaluative

You Are Here

1. Has the organization added value? How much?
2. How does this compare to the organization's peers and competitors?
3. Has the organization been managed such that each sector has added value?
4. Has the organization been managed such that each product, service, distribution channel, or process added value?
5. Has the organization been managed such that each customer relationship added value?
6. What are the major drivers of value creation for the organization?
7. For all of the above, how has this changed over time?

Predictive

8. How much value does the organization expect to create?
9. How much value do capital providers (shareholders, if publicly traded) expect the organization to create?
10. How much value does the organization expect to create by sector, product, service, distribution channel, process, and customer?

EXHIBIT 6.5 The Questions

(continued)

EXHIBIT 6.5 The Questions *(Continued)*

11. What are the expectations related to the major drivers of value creation over time?

12. What are the capital provider's expectations for the organization's peers? What are the peer's expectations for itself by sector, product, service, distribution channel, process, customer, and major drivers of value creation?

13. How do internal, peer, and capital provider expectations differ from current steady-state value creations?

14. For all of the above, how will this change over time?

TIME

Although it can add complexity, the time horizon question is one that inevitably elicits controversy. How far back should we look? How far forward should we estimate? In general, the longer the time history used to answer the question of whether the organization has created value, the better the answer will be. By having a long history, the ability to compare and contrast time-period results and generate the important "ahas" is increased geometrically.

Economic Value Management measures may naturally be captured on a monthly, quarterly, and annual basis. Particular studies may require particular groupings of time: For example, one may want to choose unique periods to understand the results of one management team compared to another.

A perspective of value over time can provide several kinds of information. One is an understanding of the business cycle and its impact on value creation. Some organizations have found that it can provide a means of knowledge transfer to those individuals who are newer to an industry or business segment. Having a value history can also demonstrate the impacts of management and strategic changes. "CelebrateBank," upon reviewing its value creation over time, was able to see how changes in management teams had changed the results of the business, although the earnings numbers had simply shown gradual increases over time. One change was observed by Mark, the finance manager at CelebrateBank, while he was looking at the value pattern graphs. "Oh," he said, "Here is where O'Reilly's team came on board. It didn't show up in the earnings, but they had a rocky start operationally. You can see the pattern changing right here, just as they came on board." This technique is referred to as a review of patterns of value creation (see Exhibit 6.2's integration of techniques).

Another illustration of the benefit of examining value over time can be gleaned from the sample bank example in Chapter 5's "Sample Value Calculation" section. In that example, the increases in reserves at RealBank were reversed to better understand the current year's results. With multi-period information, both before and after as shown in the example, it would be possible to evaluate the extent to which RealBank's management understood and accurately predicted needs for reserves, or if reserve needs were different than management had predicted, that is, management:

* Did not understand its business well, or
* Was unable to predict the future business climate, or
* Was gaming the result

This provides insight into who management is and what can be expected of them. Time is also an important component in understanding options values (see the section in this chapter on "Types of Adjustments").

While the strict answer to Question 1 is evaluative from a time standpoint, it helps to inform estimations of the future (i.e., form the basis for prediction). Organizations that do not understand whether they have created value and by how much are in the dark. They may have ideas and plans; they just never know if they are getting anywhere. Boards cannot perform their oversight role without this information, and other constituents cannot make the assessments they need. Really understanding the answer to this first question, then, is important to all constituents in their decision making.

TYPES OF CAPITAL

One area that continues to evolve is that of capital. (See Exhibit 6.1: How Economic Value Management Differs.) Some organizations are much more sophisticated than others in their use of types of capital to answer different but related value questions. Our explanation will include insights from specific kinds of organizations that can be applied to organizations in general.

Debt and Equity or Equity

As discussed in Chapter 5, from the point of view of the organization, making decisions as stewards of the shareholder's capital, a number of approaches work:

* Approaches that adjust for equity cost and recognize the tax benefits of debt in its *native* income statement form (as shown in the example on Exhibit 5.3)
* Approaches that remove the income statement effects of debt and calculate a weighted average cost of capital (as shown in Exhibit 5.11)
* Approaches that begin with equity-only analyses and then layer in separate analyses of tax and financing effects (as does APV, which is described

in Chapter 5's section on "To WACC or Not to WACC and the Use of APV")

Any approach will work as long as it accurately reflects the cost of capital in the calculation, and any unusual events or circumstances are properly considered. All approaches properly applied include the use of equity equivalents, of which there are special cases:

* Human capital (employees)
* Customer capital (marketing and sales)
* Product capital (R&D and product enhancements)

Human Capital (Employees)

There have recently been many new discussions on the topic of human capital. Some obfuscate the real relationship between human capital and the operations of the workforce, whereas others provide better mechanisms for understanding the company's operations.

One useful idea used in Economic Value Management is the adjustment to capital of certain human resource expenditures. These adjustments are handled in a way that is similar to R&D. One-time costs are capitalized and amortized in the value equation. These costs can include recruiting, interviewing, and hiring; one-time hiring bonuses and relocation expenses; and training costs. The costs are capitalized and amortized over the average employee tenure with the company. If employee turnover is high, these costs would be amortized over a shorter time period (and thus be higher) than if tenure of the workforce is longer and costs can be spread over a longer time. The behavioral impact is to encourage training and improve hiring and retention practices.

Another one-time human capital expenditure is severance costs. If the organization is subject to frequent layoffs and contractually obligated to given levels of severance, one may want to understand value creation reflecting the likely severance cost over the working life of the human capital (from hire to termination) rather than have it appear periodically as a one-time event. Similarly, if the CEO is paid to leave at will (or the company fires its CEO every three years, which actually happens in some firms), final payoffs may need to be reflected in the operational costs by moving a one-time cost in the future forward and capitalizing and amortizing these future payments. The same principles can be applied to any compensation cost not adequately reflected on a current period basis. Stock option costs are a prime example. While the organization already has this information, other constituents will need to better understand what the organization is really doing. More disclosure on these human capital issues would be useful so that investors and other constituents can make these estimates as well.

Another controversial human capital area is that of pension costs.[3] Because of the U.S. accounting rules for pensions, there may be mismatches between accounting costs and the cost related to current employees. In addition, the organization may smooth the costs by setting assumptions of expected rates of return on pension assets.

Although comparisons have been made in the literature between employees and leased assets, employees do have the ability to walk and tend to leave employers more frequently than ever before.[4] As the lease analogy aptly suggests, however, compensation does represent a rental cost on the capital value of an employee's efforts. It is important that organizations recognize these assets and understand the financial consequences of not providing the maintenance required to ensure their long life with the organization. In addition, understanding the capitalized value of future compensation when analyzing market value may be of interest as well.

Customer Capital

Customer capital, investments associated with marketing to the customer, is another special category of equity equivalent, as discussed in Chapter 5. Although the rules for financial accounting do not generally permit the capitalization of certain expenses related to advertising or sales acquisition, the organization may wish to capitalize and amortize them for certain value measurement purposes.

Some organizations have found this adjustment to be especially useful when there are a few large campaigns that distort the spending picture. The behavioral consequences of the capitalization and amortization are to:

* Encourage spending on worthwhile efforts
* Not delay spending to hit arbitrary year-end earnings targets, thus destroying longer-term value creation

Product Capital

Product capital, investments related to developing and improving product lines, is another special category equity equivalent. The prime example is the capitalization and amortization of research and development costs. The behavioral consequences, as with the others, are to encourage worthwhile investments, which, in this case, are in product improvements and capabilities.

Regulatory Capital

While rules of GAAP (generally accepted accounting principles) in the United States govern which items are classified in the capital accounts for financial statement purposes, some organizations are required to hold certain *levels* of capital by regulatory requirement. Financial services fit this category. In this case, regulators specify the levels of equity and equity equivalents these firms must hold in their capital base. Most of the regulatory schemes are intended to require a minimum level of equity-related capital to limit the risk of the financial institution. In the United States today, different regulatory schemes apply to different types of financial institutions.

Why is the level of capital specified for financial services? It is well recognized that they have important stewardship responsibilities, not only to their investors, but also to customers and communities.

Does this mean that value concepts cannot apply to them? Although this argument has been tried, it is simply not the case. Economic Value Management concepts do work even though their capital structure is not completely determined by the organization.

Organizations with regulatory limits on their capital structure often want to understand both the amount of value they created with the capital they had and the amount they would have created had they held capital at the minimum regulatory level required or at the minimum plus some self-designated cushion.

The calculations of value are similar to those shown in Chapter 5. The primary difference is that *required* regulatory amounts are substituted for the *actual* equity amounts in the formula.

Risk Capital

Although standards exist for regulatory capital, they are often developed in committee processes and take a one-size-fits-all view of determining risk and capital needs for an organization. Because of the arbitrariness of the regulatory bases, financial institutions (and other organizations that understand the application and benefits of these analyses) attempt to quantify the risk and capital requirements at given risk levels for their own organizations.

What are the benefits? An understanding of inherent risk can help an organization understand the return it is earning vis-à-vis the risk in its business. Traditional CAPM (capital asset pricing model) includes only market-related risk, whereas risk analysis also includes the specific risk of the organization. (More on this in the cost of capital section that follows.)

Estimates of risky capital should include analysis of items both on and off balance sheet.[5] Just as commitments of future payments to employees are not necessarily on the balance sheet, organizations may have other off-balance sheet commitments that impact the risk of the organization. In financial institutions, securitizations of loans are a good example. Although the loans may be off balance sheet, they may still require nearly as much risk capital as they did while on the books. Conversely, off-balance sheet items may also lower risk for the financial institution: Collateral for loans, for example, may be off balance sheet yet lower risk.

In financial institutions, many practitioners think about risk in two categories:

1. Expected risk (the mean or probable risk)
2. Unexpected risk (the volatility of the risk)

Reserves, a form of equity equivalent, are held to cover expected risk. The reserve for loan losses, discussed in the analysis of RealBank presented in Chapter 5's "Sample Calculation" section is an example of this kind of reserve. Some *expected* risks, however, may not be required to be held as reserves under standard accounting practices until they are completely known. One such example is unspecified litigation risk. Although not specified, this risk exists in certain businesses, and there may be a general level of expectation related to its magnitude.

The "Salamander Trust Company" had a litigation risk reserve that was related to specific lawsuits. Their experiential rate, however, was higher. For its risk capital analysis, Salamander added additional amounts to the reserve to reflect the expected level. In a risk capital context, generally the estimates of these expected risks—equity equivalents—are made using past experience along with estimates of future conditions. These amounts are often quantified using statistical prediction rules (see Exhibit 6.2's integration of techniques).

In addition to expected risk, the other component to be considered is unexpected risk. Equity requirements are calculated to cover this *unexpected risk*. When practitioners talk about unexpected risk, they mean outlier events: risk due to the organization's volatility. Today, because of data problems in understanding historical volatility, many financial institutions use the level of expected risk as a proxy for an associated level of unexpected risk. There are issues with this approach in that expected and unexpected risk do not always neatly correlate. Some organizations use insurance prices as a proxy for risk cost. This may cause them to understate their risk if the organization is not as diversified as their insurance carrier. In practice, insurance firms, as a subset of financial institutions, generally use regulatory capital as proxies for risk capital in analyses of their own firms rather than perform a separate calculation, although this is an area that is changing. Others use multiple approaches that combine these approaches with other analyses. Chapter 8 provides more detail on the issues, methods, and benefits of calculating value creation on a "risk" basis.

Cost of Capital

A relationship exists between the form of capital and its cost. While traditional theories (CAPM) suggest that only market-related risk be included in cost of capital, investors may require compensation for specific risk as well.[6]

As a class of investors, internal suppliers—directors, managers, or employees—may not be able to adequately diversify the risk in their portfolios for the shares they hold in the company. They may view these investments from a total risk, rather than a market-related, perspective. One way to understand the issue of specific risk is to use the risk capital approach discussed in the previous section and detailed in Chapter 8.

There are other issues with board- and management-held stock. If managers are not able to diversify away the non-market-related risks of their organization because their net worth is tied to the organization, their view of risk may be different than the average investor. This could impact their view of risk capital or cost-of-capital issues. From a value creation standpoint, this has great importance: Depending on the riskiness of the organization, they may wish to "play it" more safely than would a fully diversified investor (or in certain circumstances, more aggressively).

Another cost-of-capital issue exists in methodologies that use a real instead of a nominal cost of capital. A real cost of capital is the cost of capital required by investors, with inflation expectations stripped out. Since inflation is not included in the cost of capital, if real rates are used, inflation must be considered in the capital values (when inflation is significant).

Finding the right inflation rate to use to adjust capital values is much more difficult than many practitioners understand. General inflation rates may not apply. Certain aspects of the business may be deflating, while others inflate. If precision is required, much study and many assumptions will be necessary.

In calculating a dollar measure of value, whether inflation is calculated in the cost or in the capital itself does not matter. When calculating a percentage, however, the number in the denominator does matter. To achieve consistency, adopting the adjustment to capital for inflation may be worth considering when inflation is a significant factor.[7]

Market Value versus Purchase Price

Individually, shareholders have their own tax considerations (basis in the stock[8] and applicable tax rate at various points in time), time horizons, and purchase prices. As the market value for the stock changes, shareholders must determine whether they believe, based on the value the organization is creating and will create, that the stock will continue to be a worthwhile investment for them. When an *organization* wants to know if it is creating value, from the viewpoint of the shareholder, it becomes a question of shareholder expectation and the value created relative to that expectation. To avoid confusion, the approach to take is to understand shareholder expectation (see Question 9 in Exhibit 6.5) and then judge the extent to which shareholder expectation has been met.

Exhibits 5.17 and 5.18 show the issues regarding using the organization's market value to evaluate whether value has been created by a manager in taking a given action. This use of market value as the capital basis creates a misunderstanding about whether value has been created or destroyed, leading to a "catch-22" that produces value-destroying behaviors.

That said, is there an instance when an organization would use market value as the capital basis? In the *incentive* processes of value management, Bruce Jurin, an expert in the area of value, says that there is a use for an "economic market value capital."[9] This economic market value capital is the market value not that the organization itself has achieved, but rather it is the market value of the "average peer management team." This standard defines value creation not based on the capital the organization has had to work with, but based on the level that investors would expect from the average firm. If an organization produces adjusted net income at a level over and above this investor requirement, value has been created for *incentive* purposes. (This approach, unlike the pure market capital calculation, will not punish the management team for a higher market value in their own company; rather it holds them to an investor requirement for their average peer for *incentive* purposes.)

Another use of market value is in specialized analyses. As a *buyer* determining the economic feasibility of an acquisition, for example, management will want to use the acquisition candidate's market value as the capital amount when calculating the economic value expected from the acquisition's operations. The market value used in this case might be the stock market value with whatever premium the purchasing organization might be required to pay. As in other circumstances, the analyses would provide maximum insight if calculated over time.

As a *seller,* an owner wanting to sell a business for a specific amount might want to understand what adjusted net income would be required by the buyer. To be value neutral to the buyer, how much adjusted net income should my business generate? In calculating the buyer's requirement, it makes sense to examine the calculations of adjusted net income in light of any restrictions that the new buyer may have with the operation (i.e., if its European operation would have to be shut down or run at 30% capacity). Where long historical periods are used, it may be important to restate the information on a consistent dollar basis in each of the historical periods studied.

Types of Organizations and Capital Terminology

Different organizations have different sources of capital, but these distinctions are more terminology than substantive. Governments, for example, calculate capital based on taxpayer dollars collected (equity) and the cost of borrowing. Unlike other organizations where it is easier to make the calculations from the top down (from whole organizations to smaller parts), with the government, bottom-up calculations are easier to apply (from smaller organizations to the whole). Thus, governmental entities would start with Questions 3 and 4 and then work up to Question 1 (see the questions in

Exhibit 6.5). In municipalities, different departments would have different calculations. Miami, for example, has measured the economic impacts of high crime and lack of police protection on tourism. For governmental entities, as with all entities, understanding whether value has been created is a matter of calculating benefits less all-in costs.[10]

Another variation on Question 1 is to ask whether the organization has created value compared with an alternative. In other words, compare the value created less the alternative of using those funds to create value for the same purposes elsewhere. An example of this is the classic outsourcing problem. Should the organization—business, governmental, or otherwise—perform the service themselves, or would the sought-for benefits be more productively and economically achieved through private outsourcing? For example, governmental agencies have most notably used privatization alternatives for licensing bureaus and, more recently, schools.

In making outsourcing decisions, the issues to be addressed include not only whether expenses are increased or decreased, but also whether outsourcing raises or lowers risk. To make a good decision, the organization must determine:

- Whether the item to be outsourced is part of its core competency
- Who can best perform the task
- What controls and monitoring costs are required
- What will add value

Churches and other religious organizations are other examples of organizations that would use the bottom-up approach to answer Question 1 for the overall organization. Capital in this case comes from members' contributions. As with governments, assessments of outcomes can be made, and many are more quantifiable than some would like to admit. Have the organization's efforts provided the intended benefits? Have they provided benefits from the perspectives of the members who supply the capital for the organization's functions? To what extent has the health of the members improved through parish nurse programs? To what extent has pastoral counseling and spiritual guidance obviated the need for psychological counseling? The results of the efforts of religious organizations to serve their members can, and should, be measured. This is especially true today as taxpayer dollars may become available for their use. Governmental authorities will need to ensure stewardship of taxpayer contributions by establishing mechanisms to ensure results for the dollars provided.

FORM OF METRIC

The form of the value metric can impact the calculation of value. Strictly speaking, the answer to how much value has been created from the organization's point of view will be a dollar amount. A percentage, however, may be used as a handy way to compare this amount across different organizations from the standpoint of rate of return.

The form used for the metric can make the calculation more or less complex (see Exhibit 6.6). A dollar amount might be calculated for Company X as $200 − ($1000 × 10%) = $100. This amount can be compared across organizations, no matter the particular capital form, as long as all costs are accounted for. A second organization (Company Y), for example, might have a dollar amount for value creation that is $300 − ($2000 × 15%) = 0. A percentage measure of value creation for Company X could be calculated as ($200/$1000) = 20%. However, because of the nature of percentages and the importance of the denominator in ensuring comparability, there are issues with using them related to capital (as described in the section in this chapter on "Types of Capital"). In Exhibit 6.6, to have the numbers on a comparable basis, the calculations might need to include adjustments so that the 1,000 in capital for Company X is made comparable to the 2,000 in capital used for Company Y. In this example, while the dollar amounts do not change, changing the relationship among capital, cost of capital, and adjusted net income to put the denominators on a comparable basis impacts the percentage calculation and its description of relative returns.

Standard deviation is another form of metric that is used for measuring value creation. Standard deviation is a measure of the differences from the mean or average, in other words, a measure of variability. Exhibit 6.7 shows two examples of the use of standard deviation. In the first example, two companies both produce the same amount of value over a three-year period. If the numbers for each year are available, it is easy to see from the chart that Company A's economic value is more variable over the three years than Company B's. However, if there are many numbers involved, standard deviation is a method that can be used to quickly see the same volatility. Company A's standard deviation (average difference from the mean) is much higher than that of Company B's, although their level of value creation overall is the same. Standard deviation of the dollar amounts of value creation provides a good understanding of not only the amount but also the nature of value creation. This kind of time-based analysis is used in the technique called *volatility analysis* and in the determination of risk capital amounts.

The second example in Exhibit 6.7 shows the results for Companies A and B in 2002 for their three customers. In that year, both companies had total economic value of 70. The average per customer was the same, 23. If the boards of the companies asked what the average economic value per customer was, they would receive the answer of 23 in both cases: a positive number and the same as their peer organization. This information would miss an important insight. While the values on average are the same, asking for the standard deviation would provoke new insights. With a standard deviation of 956 and an average of 23, the board of Company A would want

	(A) $ Measures	(B) % Measures Unadjusted	(C) $ Measures Adjusted	(D) % Measures Adjusted
Company X	200 − (1000 × 10%) = 100	200/1000 = 20%	250 − (2000 × 7.5%) = 100	250/2000 = 12.5%
Company Y	300 − (2000 × 15%) = <u>0</u>	300/2000 = <u>15%</u>	400 − (4000 × 10%) = <u>0</u>	400/4000 = 10.0%
Difference	100	5%	100	2.5%
		5%/20% = 25% higher		2.5%/12.5% = 20% higher

EXHIBIT 6.6 Using Dollar and Percentage Measures

	Economic Value	
Example One	**Company A**	**Company B**
Year 2000	−200	90
2001	330	40
2002	70	70
Three-Year Total	200	200
Average	67	67
Standard Deviation	216	21
Example Two—Year 2002		
Customer Acme Inc.	−1000	20
State University	−230	15
Defense Dept.	1300	35
Customer Total	70	70
Average	23	23
Standard Deviation	956	8

EXHIBIT 6.7   Comparison of Economic Value for Two Companies

to dig deeper. An average that is so much smaller than the standard deviation indicates huge differences from the mean. In this case, it implies customer relationships where the company is losing huge value offset by those where it is making lots of money. For Company A, the Defense Department is clearly subsidizing the unprofitable customers, and perhaps paying more than it should. With one customer providing all the value, if the defense contract is pulled, Company A is sunk. For this reason, the CEO and the boards need to use a ValueMap™ (one of the techniques discussed in the section on "The ValueMap™" in this chapter), to effectively do their jobs. They need to understand the value each customer is creating for the organization and the value they are creating for each customer.

TYPES OF ADJUSTMENTS

Typically, to understand whether an organization as a whole has created value, the kinds of adjustments made in the calculation are less detailed than for some of the questions that follow (Exhibit 6.5). Some items at the total organization level just will not be as material as that in subunits of the organization.

Availability and Complexity of Information

Often the issue of adjustments can be influenced by the availability of historical information. When re-creating a long time sequence or history, certain data may not be available. For example, where U.S. companies engaged in mergers use pooling accounting, resetting the information as if purchase accounting had been used can help improve understanding of the historical look. To make this adjustment, being an internal supplier offers an advantage, as many organizations do not provide this kind of historical information to the public. If the information is to be gathered, finding someone in accounting who has been with the organization long enough to track the information can be valuable. Because this information was often difficult to obtain, published calculations in business periodicals often excluded this adjustment, thus limiting their ability to make like comparisons between multiple organizations' results. Recently, the accounting standard for goodwill was changed to eliminate pooling, thus ameliorating this difficulty going forward.

Internally, it is generally worthwhile to make the effort to obtain the information needed to achieve maximum understanding. The criteria suggested in Chapter 5, Exhibit 5.4 can provide a useful guide.

Changes in accounting reporting requirements form one important area that impacts the adjustments made in a historical look. The changes to accounting rules are never ending. As a result, it is not at all useful to say after some study: "OK, here are the three adjustments we will make—now we will apply them historically to see if the organization has created value over time and by how much." From a time perspective, the numbers may not be comparable. The solution? Understanding the historical accounting changes or making friends with the accountants in the organization can help make it easier to create the simplest calculation with the most important adjustments.

Since accounting numbers are the basis for the calculations, it is important to understand their makeup. As an external participant, this is also important. Reading the business press, discussions of financial changes, and reading annual report disclosures including the footnotes can help keep one apprised of significant changes before and as they occur. Probing issues and challenging the accounting are part of calculating the numbers, and this process is critically important to achieving the desired result. Investors should take opportunities to ask specific accounting and audit related questions. If they cannot obtain answers readily, the company may be providing an important signal that the investor should weigh in terms of whether or not the company should receive their capital or be expected to achieve a higher stock price. As mentioned in Chapter 2, the answer to Question 1 will be used on its own and as a comparison to other organizations. Whether one is an internal or external constituent, the general level of information will be lower when used to compare organizations. To answer the question for those purposes, due to lack of data, the level of adjustments will be less complex.

Changes made to regulatory capital are another example of external change. These changes can impact the calculations of value when an organization wants to understand whether it would have created value if it had held capital at regulatory minimums (or minimums plus some cushion). If the basis of the capital amounts change, the organization may wish to restate the numbers.

Similar issues also hold for risk-based capital. It is important for organizations to make improvements to their calculation methodologies.[11] Sometimes, given the initial heavy investment, there is resistance to such change. At these times, remembering Emerson's admonition about foolish consistency can be useful. Although there may be resistance to change, there *is* room for improvement in the calculations of risk capital. (See also Chapter 8's section on "Types of Capital.") Organizations today can become more sophisticated in their calculation of risk capital, and it is important that they continuously incorporate new knowledge into these calculation methodologies. As they become more sophisticated, they may wish to restate historical risk capital amounts as well.

In addition to improvements in calculation methodologies, changes in risk capital estimates may also be impacted by changes in the organization itself. In most organizations, internal units act as natural hedges to each other. A mortgage company with both mortgage-lending and mortgage-servicing businesses is one example. These two pieces of the company act as natural hedges and tend to reduce the amount of risk capital required overall. Changes in the composition of the organization can impact overall views of risk.

Fixed or Changed Boundaries

Fixed or changed boundaries will also impact the value creation question. (See Chapter 4's section on "Different Kinds of Decisions" for a discussion on boundaries.) If the organization is a going concern, then it will treat adjustments on that basis. Potential buyers of the firm, however, will also be concerned with current asset values, liquidation values, or market values as discussed in the section on 'Types of Capital: Market Value versus Purchase Price" in this chapter. In most instances, changing boundary analyses are primarily predictive (what-ifs), answered by the predictive questions.

However, the extent to which the answer to Question 1 is useful in a predictive sense as well as an evaluative one depends on the nature of the adjustments chosen. Are there elements that were core to the organization in the past but are now no longer part of the business proposition and now need to be excluded to better understand what the future holds? Has the model of the business changed, and if so, has this been reflected? In some organizations, fixed boundaries may dissolve. In financial institutions, loans, for many years a buy-and-hold strategy, were made to individuals or institutions and held on the organization's books until paid off by the borrower. Sales or securitizations of loans were unusual events. More recently, some financial institutions have changed their strategy to selling off some of the loans and holding less of the portfolio. Such a strategy change represents an example of modifications to the way sell-offs might be handled from an adjustment perspective. No longer one-time events, proceeds on sales of loans might now represent core earnings to be included in, rather than excluded from, economic value calculations.

Options Value

Options value is a fascinating area. An option has been defined as "the opportunity to make a decision after you see how events unfold."[12] Certain actions taken today can create those opportunities. The idea behind options value is to quantify the value of those opportunities.

As an example, in our work lives, attaining a certain credential or degree may give us the right, but not the obligation, to take a certain job or to speak on a given subject. It creates an option beyond the immediate value created at that time. Options are created and eliminated in every moment — some by actions of the organization, some by constituents, some by external forces, and some by a combination of all three. Options value and time are intimately linked. Once exercised, options cease to be options and become actualizations, measurable in terms of result.

Most answers to the question of whether the organization has created value and by how much do not include the value of the options that have been created. The organization and its constituents most often want to know what has been actualized (i.e., how well the organization has actually done and not just what is possible). Embedded in the stock price are investors' estimations of the organization's future value creation (see Question 9 in Exhibit 6.5). In their estimations, investors do consider options value. What options has the organization created? Will management be able to profitably exercise them? These are key questions investors must answer in formulating their expectations of future value creation, which is the basis for market value pricing.

Options value analysis can be useful to the organization in choosing between alternatives (which creates the most value including options values?) and predicting the future potential of the organization (see Question 8 in Exhibit 6.5). It can also be useful in pointing the way toward future value drivers for the organization, as discussed in Chapters 9 and 10. A review of an organization's ability to see its inherent options and to exercise and execute them wisely provides an understanding of the organization's potential to create value, which can then be compared with the amount of value it actually created (Question 1).

Another practice employs using options value analyses to analyze human capital investment decisions.[13] Training is an example of a human capital investment that provides options values to the organization. To fully understand the value of training to the organization, these options values must be considered. The organization must recognize the potential options values and then take the necessary steps to maximize the value created by those options.

Options value information can help the organization and its constituents understand to what extent the organization has made good business decisions for the future, maximized options value, market value, and the value currently being created. Often these analyses are performed for subcomponents of the organization, as discussed in Chapters 7 and 8.

CONSTITUENT FOCUS: THE ALLIANCE

It is tempting to criticize organizations for doing the wrong thing. However, until everyone uses their ability to influence outcomes for the better, real change in the way organizations operate will be limited. The responsibility of stewardship is in the hands of everyone who coparticipates with the organization in its endeavors.

Whether the organization has created value may indeed be in the eye of the beholder. There are multiple aspects to be understood. Understanding value creation is like looking in a three-way mirror (see Exhibit 6.8) and provides answers to the following questions:

1. Has the organization created value, given what it has to work with (the capital provided to it); that is, has it created value via its investments? Has the organization created value through its relationships with its constituents?

2. Has the organization created value for each of its constituents? Has each constituent of the organization been wise in its coparticipation in the organization's endeavors?

3. Has each constituent created value for itself?

For example, "The Alliance Company" has a major customer, "The Solo Firm." To calculate the left-hand side of the mirror, Alliance calculates how much value Alliance has created in total and by sector, product, and so forth. This includes how much value it has created by customer. For Solo, it represents how much value Alliance has created for itself in its relationship with Solo (as demonstrated in Example 2 in Exhibit 6.7). To calculate the middle mirror, Alliance calculates how much value it has created *for* each constituent. For Solo and each of its other customers, Alliance's calculation reflects the value created for each customer by their purchase of Alliance's products. (This is described in more detail in Chapter 9.) Finally, to calculate the right-hand mirror, Alliance calculates how much value its constituents have created themselves. To better understand Solo, Alliance calculates how much value Solo has created in its own business.

Win–Win?

The Value Map™ Perspectives

EXHIBIT 6.8   Three-Way Mirror

Most discussions on value focus on the left-hand mirror. Economic Value Management looks at the middle and right-hand mirrors, as well, both of which are critical to understanding value from all angles.

An organization is wise to answer all parts of this question (i.e., from its own perspective and from those of its constituents as well). If the organization has created a win–lose situation in its relationships, it may predictably have created a situation that is out of balance (uneconomic) and will find balance (equilibrium) at a later point. This applies to all constituents: Any constituent is better informed by understanding other constituent perspectives.

The ValueMap™ (see Exhibit 6.2) provides a framework for answering the questions in this multidimensional way. Organizations are so used to focusing on the left-hand mirror (the organizational perspective) that when the other two perspectives are discussed, there can be confusion.

Melvin, an operating manager at "PecanTrust," described it this way: "We calculate customer value, that is, how much value the relationship with our customer creates *for us.* We never thought, though, of calculating what our products or services create in terms of value *for the customer.* That's a different way of looking at it. It's interesting. We want to understand our customers better but we never thought of trying to understand how much our customers and prospects are creating for themselves through their relationship with us, nor *what they are creating with or without us.*"

Community and External Governance

The impact of the organization on constituent value can be measured in different ways. Citizens may measure value creation in a way that reflects the economic value created by the organization for the benefit of the community (e.g., taxes paid, community donations, investment in human capital, employee income, and sales tax) less the resources of the community consumed (e.g., clean air, clean water, destruction of land resources). Benefits are generally easy to quantify. Replacement cost can be used to quantify intangibles.

Option values are another consideration. Corporations located in a given area can revitalize a district creating other community options (follow-on effects). Polluters may have opposite effects, discouraging other options that may otherwise exist. Options values can also be seen in diversity of employment, encouraging equal opportunities and role models for changing demographic times. As with all good decision making, these analyses may need to be compared with other alternatives to understand the wisdom of allowing full access to the community and its resources to one organization versus another one.

Regulators may make similar calculations. Another consideration for regulators is the cost of regulating an industry or an organization versus the benefits to be gained.

From their own perspectives, organizations need to determine the value that has been added by regulation and the benefits it provides to various constituents. The benefits of regulation, where there are benefits, generally materialize over time, and therefore a long time horizon is required to understand them. Since all constituents are impacted, organizations should communicate to shareholders (and other constituents) the cost of regulation. For example, regulations that cost them $1 million a year could translate to $10 million in market value or $1 per share. Of course, wisdom needs to be applied in the calculation of cost. From an organization's perspective, the regulation could actually help limit the litigation and reputation risk that could offset the expenses for compliance.

Regulators must weigh these costs to understand if their regulation is creating value. Following Al Gore's task force on performance measures and Congress's passage of the Results Act, administrative agencies in the United States became subject to performance measures. (Lawmakers should be subject to similar guidelines as well.) Both lawmakers and regulators should be addressing results from a value perspective. They need to understand the impacts on consumers, shareholders, the community, and taxpayers. Rigor needs to be part of the calculations of value. The environment represents a particular area of importance where true costs and options values must be considered.

Providers of Capital

Providers of capital need to determine if they have been wise in their coparticipation with the organization. When individuals talk about shareholder value, often there is confusion between the organization and their capital providers' perspectives and spans of control.

Providers of capital decide for themselves the timing of their investments. These decisions are outside the control of the organization and may greatly impact whether and by how much the providers of capital are able to create value for themselves. The price of the company's stock to new equity holders is based on the market's current anticipation of future profits. If investors gauge this incorrectly, they will find they have paid too much, even if the organization is creating value with the capital it has to work with.

For equity investors, the question about value is related to the price they pay now versus the price they will receive sometime in the future, plus any dividends they will receive along the way. (For bondholders or lenders, it is the price they pay versus the interest and principle they will receive or the price they would receive if they later sell the bond or loan.) While investors must care about the answer to Questions 1 through 7, they must also focus on answers to Questions 8 and 9 (see Exhibit 6.5).

Capital providers often like to use percentage measures in comparing alternative investments. Why, in this case, might percentage measures be preferred? In making choices, capital providers compare alternative uses for the same capital (i.e., what is the total return if $100 is placed in one investment versus another?). Because of this "like capital amount" analysis, the answer, on a percentage or dollar basis, will be the same. The percentage measure will not distort the result. (See the example of Athens Bank, Exhibits 5.13 through 5.15.)

Organizations have an important role to play in allowing capital providers to make intelligent decisions. And the issue is getting more and more press. "Lost and Found: Did accounting hanky-panky tank your stock? Here's how to get some money back," a recent headline reads.[14] "Find out about class actions," a subheading reads. Of course, understanding the organization's perspective on value creation can help capital providers look through the accounting numbers and understand whether the organization has created value so they do not get taken. As Exhibit 5.4 outlines, there are a number of items to review in making the value calculation, which will also alert investors to manipulative "dirty tricks" that the organization may be employing (including issues related to revenue and expense recognition, reserving, and so forth).

For their part, organizations need to do the best job they can to report their results fairly. In addition, they need to communicate openly so that the value they are both creating and have the potential to create will be reflected in the marketplace, specifically in the price investors are willing to pay.

Investors in an organization have a big responsibility. Equity investors own shares in the firm and have the ability to significantly influence what the firm is about. (Today, they exercise that power more than ever before at both the institutional and individual levels.) They can weigh their own interests and that of the community. They need to understand not only how their investment is impacted, but also how *all* constituents view value vis-à-vis the organization. This analysis can provide them with useful information in terms of future value creation that will ultimately impact their ability to create value for themselves.

Suppliers

Suppliers of all kinds are interested in answers to all three parts of the question of whether value has been created. Board members need to understand how the organization impacts value creation from the point of view of all constituents and monitor that ValueMap™. It is one of their primary jobs, often receiving too little focus because of the lack of availability of information in an organized format.

Although not obvious, external suppliers are also interested in whether the organization has created value and whether value has been created in their relationship with the organization. As negotiators like Chester Karrass[15] will tell any supplier, understanding as much as possible about the organization and the bargaining position of each side is very helpful in any negotiation. As the first-order concern, the supplier will want to understand the value creation of the organization, as well as its practices, to determine if the supplier would wish to do business with the organization. Once the supplier determines it wants to do business, it will want to understand the value it brings. External suppliers can provide many potential benefits to an organization, measured in terms of their ability to:

- Reduce risk within the organization
- Help the organization generate revenue
- Lower expenses or capital requirements
- Make better decisions

Once a supplier understands the value it brings, it can accurately set prices for its goods and services. In its negotiations, the organization will also want to understand if it has created value vis-à-vis the supplier. Has the supplier lost or has this been a win–win? Such feedback is crucial to future agendas and negotiations. If the supplier has lost, the organization may find that additional requests for services may not be enthusiastically satisfied. Win–lose situations do not long-term relationships make.

Internal suppliers, such as employees and managers, also need to understand whether the organization has created value in its relationship with them and whether they have maximized their own value creation through the activities.

Whether the organization has created value in its relationships with the manager or employee usually changes over time. From the organization's perspective, there may be investments by the organization upfront that need to be amortized over the life of the relationship. The work of an internal supplier may also create options for the organization. Options values reflect the potential to create value for the firm in the future.

Internal suppliers need to understand whether they have created value for the organization and by how much. Sometimes this is best measured as part of a member of a team. Sometimes it is possible to measure for an individual. Unfortunately, too often internal suppliers little understand the extent to which they have contributed to value creation. They should make it their business to understand. Just as external suppliers use this information to set prices, understanding the extent of their own value creation can help employees assess the value of their contribution. This provides a measure of contribution or worth to the organization, which should be reflected in employees' and managers' pay.

Internal suppliers should also understand whether their relationship with the organization is creating value for them. This value may include training and exposure that provide options benefits, plus tangibles such as salary, benefits, and so on. In quantifying the value of the experience, employees can consider the benefits they may obtain as analogous to tuition at school. What are the experiences worth? Some jobs have low reward in that regard; others, very high. This thought process becomes a better way to view the dollar-per-hour remuneration.

There are also other kinds of intangibles to be considered. It is possible for internal suppliers to quantify their own estimate of the worth of intangibles by placing a dollar value on a particular item. Some intangibles such as freedom from discrimination, for example, may not be worth giving up at any price, making them nonnegotiable. Careful analysis by internal suppliers can provide an opportunity to properly value non-salary-related items and provide a better comparison among alternative employers. Ordinal statistics can be used as a way to quantify the value of a combination of different attributes.[16] (See the example in Exhibit 10.7.)

The world is changing. Recent books have discussed the growing disillusionment by twenty-something's in their work life; these treatises are testimony to the fact that more and more employees are operating at or near the top of Maslow's hierarchy.[17] This fact creates new challenges for organizations and for employees to find their place in the world. To create value, organizations need to understand these sea changes from the point of view of their suppliers, both internal and external. From an external supplier perspective, the issues are as relevant as for internal ones. To wit, more and more consulting firms (not all, mind you) are interested in taking on projects that will make a difference—create real value—rather than ones where they are only well paid.

Understanding the value creation practices of the organization as a whole is also an important, though too little used, screening tool for individuals choosing an employer. Many employees trade their precious, limited lifetime in the service of an organization, and yet they do not know the basis or the real process for decision making within the organization. (This is certainly true of many of the employees of Honeydo, Melon, and Cantaloupe, as described in Chapter 2's "Organizations Today and Why Everyone Should Get Involved section.) Given the knowledge-worker world we live in, how aware is that? Employees have a responsibility, a stewardship, to their own lives to understand this. If the organization is not aware or honest with itself, as in any relationship, the question must be asked, will they be honest with me and for how long?

Too many employees place themselves in a relationship of dependency as it relates to the organization they work for, attempting to absolve themselves and blaming the organization when it does not work out. This can create huge costs for them. Giving a large chunk of one's life to something is no small matter. Rather than failing to encourage employee stewardship, organizations, of course, would benefit if their employees exercised stewardship toward themselves in this regard by understanding the organization's value creation process.

Just as investors rank an organization's internal operations, employees need to do the same. To do this effectively, employees need to be literate in the concepts and calculations of value. Reviewing an organization's value creation from the past and the reasons for the inevitable ups and downs can provide invaluable insights in assessing the organization and, importantly, discovering ways in which the employee may add value to it. Employees who do not take the path of awareness are apt to end up as dependents, subject to the whims of the paternalistic organization, never becoming what they can be. In this regard, both the employee and the organization lose. Today, fortunately, the tools and the information for these analyses are more available than ever before and value management provides a comprehensive toolset.

Consumers

Consumers need to understand their coparticipation with the organization. Next to suppliers, they probably most impact the answer as to whether the organization has created value on a day-to-day basis. In that sense, they often have a great deal of power and can choose to represent not only their own economic interests but also those of the community.

Consumers who want to understand future trends will want to be able to answer how much their own relationship has added value to the organization. They also will want to understand to what extent the relationship has created value for them.

While most organizations seek to understand the answer to the question of whether the customer has added value to the organization, organizations are now starting to recognize that understanding whether the relationship has added value to the consumer is a question they should be able to answer as well. "Global Galaxy," a major financial services organization, has reaped tremendous benefits by employing a two-pronged approach in this regard. To provide more effective consultations with their major clients and add value to them, Global Galaxy has sought to understand the answer to two questions:

1. Have its customer organizations, in the course of their own businesses, created value and, if so, by how much?

2. How has its own relationship created value for the customer?

As Mary Beth, a customer relationship manager at Global Galaxy explains,

Understanding whether a customer organization has created value in the course of its own business, and what their peers have done in terms of value creation, has given us a much deeper understanding of our customers, the issues they face, and the strategies that have, and have not, been successful to our customer base. When we share the information with our customers, they are very interested in the insights, and it improves our ability to communicate with them. The discussions have helped to solidify our relationships and create a sense of partnership between us. We have also attempted to understand how our relationship has created value for our customers. It gives us a new perspective on our products from our customers' viewpoints. We think these analyses have given us a much better understanding of what products have helped our customers most. With a better understanding of our customers' own situations and what products have benefited them most, we've been able to work with our product managers on the development of new products that could benefit our customers even more.

Related to coparticipation, customers need to assess the benefits provided to them by the organization (their supplier). Assessing how much value has been created for the organization because of their relationship and the trends in the organization's own value creation are also important. While it may seem plausible at a corporate customer level to perform this level of scrutiny, does this make any sense at the retail level? The nature of the relationship, of course, determines some of this. When consumers go to buy a car, they try to understand the value proposition (what the dealer paid for the vehicle) to negotiate the best price.

Twenty to thirty years ago, few imagined the level of information that would be processed effectively by so many individual investors. As the information revolution continues to grow, retail customers can and will be able to make more determinations for themselves. For longer-term relationships, such as often exists with financial services providers, the cost/benefit will exist for customers to perform the analyses to understand the nature of the relationship and also the patterns of value creation of the service provider.

Organizations are becoming more aware of the importance of the information that is publicly available to consumers. Nell Minow,[18] a writer on corporate governance, advises that to find out what is being said and understand what is happening in the organization, board members should check out the online chat rooms. There is a wealth of information to be tapped there. For the organization wanting to create value, knowing the information is not enough. Rather, this information must be used correctly to be of benefit. Leadership in this regard by board members and the CEO is critical. Organizations need to understand what value they have added to the customer (or destroyed). This is critical information in informing their strategy. Over the long run, customers will pay when value is created and walk when it is not.

Critics and Observers

Critics and observers serve an important role in providing the information that other constituents can use. Many times the quality of information provided by critics and observers is filtered through their own ethical and knowledge frameworks. To wit, the outcry of late about the role of analysts revolves around many of these issues. All constituents must keep critics and observers honest and have their own understanding of the principles so that the information provided can be properly used.

Because of their important roles, observers and critics in particular need to be experienced drivers. Often other constituents are depending on them to form their judgments. Exhibit 6.3 lists some of these critics and observers. Examples include analysts, rating agencies, consumer groups, surveyors, journalists, and special interest groups.

Two of these groups are worthy of particular mention. Analysts are one group that has been receiving more attention of late. And that attention has been long overdue. Analysts provide information that is important to investors and are touted as creators of efficient markets. A well-known investment textbook states: "The more analysts following a stock, the more likely its price will reflect all available information. The investor's risk is lessened — as well as the attendant return."[19] The hue and cry of late with the tech bust at the turn of the century is that perhaps investors' risk has been increased, not lessened, by the role of analysts. This is the case most particularly when analysts may *hype* stocks without study of the fundamentals or calculations of true value creation.

In some cases, analyst organizations may have biases because of their other business connections with the firms under review. In addition, competence (or lack thereof) exists in all professions universally, and in this case, as all, buyer beware. Some analysts understand the basics discussed in Chapter 5. Some do not. With the tools outlined in Chapter 5 and our continuing discussions, investors have a way to gauge not only what is happening in the organization but also whether the analysts are making good sense. Have they looked through the earnings picture to the real story?

Some remark that CEOs go to school to learn how to confuse rather than illuminate the activities of the organization. *Business Week*'s May 14, 2001, cover reads: "The Numbers Game: Companies Use Every Trick to Pump Earnings and Fool Investors." Analysts and investors need to be educated enough to see through what may appear to be true. Obfuscation by the organization represents a wasteful focus outside the bounds of stewardship.

One potential interaction between the analyst and the organization that constituents should be alert to occurs when analysts' predictions on the stock seem to neatly arrive at a similar consensus and the company always seems to hit those numbers. In such a case, this ongoing "coincidence" may represent an organization with a clear earnings management focus, and analysts, on that basis, can feel sure that the numbers will be hit.

Analysts who understand value concepts regularly make calculations of the organization's value creation. Simply accepting them verbatim, however, is a surefire way for investors to miss important insights. Investors and other constituents can study these calculations and, using the knowledge gained in these chapters, change the calculations to suit their own purposes. At the least, the numbers provided by analysts can serve as a way of looking at the calculation methods of others.

Rating agencies are another group of critics and observers that have an important role to play, one to be considered by investors, lenders, suppliers, and consumers. Suppliers, investors, and lenders are interested in understanding rating agency's views of the likelihood that the organization will fail. Rating agencies are concerned with the risk of the firm; therefore, these questions are related to the area of risk capital mentioned earlier. For retail consumers, insurance companies represent a relatively long-term relationship. In choosing a provider, consumers must understand the likelihood that the insurance company will fail. Failure of the insurance company can mean loss of the value of their premiums and loss of coverage. Rating agency staff that understand value creation concepts ultimately do a better job in assessing the solidity of the organization and its business.

INTEGRATION OF METRICS

One of the key areas in understanding how the organization has created value is to understand the organization's value drivers. Outside the value context, metrics may have already been created for the organization that provide useful information about these drivers. Examples of these metrics processes include total quality management, activity-based costing, and the balanced scorecard. Integrating these metrics from multiple perspectives into the value perspective helps the organization understand the drivers of value and enables the creation of a value-based balanced scorecard. Discussion of the integration of these metrics will be addressed in more detail in Chapter 9 when we discuss Question 6: What are the major drivers of value creation for the organization? (See Exhibit 6.5.)

INTEGRATION OF TECHNIQUES

Simply having a metric, on its own, robust as it might be, will not lead to the range of insights that the techniques discussed next make possible. Using these techniques, the organization has information not only about whether (and how much) but also how the organization has created value. By providing an understanding of how value was created, the techniques make it possible to evaluate the nature and quality of the value created to produce better forecasts and create better strategies (whether these are for the organization or everyone involved with it).

Patterns of Value Creation

With the information of value creation in hand, illusions have been stripped away. In the development of the Economic Value Management metrics, value creation and its component elements have been understood. With its development, constituents can develop a solid understanding of the past. Economic Value Management, therefore, provides an ideal framework for using analyses of the past to assess and shape events in the future.

A review of past value creation and its pattern can provide a sense of the cyclicality and inherent attributes of the business. Studying the pattern of past value creation can also help inform the likely pattern of the future. Organizations that use this technique review value creation over time to discern these patterns and compare them to the results of their peers as demonstrated in Chapter 7.

Organizations that use this technique have gained insights into the factors that have influenced their ability to create value. These *ahas* create the potential for the organization to make significant strategic changes that allow it to create even more value going forward. One example is the use of the technique to analyze customer value added to understand if certain investments by the organization in customer relationships pay off over the long run. (See also Chapter 9's discussion on Customer Value.)

The "Bostern Medical Corp." used the patterns of value creation analysis to understand how to maximize value for different retail segments of its business. As Alfred, the CFO of Bostern Medical explained: "This insight would not have been possible if we had only looked at our earnings results. That's what we used to do. We had a fairly rigorous process of analyzing actual earnings against budget. We were very surprised by how our earnings results were not giving us a clear picture. We could not have imagined the significance of what we would discover in this analysis."

By reviewing the patterns of value creation, Bostern Medical had determined that two of their retail segments had very different profiles. Although economic factors impacted one of the retail segments, value creation and destruction for this entity was much more dependent than they had realized on managerial action and the merger and acquisition strategies they had employed. In another retail segment, they were surprised when the patterns of value creation revealed a much greater dependence on economic factors in the value creation of that unit. Both revelations suggested strategy changes. For one unit, it meant changes in the way the organization ran the business and in its merger and acquisition decision processes. In the other, it meant a review and analysis of the external economic factors and the development of financial strategies to hedge those elements. The patterns of value creation will be discussed further in Chapters 7 through 10.

Volatility Analysis

Volatility analyses help constituents understand the nature of value created and how changeable or variable it is. Variability of value creation can signal risk issues and important opportunities to the organization. The form of metric used for these analyses is standard deviations. (See the discussion of standard deviations in this chapter's "Form of Metric" section.) These standard deviations can be calculated over a time series or other dimensions such as across customers.

Organizations that use this technique have become alert to issues that were not otherwise discernable. "Carboco" had a product line that had been a steady cash cow for the organization. Their earnings had been declining slightly, but there was really no cause for alarm on that basis. Stan, Carboco's CFO stated, "We knew that earnings were declining slightly, but we really couldn't pinpoint the root causes. Once we developed the value metrics, we also put together volatility analyses for each product line. We sat down to review them, and it was then we understood that we had some new issues that we were dealing with in the market, related to one of our steady cash-cow product lines. Until we reviewed the volatility," he said, "we had not understood the magnitude of the issues we were dealing with. With this new information in hand, we set out a plan to do business differently in that product line, in a way that better reflected the current environment. As a result of our findings, we also established a process to monitor all our products on a volatility basis."

Volatility analyses are used to inform risk capital calculations, to understand the nature of the value being created and as an input to the ValueMap™ discussed later. The specific techniques and applications will be discussed in more detail in Chapters 7 through 10.

Information Gap Analyses™

Many organizations operate in an environment of data overload. There are too much data, conflicting data, and ineffective processes to utilize the data that exist. While data may be overflowing, information, however, may be in short supply. The purpose of Information Gap Analyses™ is to determine where information gaps exist and understand the value of correcting them. These analyses inform process improvements, the process and technology section of the Value Management Wheel™. The process improvements ultimately influence the drivers of value (Question 6, Exhibit 6.5) and the creation of value itself.

A robust understanding of value concepts is required to make the gap analyses most useful. Without the understanding of the value of the information, any gap analyses will be incomplete.

Statistical Prediction Rules

Statistical Prediction Rules (SPRs) are mathematical algorithms that help predict the nature or amount of a variable. A *Scientific American* article, "Better Decisions for Better Science," discussed the need and usefulness of robust SPRs in the area of medical science.[20] In these cases, using SPRs effectively can mean the difference between life and death. For example, will the SPR, the information used to diagnose ovarian cancer, be robust enough to detect ovarian cancer early on and not miss important parts of the population (false negatives)? And will it be accurate enough not to shock those who do not have the cancer (false positives)?

Likewise, organizations need to use SPRs to determine the likely impacts of changes in strategy and to diagnose the health of a segment of the business. One example of an SPR in business is determining risk capital by using a math algorithm that links a series of data with a determination of the general level of risk.

Value creators use SPRs to help determine strategies and then make the SPRs more robust with the feedback from the information they continue to gather. There are many very useful applications of SPRs for all constituents and for prediction in general. These will be discussed in greater detail in the chapters that follow.

Market Value Analysis

Market value analysis is a technique employed to understand the implications of current economic value in terms of market expectation. This analysis (rather than a metric per se) is the way an organization is able to understand how it has performed vis-à-vis investor or market expectations. The analysis also provides a way for the organization to set expectations for its own improvement goals, centered in a measure that will directly impact shareholder wealth. The analysis is required to answer Questions 9 and 13 of Exhibit 6.5. When "BlueKnows Enterprises" provided this information to its customers about themselves, the strategic discussions that ensued enhanced the organization's knowledge about their customers' businesses and the customers about their own.

Pictures and Analyses (also known as Visualization)

With all the techniques, the use of graphical displays of the results can increase greatly the number of aha moments. In this case, pictures can be worth a thousand numbers. As each technique is discussed in more depth in Chapter 7, examples of useful graphs will be provided.[21]

Scenario Planning and Monte Carlo Simulations

These techniques are used in answering the predictive questions and will be discussed in Chapter 10. They also play a part in understanding risk capital and developing SPRs.

The ValueMap™

The ValueMap™ is an analysis tool that provides the board and CEO with the information they need to fulfill their obligations. It is technique that can be used by all serious constituents. It provides a map of value creation, a way of presenting the answers to the key questions from the perspectives of multiple constituents using the concept of the three-way mirror depicted in Exhibit 6.8. The map not only presents the answers but also puts them in context. As Example Two in Exhibit 6.7 shows, often the contextual information, in this case the standard deviation, is critical to understanding what the answer means. The answer to and context for "has value been created and how much?" is a key centerpiece to the ValueMap™. *The ValueMap™ is a tool that encompasses all 14 questions, constituent perspectives, and techniques outlined in this book.*

APPLICATIONS OF METRICS

Metrics can be used not only to increase understanding; they also can and should impact the critical management processes.

Performance Assessment

Answers to the question of whether value has been created and how much provide performance assessment information about the organization from the organization's perspective, or about other constituents' coparticipation that is superior to that generated by any other methods. In dollar form, it represents the most complete assessment available, including all costs and benefits. In percentage form, it provides a rate of return assessment. In standard deviation form, it provides an assessment of variability. The answers to these questions provide the basis for assessing past performance in the most complete way possible at the total level. Study of the component line items that make up the answer provide important performance assessment information at other levels as well. The assessment of RealBank in Exhibit 5.3 not only assesses performance of the bank overall but can also be used to assess credit issues by reviewing the actual loan loss (or net charge-off) component of that calculation. Whether overall value has been created and by how much represents a starting point in assessing value creation at more specific levels as well.

Strategy

Understanding whether value has been created and by how much is an important feedback component for any strategy process. Organizations that do not have this information in developing strategy are like individuals in a maze, unsure of the impact of a turn to the right or left. Organizations with the answer to whether value has been created can see over the hedgerows. They may not know exactly where to go, but they do know the impacts of their latest moves. With this information in hand and with more detailed information from the other questions, constituents can then begin to discern: Is it our strategy that could be improved? Is it our execution? At the line item level, strategy changes may also be suggested: Should capital, credit risk, or tax strategies be changed? Since the answer to whether value has been created provides the impetus for better strategy, it also provides the impetus for better future results.

Process, Technology, and Organization Structure

Process, technology, and organizational structure represent major components of strategy execution. Whether the organization has created value and by how much can provide overall information about the extent that changes to process, technology, or organizational structure are urgent. Since the answer provides information on potential improvements, it helps the organization enhance value going forward. Answers to questions below the total level will provide more specific information that can be used to inform the detailed nature of changes required.

Rewards Process

For the board, the CEO, and other executives responsible for the results of the entire organization, the answer to Question 1 (has value been created by the organization?) is the most important answer in determining what their overall compensation should be.

Also important is understanding what peers have done (Question 2 of Exhibit 6.5), what value has been created on an "economic market value" capital basis (as discussed in this chapter's section on "Types of Capital"), and what the market expects the organization to produce in terms of value creation in the future (Question 9 of Exhibit 6.5).

In determining compensation levels for the board and these executives, the rewards process should be based on the extent to which value creation has been improved on a sustainable basis. In other words, has the leadership team improved value over the long term? The board and top executives' compensation should then be based on sharing in this improvement in value creation over a multiyear period. Using sustainable value creation as the basis ensures fair compensation for the results obtained. As with all Economic Value Management processes, reward systems in Economic Value Management are designed to minimize manipulation and promote stewardship. While today more and more CEO compensation is based on the market value of the firm (a function of the stock price), market value includes future expectations. Compensation programs that emphasize *future* expectations encourage manipulation of *current perceptions,* rather than the straightforward openness that stewardship demands. Although it is true that executives create options value that may be actualized by the organization in the future, executives need to have a stake in ensuring that, in fact, they are actualized. Economic Value Management compensation is structured so that executives are paid once the value has been realized—on a sustainable (as opposed to manipulated) basis.

Training and Communication

To enhance value creation, all constituents, particularly investors, analysts, rating agencies, journalists, and internal suppliers should receive communications about the value that has been created by the organization. These communications should go beyond the total organization to the subunits as well.

Training should exist for all constituents in understanding what the value creation information means and how to use it. Organizations that employ this kind of training internally with their employees see the benefits in the ability to increase value in the future. At the line item level, the answer to the question of whether value has been created provides indications to the organization of areas where greater training and value creation would be useful and thus how the training process could be improved.

Whether the organization has created value and how much is just the first question to be answered. Now that the basics have been covered, the next chapter will discuss how to generate even more *ahas.*

NOTES

1. "A Reading List for Bill Gates—and You: A Conversation with Literary Critic Harold Bloom," *Harvard Business Review,* May 2001.

2. Eleanor Bloxham, "Better Forecasts for Better Decisions," *Bank Administration Institute—Performance and Profitability Conference,* Orlando, FL, March 2001.

3. To reflect only the cost of the current employee benefit, only the service cost is reflected as an expense in operating profit. Any difference between projected benefit obligations and plan assets can be treated as a form of capital and a cost charged for its use. For more information, see Bartley J. Madden, *CFROI: A Total System Approach to Valuing the Firm,* Oxford, UK: Butterworth–Heinemann, 1999, pp. 136, 141.

4. For further information on this interesting topic, see Mark Ubelhart, "Value Measures: Exploring the Frontier," *Shareholder Value Magazine,* July–August 2001; and Joshua G. Rosett, "Capitalized Labor Contracts," Tulane University, National Bureau of Economic Research Working Paper, November 22, 1997.

5. The term *off balance sheet* refers to items that are not captured on a standard balance sheet. For example, an off-balance sheet asset would be human capital. A liability example would include the uncertain potential for future product liability litigation.

6. Yexiao Xu with Burton G. Malkiel, "Idiosyncratic Risk and Securities Returns," School of Management, University of Texas at Dallas Working Paper, July 2000.

7. For more information on this topic, see Madden (note 3), pp. 95–97; and Stephen F. O'Byrne and S. David Young, *EVA® and Value-based Management: A Practical Guide to Implementation,* New York: McGraw-Hill, 2000, pp. 403–408.

8. Basis in the stock refers to the value upon which the sales will be matched to determine profits (FIFO, LIFO, or specific assignment).

9. In conversations with the author.

10. All-in costs include real costs whether or not included on financial statements.

11. Unlike "BetaCorp"; see Chapter 4's section on "The Question of Standardization."

12. Martha Amram and Nalin Kulatilaka, *Real Options: Managing Strategic Investment in an Uncertain World,* Boston: Harvard Business School Press, 1999. This is a very useful resource on the topic of real options.

13. Eleanor Bloxham, "Intangibles, Human Capital and Options Value Management," *Journal of Cost Management,* November 2000.

14. Carrie Coolidge, "Lost and Found: Did Accounting Hanky-Panky Tank Your Stock? Here's How to Get Some Money Back," *Forbes,* October 1, 2001, p. 124.

15. Chester L. Karrass is a well-known author, speaker, and expert on the subject of negotiating.

16. Ordinal statistics involves data that can be ranked. An excellent text on statistics is Ken Black, *Business Statistics: Contemporary Decision Making,* St. Paul, MN: West Publishing Company, 1997.

17. Abraham Maslow described a hierarchy of needs that explain human motivation. According to this theory, once lower-level needs are satisfied, individuals move up the hierarchy. Physiological and safety needs are at the bottom of the hierarchy; self-actualization is at the top.

18. Robert A. G. Monks and Nell Minow, *Corporate Governance* (2001) and *Watching the Watchers: Corporate Governance for the 21st Century* (1996), both from Blackwell Publishers, Oxford, UK.

19. Jerome B. Cohen, Edward D. Zinbarg, and Arthur Zeikel, *Investment Analysis and Portfolio Management, Fifth Edition,* New York: McGraw-Hill, 1986.

20. John A. Swets, Robyn M. Dawes, and John Monahan, "Better Decisions for Better Science," *Scientific American,* October 2000.

21. For more information, the following two books are recommended, both by William S. Cleveland: *The Elements of Graphing Data* (1993) and *Visualizing Data* (1994), both from Hobart Press, Summit, New Jersey.

Edward R. Tufte, *The Visual Display of Quantitative Information* (2001) and *Envisioning Information* (1990), both from Graphics Press, Cheshire, CT.

CHAPTER 7

Evaluations of the Past to Strengthen the Future: Peers and Sectors

O rganizations and constituents that stop with the question, "Has the organization created value?" will not create the robust information required to secure continued strategic advantage. This chapter will focus on two questions that help an organization and its constituents to evaluate and monitor their reality in terms of the organization's peers and sectors (Questions 2 and 3 in Exhibit 7.1). Following the same pattern as Chapter 6's discussion of Question 1, this chapter discusses the questions of peer and sector value creation in the context of the metrics choices and uses outlined in Exhibits 7.2 and 7.3. The discussion focuses on the

---

Evaluative

1. Has the organization added value? How much?

You Are Here ▷ 2. How does this compare to the organization's peers and competitors?

And Here ▷ 3. Has the organization been managed such that each sector has added value?

4. Has the organization been managed such that each product, service, distribution channel, or process added value?

5. Has the organization been managed such that each customer relationship added value?

6. What are the major drivers of value creation for the organization?

7. For all of the above, how has this changed over time?

EXHIBIT 7.1 The Questions *(continued)*

EXHIBIT 7.1   The Questions *(Continued)*

Predictive

8. How much value does the organization expect to create?

9. How much value do capital providers (shareholders, if publicly traded) expect the organization to create?

10. How much value does the organization expect to create by sector, product, service, distribution channel, process, and customer?

11. What are the expectations related to the major drivers of value creation over time?

12. What are the capital provider's expectations for the organization's peers? What are the peer's expectations for itself by sector, product, service, distribution channel, process, customer, and major drivers of value creation?

13. How do internal, peer, and capital provider expectations differ from current steady-state value creations?

14. For all of the above, how will this change over time?

Metric Characteristics:	From (Traditional Implementation)	To (Economic Value Management)
Time	Evaluative, Primarily Annual	Evaluative and Predictive, Variable Time Periods
Type of Capital	Debt and Equity	Multiple Types of Capital
Form of Metric	Dollars or Percents	Dollars, Percents, Standard Deviation, i.e., Multiple Forms
Types of Adjustments	Simple	Simple and Complex

Measurement and Management Perspectives:

Constituent Focus	Shareholder	Alliance of Constituents
Integrating Metrics	None or Few	Multiple—Optimal Number
Integrating Techniques	None	Multiple
Applications of Metrics	Strategic, Valuation	Broad Applications

EXHIBIT 7.2   How Economic Value Management Differs: Evolution of Value Practices

Metric Characteristics:

Time	Types of Capital	Form of Metric	Types of Adjustments
※ Evaluative and/or predictive ※ Time horizon	※ Debt or equity ※ Equity ※ Special case equity equivalents – Human – Customer – Product ※ Regulatory ※ Risk ※ Cost of capital ※ Market value/ purchase price ※ Taxes, dues	※ Dollar ※ Percentage ※ Standard deviation	※ Availability ※ Complexity ※ Fixed/changed boundaries ※ Options value

Measurement and Management Perspectives:

Constituent Focus	Integration of Metrics	Integration of Techniques	Applications of Metrics
※ Community and external governance ※ Providers of capital ※ Suppliers ※ Consumers ※ Observers/ critics (see Exhibit 6.3)	※ Value drivers (the value-based balanced scorecard) – Relationship – Process – Choices ※ Activity-based information – Cost, revenue, capital ※ TQM process measures	※ Patterns of value creation – Trend and regression analysis ※ Volatility analyses ※ Information Gap Analyses™ ※ Statistical prediction rules ※ Market value analysis ※ Pictures ※ Scenario planning ※ Monte Carlo simulations ※ ValueMap™	The Wheel™: ※ Performance assessment ※ Strategy ※ Process and technology ※ Organizational structure ※ Rewards process ※ Training and communication (see Exhibit 6.4)

EXHIBIT 7.3 Economic Value Management: Metric Choices and Uses

discoveries that can and have been made and the particular tools required in making those discoveries that most enhance the organization and constituents' ability to chart their course for the future.

PEERS AND COMPETITORS

Has the organization created value in comparison to its peers and competitors? The insights organizations have gained from the answer to this question have been truly astounding. That's because the best value creators are not always the headline makers that may be in the news spotlight. "LoanDepot," a large financial services firm, discovered that the patterns for a variety of peers were very different than they might have thought were true without in-depth examination of the issues. Bob, the finance manager at LoanDepot, said, "We were surprised. The net income numbers did *not* mirror the value information. Rather, the value insights provided a very different picture." Exhibit 7.4 shows numbers LoanDepot calculated for a portion of their peer set over an 11-year period.[1] Bob explains, "Our initial comparison covered an 11-year period so that trends (and changes) could be gauged over a 10-year period."

Time

Although the information may be available, there are challenges in developing a time history for a number of peers or competitors. Some areas of difficulty include:

- *Gathering the information.* Surprisingly enough, this may be the first time an organization or investor has attempted to gather information of this sort. In addition, the information that is gathered must be reviewed carefully. Different firms may employ different accounting methods.
- *Complications caused by mergers.* This may require gathering information under several names and determining which of the data to include. It also includes deciding whether to show the data *as-is* or restated to *as-if.*

Since one management team or culture generally becomes dominant after a merger, it often makes sense to trace the efforts of the dominant party through history. (The dominating party may not retain its name after the merger, so some research in this regard may be required.) The ramification of tracing the dominant party is a resulting peer set for comparison purposes that is made up of only the strongest peers—those that survive mergers.

Of course, current period analysis can only include survivors, those that still exist today. When these are selected for the peer set and historical review, some managers in tough industries comment that the only peers in the comparison set are those that survive. This is generally not problematic,

LoanDepot (in $ millions)

	1*	2	3	4	5	6	7	8	9	10	11*	Sum	Std. Dev.
Organization													
Net Income	200	209	340	363	423	529	781	1,140	1,005	1,278	1,427	7,695	426
Value Created	33	18	37	62	29	69	81	222	(33)	202	81	800	73
Peer 1													
Net Income	155	103	213	51	308	122	369	559	749	914	1,020	4,564	328
Value Created	33	11	(69)	(242)	(377)	(422)	(231)	(143)	(77)	29	409	(1,080)	219
Peer 2													
Net Income	157	199	226	257	101	124	208	421	488	533	564	3,279	163
Value Created	37	3	23	18	1	11	(204)	3	38	75	81	(79)	86
Peer 3													
Net Income	233	20	322	70	(395)	(27)	263	299	435	541	650	2,412	279
Value Created	43	84	(125)	(265)	(837)	(317)	(222)	(277)	(71)	(20)	(297)	(2,304)	240
Peer 4													
Net Income	428	1	648	(980)	665	667	761	995	615	215	612	4,627	511
Value Created	85	185	(30)	(173)	(521)	(322)	90	(60)	(344)	(959)	(273)	(2,321)	314
Peer 5													
Net Income	(518)	(955)	726	1,103	1,115	1,124	1,492	1,954	2,176	2,664	2,873	13,754	1,143
Value Created	(1,057)	(798)	617	497	24	(599)	(1,059)	(719)	(595)	(494)	(797)	(4,980)	552

*1 = 10 years before current year just ended; 11 = current year just ended.

EXHIBIT 7.4 Peer Comparison Performed by LoanDepot (partial)

however, since most management teams have (or should have) survival as a minimum goal.

Another reason for choosing the survivors in the peer set comparison is the desire to capture the "organizational memory" that so often impacts current decisions and their consequences in the future. The impact of this organizational memory can often be witnessed over long periods in the time-series data. By having the opportunity to gain these insights, better predictions can be made—something important to most constituents.

A long historical view, such as that chosen by LoanDepot, provides information that helps organizations to begin to understand the causality in the numbers, to separate business cycle from individual performance issues. A long time history provides the basis to investigate key impacts and value drivers and to understand their volatility.

LoanDepot calculated value created using capital amounts that the organization and its peers had at those times. (No as-if or restated calculations are used.) LoanDepot used an equity capital approach in its calculations and applied this approach to the value calculated for LoanDepot and its peers. A review of their numbers in Exhibit 7.4 reveals that LoanDepot and its peers did not experience issues in creating value at the same time though some patterns are evident. Bob recalls, "I had several observations when I first saw the numbers. One was the rough patch that we all experienced in years 2 through 5. The long history really helped us to see this. Another thing I observed was the striking difference between value and net income. Although our peers (shown in Exhibit 7.4) experienced increases in net income from year 2 to year 3, four of the five experienced lower value creation. (Only Peer five improved from negative $798 million to positive $617 million.) From year 3 to year 4, all of our peers experienced a downturn in value. However, from year 4 to year 5, not only did they see a downturn, but we experienced it as well, and this in a year when four of the six of us reported higher net incomes. Given our own nearly stellar record on net income, it was surprising to see the bumps we experienced over time in creating value. For me, one of the major conclusions I draw from the information is that, while patterns can be identified, the differences in the results for us and our peers clearly indicate that our choice of, and ability to execute, strategies are very important factors in our ability to create value."

Despite the bumps in value creation, it is interesting to note that, in this sample of LoanDepot's peer set, only LoanDepot itself actually generated value over the time period reviewed, generating $800 million in value over the 11-year period. (See the sum column in the value-created line in Exhibit 7.4.) All of the peers shown destroyed value, ranging from −$79 to −$4,980.

Although not shown in this peer set snapshot, many organizations included in LoanDepot's total peer set also destroyed value over the time period studied. Although LoanDepot used objective, comparable measures of value, it generated more value than any of the peer competitors in the *total* peer set—whether those competitors were larger or smaller organizations. (Could it be that high performers tend to act like high performers, caring enough to understand the value consequences of their own actions and those of their peers? Perhaps this "coincidence" is one reason CalPERS looks for evidence of use of value management techniques in its investment selection criteria.)

Types of Capital

Either equity or debt and equity capital may be used in the peer comparison along with costs of capital that differ from organization to organization based on the agreed-upon calculation methodology.

Lack of data for peers can sometimes make it difficult to perform some of the equity equivalent adjustments if these items are not disclosed on a regular basis. The human capital equity adjustments are often particularly difficult. Since the process of making these adjustments can often yield very useful value driver information and insights, creative efforts to obtain the information is often worthwhile.

Where regulations govern the capital of peers, regulatory capital may also be used to perform a "what-if" calculation of value generation. This analysis is a comparison of peers as if all had held capital at the minimum levels required by regulation. Such analyses, used in conjunction with actual capital comparisons, can help pinpoint the impacts of capital strategy on value. Similarly, a risk capital review is another analysis that can provide an interesting look for organizations that have, and those that do not have, regulatory capital requirements. Risk capital analyses put peer comparisons on a like-risk basis, creating comparisons of value on an apples-to-apples basis from a total risk standpoint. This would have been useful to thousands of investors and lenders when "Exiscorp" went bankrupt. While Exiscorp earnings grew dramatically, it did not hold enough capital for the risk it had taken on. Understanding this would have helped employees as well.

Understanding risk capital can be somewhat challenging to determine on a comparison basis. In FAS 131 (segment/business line) reporting, peers and competitors in financial services organizations will often provide their own calculations of risk capital. This information may have limited use if:

* The bases of the calculations of risk capital are difficult to determine.
* The bases vary widely from organization to organization.
* The organization arbitrarily assumes their risk capital to be the same as (a) book or accounting capital or (b) regulatory capital.

Methods of performing risk capital calculations will be discussed when product level calculations are covered in Chapter 8. In particular, top-down calculations can broaden the usefulness of risk capital analyses for all types of organizations and be used in peer analyses.

Form of Metric

All forms of metrics may be used to compare peers, although a dollar-based version as a starting point (as used by LoanDepot; see Exhibit 7.4) is most useful. It provides a sense of the absolute magnitude of value creation. In contrast, a percentage-based measure is open to misinterpretation. Percentages must be compared to the cost of capital itself to determine if value has been created or destroyed.

For example, if two peers have different market-risk-related profiles and different costs of capital (and many do), a comparison of their value percentages can lead to incorrect conclusions. This is the case with "Crazy Burger" and "Big Burger." Crazy generates a 20% value return on capital, whereas Big generates only 12%. On that basis, Jim, the CFO of "Danver's Toy Company" tells a group of friends at the local pub, "I've looked at it—and Crazy appears to be doing better than Big." Is that true? Is Crazy dong better than Big? (See Exhibit 7.5.) Although Crazy's value return on capital is 20%, which is 5% higher than Big's, Crazy's investors require a 25% return on that capital, compared to only 12% for Big. Crazy Burger has actually destroyed value since investors need to get 25%. In contrast, Big Burger has more than satisfied the cost of capital requirements of its investors. One way to solve the dilemma is to understand the percentage return over and above the cost of capital. In the case of Crazy, value, on a percentage basis over and above the cost of capital, is *negative* 5% (20% less 25%); Big generated value, over and above the cost of capital, of 3% (15% less 12%). Even with the cost of capital numbers as an adjunct, however, the real magnitude of value created or destroyed is not understood using percentages. The dollar measures include the perspective of size as well as relative rate. (See Chapter 5's section on "Choosing the Measures: Dollars and Percents" for additional issues and discussion.)

The absolute magnitude of value creation can be seen in Exhibit 7.4. LoanDepot and its peers produced positive net income over the 11-year period (see the sum column and the net income line). Of the 66 data points that made up the totals, only five of the net incomes for the entire group were negative. In terms of value creation, however, 36 of the 66 data points (slightly more than half) were *negative,* a demonstration on a total basis of the difference in the measures.

	Value in Percentage	Cost of Capital	
Crazy Burger	20%	25%	Destroyed value—how much?
Big Burger	15%	12%	Added value—how much?

EXHIBIT 7.5 Burger Wars: Percentage Measures

Exhibit 7.4 also shows the standard deviation in value creation over the time period for LoanDepot and each of its peers. Standard deviation provides a measure of the variability of the results. A review of LoanDepot's calculations for Peer 4 and some of its comparables is instructive:

* Although Peers 1 and 4 had approximately the same net income for the total period ($4,564 million versus $4,627 million), Peer 4's was more variable, with a standard deviation (difference from the mean) of 511 versus 328 for Peer 1.

* Peer 4's value destruction over the period was very close to Peer 3's at about *negative* $2,300 million. The variability or standard deviation of Peer 4's value creation was higher at 314 compared to 240 for Peer 3.

* Peer 4's net income was nearly twice that of Peer 3, while value destruction was nearly identical.

If Peer 4 had the calculations that LoanDepot had made, it would be a wake-up call to them to further examine their value creation and the issues in their business.

This analysis demonstrates how important it is for investors, analysts, employees, and the board to understand the implications of the value creation analysis.

Some of LoanDepot's peers did not survive into future periods when they were bought by other firms. Although LoanDepot's information is of the past, the information in Exhibit 7.4 is instructive, particularly as the information is reviewed in greater depth.

Adjustments

For those who question the impact of adjusting net income to arrive at value created, a review of the LoanDepot case demonstrates the importance of the adjustments in the analyses. Exhibit 7.6 shows the adjustments to net income for LoanDepot and its peers. In general, the adjustments represented a decrease in net income to get to value created, although in four data points for Peers 3, 4, and 5, perhaps because of reserves or one-time events, value was actually greater than net income (see year 2, Peer 5, for example). As can be observed, the amounts are not insignificant. In fact, on average, the adjustments themselves ranged from 0.9 to 1.95 of net income (see the sum column). The level of adjustments LoanDepot made also varied in each year, as shown in Exhibit 7.6. A shortcut that derived a rough number for value in previous years based on the calculation for the current year, therefore, would simply not provide an accurate picture.

Although data availability was an issue for LoanDepot and caused it to simplify the calculations for itself and its peers to compare results, the adjustments made are *still* significant. Although not the case with LoanDepot, when there are severe data problems in the reports generally available,

	1	2	3	4	5	6	7	8	9	10	11	Sum	Std. Dev.
Adjustments													
LoanDepot	(167)	(190)	(303)	(301)	(395)	(460)	(701)	(918)	(1,038)	(1,076)	(1,345)	(6,895)	390
Peer 1	(122)	(92)	(282)	(293)	(685)	(544)	(600)	(702)	(826)	(885)	(611)	(5,644)	261
Peer 2	(121)	(163)	(203)	(238)	(140)	(270)	(412)	(418)	(450)	(459)	(483)	(3,358)	134
Peer 3	(190)	64	(447)	(335)	(442)	(291)	(485)	(576)	(506)	(561)	(947)	(4,716)	242
Peer 4	(343)	184	(677)	807	(1,186)	(989)	(671)	(1,055)	(959)	(1,174)	(885)	(6,948)	596
Peer 5	(539)	157	(109)	(606)	(1,091)	(1,723)	(2,551)	(2,673)	(2,771)	(3,158)	(3,670)	(18,734)	1,269
Adjustments													
LoanDepot	83%	91%	89%	83%	93%	87%	90%	81%	103%	84%	94%	90%	6%
Peer 1	79%	89%	133%	577%	222%	446%	163%	126%	110%	97%	60%	124%	159%
Peer 2	77%	82%	90%	93%	139%	218%	198%	99%	92%	86%	86%	102%	47%
Peer 3	81%	326%	139%	476%	112%	1093%	184%	193%	116%	104%	146%	195%	283%
Peer 4	80%	15620%	105%	82%	178%	148%	88%	106%	156%	546%	145%	150%	4445%
Peer 5	104%	16%	15%	5.5%	98%	153%	171%	137%	127%	119%	128%	136%	50%

*Note:

Net income plus adjustments = Value

For example: LoanDepot year 1: 200 + adjustments = 33; therefore, adjustments = –167

For example: Peer 3, year 2: 20 + adjustments = 84; therefore adjustments = 64

For example: Peer 1, year 3: 213 + adjustments = –69; therefore adjustments = –282

If sum of adjustments are negative, net income is greater than value.

If sum of adjustments are positive, net income is less than value.

Percentages are calculated as absolute value of adjustments divided by absolute value of net income.

EXHIBIT 7.6 LoanDepot's Adjustment Analysis*

organizations may need to tap nontraditional data sources to fill in the missing peer information. This may involve using subscription services that provide the necessary information directly or provide statistics that can be used to make reasonable estimates. Each situation is unique. In some cases, all the data desired is not available, and simpler calculations are required across the board to understand the information for comparison purposes.

Constituent Focus: The Alliance

Since decisions are choices among alternatives, all constituents take a keen interest in comparison information. Information from the past can point to which organizations have the best strategy, execution, and management teams—useful to both employees and investors in making career and investment decisions.

The employment and capital worlds today have changed in that there is more liquidity and there are more free agents than ever before. This creates additional opportunities of choice for employees and investors. Organized sports have clear rules that determine who the winning teams are. In the business and nonprofit world, however, existing rules of GAAP provide such an incomplete answer (as LoanDepot's analyses in Exhibits 7.4 and 7.6 demonstrate), that employees and investors have no idea whether they are supporting a "winning team."

Providers of capital, of course, are interested not only in how the organization has done with the capital it has been given, they also want to understand what has happened in the market with the capital they have provided. Changes in market value are precipitated by expectations. Those expectations are, in part, determined by the demonstrated capacities of the organization, shown in its prior value creation track record. Exhibit 7.7 provides a pictorial representation of LoanDepot's calculations of net income and value for Peer 5. This exhibit demonstrates the reasons that investors need to understand how an organization has performed with the capital it has been given. Although in year 2 this entity experiences an increase in net income and "never looks back," Peer 5 creates *value* only in years 3, 4, and 5 and then continues to *destroy* value from then on. Investors enjoy above-average returns when they understand these phenomena in advance of the crowd. To wit, the London-based investment firm, Odey Asset Management, studies the value creation of all their potential investments.

Exhibit 7.8 shows the value creation of LoanDepot and the five peers that LoanDepot studied in Exhibit 7.4. Clearly, each peer is unique. Some are much more volatile in their creation (destruction) of value, and some create (destroy) significantly more value than others.

Although four of the peers have similar value creation in the first period, the time series is required to truly understand the different paths these organizations have taken. Although in year 11 LoanDepot and Peer 2

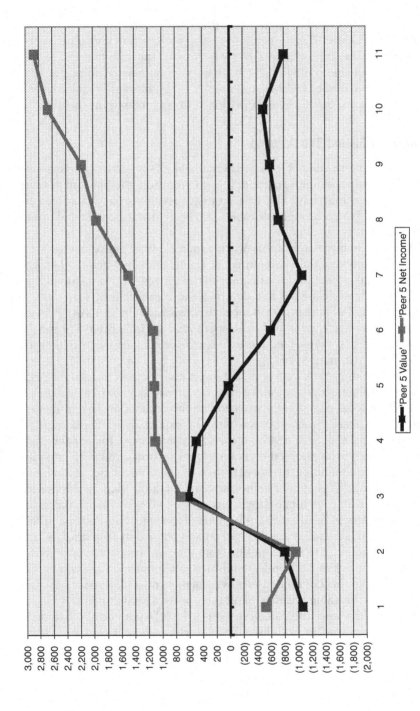

EXHIBIT 7.7 LoanDepot's Peer 5 Graph

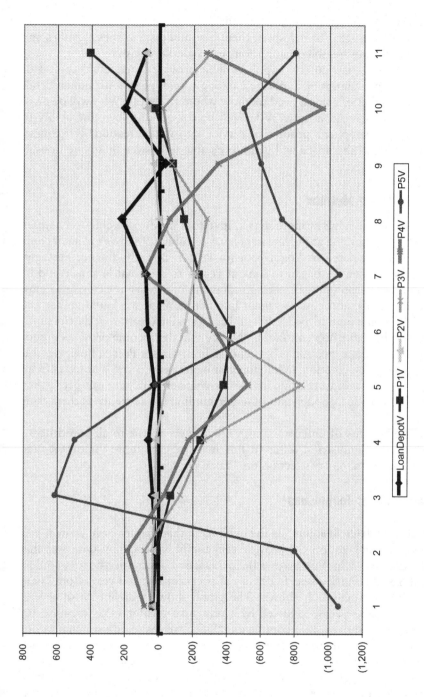

EXHIBIT 7.8 LoanDepot and Peer Value Creation

both created the same amount of value, the paths they have traveled are unique. A first step for investors, then, is to understand these profiles and what they mean for the organizations in which they wish to invest.

Suppliers, particularly suppliers who provide intellectual capital or resources that cannot be duplicated among several peers with similar product and market offerings, need to know whom to supply. Who will be prospering five years from now? Who will be solvent and have the ability to leverage the supplier's product or service into value creation? (Of course, executives and the board will want to be able to answer these questions in detail as well.)

Integration of Metrics

To understand value in more depth, investors need to be able to compare what is driving value at the line item level. Exhibit 7.9 shows the net income and value calculated by LoanDepot for Peer 5. Bob, the finance manager, explains: "When we began to look at Peer 5 to see what lessons could be learned, we began to break its results down to line items: revenue line items, cost line items, and cost of capital line items. What we found is that one substantial line item helped 'explain' Peer 5's value creation or destruction." (See Exhibit 7.9.) Bob continues: "Notice that net income provides a poor indicator of value creation. This expense line item for Peer 5, however, was *driving* its value creation. While forecasting its net income is not very helpful, if we can forecast this line item somewhat accurately for our peers, then that will provide a good means of understanding future trends in their value creation."

The benefits of understanding value drivers accrue to all constituents. For different industries, different line items will be more important than others. (See Chapter 9's section on "Value Drivers.")

Integration of Techniques

Patterns of Value Creation. As the exhibits in this chapter have shown, patterns of value creation can provide very useful information. One area that these patterns help illuminate is the presence of issues specific to an industry. In Exhibit 7.10, a selected group of peers for selected years from Loan-Depot's peer analysis is shown. The graph shows a downturn of several years for these peers, followed by a return to greater value creation for all the peers shown. Bob comments, "Since we made adjustments in our calculations of value to better reflect the true operations, the downturn observed in the value numbers for these peers represents a real slump. Reviewing the patterns of value creation at a high level and at more detailed levels over longer time cycles, we noticed repeats of these general patterns over time."

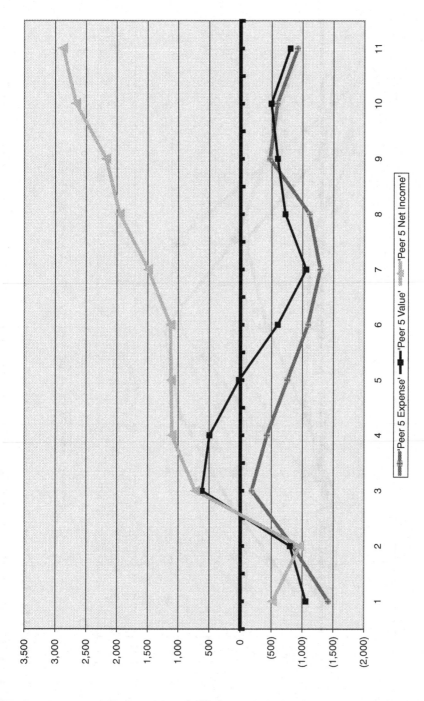

EXHIBIT 7.9 Peer 5: LoanDepot's Line Item Analysis

189

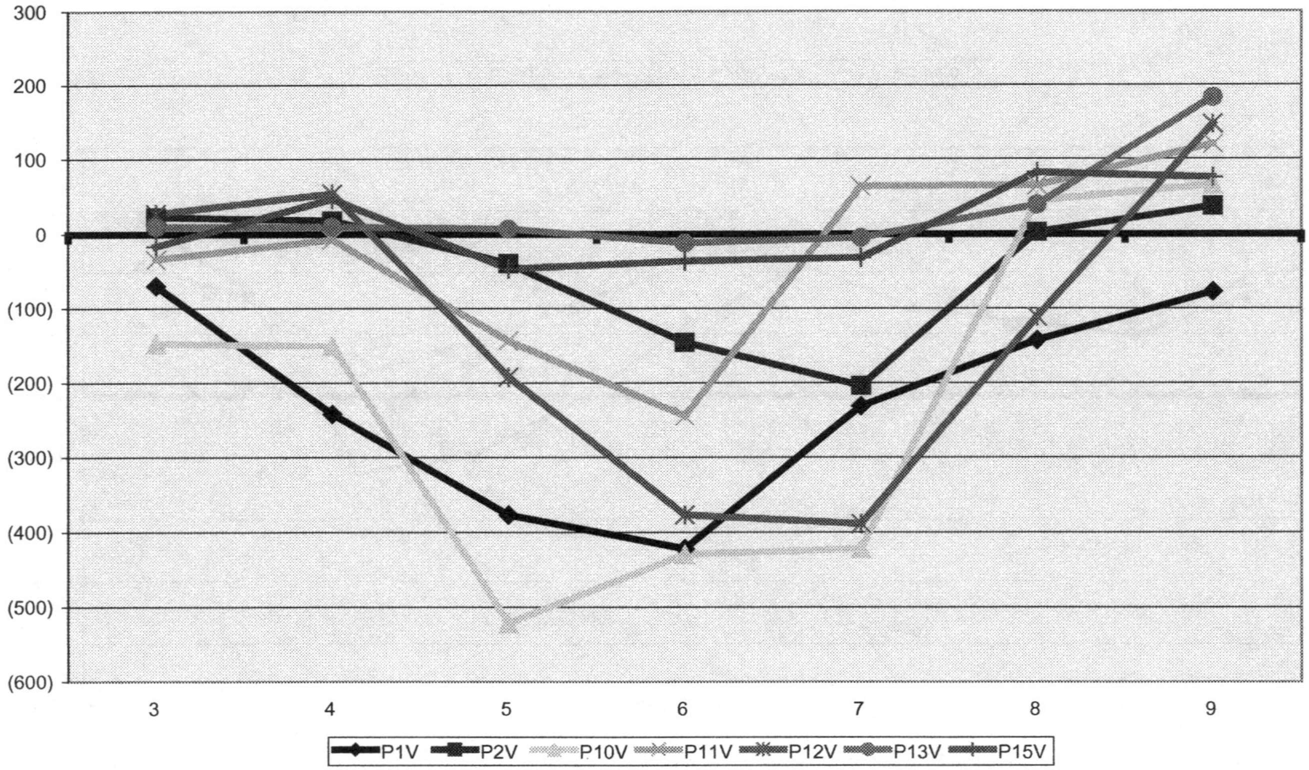

EXHIBIT 7.10 LoanDepot's Peer Comparison of Value Creation

In Exhibit 7.10, Peers 13 and 15 stand out as being less impacted than the others by this cyclical pattern. With this information in hand, LoanDepot can study the strategies of *Peers 13 and 15* to understand how they were able to *avoid* the dramatic slump that *the other peers* experienced.

Such analysis, when engaged in conjunction with a line item analysis, can provide important information about the real drivers of the business. These insights provide a way for the organization to integrate existing detailed metrics into a meaningful value context.

Volatility Analysis. While the cost of capital chosen in the calculation incorporates volatility vis-à-vis the market and the varying return expectations among peers, volatility analyses review total risk. Volatility analyses can be very useful in understanding the volatility of value creation and of specific line items as well. In pictorial form, Exhibit 7.11 shows the volatility of one expense line item for LoanDepot and 15 of its peers. The picture *shows* the volatility reflected in the standard deviations for the line item presented in Exhibit 7.12. As the graph reflects, Peer 7 has the most volatility with a standard deviation of 1,081. Peer 6 and Peer 5 also have high standard deviations of 480 and 368, respectively. Peer 8 and Peer 15 have the lowest standard deviations of 33 and 44, respectively. They show up on the graph as relatively flat lines throughout the 11-year period.

Another way to view the analyses is to review volatility without the growth in the business. Assumptions are made that serve to strip out the growth in the line item or total number and calculate differences from a trend line rather than the mean. (For more information on this technique, see the discussion on trend analyses in Chapter 10's section on "Integration of Techniques," in the "Patterns of Value Creation" subsection.) In the case of Exhibits 7.11 and 7.12, however, such analysis, while a refinement, was not relevant for LoanDepot because there was no readily apparent trend in the information.

Where possible, it is most useful to gather monthly or quarterly information for the organization and peers when reviewing volatility information. This can often provide detail that is useful in understanding trends in value and changes in value drivers such as consumer behavior and other economic factors.

Information Gap Analyses™. Information Gap Analyses™ comes into play at the peer and competitor level when the impacts of the lack of information are measured. Information properly understood and used does make a difference in creating value. Warren Buffet has said, "The CEO who misleads others in public may eventually mislead himself in private."[2] Being misled can involve lack of information—lack of reliable information or lack of the right information. Having the right information is important not only to the organization but to investors, suppliers, and other constituents as well. A

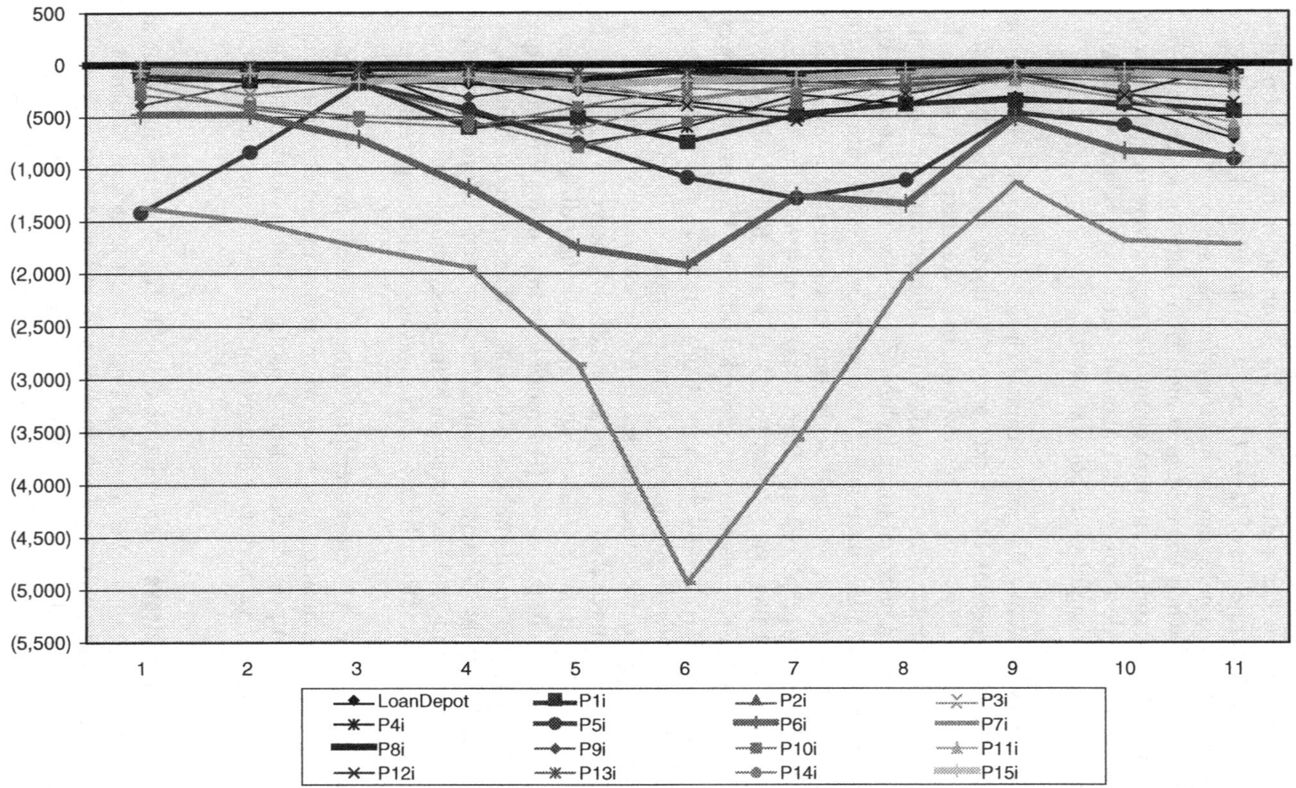

EXHIBIT 7.11 LoanDepot's Analysis: Line Item Volatility

LoanDepot	169
Peer 1	188
Peer 2	77
Peer 3	147
Peer 4	227
Peer 5	368
Peer 6	480
Peer 7	**1081**
Peer 8	**33**
Peer 9	83
Peer 10	195
Peer 11	151
Peer 12	158
Peer 13	68
Peer 14	171
Peer 15	**44**

EXHIBIT 7.12   Standard Deviations of
Line Item for LoanDepot
and 15 Peers

competitive analysis allows organizations to witness the standards others
have set for themselves and to set the bar even higher. In a recent article,
"Silent Warning: When Companies Clam Up, Trouble May Lie Ahead,"
Herb Greenberg of *Fortune* magazine tells investors, "What you don't know
can hurt you. . . . What we're talking about here is disclosure, or rather the
lack of it."[3] To begin the process of Information Gap Analyses™, organizations need to assess the gaps between the information they provide, that
provided by competitors, and what would be provided in an ideal world.
These analyses provide insights that are beneficial in the development of
information systems that have not only tactical and day-to-day relevance but
also have beneficial strategic and long-range impacts. FAS 131 and the
requirements of sector reporting have been areas where firms have had the
opportunity to differentiate themselves.

While it is clear that this kind of open book management is important
for the organization and its employees and investors, these principles also
benefit suppliers who, in many instances, act more as partners and facilita-
tors. To be effective, the information reported needs to measure true value
creation, or at least to provide all the components necessary to the calculations and analyses, because in the final analysis what is misleading is misleading.

Statistical Prediction Rules. Often, certain patterns in a large population set (of peers) will provide information on the drivers of value under a number of different strategic scenarios. For example, economic conditions drive the expenses for the peer shown in Exhibit 7.9. These drivers or relationships can be quantified in SPRs to forecast what may occur in the future. (Chapter 10 will discuss SPRs in the context of the predictive Questions 8 through 14 in Exhibit 7.1.)

In addition to the organization's own efforts, peers and competitors may also be developing their own SPRs to drive competitive advantage through better decision making. By studying a peer's use of SPRs (often reported in the press), organizations can learn how to take their own existing models and improve and enhance them. It is curious that, citing competitive concerns, some organizations will not disclose certain information. Would one imagine that Peer 5 would joyfully disclose its value creation as shown in Exhibit 7.8? However, the invention of new approaches that involve complex algorithms will often be disclosed by the inventor as a source of pride. By understanding competitors' work in this area, it is possible for an organization to raise the bar.

For example, "Huddley Savings Bank" needed to improve its marketing effectiveness. By studying the quantitative methods and techniques of one of its competitors (touted in the press), Huddley was better able to determine its own approach to gathering driver information and constructing models for evaluating customer behavior. (We will discuss this further when we discuss customer value in Chapter 9.)

Market Value Analysis. Many CEOs complain at analyst or investor meetings that their PE is too low. Given the mismatch between earnings and reality, it is easy to see why comparisons of market price to earnings could yield results that would be difficult to understand. Peer 5 is off the chart in terms of earnings growth. Should its PE be high?

Market value analyses provide a critical framework for understanding the market's expectations of value creation for an organization and its peers. Developing market value analyses provides CEOs with much better information than PE does and provides a clearer view of the meaning behind the market expectations as well. Examples of the pictures that emerge are shown in Chapter 10's section on "Comparing Expectations: The Market's Expectations and the Remaining Predictive Questions."

Market value expectations form one of the frameworks used in developing compensation for those responsible for the results of the organization as a whole. In addition, outcomes of market value analyses include a deeper understanding of the implications of certain strategies and approaches as reflected in future expectations. One example where organizations can benefit is by understanding the linkage between market value and Information Gap Analyses™ (i.e., the relationship between disclosure and expected value creation). A critical outcome of this effort within the organization may include a reassessment of, and improvements in, the organization's communication efforts.

Pictures. The use of graphs has been illustrated in the exhibits in this chapter. The exhibits are a small sample of the kinds of items that can be reviewed and the benefits that can be gained. Standard deviations of particular measures can provide clues as to what information may be better demonstrated graphically. Decomposition of the value information can also be very useful. Pictures help organizations and constituents explore the value information for insights and the "ahas" they seek.

The ValueMap™

The ValueMap™ provides the three-way mirror perspective not only for the organization but, to the extent possible, for peers as well (see Exhibit 6.8). The ValueMap™ highlights for organizations and constituents where information is lacking and what is unknown from a decision-making standpoint. Comfort with ambiguity and risk taking is important to value creation. Therefore "uncharted" parts of the map (often the case for peers) serve to represent the unknown and make clear the limits on information important for decision making.

Applications of Metrics

Performance Assessment and Strategy. By providing comparison information, peer value analyses help an organization to better understand what it has done to effectively assess its performance and its strategies, and, by performing detailed reviews, understand its areas of over- and underperformance.

If the peer numbers are far different, understanding the differences helps the CEO and board understand the extent to which their own numbers can be trusted. The process of developing these analyses provides a mechanism to help identify adjustments that should be made in their own calculations, in disclosures to investors, and in the accounting itself.

Exhibit 7.8 shows the value created by LoanDepot and five of its peers. By decomposing the information on a line item basis and integrating other metrics and analyses, LoanDepot can understand not only that it has done better than its peers, but also discern what factors are contributing to their relative success. Although challenging for large and complex organizations, this process allows them to better plot their future paths by understanding the ones they have just walked.

For example, LoanDepot, upon review of Exhibit 7.8, may wish to examine why Peers 1 and 2 have experienced recent upturns while their own recent value creation has been more volatile. Getting these clues early on can help the organization protect its own efforts. It can also help organizations that want to acquire other companies at a fair price. By creating a systematic approach to calculating the historical value of the organization and its peers, the board is positioned to perform its supervisory duties and has the knowledge to competently inspect proposed future strategies.

The benefits of the analysis are clear if examined from the perspective of the board of Peer 5. If that board is unaware of the value creation exhibited by its own organization and is instead operating under the illusion of the reported net income as shown in Exhibit 7.7, it cannot perform a respectable job of overseeing the organization's activities. By developing the systems to understand the *bad news* as well as understand the activities of its peers (see Exhibit 7.8), the board is much better positioned to protect the organization. Rather than allowing itself to be misled by the net income picture (Exhibit 7.7), with the right information, the board is positioned to take corrective action to prevent the dive in value creation to value destruction that occurs in year 5 and continues through the next five years as well. Investors, of course, also need this information to determine their strategies and how best to protect their investments and properly allocate capital in their portfolios.

Rewards Process. Boards are responsible for ensuring fair compensation. When organizations genuinely want to create respectable, fair, and yet generous rewards, they cannot do it without the information obtained through this peer analysis. How can the board of Peer 5 protect its shareholders and their own reputations from attack if they reward the executives based on net income (see Exhibit 7.7) instead of value creation? Executive management has destroyed value while bolstering reported income. How is this possible? Several reasons may be the cause:

* Being less conservative in the application of accounting principles
* Being less conservative in its reserving policies or reversing earlier reserves
* Making acquisitions that generate net income but destroy value and dilute shareholder returns
* Slowing down investments to generate short-term earnings and lower long-term value
* Selling off pieces of the business
* Aggressively recognizing revenues

In any event, until the board answers the question of whether the organization and its peers have created value, it cannot respectably supervise the pay of top executives. Boards that fail in this regard are subject to criticism and open to potential litigation. Sure, the reported net income has risen for Peer 5, but the value it has created with its capital has been negative for many years. In the most recent year shown, in fact, the organization has destroyed value by $800 million.

Far from creating improvements in value, the organization has generated $1.4 billion less in value than it did eight years before! A board handing out bonuses in such a situation should be subject to rigorous scrutiny. And not only does the story of Peer 5 look sad on its own, the fact is that this is *not* an industry-wide phenomenon. (See Exhibit 7.8). Looking at even a larger peer set (using LoanDepot's calculations of value for 15 peers in Exhibit 7.13), the board still has cause for alarm. Over the last nine years of the study, Peer 5's ranking has moved from number 1or 2 three years in a row to the bottom quintile consistently ever since. In the last five years, it has given the worst or second-worst performance of the peers. Notice that Peers 6 and 7 look even worse than Peer 5 in certain periods and Peer 7's dip in year 5 is truly spectacular. If it has the value analysis on a line item basis (see Exhibit 7.11), the board of Peer 5 knows exactly why Peer 6 and Peer 7 look the way they do. Peer 5's difficulties also stem in part from issues related to this line item. Although at times Peers 6 and 7 destroyed more value, the board of Peer 5 should still be *very* concerned. Peer 7 has been making progress and is now creating value. And in the current year not only is Peer 5's value creation lower than the year before, but it is also the most value destroying of all the peers (and this in a year where 11 of the 16 are actually creating value).

Investors also need to inspect the level of compensation vis-à-vis the sustainable improvement in value created by the organization. The measure should *not* be the executive's pay compared to peers. The pay of peers may be inflated (or deflated). Nor should it be based on earnings (for obvious reasons) or market value (which is a future expectation). The measure of what the executives have been able to do with the capital provided to them *and their ability to improve value creation over time* should be the measure used to assess their pay and inspect the degree to which *pay for performance* rather than *pay for mere existence* exists.

The rest of the story for Peer 5? About one and a half years later Peer 5 was bought by one of its competitors. This purchase has been a difficult one for the buyer and its employees and investors, as well as the employees and investors of Peer 5. The current, relatively low stock price of the new company indicates the market is not that hopeful about future prospects either.

The peer value information in conjunction with the information about the organization's value creation are not only important in *judging* an organization's compensation and rewards process, they are also important in *constructing* it. Understanding market expectations (market value analysis) plays a role as does understanding the potential volatility of the organization. (See the "Rewards Process" sub-subsection in the "Applications of Metrics" subsection in the "Sectors" section in this chapter, and similar sections in Chapters 9 and 10, for some of the construction issues related to value-based compensation plans.)

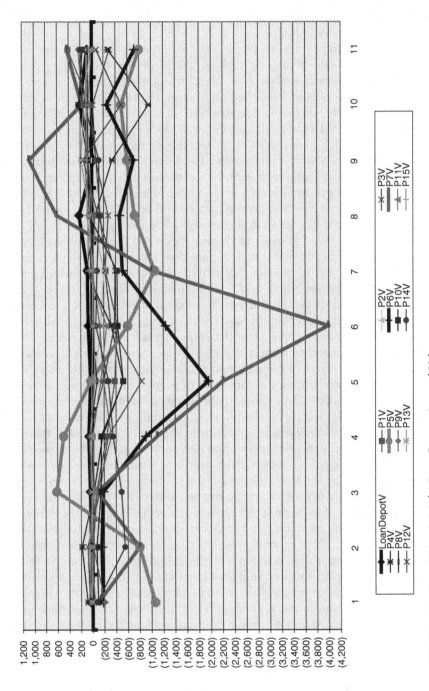

EXHIBIT 7.13 LoanDepot's Multi-Peer Comparison of Value

Training and Communications and Other Processes. Peer value information in conjunction with information about the organization itself is very powerful and will inevitably impact the organization's training and communications processes. What the board knows, executive management should know. Employees should understand what is driving value in the firm, and this should impact the organization's priorities, processes, and technology. Information gaps should be addressed as needed. And a new dialogue should begin (1) to explain the turnaround, if that is the case or (2) the good works in value terms that mean something and have the capability of producing real insight and wisdom and protecting the shareholder, employees, and customers from financial and other hardships. Likewise, shareholders, employees, customers, and suppliers should enter into a dialogue with the organization to discuss value implications from their own points of view. If peers create more value for these constituents, communicating their concerns can improve their own options and alternatives and change the way in which business is conducted.

SECTORS

The first section of this chapter addressed the value creation of peers by a review of calculations made by LoanDepot. This section will discuss the next question an organization needs to address: whether it is creating value in each of its business sectors (and whether its peers are as well). (See Question 3 in Exhibit 7.1.) As with the discussion of peer value creation, this section will follow the format of metric choices and uses outlined in Exhibits 7.2 and 7.3. For certain organizations, such as nonprofits or government bodies, the sector level (or even a level below that) may be the starting point for value measurement. Churches and other religious organizations, for example, may begin by reviewing value from their philanthropic (outreach) efforts as a sector separate from their counseling and pastoral efforts.[4]

The question of sector value is generally where the rubber meets the road in an organization. Managers of the sectors, whether they are product related or geographically based, or a combination of both, have natural interest in the value creation numbers for their sector.

Sector information is very important to constituents as well. Organizations should be aware that customers do watch and monitor them as suppliers in this regard. "FRO," a financial services research organization, for example, received questions posed by corporate customers whenever a financial services firm was experiencing difficulties. The corporate customers were concerned about doing business with the firm and would ask:

- How serious is this?
- Do we need to be concerned about the sector of the business we interact with?

- Will their current problems impact continuation of service?
- Should we diversify away from this supplier?

Sector information, properly understood in a value context, provided the reassurance that was required.

Time

Understanding sector value can be a challenge to both insiders and outsiders. As they attempt to construct a story over time, everyone finds it challenging to trace history with conviction. Primarily, this is a result of two factors:

1. The fact that organizations are continually reorganizing so that their management organizational structures may be radically different in different years

2. The fact that organizations are continually changing their calculations and allocations so that their reporting methodologies may be radically different in different years

(The section on "Constituent Focus" later in this chapter will expand on this discussion.)

Types of Capital

While it is true that, at the total level within an organization, there may be some contention about the calculation of value creation, these discussions are usually more exploratory than heated. As long as the principles are understood and fairly applied across peers, agreement on objective calculations is not very difficult to obtain. At the total level, there is general recognition that there may be new insights and that the organization may now see need for improvements that were not clear before. The issues occur, however, most directly when the next layer (the sector level) is examined and, seemingly uncontrollably, fingers begin to point and sector leaders may start to scrabble for certain seats on the de Mello bus. This is why this step must be approached with both reason and sensitivity.

At the total level, the business entity has a calculation of net income and of assets, liabilities, and equity as a starting point. Unless the sector represents a separate legal entity, this accounting foundation may not be available at the sector level. For some, then, it is easier to view the calculation of value as a two-step process:

1. Construct net income and balance sheet information at the sector level.

2. Develop value creation calculations.

Some organizations already develop net income and balance sheet information for nonlegal entity sectors. Others must develop this information and, if there is going to be a battle, this is generally the first battlefield. That is because it is a matter of contention who gets credit for which revenues and charged with which costs. The balance sheet is generally not the initial source of contention, particularly if current goal and reward systems are net income focused. However, once the holistic approach of Economic Value Management is considered, apportionment of the balance sheet becomes a more important issue.

If availability of information is an issue, organizations may find it easier to use a combined debt and equity capital approach at the sector level. Other organizations with detailed balance sheets are able to more neatly attribute equity and debt costs. In this case, an equity capital approach may be used as the starting point. If there are particular or peculiar financing decisions made at the sector level, this is indeed the best approach. (See Chapter 5's section on "To WACC or Not to WACC and the Use of APV.")

The balance sheet and income statement are linked. Economic Value Management practitioners realize this as they make the adjustments outlined in Exhibit 5.4. There are other ways that revenue, expense, and capital are linked as well. These include issues that are more managerial and behavioral than strictly measurement related. One of the basic managerial issues of any organization involves authority, responsibility, locus of control, and organizational structure. This set of issues involves a wide range of decisions an organization makes. For example, a decision that all organizations face is: *Where should a give function reside?* What are the capital implications of this decision? Should it reside at the head office, at the sector, or with an outside supplier? *What are the implications for value creation?* Because Economic Value Management is so robust, unlike other approaches, the impact of this issue is reflected in the value metrics.

Where a given function resides, of course, is very important to the calculation of value at the sector level. Because of the many issues involved in making the calculations, it is important for the organization to take the calculation process step by step, addressing the issues one by one. In its approach, the organization must look to ensure the right outcomes and behaviors from the process. Egos must be placed aside while authority and responsibility are given out in pairs. A sector manager who does not take responsibility must not be given authority. A manager who has responsibility must be given authority. This is a key attribute of true Economic Value Management organizations. They determine consciously (and this is a human capital issue of strategic importance that should be reviewed by the board) the division of the pair combinations of authority and responsibility in the organization.

A behavioral and managerial approach should be taken to the calculation of value at the sector level. The question to be addressed, for example, should not be as simplistic as to whether certain costs, revenues, or capital get allocated to certain sectors. This is not a question for the finance team alone to answer, but one in which operating managers should play a shared role in developing a consensus and understanding that includes answers to key questions like:

- Who will have authority over the resources to generate this activity?
- Who will have the responsibility for the results and the costs?

As the answers to these questions are determined, these decisions will impact the organizational structure. (See the section on "Application of Metrics, subsection "Organizational Structure" later in this chapter.) Reviewing the issues carefully protects the organization from problems that otherwise might not be addressed (and if unaddressed, could create unnecessary risks).

Organizations that have addressed these issues can and do take a number of different approaches, depending on their objectives.

One decision related to authority and locus of control has been made by "LoTech Industries." LoTech does not delegate authority (or attribute costs) for certain items to its sectors at all. These costs are for services that are controlled by the head office. Vicki, the CFO, says: "The head office makes the determination as to whether these services should be performed in-house or outsourced. We work to keep these costs at a minimum level. And to maximize our results, we try to get the sectors to focus on what they control and leave these expense decisions to us." In an Economic Value Management context, the decisions about these services are not made purely on a cost basis. Capital is also a very important consideration.[5]

The impact of Economic Value Management, versus other approaches, can be gleaned from this example. Related to locus of control, the head office's decision to outsource or not outsource these services can impact both the book capital of the firm *and* its cost structure. Often overlooked, particularly from a quantitative standpoint, but also important, decisions about costs (whether they are incurred and who controls them) can affect the *risk profile* of an organization. And thus its risk capital.

Insufficient spending can impact risk and future value. The locus of control of activities can also impact risk and future value. (This is another reason that organizational structure is an important value consideration.)

Spending on items as diverse as legal advice, advertising, and risk control can impact the organization's value creation. For example:

1. Not spending on legal advice can mean an increase in future litigation.
2. Not spending on advertising can mean a loss of future sales.
3. Not spending on risk control processes can affect future revenues and costs.

Beyond the potential income statement effects, these items also impact the organization's risk profile:

- Not spending on legal advice can mean increased litigation risk.

▪ Not spending on advertising can mean increased business risk.

▪ Not spending on risk control can mean increased business and operating risk as well.

A focus on the short term may cause organizations to make reductions in these types of expenses. From a future value perspective, however, those decisions are generally not wise. As anyone who has worked with risk capital concepts can attest, cost of the risk capital required to be held for contingencies is nearly always much higher than the cost of regular expenses that fund prevention. For example, spending adequately on legal advice upfront is usually much less expensive than the risk capital required to be held for litigation that otherwise would have been preventable.

In part because of the larger impact, some organizations structure control for items such as these in a head office. To the extent that central management determines the spending on these items, they control the effects and the risk profile of the organization. Thus, actions the central corporation or head office takes in this regard can impact the organization's cost of capital.[6] (Or, in a risk capital framework, the amount of capital the organization requires). This understanding reveals that the expense and the capital cost decisions are linked. In most organizations, the central or head office makes most financing decisions and sets the organization's standards for controlling risk within the organization. These risk mitigation efforts have a cost. When capital cost is included in measuring performance—as it is in Economic Value Management, these efforts also have an immediate *benefit:* risk mitigation reduces capital cost.

Because the expense and cost of capital issues are interwoven, as long as the expenses are not material, some organizations attribute them to the sector even though the sector does not have authority or control over them. The rationale is that the benefit the sector receives in a lower cost of capital offsets the minimal expense load. This demonstrates the linkages and trade-offs: To solve the expense attribution question, the issue must be addressed holistically and cost of capital/risk issues *must* also be addressed.

To solve the measurement dilemmas, if organizations or constituents want to understand whether a sector created value, they must first decide in what way they want to understand it (i.e., what question they are trying to answer). There are several measurement choices (not mutually exclusive or exhaustive):

1. Sector as it is, as direct revenues and charges are normally recorded

2. Sector as part of a larger organization with careful attribution

3. Sector as if a stand-alone business

4. Marginal sector performance for use in what-if calculations

5. Marginal corporation performance with and without the sector for use in what-if calculations

Before analyzing these approaches, a review of the issues involved may be useful. Because we care about value and not just isolated elements of the picture, this discussion includes all aspects of the activities of the organization: revenues, expenses, and capital cost. As Exhibit 7.14 illustrates, when an organizational structure is clear (with clear accountabilities), there are often supplier relationships between the corporate office and the sectors, and between the sectors themselves.

As the de Mello bus trip (referred to in Chapter 1) begins and seats are being assigned, sector managers begin to voice their opinions. While some sector managers may begin by saying they should not be charged for expense or capital items they do not immediately control, they will usually grant that they deserve credit for activities performed in their sector on behalf of other revenue streams. Also, they will usually admit that secondary benefits often occur from cost incurred by other sectors on their behalf. (Few argue that these benefits, at least, should be stripped away.) A careful review of the activities, as outlined, is a starting point to developing a picture of potential attribution.

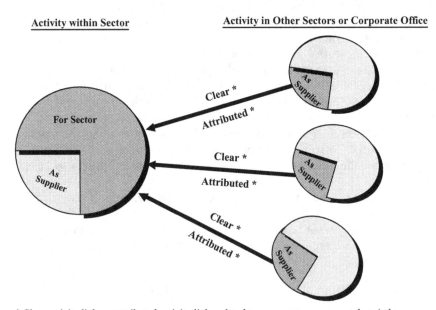

* Clear activity links or attributed activity links related to revenues, expenses, and capital

EXHIBIT 7.14   Sector Analyses

(1) Sector as It Is. Sector "as it is normally reported" is represented by the large pie on the left side of Exhibit 7.14. It presents a partial view of the sector and varies from organization to organization depending on their internal reporting structure. (It has limited usefulness other than as a starting point.)

(2) Sector as Part of a Larger Organization with Careful Attribution. This view helps determine whether the sector (defined as the series of activities that fall under the control of one manager) has created value within the context of the larger organization. The calculation of value for the sector under this view incorporates revenues, expenses, and capital. In Exhibit 7.14, this could be viewed as the four shaded areas. The sector may include capital (stores) that other sectors maintain. It may include training courses its employees attend. Some corporate functions will be clearly related to the activity of the sector. Others will represent an overhead that may be attributed to the sector using an activity-based methodology. These costs act as a corporate tax to the sector. In addition, to the extent possible, government taxes are assigned to the sector, reflecting its true benefits and costs as nearly as possible. (Related to taxes, see Chapter 5's "To WACC or Not to WACC and the Use of APV" section.). The sector may perform services for other sectors for which it will be reimbursed as well.

While the sector's activities may create the need for services from other sectors, or the corporate office, several issues rightly cause concern for sector managers:

* Control/flexibility
* Price
* Quality
* Convenience

These are no different than any other customer/supplier relationship. However, *control* is a big issue.

To address this issue, some organizations allow sectors to choose (opt in or out) on as many corporate supplied services as possible, particularly if such choices are not damaging to the organization as a whole. Economic Value Management organizations also work to manage the process so that quality, pricing, and convenience of internally supplied services will meet or beat market standards. Often this is accomplished through joint responsibility for the value-based results. For example, one Economic Value Management organization looks to its sectors to ensure that its sister operations are run excellently. If there is a problem, intervention and resolution by the affected sectors is not only allowed in the culture, it is encouraged and rewarded. (Lack of intervention meets with retribution.)

Using activity-based methods, the amount of nonspecific charges to a sector should be minimal. These charges can be viewed as representing a so-called corporate tax. Just as governments use taxes to provide protections to its constituents, the corporation can be viewed as providing protection to the sectors, often in the form of risk mitigation. For its tax dollars, the sector enjoys:

- *A lower cost of capital as part of a larger organization.* Smaller companies usually have a higher cost of capital than larger ones.

- *Lower risk, provided by the overall corporate structure.* This can also lower the sector's cost of capital or, if risk capital is used in the value calculation, lower the amount of allocated/required capital.

In determining the exact calculation of the sector's cost of capital, for these purposes, the corporation's cost of capital may or may not be a viable surrogate. Aside from clear differential risk in different sectors, one reason for modification could exist if stand-alone competitors have significantly lower costs of capital. In that case, an analysis would need to be undertaken to understand why. Such an analysis could have important strategic implications. Why and how are these lower capital costs being achieved? Another reason for analysis exists if, for example, the sectors of the organization, would, on a stand-alone basis, have widely differing costs of capital. In this case, the organization may wish to estimate a cost of capital for each sector taking into account their differential contribution to the cost and the corporate benefits outlined above. For corporations with homogeneous sectors, the corporation's cost of capital can work in many calculations. A specific cost of capital is necessary, however, when the behavioral effects would be adverse.

Another reason for analysis is to assuage sector manager anxiety. Organizations should measure the benefits of the corporate tax vis-à-vis the benefits in the form of a lower cost of capital or a smaller amount of risk capital. This can be accomplished by assessing these amounts (the cost of capital and/or the risk capital) as if the sector were stand-alone. In other words, what is the current cost of capital compared to that which must be used if the sector were stand-alone and, therefore, a small organization rather than a large one? What would the risk capital implications be if the risk mitigation efforts were not taken? Answers to these questions, of course, are essential to understanding the trade-offs. "Smartway Corp" did the analysis and found that sector managers, once they understood these issues, were much more likely to use corporate legal services for risk mitigation rather than set aside additional capital for legal issues should they arise. (Such efforts were simply more cost effective from a value standpoint.)

While the incorporation of not only the costs but also the benefits of risk mitigation is explicitly addressed in some financial institutions, their applicability is much broader. The transportation industry is one example where these techniques are applicable. It is often said that what does not get measured does not get managed. By implementing a holistic value-based approach that incorporates the benefits of risk mitigation in its measurement system, risk mitigation efforts that benefit multiple constituents are encouraged. As the World Trade Center disaster has demonstrated, understanding these issues both quantitatively and philosophically can help both government and nongovernment organizations make better choices as corporate citizens or for their citizens, as the case may be—with regard to not only the safety of employees and customers but also related to the communities in which they operate. Our discussion of product value in Chapter 8 includes discussion of approaches that all value-led organizations (government and nongovernment) should review in this regard.

(3) Sector As-If Stand-alone. This view of the sector attempts to recreate the sector performance as if the organization were a separate stand-alone organization. The calculation can be done to different levels of detail. It could include adjustments such as:

- Elimination of supplier negotiated discounts as a result of the parent affiliation
- Elimination of parent brand/image benefits
- Market-based costs for services
- Market-level reimbursement for referrals to other sectors
- Elimination of some cross-sell benefits
- Cost of capital as a stand-alone with its current size (generally calculated, if possible, including a review of other stand-alone organizations of similar size)

Since this is an as-if calculation, each organization that performs the calculation must consider the relevant elements for their particular situation.

(4) Marginal Sector Performance for What-If Calculations. Usually this calculation is undertaken at the product level, although it may be for the sector level as well. It measures the value created by capturing *additional* revenue and the marginal or variable cost (including capital cost) of capturing that revenue.

Usually sales or production volume increases in an organization require additional investments (capital) in step functions.[7] This calculation therefore may be done under different scenarios to understand value at different volume levels and to understand optimal size and growth functions as well.

(5) Corporate Performance with and without the Sector for What-If Calculations. Just as being a part of the corporation affects the measure of sector value (see contrast between 2 and 3), so too the sector's existence impacts overall corporate performance. To understand the marginal impact of eliminating the sector, corporate performance can be calculated with and without the sector.

The sector's impact on the organization, for example, may include:

* Lowering or mitigating volatility in the overall corporation. (See the section on "Integration of Techniques," subsection on "Volatility Analyses," later in this chapter.)
* The cross-sell benefits of the sector
* The expense reductions that would realistically occur if the sector were eliminated (these may be less than the costs attributed to the sector — if so, this provides valuable information for review)
* The effects of overall reduction in corporate size if the sector were eliminated
* The need for additional capital elsewhere in the corporation should the sector no longer exist

To truly understand the impacts, economic shock scenarios can also be performed to evaluate the impact of the sector on corporate performance.

Types of Adjustments

Within the organization, detailed information exists to perform analyses by sector in a robust way—including detailed equity equivalent adjustments. The details of the value calculation itself are critical from a behavioral standpoint and are often the subject of intense debate.

The section on "Types of Capital" earlier in this chapter listed five calculations using sector information. Within these five, there are two other possible calculations:

1. Sector calculations with the same adjustments that are made at the corporate level
2. Sector calculations with adjustments specific to the sector

Why might the sets of adjustments differ? Looking at a specific example may help answer this question. "Multisector Corp" was made up of multiple sectors. For most of these sectors, selling off parts of their business was an unusual, noncore event. For one sector, "Tradesect," however, the buying and selling of businesses was a key component.

As it turned out, the sales by Tradesect were immaterial to the corporation as whole. To simplify explanation of the calculation, at the corporate level Multisector chose to create a general rule to exclude all business selloffs. However, these sales were *very* material to Tradesect. Because of this materiality, and the ongoing nature of these sales for their business, Tradesect measured its value including them. This inclusion was not a free ride for the sector, however. The sales created volatility for Tradesect that was ultimately also reflected in its cost of capital.

Other reasons for differences in adjustment between the corporation and the sector include the desire to regulate behaviors at the sector level that could negatively impact the corporation as a whole, or to address an accounting issue that impacts only one sector.

For "Beehive Bank," a small sector provided government tax benefits to the corporation as a whole. To fairly measure that sector's contribution, a specific calculation was done of the tax impact of that business. An attribution of taxes paid was then made to the other businesses in proportion to their taxable income. Because they had no particular tax issues, the calculation could be done using a generally applicable rate.

When reviewing sector information for peers, the amount of disclosure by them can act as a constraint on the calculations performed. It is beneficial, however, to use as much of the disclosed information as possible to construct a value calculation for peers at the sector level as well.

Constituent Focus: The Alliance

Sector value can be one of the most important areas of analysis for all constituents. Here, the impacts of operational decisions, fluctuating environmental stresses, and the effectiveness of hands-on management can be witnessed. While sector analysis is extremely important to all constituents, the information may be difficult to obtain on an ongoing basis. In analyzing these results, the first thing observers and capital providers should do is to review previous reports of this sector information. (See Exhibits 7.15 and 7.16.) Exhibit 7.15 shows "Bridgeside Bank's" report for the year 2001. (Exhibit 7.16 shows the report for 2000.) As shown, the results, in total, for year 2000 are the same for both reports ($1,300 in both cases), but the amounts reported by sector are different. Sector A in year 2000 is shown on the 2001 report as $500. On the prior report, it was $450. To develop annual or quarterly information on a like basis requires understanding the changes in reporting. Sometimes this is difficult, particularly for outsiders. For example, if Sector A is reported on a like basis in the 2001 report at $500 and $600 in year 2000 and 2001, respectively, how can that be compared to the $400 shown for year 1999 on the 2000 report? Organizations such as Bridgeside may disclose no more than that there were "enhancements to the allocation systems" or that a "sector restructure" had taken place. Although it may be helpful to have the prior period restated, as Bridgeside did for 2000 in Exhibit 7.16, if this is the only year's information that is restated, the organization has not provided any real time history to look at. How do we think about year 1999 in Exhibit 7.16 in this context? How different would the sector results for that year appear? Organizations that provide more detail and restate the prior years' information are obviously doing a better job of disclosure. In addition, they are also demonstrating that they have a better handle on the trends in their business sectors.

Another issue important to all constituents is the way in which the organization reports corporate center results. Before determining what to report in the sector results, organizations should carefully consider the use of the corporate center. As shown in Exhibits 7.15 and 7.16, some organizations present sector information with a corporate center that may hold a negative balance. Unfortunately, it is sometimes a knee-jerk reaction of observers or capital providers to want to see all revenues, costs, and capital attributed by sector. This is not always the best practice, however. Before simply rejecting the organization's approach as flawed, observers and capital providers need to take a careful look at not only the sector information per se, but also the corporate department or corporation analysis. Questions to ask include:

- What is in here?
- Who is managing this?
- How are they managing it?

	Year 2000	Year 2001	Increase/ (Decrease)
Sector A	500	600	100
B	300	250	(50)
C	200	300	100
D	700	750	50
Corporate	(400)	(500)	(100)
Total	1,300	1,400	100

*2001 is this year and year of the current report.

EXHIBIT 7.15   Bridgeside Bank (simplified) Organizational Results—2001*

	Year 1999	Year 2000	Increase/ (Decrease)
Sector A	400	450	50
B	300	350	50
C	200	200	0
D	700	800	100
Corporate	(450)	(500)	(50)
Total	1,150	1,300	150

*2000 is the year of this report.

EXHIBIT 7.16   Bridgeside Bank (simplified) Organizational Results—2000*

Despite the elegance of having them embedded, if these amounts are not managed by the sector or specifically related to its activities, observers and capital providers are much better off with the separate entity reporting. Organizations that arbitrarily push everything out to the sectors actually may provide less useful disclosure than those that adopt the corporate center approach. If corporate treasury functions manage excess capital of the corporation, having them separated in the reporting provides observers and capital providers with very useful information. Sometimes there is also a great deal of risk in the corporate units that is better seen in the light of day than buried in several sectors. To justify any excess capital held by the corporate sector, there must be a compensating options value. To judge for themselves whether these corporate activities are prudent and represent future value potential or simply mismanagement, observers and capital providers need the distinct reporting.

Integration of Metrics

Based on the lengthy discussion on capital and adjustments, it should be clear by now that revenue, expense, and capital attribution processes are parts of the value calculation by sector. While activity based costing (ABC) information is helpful, activity based revenue and capital information are equally important as well. Most practitioners of ABC begin with the caution that ABC processes should be embarked upon with the knowledge of how the information will be used. To reap the benefits of this analysis, one must begin with the end in mind—*value creation*. That means understanding where value is created and addressing the business processes to increase value. To be effective, it is very important that revenues *and* capital are included as well. A partial review will not provide adequate information for value-added decision making. In addition, marginal and average revenue, expenses, and capital should all be considered for decision-making purposes. Many organizations make the mistake of developing average numbers alone and find that, in fact, they do not have adequate information to make the decisions they want to make.

Integration of other metrics is also important in increasing value at the sector level. What drives value will differ from sector to sector. As a result, value-based balanced scorecards that contain the value drivers of import will also differ from sector to sector. These value drivers will reflect the distinct efforts of each sector and should be developed with cognizance of the individual sector's culture to drive value-creating behaviors.

Integration of Techniques

Patterns of Value Creation. Patterns of value creation information at the sector and product levels are probably the most useful information for any constituent. As mentioned earlier, one of the biggest issues for external constituents is lack of data. However, when it can be obtained and the calculations made, the insights are extremely useful. Exhibit 7.17 depicts the sector review that "RiskLess Savings and Loan" conducted of the patterns of its value creation. As the RiskLess data shows, Sectors B through F were not on board for the first 11 months of the review, but were acquired by RiskLess over time. As opposed to the annual data used in the large corporate peer analyses conducted by Loan Depot (Exhibits 7.4 and 7.6 to 7.13), the data used by RiskLess in Exhibit 7.17 are monthly.

In contrast to the LoanDepot analysis, the RiskLess sector analysis has many data points that show positive value creation! While the later additions of business sectors adds value to RiskLess, it is clear that, of all the sectors, Sector A has created the most value over the 72-month period. Further examination of RiskLess' sector review reveals a distinct annual pattern to the value creation, with recurring patterns of peaks and valleys. Since these value numbers cut through to provide an understanding of the operating activities, they provided fodder for RiskLess to review its strategies. (In fact, organizations in the financial services sectors often, upon review of the value numbers, begin to comment on this cyclicality and its effects. These new understandings and discussions result in improvements in strategy and operations for those that see the value trends and act upon them. See the "Process and Technology" subsection in the "Applications of Metrics" section later in this chapter.) Exhibit 7.18 shows a subset of the RiskLess information from Exhibit 7.17. The total value creation of all the combined sectors since the acquisition of the second sector (i.e., the last 60 months) is plotted in this exhibit along with the value creation for Sector A alone. By looking at all sectors combined vis-à-vis Sector A, it can be seen that, in most time periods and in total, the sectors RiskLess acquired, B through F, did add additional value to the organization. Exceptions occurred in the early time periods when only a couple of the new sectors acquired were on board and also during particularly rough monthly periods for Sector A (December, three and four years ago). At those times, the acquired sectors also destroyed value (although very little). Another interesting value interaction can be seen distinctly beginning approximately two years ago, around the time of the acquisition of Sector E (see Exhibit 7.17 also). As Exhibit 7.18 shows, the total combined sector line for RiskLess is above that of Sector A throughout this period meaning the acquired sectors, B through F, combined created value. Further, the distance between the total and Sector A indicates that the largest creation of value by the new sectors occurred in the period from two years to one year ago. Because of this, the downturn experienced by Sector A during the course of that period was buffered by the other acquisitions.

Volatility Analyses. Volatility analyses are also very useful in understanding how sectors relate to each other. As Exhibit 7.17 shows, although RiskLess'

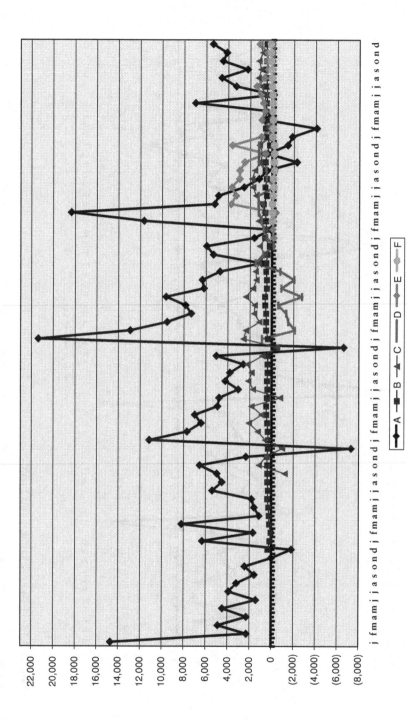

j f m a m j j a s o n d j f m a m j j a s o n d j f m a m j j a s o n d j f m a m j j a s o n d j f m a m j j a s o n d

→ A ─■─ B ─▲─ C ── D ─◆─ E ─◇─ F

EXHIBIT 7.17   RiskLess Savings and Loan's Sector Review

213

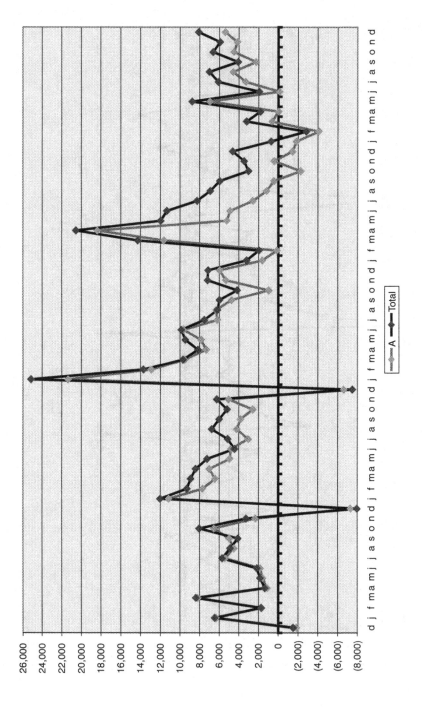

EXHIBIT 7.18 RiskLess Savings and Loan's Sector A and Total

Sector E appears more volatile than most of the other acquisitions, it trended somewhat against the performance of Sector A, particularly during its decline one year ago.

A simple volatility analysis of the sectors helps verify the extent to which our intuitions from the graph are correct. Exhibit 7.19 shows the volatility or standard deviations of each RiskLess sector and the total over the last 30 months, the last 24 months, and the last 12 months. A review of the 24-month volatility shows that, while Sector A had the highest volatility, Sector E's volatility is also large compared to the other sectors. This volatility is a measure of risk. Even in the last 12 months, Sector E has the highest volatility (excluding Sector A). In determining risk capital levels, although this volatility analysis is a small snapshot of what RiskLess examined, the trends in these data were confirmed in its other analyses and RiskLess did attribute the most capital to Sector A, on a risk basis, and the next highest level to Sector E (for more information on risk capital, see Chapter 8's section on "Types of Capital," subsection on "Risk Capital"). The far right column of Exhibit 7.19 also shows the calculation of the volatility or standard deviation of the sectors not only 12 months ago, but also for the 12 months prior to that (i.e., the 12-month period beginning two years ago

Volatility	30 Months	24 Months	12 Months	Prior 12 Months
A	4,398	4,652	3,132	5,697
B	107	97	46	126
C	423	354	231	408
D	931	569	145	457
E*	1,328*	1,328	362	1,656
F*	94*	94*	71	74*
Total	4,315	4,814	3,288	5,364
Value				
A	107,706	68,561	25,732	42,828
B	16,183	12,924	6,185	6,740
C	34,655	24,735	10,856	13,880
D	5,700	9,945	(511)	10,456
E*	31,969*	31,969	9,128	22,840
F*	(921)*	(921)*	162	(1,084)*
Total	195,291	147,213	51,552	95,661

*Sector E on board last 24 months; Sector F last 22 months.

EXHIBIT 7.19 RiskLess Savings and Loan Sector Volatility and Value (in thousands)

running to one year ago). The numbers reflect very high volatility over this one-year time horizon, as we saw graphically in Exhibit 7.17.

Notice that the volatility results for the last 12 months and the 12 months prior to that do not in any way add up to the 24-month volatility. That is because the 24-month standard deviation is measured as the differences from the average over the entire period, while each 12-month measure is a measure of value deviation from the average in that 12-month period.

There is another way that the volatility numbers don't add up. As shown in Exhibit 7.19, the volatility of all sectors (of 4,315) is less than what it would be for Sector A alone (of 4,398) over the last 30 months and only slightly higher than sector A in the last 24 and 12 months. In fact, the total volatility in the prior 12 months column (of 5,364) is also lower than Sector A alone (of 5,697). From this perspective, the sector additions have generally not significantly contributed to additional volatility and for some time periods have actually lowered the volatility.

Value creation over the time periods is also shown. Here the very positive impact of Sector E on overall value, since it came on board 24 months ago, can be seen, adding nearly $32 million ($31,969) in value. In particular, Sector E is a standout in the prior 12 month period as we noted looking at the Exhibit 7.17 graph.

Looking at the 24-month period, Sector C has also created a great deal of value, $24,735, with a very low volatility of 354.

The results of Exhibit 7.20 provide RiskLess another way to understand the impact of the acquisitions on volatility and value as well. To do this, Exhibit 7.20 provides a review of the volatility and value of all sectors in total *from the time of acquisition* of each sector. Assuming the numbers are stated in present value terms and represent *incremental* value, looking down the first column, because of the acquisition of B, RiskLess' overall value has increased $26,386; because of C, overall value has increased $57,370. If B had not been acquired, volatility would be 57 lower over the time period. If C had not been acquired, volatility would be 381 less. D, since its acquisition, has increased value by $1,118 and also decreased volatility by 106, acting as a natural hedge. Remarkably, E has also lowered overall volatility while increasing value. F is the only acquisition that to date has not added overall value for RiskLess. It has some catching up to do—since E has only been on board two months longer than F and generated $31,969 since acquisition compared to −$921 for F. To show the acquisitions over a comparable time frame, the 24-month and 12-month results are also shown. Since E came on board exactly 24 months ago, the results are the same as since inception. The overall impact on value for the 24-month period of each sector is identical to that shown in Exhibit 7.19 since the total is arrived at by adding together all of the sectors. The only sector to destroy value in the last 12 months was Sector D; Sector F was positive in that time period.

($000)		B Start	C Start	D Start	E Start	F Start	24 Months	12 Months
Total	Volatility	5,172	5,336	5,218	4,814	4,900	4,814	3,288
	Value	372,219	341,201	261,514	147,213	142,007	147,213	51,552
Total minus B	Volatility	5,115					4,793	3,306
	Value	345,834					134,288	45,367
Impact of B	Volatility	57					21	(18)
	Value	26,386					12,924	6,185
Total minus C	Volatility		4,955				4,722	3,151
	Value		283,831				122,477	40,696
Impact of C	Volatility		381				91	137
	Value		57,370				24,735	10,856
Total minus D	Volatility			5,324			4,651	3,403
	Value			260,396			137,268	52,063
Impact of D	Volatility			(106)			163	(114)
	Value			1,118			9,945	(511)
Total minus E	Volatility				4,846		4,846	3,178
	Value				115,244		115,244	42,424
Impact of E	Volatility				(32)		(32)	110
	Value				31,969		31,969	9,128
Total minus F	Volatility					4,883		3,245
	Value					142,928		51,390
Impact of F	Volatility					16		43
	Value					(921)		162

Assumption: Numbers are stated in present value terms and represent incremental value.

EXHIBIT 7.20 RiskLess Savings and Loan Impacts of Sectors*

Sector information can represent approximations of contribution or may represent the variable impact of the sector on the organization's value. At times, these numbers may be very close. The variable impact of the sector on value is the impact of variable revenue (i.e., the revenue that would go away if the sector were not present), variable cost (i.e., the costs that would go away—some shared costs might not), and the variable capital that would be eliminated. If the values shown approximate the variable sector contribution, then indeed the impacts of not making the acquisitions are appropriately reflected. Although value is the most important issue, volatility represents an interesting area as well, particularly to those who are required (or encouraged) by regulation to tie their capital to total risk.

As Exhibit 7.19 shows, the volatility of the parts is not equal to the volatility of the whole. As noted earlier, in Exhibit 7.19, for example, the total volatility of 4,814 for 24 months is not the sum of the sectors. That is because as noted on the graphs in Exhibits 7.17 and 7.18, some sectors may offset the results in other sectors—acting as a hedge and smoothing volatility. The volatility impact numbers in Exhibit 7.20 show RiskLess the result of not making *one* of the acquisitions. To show the impact of not making *two* of the acquisitions, RiskLess would have to construct a separate analysis to calculate the effects. For example, if RiskLess wanted to assess the impact of not making two of the acquisitions, B and C for example, the value and volatility of all sectors *excluding B and C* would have to be calculated. Covariance matrices could also be developed. The simple math used here, however, presents the impacts. Again, to do all of this properly, the value information needs to approximate the variable or marginal value.

Our review shows the volatility analysis does support what the graph 7.17 showed: E does act as a hedge for RiskLess, moving opposite to A during the first year on board. D also acts as a hedge, and the graph shows this. And after a rocky start, D adds value, although recently it has dipped slightly into more negative territory than we would wish.

All in all, again, the value information is most important. The volatility information, however, can help us to better understand key value drivers and risk capital requirements, as well as how various sectors relate to each other. In some organizations, these relationships are more dramatic than those present at RiskLess, with nearly opposite results in various time periods for various sectors.

In the financial services world, as organizations become more diversified, understanding these trends can alleviate a lot of heartburn. Without this understanding, organizations have made acquisitions or built sectors only to sell or eliminate them a short time later because these factors were not fully understood at the outset. Employees owe it to their boards to inform them of these issues, as well as the value ones, in advance.

Information Gap Analyses™. Information Gap Analyses™ are often performed at the sector level. For corporate-wide information needs, however, these analyses must be performed to integrate the information across sectors. Corporate-wide Information Gap Analyses™ are complex but can address major information issues. Territorial claims and lack of ownership (issues of authority and responsibility) tend to be the biggest challenges.

Whether performed at the corporate or sector level, the purpose of Information Gap Analyses™ is to provide a mechanism to protect the organization from the too frequent value leakage that occurs with information systems. In this case, value leakage takes many forms. In simple terms, the high cost of information systems is just not warranted based on the benefits received.

Information Gap Analyses™ involve an objective review of the organization's information needs, the processes that support (or do not support) these needs, and the value implications of the current processes. Information Gap Analyses™ include review of the who, what, where, when, and how of the capture, manipulation, availability, and usage of data.[8]

Exhibit 7.21 represents some of the questions that form the basis of Information Gap Analyses™. Performing first high-level and then detailed assessments, as needed, can help organizations get information systems on track—and ultimately achieve the benefits that served to justify the purchase and implementation of the system in the beginning. "BestBank" used a similar process to assess its new sector information project. Through the course of meetings, areas were identified that offered significant potential for savings and enhancements to the decision-making process by using existing infrastructure. Information Gap Analyses™ of this kind help organizations create value by providing mechanisms for the organization to:

* Assign ownership for information (one of the organization's most important assets)—whether it be information that is developed internally or externally.

* Resolve major data quality issues that either prevent the use of available information or result in bad decision making.

* Make data available that is significant but missing.

* Make data available when and as it is needed.

* Eliminate multiple forms of data that add cost with no concomitant benefit.

Tracking these issues can provide an organization with a sense of progress and better inform information strategies going forward. Doing so in a value context ensures that the data issues are appropriately prioritized based on their value impact including:

* Revenue, expense, and capital cost
* Risk capital, as appropriate

Use of the Information/Decision Context:

For what purposes is information of the kind outlined used today?

For what purposes will it be used going forward?

In detail, what is the decision process context (current and future) for each piece of data and each data calculation? Specifically, who are the users and how do they and will they use the data? Specifically, what decisions are or will be made with this information?

Data Quality Baseline:

What assessments of data quality exist today? How often are they performed and by whom?

What assessments of data quality have been envisioned for the future? What are the views related to how often they would be performed and who would perform them?

What specific measures are used or will be used to measure data quality?

What are the current assessments of data quality for each piece of data? What issues (real and perceived) are known to exist in the current data?

For each piece of data, what is the cost of gathering accurate versus inaccurate data?

Data Calculation Quality Baseline:

What assessments of data calculations have been performed and by whom? What specifically has been addressed in these assessments?

What assessments of data calculations have been envisioned for the future? What are the views related to who would perform them?

What are the current assessments of each data calculation? What issues (real and perceived) are known to exist related to them?

For each data calculation, what is the cost of developing the information best suited to the decision context versus another alternative?

Decision-Making Impacts/Consequences:

To what extent are the implications for using or not using each piece of information understood? What would have to happen to have it taken seriously?

For each piece of data specifically, if the data are not used because the quality is suspect, what is the potential impact on the specific decisions for which the data were designed? If the data are used and the quality is suspect, what is the potential impact (on average and at the tails, i.e., a catastrophic error)?

(continued)

EXHIBIT 7.21 Information Gap Analyses™ Questionnaire

EXHIBIT 7.21 Information Gap Analyses™ Questionnaire *(Continued)*

For each data calculation, if the data calculation is not used because the quality is suspect, what is the potential impact on the specific decisions for which the data were designed? If the data calculation is used and the quality is suspect, what is the potential impact (on average and at the tails, i.e., a catastrophic error)?

Use of the Information Going Forward:

For each piece of data specifically, what would need to happen to adequately assess data quality on an ongoing (rather than a spot) basis?

For each data calculation specifically, what would need to happen to adequately assess the data calculations and update them appropriately along the lines of best practice for each decision context?

For each category of information, what would need to happen to adequately assess the positive benefit of (or detrimental impact of lack of) accurate data and proper use of data calculations for decision making on an ongoing (rather than a spot) basis?

Overall, what is necessary to make this database a "killer ap" for decision making purposes?

And it ensures that data and the calculations of the data within systems are designed to support the organization's needs from a value decision-making standpoint.

In addition to the organization itself, Information Gap Analyses™ should be undertaken by other constituents as well, including investors, suppliers, employees, and customers. These assessments should address the constituent's own use of the information, the quality of data, and its availability. Investors and others who calculate the organization's value creation for themselves will be able to assess information gaps as they perform their own manipulations of the data. In addition, constituents can and should rank peers on the information they provide, including its quality and availability as well.

Statistical Prediction Rules. Statistical Prediction Rules (SPRs) are generally developed at a more specific level than that of the sector. Sometimes, however, they may be used by an entire sector to forecast customer demand or potential losses based on econometrics (multifactor economic value driver models). "TechBank.Com," which regularly uses SPRs at the sector level, uses econometric modeling to not only forecast its anticipated revenues, expense, and capital requirements, but also to determine its organization and human resources planning and facility requirements.

Market Value Analysis. Market value analysis is related to understanding market expectations for an organization. At the sector level, there are generally no market prices per se. Stand-alone peers, in similar businesses as those of the sectors of a conglomerate, however, can be analyzed to understand market expectations of value creation for firms in that general industry. This information can then be compared to the sector's performance.

Pictures. Exhibits 7.17 and 7.18 for RiskLess show some of the uses of graphing. Similar graphs can be constructed to compare a specific sector to other sectors of the organization, similar sectors of peers, or stand-alone peers in similar businesses.

ValueMap™. The ValueMap™, at the sector level, is similar to that at the total level, with value information for each constituent in numerical, graphic, and written form. The three-way mirror (Exhibit 6.8) provides an outline of some of the relevant information that is addressed at the sector level.

Applications of Metrics

Performance Assessment and Strategy. Value is the quintessential tool for performance assessment. Understanding sector value and sector interactions is key to evaluating the organization's ability to add value into the future. As discussed earlier, different calculations may be needed to answer different questions. For example:

- How much value would this unit create stand-alone?
- How much value did it create generically?
- How much value would be lost if it were sold?

This performance assessment, as noted earlier, should also include sector peer analyses. How well have similar sectors of peers performed, from a value perspective? How well have stand-alone peers in the same sector business performed?

In addition to understanding how much value the sector has created vis-à-vis its peers, to understand its strategic options, an organization will also want to assess how much value would be lost if the sector were sold (a marginal analysis) and the potential value of the sector to another buyer.

For example, another organization, purchasing the sector, might be able to generate more value from it. They also might achieve volatility benefits that add value to the overall organization. (As noted in the explanation of Exhibit 7.20, different sectors have different impacts on overall organizational volatility. As with value interactions and synergies, this is due to the distinct attributes of the sectors and their unique combinations.)

Although the value impact is primary, understanding the volatility impact for prospective buyers can be useful in performing the overall analysis. It may be argued that diversification of risk or amelioration of volatility through acquisition of the sector by another organization is not that important since many investors are able to create the same diversification in their own portfolios and do not need an organization to do it for them. However, the importance of volatility is also influenced by other factors as well:

 Some investors may not be able to diversify, for example corporate management (a reason to not provide large stock grants or options on the stock of their own organization since their ability to diversify may be limited, giving them different aims than the average investor).

 Information gaps may, in reality, prevent outside investors from efficiently hedging the risks or adequately diversifying them.

 Where risk capital is involved, lower overall volatility may lower regulatory capital requirements and thus capital cost, making these factors important in overall value creation.

Whether volatility per se is a factor, the value implications of sector interactions are pertinent. Organizations often find it useful to add sectors that capitalize on the existing infrastructure and customer base thereby enhancing revenues while expenses and capital costs are spread over multiple sectors.

Organizations can inadvertently make the grave mistake when first beginning the sector value assessment process to rush into decisions about which sectors to keep. There can be a natural inclination toward using the value information to immediately decide which businesses to be in. (Many a consultant has suggested it.) Rather than rushing to such conclusions, however, the value assessment information should be used *first* to inform strategies to improve a sector's value performance. After all, prior to the measurement, the information to inform strategy adequately and provide necessary feedback was not available. First, sectors need to be given the opportunity to improve value creation. Only after the sector has had sufficient opportunity to improve value creation should assessments be made related to its fate. In addition to avoiding decisions that may not ultimately be in their own best interest, this approach also helps to address resistance to *new insights*. What sector managers would want to develop value information only to have it used to immediately dispose of their business (and their job)? By focusing first on value improvement and then on sector alignment, not only employees, but all the organization's constituents win.

Process and Technology. Information Gap Analyses™, often performed at the sector level, can also be used to enhance value through improvement in the use of technology. Line item analyses, for example specific revenue, expense or capital items that are part of the sector value equation, can provide important insights for improving the sectors' processes and overall value creation. Many organizations have found that developing value calculations for the sectors generates numerous process improvement ideas.

One organization held meetings with each sector to discuss the metrics and their implications. While in the meetings, operating managers were able to generate many ideas to add value, including numerous process improvements. These ideas included not only cost savings and efficiency improvements, but also better ways to handle processes to enhance revenues and lower capital costs. As mentioned in the section on "Integration of Techniques," subsection "Patterns of Value Creation," organizations in similar industries looking at sector value analysis for their industry for the first time often have similar insights. "CrescentCiti Savings," which operates in a financial services sector similar to that of RiskLess, immediately recognized the cyclical trends in its business upon review of its own value information. This review sparked not only new insights into the business, but also ideas to help improve the organization's processes. The patterns of value creation sparked further realizations as well. Not only were there annual patterns of value creation but also patterns over the course of the month. CrescentCiti managers discovered that by changing longstanding procedures, they could reduce costs and improve quality while also lowering overall volatility. A TQM-type analysis would produce similar understanding from the bottom up (charting the volatility of each distinct process). Starting with the sector value analysis provides the big picture context that can then be used to drill down to individual processes. Using value as the starting point provides resolution and understanding of the relationship of the parts to the whole. In this way, the value enhancements to processes are completely harmonious with TQM enhancements. Both TQM and value provide a range of insights. They not only consider the insights available in the study of the results (the numbers, the percents), but also in the study of change (or volatility).

Organizational Structure. Understanding whether and how the sector has added value also helps the organization to structure support mechanisms and carefully think through the issues of accountability. Balanced accountability and ownership, responsibility and authority are necessary to value creation. Going through the process of sector value assessments provides organizations with insights on organizational structure that otherwise might not be addressed. Understanding how the operations interact from a value and volatility standpoint provide insights into potential overlaps, downtimes versus crunch times from an operating perspective, and the potential to create organizational realignments that take advantage of this information. For example, can operational management resources be more efficiently placed in charge of the work of two sectors, taking advantage of the new understandings? These considerations represent opportunities for redesign of organizational structures that create value. (See also Chapter 9's section on "Value Drivers," "Applications of Metrics," "Organizational Structure" for additional discussion.)

Rewards Process. Sector value creation should form the primary basis for sector manager compensation. Where a sole focus on their own sector would act against the benefit of the organization, a portion of compensation should also be based on the value creation of the overall firm. Compensation should be based on improvement over a multiyear period. And that improvement should be in the context of the sector's performance as compared to similar sectors in other organizations. By developing value improvement as the measure, managers are encouraged, as is the whole organization, to do their best with what they have to work with. As Michael, the CEO of "Branford Industries" remarked, "By constructing a reward process in this manner, the arbitrariness used to determine who gets paid what based on whom they lunched with is eliminated." A speaker at a recent American Association of Bank Directors (AABD) conference stated that objective measures are identified with high performance firms. Sector value improvement measures are the most objective and comprehensive measures available. If constructed based on the encouragement of desired behaviors, the elimination of easy manipulation, and the consideration of all aspects of performance, return and growth (revenue, expense, and capital), as they should be, they are indeed best suited to be that objective measure.

Exhibit 7.22 shows an incentive plan designed for one sector of "WindiCiti Savings." The box on the bottom left of the exhibit and the graph show the impacts on compensation based on the sector's projected value creation. The new value plan includes a bonus *holdback,* or vesting concept, to ensure sustainable value creation and to help retain the value creators. Thus the amount paid in the first year to managers of the sector (value bonus paid of $1,200 (i.e., $1.2 million) is less than the amount declared (value bonus declared of $2,400). By year 5, the amount projected to be paid of $2,300 exceeds the amount declared of $2,000 because of the payout of bonus earned in prior periods.

WindiCiti's calculation of value for the sector's reward process is a specific calculation, designed to encourage value-creating behaviors. Tom, the CEO of WindiCiti, remarked: "The calculation of value was designed carefully for the incentive programs we put in place for each sector. It is natural for managers to want to game a system. Work was done to ensure the calculations of value for reward purposes were fair, were not manipulatable, and would drive the right behavior. In other words, behavior that would maximize sustainable value over time."

The plan for WindiCiti's sector is designed with an understanding of both the value that might be obtained and the volatility that might be experienced by plan participants. In constructing the plan, scenarios were run to understand the likelihood of certain bonus payouts, since the objective of

($000)

Plan Parameters

Target Bonus	2,000
50th Percentile Value Improvement	10,000

Industry Performance

How often has industry achieved 50th percentile? 2 out of 5 years

Outlook: Concerns in industry about credit losses threatening sustainable long-term profitability

Value versus Prior Plan—Last Year

Prior Plan Adjusted Net Income	45,000
Prior Plan Payout	50%
Value Improvement	(8,000)
Value Plan Payout	0%
Value Plan Balance	(1,500)

5-Year Strategic Plan	Year 1	Year 2	Year 3	Year 4	Year 5
Pre-Tax Net Income	60,000	100,000	120,000	150,000	180,000
Value	23,000	33,500	40,000	54,000	64,000
Value Improvement	12,000	10,500	6,500	14,000	10,000
Value Bonus Declared	2,400	2,100	1,300	2,800	2,000
Value Bonus Paid	1,200	1,600	1,800	2,200	2,300

EXHIBIT 7.22 WindiCiti Plan Illustration

the compensation plan is to "incent properly." Tom remarks: "On the one hand, we did not want to over pay. On the other hand, we wanted to drive behavior, not demotivate. In this sense, the holdback or vesting concept serves multiple functions. It is important as a retention vehicle. It acts as an enforcer from a sustainability viewpoint. And it helps smooth volatility. The value results are much more volatile than earnings are. The vesting helps smooth volatility in the plan, which might otherwise be objectionable to employees. We are also pleased with our ability to clearly demonstrate true pay for performance. It is significant that the use of value creation and the design of the plan allow us the ability to demonstrate the relationship among value created, improvement in value creation, and the bonuses earned and paid. For example, $23,000 represents the all-in costs, including capital costs, and the total amount of value that has been created by the end of year 1. $12,000 represents the value improvement from the prior year, a significant increase. Of that, four-fifths goes to investors and one-fifth ($2,400 bonus declared) goes to compensation. Further, before there is positive value improvement in a subsequent year, the improvement in value from the year before will have to *continue* to be created in all subsequent years as well. From that perspective, managers are only sharing about 2% of the *sustainable* value improvement (i.e., 2% of the *additional* value they have created)."[9]

The ability to quantify the relationship between bonus and value creation is significant. This tool gives boards and top management an eagle's eye view of true pay for performance. As shown here, the WindiCiti plan is constructed so that sector management shares in just a fraction of the value produced and yet, in this case, is incented in a healthy enough fashion for them to wish to add as much value as possible.

Training and Communication. At the sector level, to increase the momentum behind value creation, it is very important that targeted messages be developed by each sector for its employees. Truly seeing how the sector is performing is essential to generating the momentum for increased value. It provides a mechanism to generate the ideas and actions that will fuel the value creation process. As discussed in the process and technology section, these communication forums often provide the give and take many individuals need to connect the numbers with new insights and value-creating initiatives.

With the insights about peers and sectors in hand, what can value metrics teach us about products, services, distribution channels, and processes?

NOTES

1. The standard deviations calculated are population standard deviations. If inferences for the future were to be drawn, sample standard deviations could be calculated.

2. Robert G. Hagstrom, Jr., *The Warren Buffet Way,* New York: John Wiley & Sons, 1995.

3. Herb Greenberg, "Silent Warning: When Companies Clam Up, Trouble May Lie Ahead," *Fortune,* October 1, 2001.

4. For example, what has been the effect of the philanthropic efforts? What has been the effect of the counseling efforts? Ordinal statistics can be used to calculate value by sector and compare the results to peers. See also Chapter 6's section on "Types of Organizations and Capital Terminology."

5. See also Chapter 6's section on "Types of Capital." This is not a new concept; costs and capital are often linked. As noted in the discussion on human capital in Chapter 6, certain costs for accounting purposes are, in reality, investments in the future. Strategic investments that provide unique advantages to customers, employees, or suppliers may be costs for accounting purposes, but from a value perspective are capital in nature.

6. Depending on one's views of cost of capital. See Chapter 6's section on "Cost of Capital."

7. *Step function* refers to the fact that capital investment must often be made in chunks or blocks. Computer capacity is one example. As volume increases, one is not able to purchase the exact computer capacity one needs. Rather, one must buy it in some increment. This is called a step function because graphically it is not a smooth 45-degree angle line; rather, it looks like a staircase.

8. I am indebted to Mary Ann Beach for her insights on this topic.

9. Approximately 2% of the additional value, calculated on an NPV basis into perpetuity.

CHAPTER 8

Placing Detailed Evaluations in Context: Product, Service, Distribution Channel, and Process

Measurement at the product, service, distribution-channel, and process level is even more complex than it is at the sector level. The issues of the measures themselves, the attributions that may be required, and the care in decisions made based on these numbers, which were discussed for sectors, are amplified at the product, service, distribution-channel, and process levels.

Although the issues are greater as more finite levels (i.e., products, etc.) are measured, one advantage (if it can be characterized as such) is that there are often less clear or powerful champions at these levels. Because there are often no equivalents to sector leaders, the discussions may, in fact, be quieter. The advantage comes with a related disadvantage. Because there are fewer clear or powerful champions, there may be a tendency toward impatience in working through issues to develop meaningful information. The purpose of the results must be kept at the forefront to achieve an appropriate, efficient, and balanced approach.

This chapter will discuss the answer to Question 4 (see Exhibit 8.1) and explain the metrics choices and uses as outlined in Exhibits 8.2 and 8.3.

Evaluative

1. Has the organization added value? How much?
2. How does this compare to the organization's peers and competitors?
3. Has the organization been managed such that each sector has added value?

You Are Here ⟩ 4. Has the organization been managed such that each product, service, distribution channel, or process added value?

EXHIBIT 8.1 The Questions

(continued)

EXHIBIT 8.1 The Questions *(Continued)*

5. Has the organization been managed such that each customer relationship added value?
6. What are the major drivers of value creation for the organization?
7. For all of the above, how has this changed over time?

Predictive

8. How much value does the organization expect to create?
9. How much value do capital providers (shareholders, if publicly traded) expect the organization to create?
10. How much value does the organization expect to create by sector, product, service, distribution channel, process, and customer?
11. What are the expectations related to the major drivers of value creation over time?
12. What are the capital provider's expectations for the organization's peers? What are the peer's expectations for itself by sector, product, service, distribution channel, process, customer, and major drivers of value creation?
13. How do internal, peer, and capital provider expectations differ from current steady-state value creations?
14. For all of the above, how will this change over time?

Metric Characteristics:	From (Traditional Implementation)	To (Economic Value Management)
Time	Evaluative, Primarily Annual	Evaluative and Predictive, Variable Time Periods
Type of Capital	Debt and Equity	Multiple Types of Capital
Form of Metric	Dollars or Percents	Dollars, Percents, Standard Deviation, i.e., Multiple Forms
Types of Adjustments	Simple	Simple and Complex
Measurement and Management Perspectives:		
Constituent Focus	Shareholder	Alliance of Constituents
Integrating Metrics	None or Few	Multiple—Optimal Number
Integrating Techniques	None	Multiple
Applications of Metrics	Strategic, Valuation	Broad Applications

EXHIBIT 8.2 How Economic Value Management Differs: Evolution of Value Practices

Metric Characteristics:

Time	Types of Capital	Form of Metric	Types of Adjustments

▓ Evaluative and/or predictive
▓ Time horizon
	▓ Debt or equity
	▓ Equity
	▓ Special case equity equivalents
	  – Human
	  – Customer
	  – Product
	▓ Regulatory
	▓ Risk
	▓ Cost of capital
	▓ Market value/ purchase price
	▓ Taxes, dues
		▓ Dollar
		▓ Percentage
		▓ Standard deviation
			▓ Availability
			▓ Complexity
			▓ Fixed/changed boundaries
			▓ Options value

Measurement and Management Perspectives:

Constituent Focus	Integration of Metrics	Integration of Techniques	Applications of Metrics

▓ Community and external governance
▓ Providers of capital
▓ Suppliers
▓ Consumers
▓ Observers/ critics (see Exhibit 6.3)
	▓ Value drivers (the value-based balanced scorecard)
	  – Relationship
	  – Process
	  – Choices
	▓ Activity-based information
	  – Cost, revenue, capital
	▓ TQM process measures
		▓ Patterns of value creation
		  – Trend and regression analysis
		▓ Volatility analyses
		▓ Information Gap Analyses™
		▓ Statistical prediction rules
		▓ Market value analysis
		▓ Pictures
		▓ Scenario planning
		▓ Monte Carlo simulations
		▓ ValueMap™
			The Wheel™:
			▓ Performance assessment
			▓ Strategy
			▓ Process and technology
			▓ Organizational structure
			▓ Rewards process
			▓ Training and communication (see Exhibit 6.4)

EXHIBIT 8.3 Economic Value Management: Metric Choices and Uses

TIME

While organizations may continually reorganize and sectors may come and go, this is even more the case in the product and service area. In terms of distribution channels, technology has provided the impetus for much change. The Internet, for example, has created an additional distribution channel for many organizations, including organizations such as churches and the government. Often, to fully understand the impact of a product, service, distribution channel, or process, an organization must measure more than its own results at that level. To be understood fully, the measurement must be placed in context and reviewed over a sufficient time period. To gain the best understandings and monitoring capabilities:

- An organization knows how its peers have done with the specific (or similar) distribution channel, process, product, or service.

- An organization places the results of its products, services, and so forth, in context. To do this, the results of products, services, distribution channels or processes, and the organization as a whole, and their inter-actions over time, are understood. What are the value and volatility interactions? To what extent are there synergies and/or cannibalization among products, services, distribution channels, or processes? (See sector discussion in Chapter 7 for more on this.)

- To the degree possible, the results of peer products, services, distribution channels, or processes are placed in context (in terms of their inter-actions within the peer organization over time).

- The impacts of product, service, distribution channel, and process offerings on constituents, particularly customers, are assessed over time.

It is easy for information that is misapplied to misguide rather than illuminate (as discussed in Chapter 5's section on "Choosing the Measures: Dollars and Percents"). At increasingly finite levels, this becomes even more true as the tendency exists to want to witness the part, the more finite piece, separate from the whole. This natural tendency exists because of the desire to break the pieces into small enough parts so that action can be taken. To gain real insights, this tendency must be balanced.

To understand the part, the context (or the whole) must be understood as well. The example of Peer 5 related to board oversight of the rewards process demonstrates the importance of context in understanding value creation. (See Chapter 7's "Peer" section, "Application of Metrics: Rewards Process" subsection.) To be useful, it is important that the impact of products, services, distribution channels, and processes be placed in the larger context. To acquire this understanding requires discernment. While there are no magic bullets, there are more complete views.

The importance of context is demonstrated in the benefits organizations and constituents obtain in understanding value from the perspectives of other constituents as well. This is a matter of understanding value from many perspectives and, thus, understanding it more fully. The benefits of concepts like the balanced scorecard are in drawing multiple perspectives into the understanding of the whole. Value driver information also must be put in the context of overall value creation.

Placing product, service, distribution channel, and process information in context over time does not only apply to the corporate sector. It is important that governments and nonprofits have the will to reevaluate the effectiveness of services over time and develop the capabilities and will to do so. This is particularly true as government uses private entities to distribute and carry out its missions (i.e., by exploring alternative distribution channels). For what services do private entities make sense? Where do public servants with public aims better serve long-term stewardship?

Just as in sector analysis, frequent changes over time can make it difficult to consistently understand value creation at the product and service level or distribution-channel level. To achieve a consistent understanding, allocation issues must be addressed below the total organization level. (See particularly Chapter 7's "Sector" sections on "Time" and "Types of Capital.") At the product, service, distribution-channel, and process levels, understanding the purpose of the information is necessary so that information is not misapplied and can be used to generate true insights.

TYPES OF CAPITAL

Multiple forms of capital may be used to analyze the value creation of products, services, distribution channels, and processes. For many organizations, it can make sense to view these slices of the data first, as if entirely equity financed, and then layer on the financing aspects of the operations (for example, the use of debt obligations and the concomitant tax benefits). (For others a WACC approach may be simpler; see Chapter 5's "To WACC Or Not to WACC and the Use of APV" section.)

Equity equivalents (such as human resource or marketing investments) may or may not already be attributed at the product or distribution channel. To address this, the components of sector or corporate capital may have to be broken down. (See "Integration of Metrics" section later in this chapter.)

Risk Capital

One capital area that is often performed at the product or process level is risk capital analysis. Chapter 6's "Types of Capital" section provides an introductory discussion of what is meant by risk capital. While a general measure of value creation is based on the capital an organization has available to it, the purpose of risk analyses is to understand the value created based on a level of capital determined by the riskiness of the organization. These risk analyses can be conducted for the organization itself, peers, sectors, products, distribution channels, processes, and so forth. In each case, value is based on a capital level determined by risk. This value represents a reward less a charge for the risk taken on.

Risk analyses are of interest to all kinds of organizations. As a matter of practice, many financial institutions use risk as the basis of attributing capital to products. These measurements are then aggregated to arrive at sector attributions and measurement of sector value. Other kinds of organizations also benefit from a review and attribution on this basis. One important reason is highlighted when events like extremely damaging floods, earthquakes, military crises, unanticipated business cycle reversals, or terrorist attacks take place. When events like these occur, the understanding of an organization's consistent value creation based on the capital it has on board can be disrupted. Risk capital analyses attempt to quantify value creation with an amortization of these risk costs. This is done by holding capital as a cushion for risk and charging for that capital. As noted earlier, quantification can help to encourage risk mitigation efforts. (See also Chapter 6's "Risk Capital" section for a definition of expected risk and unexpected risk and the relationship to this capital discussion.)

In particular, the issue of risk capital can be important in analyzing peers. For example, suppose Peer A and Peer B produce similar kinds of results, with a similar capital base. Unlike Peer A, Peer B has purchased an insurance policy that covers major business interruptions. The costs of the premiums for that policy are deducted from Peer B's earnings on an ongoing basis. It might appear Peer A is getting a "free ride." If one of the unexpected events mentioned above occurs and the firm's insurance policy covers those losses, Peer A's requirements for capital will be higher than Peer B's. Peer A will have to pay the losses out of its capital. In answering the questions of value creation, we often want to know what value is created with the capital on board. And we want to know what value is created when capital is placed on a like basis given the risks taken on. Or stated another way, what value is created if our capital level were high enough to cushion for a given level of risk?

In choosing what the organization is and is not, what activities it will engage in and how, executive management and the board of directors determine the risk level of their organizations. This process is conscious in some organizations and less so in others. In either case, the impact, in some measure, influences all constituents, even investors, albeit less directly.

While risks that are specific are often discussed as irrelevant to investors, there are ways in which we can understand their relevance to investors and to other constituents as well. In deciding whether to purchase Enron, for example, understanding these *specific* risks were very relevant to prospective investors. Market-related and specific risks become intertwined when some organizations hedge or otherwise address the risks that they understand best and when some organizations in the very same situation do not. What investors were exposed to if they invested in Enron, for example, were the ways in which Enron chose to manage their risks. While many of the risks Enron faced were *market related,* how Enron chose to address those risks was *specific.* Enron is an example of a firm that most would say in 2000 and 2001 held less capital than most investors and creditors would consider (in hindsight) adequate vis-à-vis the risks they had taken on. Those who invested in Enron were subject to returns for that stock based, in part, on Enron's decision to hold less capital than required, to avoid bankruptcy court and to handle a given change in markets or energy prices, or to cushion the *specific* risk effects that are generally called reputation risk. Because of the specific choices made by Enron, and its level of disclosure, investors and third parties, such as rating agencies and analysts, did not adequately understand the risks. If, however, all had been performing risk capital analyses, they would have been better positioned to forecast potential problems. Because the risks were relatively unstudied, the issues that emerged came as a surprise to many constituent groups, including investors, employees, and customers; because of the surprise, the natural reaction to the risks once known was even more severe than it otherwise might have been.

In some instances, even more than investors, other constituents may not be able to easily diversify. Many employee-hiring requirements do not allow employees to work for multiple businesses. Because employees often work for one or at most two firms, they may suffer if the organizations they work for suffer as part of a crisis, whether the risks involved are market related or idiosyncratic. Similarly, suppliers may not be able to diversify away the specific risks of their customer firms. And customers may also suffer if their supplier relationships are disrupted. (See also the FRO company example in Chapter 7's section on "Sectors.") Constituents, therefore, *are* concerned not only about market-related risk but about total risk, including idiosyncratic risk. Since these constituents are integral to future value creation, these perspectives are important to diversified investors as well.

Before discussing the methods of calculation and their application, an understanding of the different purposes of these analyses is important. Exhibit 8.4 demonstrates the key uses of risk capital.

There are two primary ways in which risk capital is conceived. One way is as a mechanism for setting a target or ideal capital level (i.e., a certain level of capital associated with a given level of risk in the business). Another way it is conceived is as a mechanism for apportioning existing capital. Measuring value at a granular level includes an estimate of capital used at a granular level. One way to understand capital at a granular level is to understand risks at that level and those risks relative to the other risks that are taken on.

Two Views / Conceptions
* Set target or ideal capital level
* Apportion existing capital based on risk

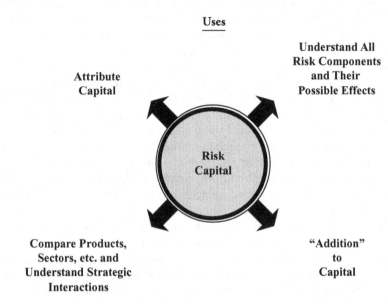

EXHIBIT 8.4   Risk Capital Purposes

These two primary ways of conceiving risk capital act as filters or lenses for discussing the subject. It is useful to be clear about these lenses to understand the value and benefits of the metrics themselves. This is particularly true because often it is so-called quantitative experts who will derive the risk capital calculations. As a means of evaluating the validity of their modeling assumptions, it is often helpful to discuss in depth the ways in which risk capital is conceived.

Risk capital analyses are used in several ways. One way is to attribute capital based on the relative riskiness of the sector, product, and the like, frequently by taking current capital and dividing or attributing it on the basis of relative risk. Financial services firms often do this when they are meeting the sector reporting requirements of FAS 131.

In other cases, an organization may conduct an overall review of its capital levels based on the risk it has taken on. This is a sound practice for any organization. It is important to remember, however, that no matter how much the "quants" cloak the answers in solemnity, with reams of backup detail, these are just forecasts or estimates; *noting the assumptions is advisable*. Although fraught with difficulties, it *is* a useful exercise as the case of Enron showed. A measure of the riskiness of its trading business would have been useful to all constituents—and would have demonstrated how under-capitalized Enron was in terms of its trading operations and general business exposures. So, in that regard, the inquiry is worth the journey it creates. Whether overall risk capital is viewed as equal to existing capital or at an ideal level that is greater or less than existing capital, the risk attribution process creates differences between the amount of risk capital and the amounts of more traditional measures of capital at units below the total. These differences provide the bases for very informative analyses.

"Alfrisco Corp" used risk attribution methodologies for its retail operations. Alfrisco discovered that it could run business models with very different levels of cash capital but similar risk capital requirements. They also found, in other instances, that they could run the business with similar cash capital employment but very different risk capital requirements. Both analyses pointed to strategic opportunities. Elizabeth, the CFO, explains, "We began to ask whether the cash capital could be decreased and still achieve the same risk-adjusted return. The analyses pointed to areas where the search could begin. We also wondered, with a similar cash capital investment, which business model would be most beneficial. Are we undercapitalized? Can we and should we leverage (or de-leverage) our business model? The analyses gave us the answers we needed."

Risk capital analyses are also used as an *addition to capital*. Sometimes this addition to capital is viewed as an amount required to achieve an ideal level of capital given the risk in the business. At other times, the view is as an addendum to the more traditional capital analyses. Like human, customer, or product capital, equity equivalents can be used to encourage behavioral benefits. In this case, the addition to capital represents an estimate of risk into the future that can be capitalized and whose cost therefore can be amortized over time. An analogy to this use of risk capital is the purchase of an insurance policy. An insurance policy can be viewed as a mechanism by which risk cost is amortized over time. The amount of premiums paid monthly (quarterly or annually) represents the amortized cost of risk. Policy coverage limits represent the amount of risk being covered by the premium charge. Similarly, in this use of risk capital, the risk capital represents the amount of risk coverage; the charge for the cost of risk capital is analogous to the monthly insurance premium.

From a behavioral standpoint, the use of risk capital, whether as attributional or additive, represents behavioral benefits in sensitizing managers to risk in their decision making and ensuring adequate returns for the risk taken on. Certainly trade-off decisions related to enhancing operations are made on a much sounder basis than simply a cost that may be eliminated with no near-term consequences in the metrics being used. For example, "Bruno Financial" measured its risk capital requirements for its lines of business. A common issue was that caused by a regulatory mind-set, Bruno focused primarily on credit risk (with little in the way of market risk) in assessing capital requirements. "We don't need [risk] capital in the trust business," Rocky, the head of Bruno's multibillion-dollar assets-under-management business, stated. Despite this, and perhaps because of it, the organization's executives were always surprised when the company experienced volatility or had large unexpected losses in the business. No risk? (All business has risk.)

"Camelia Bank," which also measured its risk capital, included a broader definition of risk for these purposes. In its investment and trust area, capital was attributed for the risks taken on, including significant operational risks. These operational risks included trading settlement and accounting risks and investor litigation risks. Once those risks were understood and included as a part of a capital charge, they provided a mechanism for decision making. Should the organization self-fund the risk? Or should it offload some of the risk via insurance policies or other mechanisms? Quantifying the potential capital cost provided a basis for understanding the risk and a way to frame the problem for decision-making purposes. With this frame, Camelia could determine the appropriate actions to take, what to insure, and so forth.

Another way in which risk capital is used is in analyses designed to better understand risk and its possible effects. Unlike measures of cost of capital that are most often performed on risk related to the market (i.e., risk that cannot be diversified away), risk capital is generally based on both systematic and unsystematic risk, both diversifiable and nondiversifiable, and specific and market related. Since risk capital provides a quantitative summary of risk, the study of risk capital can provide a vehicle for understanding a number of risk components. This is generally done two ways. One is to postulate a number of sources of risk (credit, market, operating, and the like) and then to assign a value or amount to the risk type.

Another way is to study risk more generally, quantify it, and dissect the numerical information to determine and categorize the sources of risk. Using both approaches (rather than one or the other) can, in fact, yield the best information and most complete understanding of all risk components and their possible effects.

Another way risk capital is used is to compare sectors, products, distribution channels, and so forth, and to understand their strategic interactions. These analyses allow the organization to make trade-offs between not only return scenarios but also alternative risk scenarios and to understand the interactions between return and risk in a more robust way. As noted in Chapter 7's "Sector" section, "Integration of Techniques": "Volatility Analyses" subsection, understanding volatility and risk interactions can be of practical use in understanding value creation and improving it. Risk capital provides a way to accomplish these analyses. When an organization, for example, measures overall risk capital and then drills down to individual units applying similar methodologies, it is possible to chart variances, correlations, and covariances.

Rather than create a belief system, the organization is able to numerically *probe* interactions and better understand them. This approach also provides the organization a framework to experiment and measure the impact on a return and a risk basis of alternative business models, as noted in the discussion of Alfrisco Corp's use in assessing its retail operations (earlier in this section). Other examples include analyses to understand the multiple impacts of a divestiture or acquisition, or exploring the potential impacts of a reorganization. Again, these are decisions that organizations often make by forecasting earnings impacts. The risk impacts that are often ignored in the quantitative analyses are often key to the success or failure of the endeavor. Because risk capital analyses, at their best, attempt to address all risks, these analyses can provide more robust understanding of future effects. While the benefits are clear, some organizations are reluctant to tap into these potential information sources because of the changes that may ensue. For example, as every dot.com or company that really needs it knows, funding can be a primary source of risk. Being able to diversify funding sources can be valuable. While for most institutions, relatively stable sources of funding may exist, financial institutions with a deposit base as a source of funding face a number of risks. One is operational risk associated with detailed record keeping. Another, for demand deposits, is the ability of deposit funders to pull funding at any time. Some financial institutions explicitly recognize these very important risks. Those who narrowly focus on credit risk do not adequately include these risks, thus failing to best understand not only risk components, but also the strategic interactions among sectors, products, and the like. Cheap or easy-to-obtain sources of funding can be volatile and contain important risks that should be identified and quantified.

As a practical matter, organizations approach calculations for risk capital in different ways. Some organizations believe that their *on-books,* or regulatory required capital are sufficient proxies for risk capital (see Exhibit 8.5). For the reasons shown, these approaches are not sufficient. "Partisan Electric" focused on on-books capital in its decision making. Because of this focus, the organization determined that rather than expand its operations by continuing to hold real assets and sell the production from them, a trading business would require less capital. In terms of real assets, the assessment was correct. In terms of risk capital and the true business cycle requirements, it could not have been more wrong. The organization eventually went bankrupt. Because the use of risk capital concepts were not pervasive at the time, the media, analysts, customers, and employees did not focus on the risk capital requirements of the firm. While the lack of proper assessment of the risks of the trading business represents just one factor in Partisan Electric's demise, a more general assessment of risk capital for the overall firm, including assessments of business, operating, reputational, management, cultural, and other risks, would have provided an early, complete, and ugly picture of the organization's business prospects. (Dr. Robert Earle, a utilities markets

Approach	Implication/Issue	Outcome
Use of On-Books Capital in All Analyses	Lack of adequate methodologies to ascertain risk and to understand risk implications of decision-making.	Potential significant issues where disconnects between on-books and risk capital exist.
Use of Regulatory Capital	While risk measures exist, they are inadequate, inconsistent, and change based on agreed upon regulatory standards. Like accounting, regulatory capital is rules based. As the rules evolve and become more risk related, other issues emerge. Viewed as a standardized benchmark, motivation is to decrease the amount as much as possible. This can create noneconomic effects.	Potential significant issues where disconnects between risk and regulatory capital are dramatic.

EXHIBIT 8.5 Can On-Books or Regulatory Capital Act as a Proxy for Risk Capital?

expert, states: "This is what has happened with some public utilities. For various reasons, many stopped building power plants in the 1980s and '90s. Buying power on the market was viewed as safer from a returns point of view, and required little direct capital. As many have found out over the past few years, they were really putting a lot of capital at risk, so they have had to deal with credit downgrades, bankruptcy, and so forth. What's surprising is that some of the ratings firms didn't realize this until Enron.")

"Partisan Electric" was not subject to regulatory capital requirements. What about the use of regulatory schemes, if they are available? Some organizations believe that regulatory schemes are sufficient mechanisms for assessing risk capital. On the surface, this makes sense. Regulatory schemes applicable to certain industries establish minimum capital standards. (See also Chapter 6's "Types of Capital" section.) The purpose of these standards is to prevent insolvency and establish capital cushions that may be required under extreme circumstances. Regulatory frameworks differ for different types of organizations. They may include standards for asset risk; underwriting risk; interest rate risk; or credit, market, and operating risk. The issues with regulatory frameworks used as a proxy for risk capital are shown in Exhibit 8.5. Organizations, analysts, and investors that use regulatory frameworks as the basis for measuring risk can be fooled into believing that they have a good measure when, in fact, that is not the case. Investors may believe an organization is well capitalized based on regulatory capital definitions, only to find out later that there are off- or on-balance sheet exposures not adequately reflected in the regulatory equation. Some organizations have even used this to game the system, creating an impression of being well capitalized (based on regulatory standards) while taking an increasing risk precisely in the areas not measured by those standards. Some organizations do this knowingly and may even discuss these efforts at industry conferences; other organizations do not fully appreciate the significance of the differences until it is too late.

While it is clear that on-books and regulatory approaches provide poor proxies for risk capital, what is the state of the art of risk capital? While some who have spent decades in the field and seen the progress that has occurred might argue that the state of the art is quite advanced, the proof is really in its predictive ability. Here we would have to say that the results are not what might be hoped for. For example, in January 2000, *American Banker* ran an article discussing the implications of Enron for risk capital issues in banks.[1] As this article suggests, the results of credit analyses of Enron indicate issues with the current state of risk assessment, even at the most sophisticated financial institutions.

To better understand some of the issues of risk assessments, see Exhibit 8.6.[2] In concrete terms, there are a number of issues that exist in current risk evaluation systems. Once understood, solutions to creating more robust approaches can be employed.

One of the issues in common risk capital approaches (see Exhibit 8.6) is to quantify risk-by-risk type. While this approach provides flexibility in allowing measurement approaches that are customized to fit available data, one major issue is that many important risks often are unmeasured, thus severely limiting the tool as an early warning mechanism. This is because it is often the case that it is precisely what is *not* measured that will cause problems in the future; what is measured and monitored may have minor hiccups—what is not is where disaster is more likely to strike. Another issue with evaluation by individual risk type approaches is that because the measurements by risk type are often so different, organizations often do not gain a good understanding of the relationships between risks. "Standard Bank of Ohio," for example, was an organization that measured credit risk based on the probability of default of the borrower and operating risk based on the level of expenses in a unit. While the executives believed that each approach had validity, they could not use their measurement processes to discern the relationships between credit risks and operating risks, although defaults are clearly, in part, associated with the borrower's characteristics *and* also associated with the bank's operations and management of those credits. Another approach often used for quantifying risk capital is the use of expected risk information to quantify unexpected risk. Banks or other institutions in assessing credit risk often use this approach. The issue is that the relationship between expected risk and unexpected risk is indeterminate. For example, credit risk for consumers may have a high degree of expected risk but

Approach	Common Issue
Evaluation of Risk by Individual Risk Type	Leaving out significant risk, or inadequately addressing certain risks, often particularly business and operating risks; little or no understanding of relationships between risks.
Use of Expected Risk Information to Quantify Unexpected Risk	Statistical flaws in methodologies—particularly used in credit risk implementations.
Use of Top-down Models of Volatility	Lack of believable data.
Use of Consultant or Other Database for Information	False sense of security Lack of specific knowledge Lack of insights Data "manufactured"
Use of Capital Proxies	Widely different results—inconclusive On-books capital issues (see Exhibit 8.5)— particularly used in operating risk analyses.
Use of Accounting Data to Assess Counterparty Risk	Accounting data, as readers of this text understand, may not provide adequate bases for assessing the operating, credit, or business risks of counterparties.

EXHIBIT 8.6   The Poorly Clad Emperor: Common Approaches and Issues Related to Risk Capital

low unexpected risk (i.e., the average may be high, but the variance from the average low) while credit risk for commercial borrowers may have a lower expected risk but a higher degree of uncertainty. These differences occur product to product, in the context of each lending situation as well. As witnessed in Chapter 7's "Sector" section on "Integration of Techniques," the expectations of any given line item and its volatility may differ widely. To the rescue comes mathematics in the form of a statistical concept called a binomial or Bernoulli distribution. (Bernoulli distribution is the technical term for a special case of the binomial.) For these distributions, it is possible to calculate a measure of variability, that is, the standard deviation, by knowing the value of the mean, or average. Many credit risk modelers take this shortcut. The problem, however, is that credit risk is not binomial, (i.e., a distribution with just two possible outcomes). If this were so, then there could be just two possible outcomes: In the case of credit risk, it would imply that the borrower either defaults and only pays back a given amount or does not default and pays the loan in full. However, that is not the case. In fact, there is a continuum. This continuum runs from the probability that the borrower pays nothing to the probability that the borrower pays the total amount due (see Exhibit 8.7). Those using a binomial distribution to describe a credit risk analysis are not representing the risk appropriately. Why is it done? We can speculate that the reason has to do with the mathematical simplicity. If the distribution were binomial, the data requirements of the calculation of variability and standard deviation would be simpler. Using the mean or expectation in this case, however, represents a shortcut— sometimes a close approximation, but other times, not as close. Those relying on the binomial distribution are likely to miss important elements when doing a credit risk analysis.[3]

For example, use of the binomial results in lower estimations of risk capital in the example shown in Exhibit 8.8. As this example demonstrates, just a small amount of additional data can result in a better calculation without reliance on the binomial assumption. Dr. Robert Earle has found that the use of the binomial always underestimates capital requirements.

Another approach to assessment of capital risk is the use of top-down models of volatility.[4] These models can provide an assessment of relative risk contribution by any slice or cut from which data are available and can be used to understand drivers of risk. The issue in its use often comes in the availability of data and, even more importantly, in the framing of the analyses that can create concerns related to believability of the data, particularly in situations where attribution is necessary. These issues can be overcome, however.

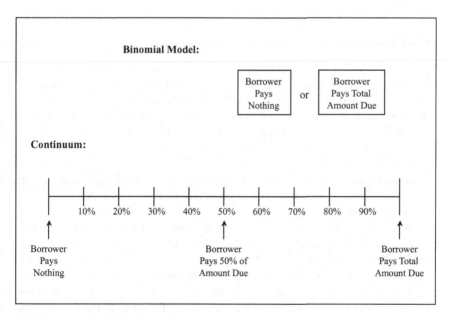

EXHIBIT 8.7   Credit Risk Analysis

Example*

Probability of Default	0.0018
Exposure ($M)	100
Recovery Rate	0.5113
Expected Loss	0.087966

Using the Binomial

Unexpected Loss	2.071512	(one standard deviation)
Capital Attribution	6.214535	(using three standard deviations)

Impact of Slightly More Data on Same Analysis and No Use of the Binomial

Probability	Loss	Payback
0.99820	0	100
0.00090	32	68
0.00046	47	53
0.00034	81	19
0.00010	100	0
Unexpected Loss	2.271727	(one standard deviation)
Capital Attribution	6.815181	(using three standard deviations)
Difference in Capital	10%	
	$600,646	

*Example found in Credit Risk Measurement by Anthony Saunders, p. 52.

EXHIBIT 8.8   Impact of Use of the Binomial

Often, an organization has much more data than it, or its information systems staff, would like to admit. Stress tests can be used to assess the impact of data quality. "Podna's Bank" used stress tests to better understand the validity of its own data. To the surprise of many skeptics, the ultimate impact on the risk capital results, based on the probable range of data, was very small.

A common approach used by firms to understand risk capital is to purchase consultant or other database information. One reason for this is that internally the organization *knows* how poor its own data and record keeping are. The organization may *assume* that the data it is buying are much better. (And the manager can transfer project risk to the supplier!) This, however, may be done to the detriment of other constituents because the quality can, and does, differ greatly from service offering to service offering. Sometimes the lack of quality or the lack of reliability is discovered too late. In one case, Sam, a finance manager, left "Roadhouse Bank" to move to "Loanshark Financial." At the new firm, Sam discovered that Loanshark was buying information that its sellers claimed included information from Roadhouse. Sam, who had worked at Roadhouse just days before the purchase of data was made, knew this was not possible because (1) Roadhouse had *not* supplied the information, and (2) Roadhouse did *not* even physically have the information to supply. Sam questioned the supplier of information as to whether Roadhouse data were indeed included. The supplier (mistakenly) verified that it was. Unfortunately, Loanshark was too far down the road to halt the use of the database information. (Foolish consistency, as Emerson said, comes to mind.) In this case, certainly, false comfort was obtained by using the purchased information.

A similar situation occurred when "VirtualTrust" and "Glenmoral Bank" bought data from the same vendor at the same time. Comparing the information provided to the firms revealed differences in the information provided for the same data sets.

In some organizations, multiple sets of data are purchased. "Rocky Bottom Savings and Loan" had purchased data from one vendor, merged with another organization, purchased a second set of data, and found that while in the case of some products the information was similar, in other cases it was different for no discernible reason. To sort it all out, Rocky Bottom had to hire a third consultant to make sense of it.

Why, then, is database information purchased (at the cost of millions of dollars)? Because *sometimes* the data are very good. Generally, however, the reason is because internal data are deemed inadequate, and although the purchased data set *may be* inadequate, it is not *known* to be so.

There is, of course, another issue with the use of database information. That is, what distinguishes one organization from another is not only its ability to generate returns but also its ability to manage its risks. Since it is this differential that creates competitive advantage, using industry information can provide false negatives, false positives, and lack of proper behavioral incentives. For example, what might distinguish one bank from another is its ability, for any given borrower, to *collect* on that loan. For another company, perhaps the firm has instituted better controls and management processes (value-based ones perhaps!) to obviate value-destroying decisions and thus within the same industry, their litigation and business risk is much smaller.

Another variation of the database approach is the use of capital proxies. These are studies made of other firms or related entities from which patterns can be discerned and information extracted and used. Often the extrapolations are difficult to make, however. Their use should be restricted because systemic problems like lack of capital may not show up when business models for an industry have changed and the marketplace has not yet reflected those changes. (See the example of Partisan Electric earlier.)

Commonly, organizations use accounting numbers to help them assess counterparty risk (that is, risk involving another entity including, for example, business, operating, and credit risks). They develop models and run numbers based on profit and loss statements and balance sheets. As demonstrated earlier, these standard accounting statements can be manipulated and do not necessarily provide complete information for assessing such risks. (See also the LoanDepot and RiskLess examples in Chapter 7, in the "Peers and Competitors" section and also in the "Patterns of Value Creation" subsection of the "Sector" section.) The Enron situation brought this issue to the forefront. "Every risk management tool remains at the mercy of the financial statements provided by borrowers and approved by auditors—and if those reports are misleading or inaccurate, as was allegedly the case of Enron, the risk models are of dubious value."[5] The solutions to the issues raised are shown in Exhibit 8.9. To clothe the emperor, it is important to recognize that economic value techniques (such as those presented in this book to date) can provide better information for risk assessment. As our examples have shown, risk measurement or any assessment based solely on accounting numbers *can* be flawed. Using economic value techniques can help an

Approach	Benefits
Use economic value techniques to separate fact from fiction	Not bamboozled by accounting data; obtain more realistic picture
Understand the detail of the assumptions behind the techniques—know what is known	Impacts of statistical, data, and theoretical flaws understood
Include a portfolio of techniques, including those with fewer assumptions and unknown variables	Able to quantify a range of answers
	More realistic picture emerges
Conduct Information Gap Analyses™ and stress tests for data and methodology quality issues	Establishes ability to continuously improve and update process (and insights)
Drill down to integrated benchmarks	All significant risks included; relationship between risks understood
Train to understand the drivers of risk: core external and internal risk drivers	Able to change organization's risk profile
	Able to evaluate strategic and tactical changes
Understand the relationships among value, variability, and expectation	**Strategic decisions that create rather than destroy value**

Key: Be clear about the purpose of the analysis and usefulness of the approach outcomes. Address purpose issues before, during, and after quantification.

Thanks to Jeff Hegan for his insights on presentation.

EXHIBIT 8.9 Clothing the Emperor: Solutions to Risk Capital

organization to better assess counterparty risk and its own internal risks as well. For constituents, economic value analyses can provide the first insights into the risk profiles of their counterparties: for employees, their employer; for suppliers, their customers; for customers, their suppliers; and for boards, the organizations they monitor. Using accounting numbers can result in misinformation and a false sense of security. Thoughtful development of risk capital analyses, using an economic value context, can rectify this.

In clothing the emperor suitably, it is clearly important to begin with careful understanding of the purpose of the analyses (see Exhibit 8.4). Purposes will drive an understanding of the usefulness and limits of various approaches. For example, if the purpose is to understand the components of risk in a quantifiable way, the approaches taken should provide a mechanism for doing this—and an understanding of the intersection or interrelationship of risk components on that basis. Because there are limitations with all techniques in current use, including a portfolio of techniques rather than relying on one approach or another is most advisable. Probably more than anything else what inhibits the value of risk capital analyses is the either/or mentality. We must use *this* approach, *not* that one. In fact, all approaches have downsides and upsides. There is no perfect science. The best approach is to use them all, or as many as possible, and recognize their limitations by performing stress tests and probing the assumptions that lie behind the results.

Techniques should be chosen based on the purpose of the analyses and used with a full understanding of the assumptions behind the techniques. Because of lack of access to internal data, external constituents may find it necessary to include techniques with more assumptions and a greater number of unknown variables. Using multiple techniques can serve as a second check on the understanding developed. Clearly understanding the detail of the assumptions behind the techniques, and knowing what is unknown, allows the user to place the information obtained in context. In addition, it is extremely useful for external constituents like investors, analysts, and prospective employees to query members of an organization to determine the extent of their understanding of risk in the business, its quantification, and the assumptions behind the calculations. The reasons for the importance of these dialogues are evident in every business failure. While understanding return information is very important, as discussed in earlier chapters, understanding risk is also vitally important. If an organization does not understand the risks in its business, it is likely not managing them and therefore much more likely to create missteps it would sooner avoid. "I don't handle that" or "I don't understand it" should *not* be acceptable answers from board members or members of executive management. Taking risk is, in fact, the true nature of any business enterprise. Saying you do not understand the risk in that business is another way of saying that you do not understand the business you are in.

To understand how good the techniques are (tolerances for error), issues with the data used as well as the techniques employed should be studied. This can be done by conducting Information Gap Analyses™ that focus specifically on the issues related to risk capital methodologies.

In addition, stress tests can be performed for data and methodology quality issues. For example, if the data were wrong by 10%, by 20%, what would the impact be on our understanding of risk? If this methodology assumption were wrong by 30%, what would the impact be? The management team at "Reunion Bank," after employing this approach, discovered that many of the issues with data that they thought might be causing difficulty in their assessments had little impact, while a couple of issues existed that created the impetus for future research. To really understand risk capital, it is very helpful not only to review and utilize specific methodologies but also to incorporate integrated benchmarks (i.e., measures of risk with multiple components of risk, both inside and outside of the organization). Measures of risk containing multiple layers of information can be dissected to understand the core internal and external risk drivers for the organization. Employees and others can also understand their own decision making by understanding what drives risk in their own decisions. For the organization, analyses of core external and internal risk drivers can help the organization understand not only the components of risk but also how the risk elements integrate and interact to form a total picture. Organizations that succeed in this endeavor not only drill down to integrated benchmarks to obtain this understanding, they also train internal and external constituents in the drivers of risk for their business. These intelligent conversations are essential to understanding the characteristics of the business. When an internal or external constituent says that more risk is bad, an informed constituent should begin to probe, since business optimization viewed as a portfolio of decisions is a matter of choosing the optimal risk return position (see Exhibit 8.10). The chart at the top left shows the typical trade-off that many think about. To be in business means to take risk. To have no risk is to be out of business (as is to have no return). Any given action may or may not optimize return for the risk taken on. The small chart at the right in the exhibit shows a slightly different view. At a certain level of risk, one is no longer paid for the additional risk taken on. (At this point, like a casino gambler, lottery player, or dot.com investor, the compensation must be in the form of entertainment value.) This is why it is very important that all constituents understand the relationships among value, variability, and expectation. The insights from this modeling can produce very useful information for decision-making purposes. (Some of this modeling was demonstrated in Chapter 7.)

When considering potential techniques for understanding risk, a way to frame the process is shown in Exhibit 8.11.[6] Techniques fall into two general categories: studies and benchmarks. Studies are actual measures of the

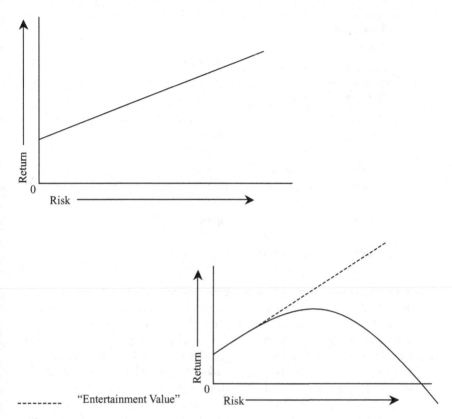

EXHIBIT 8.10 Risk Return Optimization

experienced risk. Volatility analyses, for example, represent a risk approach that falls into this category. Benchmarks are measures of outcomes from other processes, related to the risk under review. For example, measures of expected risk that are then translated into an understanding of unexpected risk, measures of levels of capital in other related industries, measures of one type of risk as a benchmark indicator of the size of another risk element, or a driver analysis that is turned into a statistical prediction rule (or another form of benchmark technique). To understand risk, the technique should be used in a framework that helps the user identify the sources of risk in the business. The sources of risk include the decisions that an organization makes, an understanding of the relative importance of each decision, and the decisions and actions of others that impact (the risk of) the business (a reason the constituent analysis is so important). Risk frameworks should also provide information on the nature of the risk (i.e., what is its pattern). Certain risks in a business, for example, may be ongoing with minor day-to-day impact; for example, routine operating decisions. While other

Techniques	
Study ⎫ Benchmark ⎭	(See text for example)

Questions to Answer	
▓ Source of Risk	(Decision making and context)
▓ Nature of Risk	(Pattern)
▓ Drivers of Risk	
▓ Techniques to Mitigate	
– Impact on Return	
– Impact on Risk	
Risk: Adverse, Unexpected Consequences	

EXHIBIT 8.11   Risk Framework

risks related to infrequent decisions or effects may have no ongoing day-to-day impact, they might have a large impact on outcomes on an infrequent basis (for example, merger and acquisition decisions). An understanding of the drivers of risk from these analyses will help an organization determine whether or not the day-to-day operating decisions in fact pose little risk or whether their cumulative effects are masked and may have the potential for further consequences in the future. Monitoring the drivers of risk as well as its effect (through ongoing studies) provides awareness that is helpful to the organization's response to the risk information (i.e., to its actions to mitigate). (For further discussion on risk drivers, see "Integration of Techniques" in this chapter and Chapter 9 sections related to value drivers.) These actions fall into two general categories: actions to mitigate or lessen risk and/or actions to enhance return by ensuring that the organization is paid for the risk that it takes on. Similarly, investors, lenders, employees, and other constituents must also make these decisions as well. It is clear that understanding risk and evaluating its magnitude (risk capital is one way to do this) is a core competency. Competency, then, as a manager, board member, investor, critic, or employee requires that risk and risk capital issues be addressed. Risk assessment includes an assessment of key risk factors. Assessments of risk can include risk or volatility studies of risk experience in the past. Benchmark and statistical prediction rules can be used to assess potential risk that may still be embodied in decisions of the past. Each constituent group will have different levels of risk tolerance that may have an impact upon their view of the risk in the organization. Thus, the amount of risk capital that each constituent will require or desire will differ. Viability of certain job categories within the organization might best express an employee's tolerance for risk; solvency, a creditor's. Boards are responsible for applying the right duty and care, appropriate to the circumstances considering the claims of all constituents. A 2002 survey by the National Association of Corporate Directors, unfortunately, showed that "when asked, only 37% of directors responded that a formal Enterprise Risk Management (ERM) process was in place in their organization—or that any other formal method of identifying risks was used. Even more alarming was the fact that 17% of directors stated they did not know whether their company had a formal method for identifying risks."[7]

This author would like nothing more than to launch into the details of all the approaches. That, however, is a topic for an entire book. Rather than rehashing specific techniques, placing these calculation methods in context is even more important.[8]

As with most endeavors, the biggest issue is "the preconceived notion." That is, entering into the calculation of risk capital with the idea that *in advance* one understands where the risks lie. "MinnieBank" executives used a variety of approaches to study its business under two models (see Exhibit 8.12). These two business scenarios are analogous to the business model choices that Partisan Electric confronted and are more and more faced by many different kinds of organizations today. In one scenario, MinnieBank originated loans and held them on the books. In another scenario, they originated loans and held some, sold some, and securitized some. To be simplistic and yet illustrate the point, in the first scenario, MinnieBank made decisions that created credit risk and created operating risk in terms of collections (i.e., can we get paid for this business?). There were obviously other business risks as well. This is simplified, however, to draw a contrast. In the second scenario, for the portion of the originated portfolio where Minnie-Bank held the loans, the risks were similar to the risks in Scenario 1. For the securitized loans, close examination showed they retained credit risk. Although the loans were not on the balance sheet, they still created credit risk for Minnie (and additional reputational risk as well). While the investment bank earning the fee for establishing the structure benefited from the transaction, Minnie lost value on its securitized portfolio. For the portion of the portfolio in which the loans were sold, Minnie was value neutral to slightly destructive. In selling loans with no recourse that it did not wish to hold, Minnie created the risk reward trade-offs shown in Exhibit 8.12. In this case, the organization had taken a portfolio business and made it into a trading business. The trading business had high risk over a short time horizon. The portfolio business had lower risk over a longer time horizon. The returns for the trading business were of short duration (until the next deal was done). The returns for the portfolio business lasted three to four years on average. Because of the nature of MinnieBank's business overall, their risk analyses showed that for them, the risk in the trading business was much higher than the portfolio business. To be value neutral, Minnie depended on their ability to sell the loans at prices that were highly advantageous to it.

To receive those prices, buyers had to believe they could better manage and extract value from the portfolio than the originators (in this case, Minnie) could. "The analysis of risks for the business scenarios initially surprised us," said Dave, the CEO. "Previously, we had thought that both the securitizations and loan sales created tremendous value. While both strategies boosted short-term earnings, further analysis showed us that both were value destroying."

Risk capital is used as a technique to calculate the value that is created under a number of contexts. Some organizations use risk as the basis for attributing the firm's existing capital (see Exhibit 8.13). In this example, "Meltdown Capital" calculates value by product in two ways. One calculation is performed using on-books capital. In this case, on-books capital for Product A is 400 and value is 10 while on-books capital for Product B is 600 and value created is 40. Meltdown also performs "Analysis A." To perform this analysis, the first step Meltdown takes is to calculate the risk attributable to each of its products. The analysis shows 30% of its overall risk is attributable to Product A and 70% to Product B. Based on this, Meltdown attributes 300 in capital to Product A and 700 to Product B. Product A generates 20 in value; Product B, 30 in value. Although this is an

Hold Loans on Books	Sell Loans with No Recourse
Risk	**Risk**
▪ Credit risk over life of loan	▪ Credit risk until loans sold
▪ Operating risk: collections on loans	▪ Operating risk: ability to sell loans
	▪ Loan price received
Return	**Return**
▪ Revenue over life of loan	▪ Upfront revenue from sale
▪ Expense of origination	▪ Expense of origination
▪ Expense of managing loan portfolio	▪ Expense of "traders": ability to find buyers at right price

Scenario 1: Originate loans → Hold on books (+)
Scenario 2: Originate loans → Hold some (+), securitize some (−), sell some (0,−)
In Scenario 1 all loans are held on books.
Scenario 2 includes three outcomes for loans.
The outcome: "hold loans on books" and "sell loans" are shown above.
"Securitize loans" has a similar credit risk profile to "hold loans" and increased reputational risk due to the public nature of securitization. Returns are lower than "hold loans" due to the cost of the investment banking fee.

EXHIBIT 8.12 Risk and Reward Tradeoffs of Loan Selloffs: MinnieBank (Simple View)

approach to attributing capital based on risk, other issues come into play as the examples that follow show.

For example, Meltdown, using various approaches, understands that its need for capital is in fact greater than its current on-books capital (see "Analysis B" in Exhibit 8.14). This determination is based on a number of

	Capital	Value Creation
Actual Capital Calculation		
Total Company	1,000	50
Product A	400	10
Product B	600	40
Analysis Ⓐ		
Attributing Actual Capital Based on Risk		
Total Company	1,000	50
Product A (30% of risk)	300	20
Product B (70% of risk)	700	30

EXHIBIT 8.13   Meltdown Capital

Meltdown Capital	Capital	Value Creation
Actual Capital Calculation		
Total Company	1,000	50
Product A	400	10
Product B	600	40
Analysis Ⓐ		
Using Actual Capital to Attribute Risk		
Total Company	1,000	50
Product A (30% of risk)	300	20
Product B (70% of risk)	700	30
Analysis Ⓑ		
Using Risk Capital		
Total Company*	1,300	20
Product A	390	11
Product B	910	9

*Not actual capital; uses "risk capital."

EXHIBIT 8.14   Risk Capital Greater than Actual Capital

assessments. In addition to its own internal models, Meltdown may have discussions with credit-rating agencies. (Understanding its balance sheet requirements to operate and their potential impact can be very important to any organization, particularly when it is dependent on a certain rating to do business or where market factors may create needs for capital that must be anticipated.) In the case of Meltdown, a determination is made that, in fact, to operate as a going concern, it needs more capital, 1,300 rather than 1,000. In Analysis B, Meltdown calculates the value it would be generating if, based on its determination, it were properly capitalized. In this case, value created in total would be 20, not 50. This result is interesting because, properly done, this means a result of 50 that might be calculated is a kind of fool's paradise. That is, if the organization needs 300 in additional capital to remain solvent or maximize value over the long run, a result of 50 is an illusion, particularly if 1,300 is an estimate based on current needs. In Analysis B, Meltdown attributes the 1,300 to the two products based on their riskiness. As shown, Product A's capital requirements are very close to its on-book capital. It is Product B, where the discrepancy is large between its current capitalization (on-books) and its requirement (based on risk). With this analysis, Meltdown now has some information with which to begin to thoughtfully make some strategic decisions about its product lines. (See the discussion of Alfrisco Corp earlier in this section.)

As with Meltdown, an organization has a serious problem if it finds that the capital it really needs to operate today is greater than what it has on-books. Obviously, in this event reassessment of risk and ways to mitigate it, of dividend policy and the balance sheet structure, must be addressed.

Of course, another possible situation is that experienced by "Radioactive Savings" (see Exhibit 8.15). In this case, Radioactive calculates risk capital to be less than its actual capital. As shown in Exhibit 8.15, risk capital is 800. In Analysis B, Radioactive attributes this risk capital based on the risk to Products A and B. This is just one of the ways an organization may present its risk capital analyses. Another approach is shown in Exhibit 8.16. Here, in Analysis C, Radioactive uses the same risk capital for Products A and B. However, at the total company level, the organization attempts to *reconcile* total on-books capital to risk capital. It does this by creating an account for this additional capital, thus explicitly providing an understanding that capital is available either for return to shareholders or for taking on additional risky activities that can generate value for the firm.

Exhibit 8.17 shows another possible analysis for Radioactive. In this case, Radioactive's executives recognize that the level of total capital they need on a risk basis (of 800) is, in part, due to diversification benefits between Products A and B. However, they do not want to attribute that diversification benefit to Product A or B in this example. Instead, they would like to understand the value created by each product on a risk basis that is stand-alone. In other words, if they sold their Product A line, what

Radioactive Savings	Capital	Value Creation
Actual Capital Calculation		
Total Company	1,000	50
Product A	400	10
Product B	600	40
Analysis Ⓐ		
Using Actual Capital to Attribute Risk		
Total Company	1,000	50
Product A (30% of risk)	300	20
Product B (70% of risk)	700	30
Analysis Ⓑ		
Using Risk Capital		
Total Company	800	70
Product A (30% of risk)	240	26
Product B (70% of risk)	560	44

EXHIBIT 8.15 Risk Capital Less than Actual Capital

Radioactive Savings	Capital	Value Creation
Actual Capital Calculation		
Total Company	1,000	50
Product A	400	10
Product B	600	40
Analysis Ⓐ		
Using Actual Capital to Attribute Risk		
Total Company	1,000	50
Product A (30% of risk)	300	20
Product B (70% of risk)	700	30
Analysis Ⓒ		
Using Actual Capital in Total:		
Risk Capital by Product		
Total Company	1,000	50
Product A	240	26
Product B	560	56
"Extra Capital"	200	(20)

EXHIBIT 8.16 Risk Capital Less than Actual Capital—Actual and Risk in Combination

Radioactive Savings	Capital	Value Creation
Actual Capital Calculation		
Total Company	1,000	50
Product A	400	10
Product B	600	40
Analysis (A)		
Using Actual Capital to Attribute Risk		
Total Company	1,000	50
Product A (30% of risk)	300	20
Product B (70% of risk)	700	30
Analysis (D)		
Using Risk Capital		
Total Company	800	70
Product A	270	23
Product B	630	37
Diversification Benefit	(100)	10

EXHIBIT 8.17 Risk Capital Less than Actual Capital

would be the value creation they would achieve with Product B, assuming there are no other effects? See Analysis D. In this case, Product A requires 270 in risk capital; and Product B, 630. These differ somewhat from a similar analysis for the two products, Analysis B in Exhibit 8.15. In this case, the products were given the diversification benefit and, thus, show lower capital and higher value creation. Analysis D, Exhibit 8.17, shows that there is a benefit from a risk standpoint to the organization of having both products rather than just one. Many organizations that perform these analyses like to (to the best of their ability) understand the diversification benefits that their products provide to each other.

Another presentation that organizations often employ is to show Product A and Product B capital without the diversification benefit and to place the net of any extra capital and diversification benefits in a single line item (see Exhibit 8.18). For example, financial services firms may show this amount in the corporate or treasury area when reporting line of business information.

Beyond reporting mechanisms, organizations also use these kinds of analyses to help them set their overall capital levels. In this case, Radioactive might choose to decrease its on-books capital by 100, keeping 100 in extra capital, equivalent to the diversification benefit, in case it wanted to rapidly sell off one of its product lines (see Exhibit 8.19).

Radioactive Savings	Capital	Value Creation
Actual Capital Calculation		
Total Company	1,000	50
Product A	400	10
Product B	600	40
Analysis (A)		
Using Actual Capital to Attribute Risk		
Total Company	1,000	50
Product A (30% of risk)	300	20
Product B (70% of risk)	700	30
Analysis (E)		
Using Actual Capital in Total:		
Risk Capital Excluding		
Diversification Benefit by Product		
Total Company	1,000	70
Product A	270	23
Product B	630	37
Net of "Extra Capital" of 200 and		
Diversification Benefit of (100)	100	10

EXHIBIT 8.18 Risk Capital Less than Actual Capital

One final note must be made related to regulatory capital guidelines. Just as some organizations "go out of their way" to use accounting rules to show high levels of profitability, organizations subject to regulatory capital guidelines often go out of their way to prove that they are well capitalized. Such actions may or may not be in the best interest of shareholders. (One way organizations do this is to move assets off balance sheet.) Suppose an organization is in the situation outlined as A in Exhibit 8.20. This is an issue that some banks find themselves in. Risk capital is less than regulatory capital, which is less than actual capital. To give the appearance of being even better capitalized, since most constituents do not study the organization's risk capital, the organization may often wish to show that it holds substantially more capital than is regulatorily required. To give that appearance, rather than increase actual capital, the management team may set a goal of reduced regulatory required capital that they believe will achieve that. To do this, "Royal Oyster Bank" engaged in noneconomic activities (i.e., non-value-creating activities) that reduced its regulatory but did not change its risk capital. In this case, Royal Oyster securitized loans for this purpose with little or no risk transfer. The term used for this activity is *regulatory capital*

Radioactive Savings	Capital	Value Creation
Actual Capital Calculation		
Total Company	1,000	50
Product A	400	10
Product B	600	40
Analysis Ⓐ		
Using Actual Capital to Attribute Risk		
Total Company	1,000	50
Product A (30% of risk)	300	20
Product B (70% of risk)	700	30
Analysis Ⓕ		
Setting/Choosing a Capital Level		
Extra = Diversification Benefit		
Total Company	900	60
Product A	270	23
Product B	630	37
Net of "Extra Capital" of 100 and Diversification Benefit of (100)	0	—

EXHIBIT 8.19   Risk Capital Less than Actual Capital

arbitrage. Royal Oyster reduced regulatory capital to 1,100. Risk capital remained at 1,000. Actual capital remained at 1,300. While the action may seem harmless, there was an economic cost. To give the appearance of being fortified from a capital standpoint, Royal Oyster had taken actions that would reduce its future returns but not change its actual capital or the level of its risk. Only its regulatory capital requirement was altered.

Example B is another example that organizations with regulatory capital requirements sometimes face. While current capital for "Royal Lobster Bank" is 1,150, regulatory capital is 1,100. Worried that as they grow their business, their regulatory capital requirements may grow and they may become less than well capitalized, Royal Lobster attempted (as did Royal Oyster) through noneconomic means to increase the spread between actual and regulatory capital requirements. In so doing, regulatory capital requirements became 950, while risk capital requirements remained steady at 1,100. The picture this presents can create an illusion that Royal Lobster is very well capitalized when it is not. For example, upon growing its business further, its risk capital might become 1,200, while its regulatory capital would become 1,000. Although it appears to be adequately capitalized for its risk, it is not, in fact, in that position.

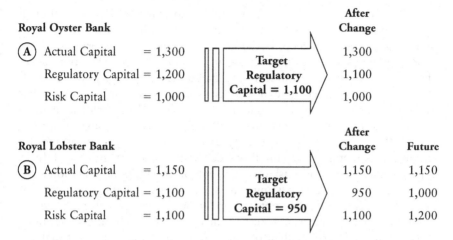

EXHIBIT 8.20 Interaction of Actual, Regulatory, and Risk Capital

Just as accounting issues can be challenged through the implementation of Economic Value Management processes, using the multiple risk capital approaches recommended in Exhibit 8.9 can also challenge regulatory capital gamesmanship. With the adoption of Basel II, many banks are creating risk information that will *drive* regulatory capital. This risk information is based on the Basel guidelines. The issue is that in this environment, there are new incentives to manipulate not only regulatory capital but risk capital as well. Charles, the risk capital specialist at "Rubberforest Bank," in describing their current initiative states: "We are currently in the process of developing risk capital models for Basel II. As we begin to develop the data, our goal is to ensure our regulatory capital will be as low as possible." Just as some organizations may "cook the books" to ensure certain earnings outcomes, unfortunately Rubberforest has embarked on a path to ensure a certain regulatory outcome, using risk numbers not for greater understanding (of itself or its constituents), but for short-term benefit. Just as the SEC becomes more vigilant on accounting fraud, the FED, OCC, executive management teams, boards, and others need to become vigilant in halting these actions before they create a lack of trust in the bank's assessment of risk and its reported numbers.

TYPES OF ADJUSTMENTS

As with sector evaluations, product, service, distribution-channel, and process calculations of value may use all forms of metrics; the inherent difficulties experienced at the sector level related to adjustments and measurement are magnified, because attribution issues can be even more difficult. See the discussion in Chapter 7.

Another area more likely to be tackled formally at this level, though equally applicable to merger and acquisition activities, consists of options value techniques. Projects or decisions related to products, services, distribution channels, or processes requiring capital investment planning are often the most common applications, including using real options to evaluate investments and create exit strategies in R&D, startup ventures, product design, contracts, and information technology."[9] In performing these calculations, one of the most difficult inputs (or assumptions) in options value is the measurement of volatility (risk or uncertainty). This is another reason that understanding volatility (see Chapter 7's "Integration of Techniques" section) and total risk can be so important. Options valuation techniques can be used in assessing past value to understand the nature of embedded options, learning options, and growth options that might rightly be assessed by an acquirer of pieces of the organization's business but not be reflected in the internal valuation the existing organization might make.[10] (See also Chapter 6's "Types of Adjustments: Options Value" section for a longer discussion and description of real options.)

CONSTITUENT FOCUS: THE ALLIANCE

In understanding their value proposition to the organization and the organization's value proposition for them, the product level is often the level of interaction at which customers may wish to perform their calculations of value. Their value proposition to the organization may be able to be estimated, depending on the organization's disclosure. To calculate the organization's value proposition for them, they will need to calculate the value created (versus alternatives) of the products/services they use and their ability to access those products/services through the distribution channel. This calculation may also include an assessment of relationship options. For example, will a relationship provide options for future activities based on the organization's overall product set? Will a consolidated relationship provide valuable options for them and for the organization?

Suppliers will frequently also address similar questions at the product, distribution-channel, or sector levels. What value has the supplier created for the organization at those levels, and what value is the organization creating for the supplier? How valuable are strong relationships? To what extent does investment today provide options value for the future? Answers to these questions for customers and suppliers influence pricing, determined on both cost and market bases. Understanding the inputs in these contexts provides the basis for understanding whether prices are *reasonable* prices and what the market will bear.

Drawing conclusions or making decisions at the product, service, distribution channel, or process level, of course, is based on interrelatedness, that is, the effect one product, service, or distribution channel may have on the outcomes of others. The earlier discussion of risk capital demonstrated this. To address this issue clearly, an assessment of both marginal and average value is important. For example, if we sell one more product, what is the marginal revenue, and what is the marginal cost, and the marginal capital, required for doing so? What is the marginal value of taking such an action? While understanding the total value and the average value created (per product or some other measure) are important, understanding marginal value creation is also important. A humorous example of this occurred recently at an analyst conference. At that meeting, Bill, the president of "MegaWorld Bank," presented the following profitability statistics for their commercial customers (see Exhibit 8.21). Bill explained: "If the customer buys three products, our profits are $8,000. If the customer buys eight products, it is $70,000, and if the customer buys fourteen products, our profit is $340,000. Cross-sell is important to us." An investment manager seeing the numbers asked Bill, "Why not just sell the last six products and make $270,000 rather than the first six products where you make something south of $70,000?" After the laughter subsided, Bill replied, "There are several answers to this. One relates to customer behavior; that is, our customers may not wish to buy the last six products first, because they may need to develop the relationship with us first before being willing to buy those products. Jim, MegaWorld's CFO, added: "Another reason relates to the fixed costs of initiating and establishing our customer relationships—because of this, the economics of additional sales to existing customers are very attractive. The marginal cost of additional product sales becomes minimal compared to costs of the initiating of a new relationship."

Although Bill and Jim did not mention it, the ability to price more profitably to longstanding customers may be a third factor. One reason why is

Profitability Statistics Presented

3 Products	=	$8,000 annually
8 Products	=	$70,000 annually
14 Products	=	$340,000 annually

Recap

First 3 Products	=	$8,000 annually	=	$2,667 per product annually
Next 5 Products	=	$62,000 annually	=	$12,400 per product annually
Next 6 Products	=	$270,000 annually	=	$45,000 per product annually

EXHIBIT 8.21   Profitability Statistics Example: MegaWorld Bank

that those customers may incur switching costs. In fact, "Researchers have found that, generally speaking, it is optimal for firms to increase prices over time . . . this is consistent with the industry observations that loyal customers are *willing* to pay higher prices. Switching costs, potential risks, and familiarity with a firm and its product are among the reasons that customers in longer customer-firm relationships are more willing to pay higher prices."[11]

This can have implications, of course, for product pricing strategy. There can be discontinuities in profit driven by upfront costs and market forces. In calculating value, if the customer relationship is long term, the upfront customer acquisition costs may be capitalized and amortized (even if accounting treatment might be different), as we have noted in discussing customer capital. If the customer relationship, however, tends to be transactional (one time, not ongoing), upfront costs may need to be calculated and viewed as an expense associated with the sale. The determination of customer likelihood to continue to buy, to be sticky, is often determined by statistical prediction rules used to model the customer's propensity to continue to purchase. Organizations with high acquisition costs will tend to focus their efforts on customers with long-term prospects.

What this means is that customer behavior may impact the calculations made for products. If product one is a door opener, its options value must be considered. These issues provide cautions in terms of interpreting product level data. Understanding context, the product calculation's purpose, customer behavior, and lifetime value are very important. While investors and analysts like to receive as much sector information as possible, product information is also highly prized.

INTEGRATION OF METRICS

Value drivers at the product, service, distribution-channel, and process level often make their way to sector-based balanced scorecards. Sector managers often review statistics at this level, including significant line item information as well. Such metrics may include the number of products sold per customer, number of new products, innovations to existing products, traffic volumes for each distribution channel, product cost, process efficiency, and the like.

Activity-based information is often captured at the product, service, distribution-channel, and process level as well. For example, cost, revenue, and capital may all be captured for processes that occur in product manufacture and sale. Risk capital may be captured at this level or the instrument level (a more specific level) as well. As noted in the section on risk capital, process risk is often reviewed at the product level. Such process analyses may impact an organization's decision to hold assets and generate profits from them or to sell, or to securitize or trade them instead. These process level reviews not only provide information about an organization's revenues and its costs, they also provide information on activities and their impacts on capital—including on-books, regulatory, risk, or other measures of capital. It is often at the product, service, or distribution-channel level that the process information is integrated into a complete activity-based framework. To ignore capital impacts in the activity analyses is to provide a partial answer at best and a false one at worst. To understand the value created or destroyed by the activities of the organization, including the differential impact of capital produces information that becomes actionable to the organization and is therefore highly useful.

Total Quality Management (TQM), customer service, and process measure data are often collected at the product, service, and distribution-channel level. Measures provide mechanisms to monitor product quality versus expectation, product processes within tolerance of variability, etc.

With the advent of the Internet and other electronic distribution channel mechanisms, understanding TQM and activity-based and scorecard value drivers at this level becomes even more important. Discussing the results in one organization related to Internet distribution channel impacts a recent article noted, "Online customers carry 20% to 30% higher balances than offline customers and have a 30% lower attrition rate, Mr. Ostler said. Bill payment customers are even more valuable; they are 50% to 60% less likely to leave the bank."[12]

INTEGRATION OF TECHNIQUES

As demonstrated in the sector discussion, organizations can gain major insights by producing information (such as shown in Exhibits 7.17 through 7.20) that compare the patterns of value creation and analyze the volatility of different products and of different distribution channels. Information Gap Analyses™ will often drill down from the sector to the product or distribution channel level to assess the quality of information and decision rules and correct issues that may occur.

Statistical prediction rules are often developed at the product level as well by testing the value impacts of alternative strategies. Using a variety of techniques, employed in combination, some organizations have become very sophisticated at testing the impact and determining the key value drivers in their marketing programs. The information from these tests is then used to formulate statistical prediction rules concerning customer response and behavior to the organization's activities. The outcomes are continually monitored, and the information is fed back to the models.

In a similar way, statistical prediction rules or benchmarks are developed that measure risk. In high-performing organizations, multiple rules are used, and their efficacy is monitored in light of experience. As noted earlier, those that use economic value rather than profit-only information have clearer pictures and better predictive information.

Information Gap Analyses™ provide a systematic way of discerning the quality of the data available for product, service, distribution-channel, and risk capital analyses. "Portside Bank," embarking on a new measurement program, found that data quality differed significantly from product area to product area, and calculations of accounting-based numbers, even for a given product, differed in different geographies. (It was a U.S.–based firm — however, this could easily happen cross-border.) Information Gap Analyses™ were required to bring order to chaos and begin to develop the information so that it could be used to create value.

The ValueMap™ is an important tool for understanding constituent value. At the distribution level, for example, the organization may show the value impact of the distribution channel on its bottom line as well as the value benefits as viewed by the customer. A framework like that presented in *Customer Equity*[13] can be used to present the customer perception of value. These value benefits may include customer assessments of expectations versus delivered quality, quality vis-à-vis price, product uniqueness, suitability, convenience, and service. Using the ValueMap™, ordinal statistics[14] may be used to present a picture of the customer's views of the product offerings or a given distribution channel. These may be presented in value terms for the organization and vis-à-vis the offerings of peers. At times, community interaction with an organization may be limited to its concerns about certain products for safety, health, environmental, or social justice reasons. The ValueMap™ can be used by the organization to chart its efforts in these areas as well, using ordinal statistics to provide quantification related to the organization's actual and perceived improvements.

APPLICATIONS OF METRICS

Performance Assessment

Product, service, and distribution channel and the processes associated with them are key to understanding the value created by the organization on average and at the margin (i.e., for the next unit sold). They are also key to understanding the value created for customers as a constituent class. Attribution processes and overhead allocation mechanisms can present issues in understanding the data. For that reason, it is important to be able to analyze the data from a number of perspectives. Investors can collect information as it is disclosed by companies for one product line or distribution

	Total: Input Known	Internet: Calculated	Retail: Calculated
Core Revenue*	100	30	70
Core Cost*	80	14	66
Capital	400	100	300
Value	(20)	6	(26)

*Adjusted as appropriate.

Information disclosed by company and other sources:

■ Internet channel represents 30% of organization's core revenues.

■ The Internet costs per dollar of revenue are half those of the retail operation's costs per dollar of revenue.

■ Internet channel capital is $100 million.

■ Cost of capital is 10%.

EXHIBIT 8.22   Gleaning Information about Other Products/Channels

channel and use it to develop a better understanding of product lines or distribution channels for which there is no specific disclosure. Exhibit 8.22 shows a simple example of this.

Strategy

Understanding the marginal impacts best supports decisions concerning changes in strategy. For example, for the company shown in Exhibit 8.22, what would the *marginal* impact be of a retail shutdown? To what extent does the retail operation cross subsidize the Internet activities? To what extent does the retail outlet marketing make possible the economies of scale shown for the Internet? Because elimination of retail might not provide the rosy picture now shown in Exhibit 8.22 for the Internet, in assessing the addition or elimination of a distribution channel or new product, it is important that both average and marginal information is developed. At times, the organization will not have the internal information to answer these questions and may need to turn to organizations with standalone products or distribution channels for additional insights into probable outcomes. In addition, analyses may also be required that involve selected testing to help determine marginal impacts in advance of full-scale rollouts.

Process and Technology

Improvements in processes, identification of quality issues, services issues, and research, and development needs come from an understanding of value creation at the level of products, services, distribution channels and processes themselves and a study of the components of those values. Information Gap

Analyses™ can provide suggestions for improvements in decision tools and in the information required to monitor product, service, distribution-channel, and process value.

Organizational Structure

Understanding the trade-offs and relationships between products and distribution channels, and understanding the ability and propensity to drive cross-sell, all represent information gathered by understanding value creation at the product, service, or distribution-channel level. This information should be used by the organization in structuring itself and its offerings to its customers. A key question is, what will the customer's experience be like under one structure of product, service, or distribution-channel offering versus another one? In the early days of the Internet, some organizations established very separate organizational structures for their Internet versus other operations. The impacts related to product availability and to customer service became a negative from the customer's viewpoint. Better integration through organizational realignment has made the Internet more seamless to customers and a more highly valued delivery source.

Rewards

While product, service, and distribution-channel value are important, incentives structure must be based on maximizing total value. This means that the organization must review the structure to ensure that incentives, in fact, encourage value creation across products, services, and distribution channels. The organization must recognize cross-organizational efforts and reward efforts to create value. For organizations, this can have process and technology implications as well. Wilma, the CEO of "Trailside Tools," while discussing these concepts with analysts, remarked, "We had to establish monitoring mechanisms to show the number of referrals from this product area to that product area. Until we had that in place, Charlie would tell me he had given Bill 1,000 referrals and Bill would say he only got 500. Now we can track it. Charlie sent 800 referrals and Bill got 800." Of course these are the kinds of processes that form the basis of establishing incentives that truly create the right behaviors.

"Bounty Bank" established an Economic Value Management pay program for the sales managers of a particular product base. In establishing the pay program, it established a mechanism to pay for improvements in the value created by the entire customer relationship, which included its referrals to another product area. The program was extremely successful, and the organization saw a huge turnaround in the unit as a result: a 30% increase in profits and value in the first year alone. Was it difficult to establish? It took some effort and perseverance, particularly in aggregating the customer

- How close are our processes, our products, services, distribution channels to the expectations of our customers?

- How well do we understand our suppliers, employees, and other perspectives on these issues?

- What do we need to do to move our processes, products, and so forth closer to expectation and understand our constituents' needs more clearly?

- What are the impacts of risk and risk capital?

- What are the impacts of:
  - Capital investment at the product and distribution level?
  - Human capital investment?
  - Product capital investment?
  - Technology investment?

- What training is required to address all of the above?

EXHIBIT 8.23 Training/Communication Issues Addressed at the Product, Service, Distribution Channel, and Process Levels

data (see Chapter 9). The benefits far outweighed the costs, however. Value increased significantly in the very first year of implementation.

Training and Communications

Training and communications at the product, process, and distribution-channel level are often driven by the insights that arise from Information Gap Analyses™ and ValueMaps™. Questions that are addressed or discussed often include those shown in Exhibit 8.23.

The analyses of value at the product, sector, process, and distribution-channel levels move into the pulse of the organization, its daily life, and what occurs at the transaction level. These analyses are closely linked to understanding of customer value and value drivers—topics discussed in Chapter 9.

NOTES

1. Rob Blackwell, "Lessons of Enron: The Limitations of Risk Models or the Freedom to Take Risks," *American Banker*, January 23, 2002.

2. There are many other risk analyses and approaches that may be of interest to the reader, including extreme value theory and external event analysis. Chapter 9's section on "Value Drivers" also provides an overall context for understanding risk driver analysis.

3. Confirmed in separate private communications with Dr. Rakesh Vohra, Dr. Robert Earle, and Drs. Linda Allen and Anthony Saunders.

4. See Dennis Uyemura's ground-breaking work in Dennis Uyemura and Donald Van Deventer, *Financial Risk Management in Banking: The Theory & Application of Asset & Liability Management,* Bankers Publishing Company, Burr Ridge, IL: Irwin 1993.

5. See Note 1.

6. The following are some resources that describe techniques currently employed: John B. Caouette, Edward I. Altman, and Paul Narayanan, *Managing Credit Risk: The Next Great Financial Challenge,* New York: John Wiley & Sons, 1998; Neil A. Doherty, *Integrated Risk Management: Techniques and Strategies for Reducing Risk,* New York: McGraw Hill, 2000; Philippe Jorion, *Value at Risk: The New Benchmark for Controlling Derivatives Risk,* Burr Ridge, IL: Irwin, 1997; Anthony Saunders, *Credit Risk Measurement: New Approaches to Value at Risk and Other Paradigms,* New York: John Wiley & Sons, 1999; Anthony Saunders and Linda Allen, *Credit Risk Measurement: New Approaches to Value at Risk and Other Paradigms,* New York: John Wiley & Sons, 2002; and Dennis G. Uyemura and Donald R. Van Deventer, *Financial Risk Management in Banking: The Theory & Application of Asset & Liability Management.* Burr Ridge, IL: Bankers Publishing Company, Irwin, 1993.

7. "After Enron: A Survey Conducted by The Institute of Internal Auditors and National Association of Corporate Directors," January 31, 2002.

8. See Note 6.

9. Martha Amram and Nalin Kulatilaka *Real Options: Managing Strategic Investment in an Uncertain World,* Boston: Harvard Business School Press, 1999.

10. For example, Learning Options provide the opportunity to learn about a business, market, or geography and exercise that knowledge gained in the future. Growth Options provide the opportunity to grow a business in the future based on what is established today.

11. Robert Blattberg, Gary Getz, and Jacquelyn Thomas, *Customer Equity: Building and Managing Relationships as Valuable Assets.* Boston: Harvard Business School Press, 2001.

12. Chris Costanzo, "Using New Sets of Metrics to Measure Web Success," *American Banker,* December 4, 2001.

13. See Note 11.

14. Ordinal statistics involves data that can be ranked.

CHAPTER 9

The Customer, Value Drivers, and Changes over Time

This chapter will address the remaining evaluative analyses, as shown in Exhibit 9.1, Questions 5, 6, and 7.

Evaluative

1. Has the organization added value? How much?
2. How does this compare to the organization's peers and competitors?
3. Has the organization been managed such that each sector has added value?
4. Has the organization been managed such that each product, service, distribution channel, or process added value?

> You Are Here

5. Has the organization been managed such that each customer relationship added value?

> And Here

6. What are the major drivers of value creation for the organization?

> And Here

7. For all of the above, how has this changed over time?

Predictive

8. How much value does the organization expect to create?
9. How much value do capital providers (shareholders, if publicly traded) expect the organization to create?
10. How much value does the organization expect to create by sector, product, service, distribution channel, process, and customer?
11. What are the expectations related to the major drivers of value creation over time?

EXHIBIT 9.1 The Questions

(continued)

EXHIBIT 9.1 The Questions *(Continued)*

12. What are the capital provider's expectations for the organization's peers? What are the peer's expectations for itself by sector, product, service, distribution channel, process, customer, and major drivers of value creation?

13. How do internal, peer, and capital provider expectations differ from current steady-state value creations?

14. For all of the above, how will this change over time?

THE CUSTOMER—HAS THE CUSTOMER RELATIONSHIP ADDED VALUE?

The question of customer value is one that has received more and more attention of late. Unfortunately, some practitioners use the term *customer value* and really mean *net income*. This section will discuss customer value from the perspective of both the organization and the customer's interaction with the organization. This discussion will follow the format outlined in Exhibits 9.2 and 9.3.

Time

The issue of customer value is closely related to the time frame for measurement. Unlike other measurements generally involving a standard period

Metric Characteristics:	From (Traditional Implementation)	To (Economic Value Management)
Time	Evaluative, Primarily Annual	Evaluative and Predictive, Variable Time Periods
Type of Capital	Debt and Equity	Multiple Types of Capital
Form of Metric	Dollars or Percents	Dollars, Percents, Standard Deviation, i.e., Multiple Forms
Types of Adjustments	Simple	Simple and Complex
Measurement and Management Perspectives:		
Constituent Focus	Shareholder	Alliance of Constituents
Integrating Metrics	None or Few	Multiple—Optimal Number
Integrating Techniques	None	Multiple
Applications of Metrics	Strategic, Valuation	Broad Applications

EXHIBIT 9.2 How Economic Value Management Differs: Evolution of Value Practices

Metric Characteristics:

Time	Types of Capital	Form of Metric	Types of Adjustments
※ Evaluative and/or predictive ※ Time horizon	※ Debt or equity ※ Equity ※ Special case equity equivalents – Human – Customer – Product ※ Regulatory ※ Risk ※ Cost of capital ※ Market value/ purchase price ※ Taxes, dues	※ Dollar ※ Percentage ※ Standard deviation	※ Availability ※ Complexity ※ Fixed/changed boundaries ※ Options value

Measurement and Management Perspectives:

Constituent Focus	Integration of Metrics	Integration of Techniques	Applications of Metrics
※ Community and external governance ※ Providers of capital ※ Suppliers ※ Consumers ※ Observers/ critics (see Exhibit 6.3)	※ Value drivers (the value-based balanced scorecard) – Relationship – Process – Choices ※ Activity-based information – Cost, revenue, capital ※ TQM process measures	※ Patterns of value creation – Trend and regression analysis ※ Volatility analyses ※ Information Gap Analyses™ ※ Statistical prediction rules ※ Market value analysis ※ Pictures ※ Scenario planning ※ Monte Carlo simulations ※ ValueMap™	The Wheel™: ※ Performance assessment ※ Strategy ※ Process and technology ※ Organizational structure ※ Rewards process ※ Training and communication (see Exhibit 6.4)

EXHIBIT 9.3 Economic Value Management: Metric Choices and Uses

(e.g., monthly, quarterly, annually), measures of customer value are often discussed in terms of a life-cycle approach.

One reason for this is because, in the initial stages, a customer may not be profitable. Why? Customers in the early stages may still be shopping for price. They may not be willing to commit to value-added services upfront, and they may take a lot of time, effort, and cost to woo for just the first product sale. (See Chapter 8's "Constituent Focus" section for more information on this phenomenon.) In general, fewer products purchased (if they are priced appropriately) will result in lower value creation. Customers who buy less will create less value.

As Exhibit 9.4 shows, after customer acquisition and initial purchase, the challenge for value creation is growing revenue through cross-selling of additional products and through referrals, which lower acquisition costs and raise the probability of acquisition and retention (see Exhibit 9.5).

It can be argued that the best customers can provide a marked difference in value creation from average customers. Even when customer analytics are not sophisticated enough to incorporate every nuance of customer behavior in the value modeling, simply understanding the distinct impacts of channel and product processes required to meet the customer's needs can produce marked differences in the calculations and thus the understanding of value creation.

More sophisticated value modeling will also reflect differential investments per customer. That is the investments the organization must make to grow their business. (A caution to customers: Additional freebies on the front end—in the wooing stage—may mean higher prices on the back end. Why does investment banking spring to mind?) Needless to say, acquisition costs can differ from industry to industry and business model to business model. (Clearly, this is an area where organizations can redefine the territory.)

Customer value, then, from the organization's perspective can be calculated on a current basis, a to-date basis, an as-is basis (reflecting no additional sales—but the benefits of current sales into the future), or a projected lifetime basis. To calculate customer value, some would argue, can only be done on a lifetime basis. A lifetime value would include projections of future

EXHIBIT 9.4 Customer

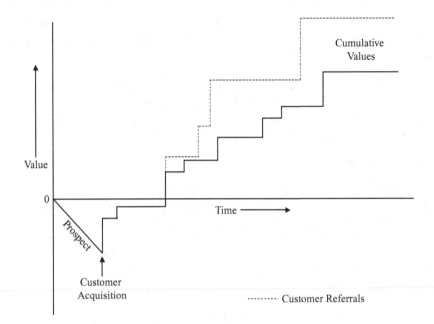

EXHIBIT 9.5   Prospect/Customer Relationship (Retained Customer)

value creation based on what are essentially statistical prediction rules (SPRs). These rules would include propensity to purchase additional products, the types of products and their timing, where the customer is in terms of life cycle with the firm, and so forth. Just as with the NPV analyses discussed in Chapter 5, this lifetime value can be represented as one number. Or, using economic value techniques, the numbers can be associated with the periods involved. In performing the value calculation, for example, it is possible to amortize customer acquisition costs as capital costs in the value equation. What is the motivation for lifetime value? Behavioral. If the organization has a long time to invest before achieving benefits from the customer relationship, it may face the issue of internal impatience, a refusal to invest to maximize value. I recommend the book *Customer Equity* because it explains these rationales with great clarity and in more detail than can be covered here.[1] The contribution I would be sure to make to the insights provided is that a customer's total value should also include the value to the organization of referrals given to the organization by that customer.

There are a number of ways this referral value can be calculated. One approach, from a customer attribution standpoint, is to calculate the amount of that value attributable to (1) the reduction in upfront capital—acquisition costs—for referral customers and (2) the potentially greater value creation from them (due to less upfront risk aversion). This recognition of additional customer value is important. This portion of value creation is not generated through direct sales to that prospect or customer but through the additional follow-on benefits they bring in terms of referrals and word-of-mouth advertising (see Exhibit 9.6). As shown, these prospects and customers can provide far greater value to the organization and may be worth far more in terms of investment than prospects that do not provide referrals, even if nonreferral providers contribute more in terms of direct sales. (A note to customers: In thinking about the value you create for the organization, this should not be discounted.)

Types of Capital

Of interest here, of course, is customer capital, which we have referred to as a special investment category. It includes acquisition costs, additional marketing costs, and giveaways. Some organizations are very good at tracking this information for individual prospects and customers. Others do this on a very segmented basis and others on a more aggregate basis. In part, size of the prospects and customer base will drive some of the cost and

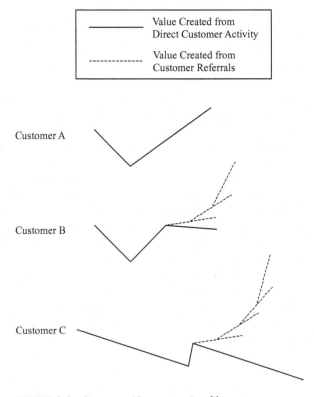

EXHIBIT 9.6   Prospect/Customer Profiles

benefit analyses related to greater information detail. Information Gap Analyses™ can be used to help determine at what level optimum information (given cost) is procured.

From a risk capital standpoint, customers represent an important counterparty risk to be measured by the organization. While this is certainly true for organizations in the lending business that must understand the credit risk of their customers, it is also true for other firms as well. Insurers, of course, assess the riskiness of their customers. So do (or should) firms whose own reputations may become associated with that of their clients. Audit firms are (or should be) an example. Specialized providers who cannot do business with competitors are one example. Any organization, in fact, (and that is most firms) that depends upon customer payment (preferably prompt payment) falls into the category of organizations that want to monitor customer risk. Certainly it is clear that employees will make the same kinds of risk assessments related to the organization they work for: Can the organization pay? For how long (prevalence of layoffs)? What is the organization's reputation or likely to be their reputation?

Risk associated with customers can also be viewed by organizations in terms of probability of occurrence and the impact if a customer leaves. This is often referred to as the "stickiness" problem. In the banking world, the discussion is often in terms of the likely stickiness of customer deposits. As with other aspects of measuring lifetime value, customer's riskiness may be studied based on certain characteristics and statistical prediction rules or multifactor models developed to benchmark potential risks. In this regard, economic value metrics can be very important in actually measuring the inherent risks in potential and existing customers. "Watery Savings," a financial services firm that used economic value analyses (and had a renowned reputation for credit risk assessment) was surprised at the results obtained and the knowledge gained. Customers, whom they thought they understood through the use of their relationship programs, were found to be not well understood at all. In fact, in some cases Watery discovered that the customers did not understand their own organizations very well either. As one example, Watery's analyses demonstrated the riskiness of certain customer strategies: Paying too much for acquisitions or limiting their business model to product areas that might represent worthwhile add-ons to other business propositions but were not that robust on the standalone basis these organizations had chosen. This review helped them to counsel their customers and become trusted advisors.

Of course, all traits that *seem* to be associated with the customer may, in fact, have more to do with the organization's own operations. For example, related to the risk of customers from a stickiness standpoint, two organizations may have different risk profiles for their customers due to the organization's own differential ability to influence customer behavior. One organization may understand how to retain customer deposits, for example. Another, which has studied their customers in depth, will understand how best to optimize the cross-sell process. Similarly, credit risk of the customer can be influenced by the organization's own interaction with them. Consumer finance firms that provide *handholding* credit counseling services provide a value added service that helps individuals establish reliable credit histories and at the same time limits the firms' downside risks on the loans that are made. This handholding is costly. For these organizations, however, it often represents a worthwhile trade-off: lower credit losses and higher customer retention offset the additional costs.

Any organization with membership must address the issue of retention and stickiness. A clear definition and understanding of customer needs is a critical first step to address these risks.

Form of Metric

As noted in Chapter 5, decision making related to customer value has created confusion for some organizations when percentages are used. See the examples in Chapter 5, "Choosing the Measures: Dollars and Percents." Using standard deviations to analyze customer groups can be very useful as well. See the example discussed in Chapter 6's "Form of Metric" section and shown in Exhibit 6.7.

Types of Adjustments

The issues discussed in terms of attribution for product or sector will also occur with the measurement of customer. In this case, there may be multiple products, sectors, and distribution channels interacting with the customer. The attribution of revenues, costs, and capital to specific customers can therefore become complicated.

To maximize value, decisions related to the customer must be made on the correct basis (i.e., marginal versus fully loaded), and reward systems must incent maximization of customer value. Some organizations end up with lengthy projects just to sort out the web of relationships a customer has with the organization. Often there are cross-sector issues and organizational structure issues that must be addressed to understand customer value creation.

Investments in customer capital will often have options values that are not always readily apparent. Follow-on referrals are an easy example. Others may include a greater market understanding of a particular client segment, thus leading to the ability to innovate products that meet the needs of that growing segment. Of course, strictly evaluative measures will reflect the valuable (or not) exercise of these options. Predictive measures can estimate these effects. Pricing to customers based on customer value, although sometimes viewed as an evaluative process, in fact is a predictive one if lifetime value concepts are employed. In that case, options value should be considered.

Constituent Focus: The Alliance

In their association with the organization, customers obviously want to understand value from both sides: what value has been created for the organization and what value the organization has created for them. To do that, customers will analyze product quality, cost, customer service, and the other factors discussed in Chapter 8's "Integration of Techniques" section. Customers will assess the benefits associated with having or maintaining a trusted supplier. They will assess the benefits of doing business with small suppliers and the level of service they can expect from those associations.

For customers for whom economic value impacts can be calculated directly (commercial customers, for example), both the customer and the organization can use Economic Value Management techniques to assess the impact of the organization's products and channels on the customer's economic value. These may include cost benefits, performance benefits, advertising or marketing benefits, risk benefits, and the like. "Shapely Savings Bank" did this, and as Veronica, the CFO, said: "We achieved remarkable insights that influenced our product innovation. The exercise required us to step into our customer's shoes. We needed to answer the question: What are the economic consequences to the customer of our products?" For customers, there is often a concern for both absolute value and peer comparisons (i.e., fairness in both what is created for them by the organization vis-à-vis other alternatives and by them for the organization). For some customers, the calculation of value may require more adaptive thinking.

Ordinal statistics can be used by the organization and by customers to rank and understand the value that has been created for them.[2] (The discussion related to Exhibit 9.7 in the "Integration of Metrics" section in this chapter and Exhibit 10.7, an employee example, helps to amplify this. See also Exhibit 8.10; some value may be entertainment value.)

Providers of capital are always interested in having information related to value creation of different customer segments. Such information, in addition to future estimates of demographics and psychographics, helps capital providers predict the efficacy of the organization's alternative strategic approaches. (Such information helps organizations, too—and many do not have it!) At the level of customer value, community and other external governance constituents often work to ensure that excess value is not created by the organization at the expense of the customer, that organizations can compete on an even playing field to win the customer's business, and that the relationships create value on both sides (a win–win).

Integration of Metrics

One of the most important sets of value drivers are those that relate to the customer perspective. In terms of understanding value drivers, and in measuring value creation, the perspective of the organization and the perspectives of both internal and external customers broadens the usefulness of the under-standings in multiple contexts. (Internal customers are employees within the organization for whom other employees supply services. Employees may have both internal and external customers.) In Chapter 3, we introduced the issue of specific value driver measures and their potential impact on behavior. In Kaplan and Norton's *The Balanced Scorecard,* there is an important sec-tion called "How Bad Things Happen to Good Measures: Using Diagnostic Measures to Balance Strategic Measures."[3] This section discusses the issue of what it calls "myopic suboptimization." It provides the example of the measure of on-time delivery and how a focus on that measure, even though it is an important measure, can create undesirable results. Recognizing that this issue must be addressed, the authors state, "A company's total meas-urement system should not encourage suboptimization. Designers should attempt to anticipate suboptimization that might occur for a given metric on the Balanced Scorecard and provide supplemental metrics that dis-courage achieving the primary scorecard objective in undesirable ways."

In Chapter 3, Exhibit 3.7 showed two metrics that might help to balance each other. One measure represented the customer's assessment of customer service; the second, the cost per transaction. These two measures obviously could help balance each other. The issue, however, noted in the Exhibit 3.7 example, is that although balanced measures in this case can help to reduce sub-optimization, they cannot provide clear direction per se. Exhibit 3.7 showed, in fact, a variety of reactions that might be had given a variety of stated goals. The organization might whimsically or arbitrarily set goals in any number of ways—that might, although balanced, be suboptimal. ("Singsong Savings" developed over 20 conflicting, and balancing, measures. "Wingsong Savings" developed hundreds of measures, more than anyone could remember or ever figure out how to balance.) The point is: How should the organization set goals and understand the requirements from a value creation perspective?

To address the issues in Exhibit 3.7, additional analyses should be under-taken. To do this, the organization will assess which factors, in which combi-nation, create value for the organization, which create value for the customer, and which together can maximize value for the firm.

Exhibit 9.7 shows three scenarios. In each case, the transaction is priced to create value after a charge for the cost of capital. Which scenario, how-ever, will create the most value from the customer's perspective? Which will maximize value for the organization? To illustrate this, a simple example is used. For customers in this example, value is driven from two factors: level of the relationship between customer service and quality/price. (In real life, of course, the model would include more factors, more scenarios, and more customer segments. The organization would have studied customer behav-ior and built marketing and retention statistical prediction rules with the most important factors for their customer base. These are not rules devel-oped overnight but via vigorous experiment and testing.)

Data	Scenarios	1	2	3
Customer Service		**3.2**	**3.4**	**3.8**
Cost per Transaction		**$3**	**$5**	**$8**
Price		**$4.00**	**$6.00**	**$9.00**
Customer Segment Viewpoints				
	Customer Service			
Segment A		3.4	3.8	4.2
Segment B		3.0	3.2	3.4
Segment C		3.2	3.2	3.8
Average		3.2	3.4	3.8
	Customer Service vis-à-vis expectation*			
Segment A		1.1	1.3	1.4
Segment B		1.0	1.1	1.1
Segment C		1.1	1.1	1.3
Average		1.1	1.1	1.3
	Quality vis-à-vis price			
Segment A		1.3	1.0	0.7
Segment B		1.1	1.2	1.2
Segment C		1.0	1.0	0.8
Average		1.1	1.1	0.9

Calculations	Scenarios	1	2	3
Customer Segment Analysis				
	Relative			
Segment A	Weights			
Customer Service	0.2	0.23	0.25	0.28
Quality/Price	0.8	1.00	0.80	0.58
		1.23	**1.05**	**0.86**
Segment B				
Customer Service	0.8	0.80	0.85	0.91
Quality/Price	0.2	0.23	0.23	0.24
		1.03	**1.09**	**1.15**
Segment C				
Customer Service	0.5	0.53	0.53	0.63
Quality/Price	0.5	0.50	0.50	0.40
		1.03	**1.03**	**1.04**

Notes: Top section provides raw data and calculates scores for each segment and scenario.
*Customer service scores listed above are converted to scale where 1.0 = meets expectation.
Bottom section calculates weighted average scores for each customer segment and scenario.

EXHIBIT 9.7   Balancing the Measures: Creating Value with Value Drivers

Scenario 1 shows a lower customer service, lower price strategy; Scenario 3, a higher customer service, higher price strategy; and Scenario 2, an in-between strategy. Average numbers do not provide the detail to map a strategic change. Looking at three customer segments, each customer segment will have a different reaction to a given level of customer service and have different perceptions of quality vis-à-vis price. Some segments will view higher prices as a sign of much higher quality, whereas others will not believe that quality is that different at all. Different customer segments will also place a different value on customer service versus value for the dollar (i.e., quality/price). These differences will be reflected in the customer's overall view of their experience and the value derived from it.

For Segment A, value has been created in all but the third scenario (i.e., where the score is less than 1). For Segments B and C, value is created under all three scenarios. For Segment C there is not much differentiation, but for Segment B there is, and higher levels of customer service and higher prices appear warranted. The exhibit clarifies that not all customers define value in the same way.

With this information in hand, an organization may then study what this information means in terms of their impact on retention, cross-sell, and referrals in the future. Are different business models warranted for different segments? What are their costs vis-à-vis the long-term benefits obtained?

On its own, it is clear that simply adding another measure to the scorecard will not help the organization determine what is in the best interests of the customers and investors. To do that requires modeling of value creation — first of the past and what drives value, then development of predictive models, next the experimentation and the testing of those models, then the refinement of them to reassess and continually act in the best interest of their own and their constituents value creation. It is through this work rather than intuitive guesses that the benefits or shortfalls of a score of 3.8 as a customer service goal can be understood.

In a similar way, activity-based information must be understood to perform these analyses — the activity of the organization and that of the customer and how these impact value creation. A common issue that is cited is convenience or ease of use. Many customers like the convenience of 800 numbers to transact business. When companies implement complicated voice menus, this can adversely impact their views of the value proposition of the supplier, however. For some organizations with significant customer segments that value convenience, cost-cutting moves of this kind have created a lose–lose situation. Customers believe the value proposition is less strong and the organization loses value creation over the long run.

TQM processes measure customer service and process quality outcomes. This information must be balanced within the framework of value to understand: Which outcomes do customers value? Which are they willing to pay for? Is reeducation possible? What will various choices mean in terms of the customer segments that will or will not buy the product?

Integration of Techniques

Patterns of Value Creation. Customer's actions (whether they purchase, refer, etc.) end up providing an outlook on their view of the organization's value creation in a larger sense. Are the products still relevant? Do the means of distribution still facilitate their ends?

Value creation related to the customer can be understood in terms of two components: (1) those activities of the organization that do not impact customer behavior (for example, the organization's efficiency in the use of its internal resources that do not impact the price or other outcomes to the customer) and (2) those activities of the organization that impact the customer experience and behavior. (See the "Integration of Metrics" section earlier in this chapter.)

Studying customer patterns of value creation can help an organization identify the most important value drivers for various segments and adjust their approaches. Clearly, not all customers are the same. And not all customers will react to changes in the same way. Some customers will opt for supplier consistency; others to keep their options open. Patterns of value creation can help organizations in the creation of relevant segments (i.e., the segmentation process) as well.

Volatility Analyses. Measurement of the changes in customer value creation over time provides good early warning signals of potential issues (for the organization and its constituents). A change in a value driver like a customer service number on its own may also provide useful information. However, as shown in Exhibit 9.7, if customer service goes down, certain segments may care much less than other segments do. Exhibit 6.7 (concerning customer volatility) shows the importance of understanding not only the measurement of value creation but its volatility as well.

Information Gap Analyses™. Some industries do better than others in understanding customer value creation. They know more about the customer; they study the customer.

Financial services organizations are believed in general to not do as well with this. "TreeTop Trust," perhaps not considered *the best,* but certainly highly regarded and in the top quartile, gathered a lot of customer information. The issue TreeTop faced was that no one trusted the quality of the information. Because of this, and for historical reasons, the organization had multiple databases. This created a situation with lots of data and no information. Data quality was suspect, as was its use.

Many organizations share this issue, particularly as it relates to customer or marketing information. Some organizations cannot tell you who their customers are (in any consolidated way). Some organizations have spent millions over and over again on marketing-related databases.

Much of the information related to customers does not come from audited financials; it is built by people with a marketing perspective (perception: less grounded), and so it may not garner respect. This is often one of the first places an organization must look at information afresh and use the Information Gap Analyses™ approach to establish rigor and credibility in the information and the analyses derived from it.

Statistical Prediction Rules. Within that culture of rigor, it is possible to develop effective marketing statistical prediction rules (SPRs) related to specific customers and specific customer segments. These SPRs can help the organization predict demand and understand and predict value creation.

Pictures of Customer Value. Pictures of total customer value creation, from the organization's perspective, can look like Exhibit 9.8. This presentation on its own can be misinterpreted to imply that all customers create some value in each period. In response, a standard picture of customer value creation breaks customers into segments to demonstrate that not all customers create value in the period being measured (see Exhibit 9.9). Of course, the issue with this common presentation is that perhaps customer segments C and D are proportionally newer customers. Or perhaps (although some organizations are reluctant to admit this) it is the organization's actions that have created the issues: mispricing products to those segments.

Exhibit 9.10 provides another picture of customer value creation. This view, over time, is in marked contrast to the one-year snapshot. While customer segment D might be discounted in traditional schema focused on the results of Exhibit 9.9, this exhibit provides a very different picture.

Exhibit 9.11 provides another picture showing the value creation by each segment, by year, providing a picture of customer value creation that is actionable. The organization can focus on addressing questions such as: (1) Can the organization take actions to make Segments C and D more valuable in earlier years? and (2) Can the trend of decreasing value for Segment A be turned around?[4]

ValueMap™. The customer information is a very important component of the ValueMap™ (see Exhibit 6.8). The map provides a way to consolidate and look at the information about value creation, the drivers of value, and multiple customer perspectives.

Applications of Metrics

Performance Assessment. Looking at value, from both the perspective of the customer and the organization, helps the organization to properly assess

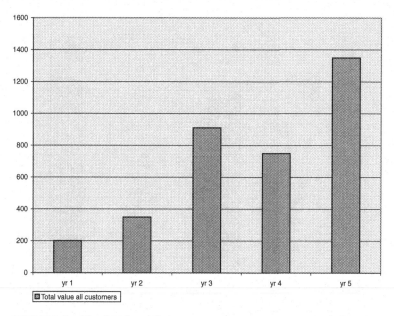

EXHIBIT 9.8   Total Value All Customers, Years 1–5

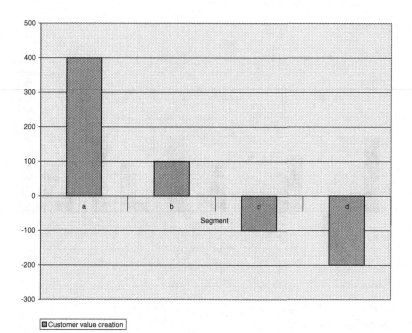

EXHIBIT 9.9   Customer Value Creation—By Segment

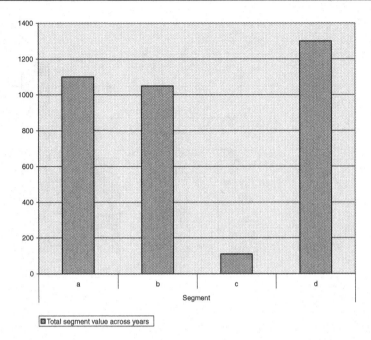

EXHIBIT 9.10 Total Segment Value across Years

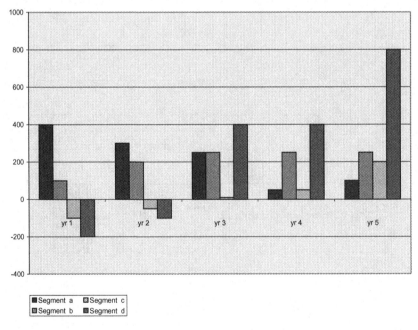

EXHIBIT 9.11 Customer Value Creation—By Segment by Year

its performance. If value is not being created, what are the reasons? As Exhibits 9.7 and 9.11 pointed out, looking behind the numbers to deeper levels is important for the organization to determine its strategy.

Understanding the value proposition to the customer is critical. An organization embarking on strategic change must not only assess current performance and likely future changes but also the impact of changes. Organizations use economic value calculations to not only understand their customers and assess their performance but also to determine which products and services would benefit their customers most.

Strategy. Strategic insights and directions can be gleaned by studying changes in customer value through volatility and patterns of value creation studies. Volatility analyses can be applied to both the review of value creation and the drivers of value (from both the organization and customers points of view). These insights provide important inputs to any strategy process. When ignored, organizations have seen their markets dry up and/or their value steadily decline. This input to a strategy allows the organization to take preemptive actions to reinvent itself—which will be rewarded in the stock price.

Such reviews can also lead to strategic shifts in employee and customer interactions. One question to address, for example, is which interactions are commodity like and which are value added?

Process and Technology. Often the study of customer value will create the necessity for changes in process and in technology. Process changes may be made to improve efficiencies (for the organization and/or the customer), to improve customer retention, referral rates, and so forth. Technology is often used to provide platforms to hold and gather more and more customer-related information. (See the example in Chapter 8's "Rewards" section.) It is customer information that often generates major expenditures in technology dollars. For this reason, it is critical that the value benefits of the information are understood.

Organizational Structure. Organizational changes can come about based on analyses of customer value. These can include changes to create better responsiveness and customer service, enhance product quality, and improve cross-sell and retention, for example.

Rewards. Cross-sell is often an important value driver in many organizations. "FrontView Partners" established incentives based on improvement in customer value creation. As a result of this clear focus, without having to make organizational structure changes, FrontView saw a greatly enhanced ability to generate additional customer business across business lines where before that activity was virtually nonexistent.

Training and Communications. In creating value, communications to customers are very important tools. "TechWorld" studied customer behavior and found for some of their customer segments that encouraging their customers not to call has, in fact, created the opposite behavior on the part of the customer and greater sales for the organization. Sometimes what is most effective is not obvious. (Which is what this book is all about.)

Training within the organization *about* customers is vitally important to the creation of value. Understanding the customer is critical to meeting their needs. Economic value analyses and driver analyses can help organizations understand individual customers and customer segments and how meeting their needs can create a win–win situation in terms of value.

VALUE DRIVERS

What are the major drivers of value creation for the organization? That is the $64,000 question. Measuring the value that has been created is essential to understanding where we are. Understanding the major drivers of value creation is a question of causality, a question that takes real digging, persisting, hypothesis, and testing to discern. It is a very key question for the organization to address. (This section will discuss Question 6 on Exhibit 9.1 using the format of "Metrics Choices and Uses," outlined in Exhibits 9.2 and 9.3.)

To understand what drives value and what destroys it requires discernment between the activities that work (produce) and those that do not. It requires the separation between those activities that are an investment and those that are a waste. The answers to these questions are found when we understand which activities create value and which destroy them, which contribute and which do not.

To understand these activities that create value we must also understand value from the perspective of our constituents—what employees value and what customers value, for example. (See the "Why Improvement Matters" section at the end of this chapter.) We may hypothesize, but we must also test, as the first section in this chapter, on customer value, suggests.

There has been much written on the topic of performance drivers, and on lagging and leading indicators. Some of what has been written has been very helpful; some, unfortunately, has caused more harm than good, more form than substance.

Of course, all organizations want to understand the causes of value creation, for themselves, their peers, their sectors, products, and the like. To do this, the organization must understand the relationship between the drivers of value and the value that is created.

Some organizations begin to understand the value drivers for their organization by constructing value driver trees. These break down the financial results into component parts.[5] Organizations also begin to understand the value drivers for their organizations by studying their organization's processes and activities, using disciplines like TQM, ABM, and supply chain management. These process views help an organization to better understand its core activities and their linkage to value.

What drives value for an organization? At the most basic level it is the unique configuration of its choices, decisions, and interactions. Sometimes these are called: "the customer experience," "the employee experience," "the market view," or "the organizational process experience." This is why often the views of constituents along with the organization's internal processes form the basis for the understandings. To understand this well and to avoid becoming misled requires two important mind-sets. One is a strategic view that looks at major strategic decisions. Another is a scientific view that hypothesizes the value drivers and tests their validity.

The first view, the strategic one, looks at the firm based on the major strategic components. There is no right way to do this. See Exhibit 9.12, which is an analysis that was put together by "Pear Advisors." It is clear to

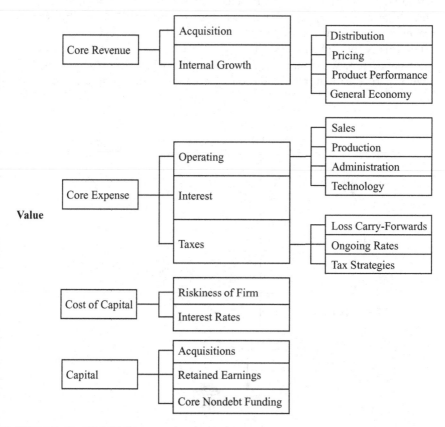

EXHIBIT 9.12 Pear Advisors' Strategic Themes

see that these items can be cascaded down further, creating a map of the organization's performance.

Another approach that is often taken is to *hypothesize* the value drivers of the organization. This can be done at a very detailed level or at a higher, more strategic level. The organization can do this by assembling the facts it knows about what drives value or by intuiting what is likely important. Information can be organized at the total level, also, by sector, product, process, or constituent.

Many organizations developing scorecards develop these hypotheses, then stop at this point and develop a set of metrics based on what they believe, that is, what they intuit are major drivers of value. As Exhibit 9.13 shows, many organizations begin with the idea that they want to create value—that that is their objective. (See "Value" at the top of the exhibit.) To drive value creation, they decide to develop a scorecard that consists of a series of value drivers. To do this, they *hypothesize* or intuit what the organization's relevant value drivers are. Moving from their objective to that action step, they then work to develop a *consensus* about the most important value drivers, which is the next step on the circle. After this step is reached, they *stop* there, and the scorecard is developed. As the chart indicates, this is the right half of the circle, or what will be designated as the right-hand view. What many organizations miss when they *stop* here is they have not really made an evaluation of what the major value drivers are.

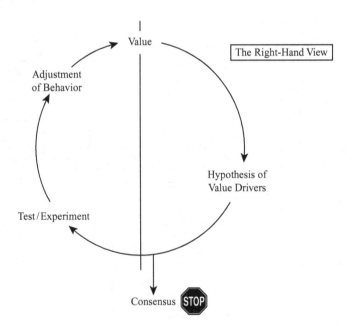

EXHIBIT 9.13   Scientific Approach

What, in fact, they have is a listing organized in some way that represents a *hypothesis* about what the value drivers are.

Measuring and monitoring the hypothesized list *can* help an organization to keep on track with the objectives it now has. It does *not*, however, provide an evaluation that can be used to confirm or deny the hypothesis.

That is where the left-hand side of the circle (see Exhibit 9.13) must enter. For those value drivers that are hypothesized as major, the organization must *test* those hypotheses. This can be done via live experimental feedback or through studies the organization performs. These tests and experiments can help the organization to validate their hypothesis, creating a fact-based connection between what are believed to be value drivers and what, in fact, may be value drivers. (See the next step around the circle.)

To make the answer to the question not only more accurate but also value creating, the organization can use its new-found information about what is and is not driving value to adjust its objectives and strategies and its operational and constituent related behaviors and interactions. (See the next step around the circle.) It is this *adjustment of behavior,* based on the fact base, that will drive real value creation.

In this case, the right- and the left-hand side each need to know what the other is doing. Environmental factors, demographics, technology, and other influences can shift what the key value drivers for an organization may be. From that perspective, it is important to see this as a process, a process that is not set in stone on a tablet but is living and breathing in the organization's enhancement of what it is.

Thus fulfilled, the objectives of the organization, are always placed in context — in the context of value creation. The value drivers are important to understand not to enforce a predetermined strategy but rather to act as a mechanism to adjust the organization's behavior in a way that will create additional value. To do that, new insights are critical. Too often, hypothesized value drivers or scorecard objectives are used in a way that says, "let's emphasize this," not understanding the value implications. Two companies in the same industry may need to do very different things to create value. For this reason, decisions based on the impact on value are much better tools than the assessment of the impact on a hypothesized driver that may or may not have a great impact.

Along those lines, there is another point worth mentioning. The picture that some people have of financials just popping out on the back end of everything the organization does is just wrong. The financials are created in each moment, interaction, behavior, and decision an organization makes. Those moments represent an investment that the organization has made. Stewardship and creating value are about ensuring that those investments are wise.

The core competencies, that is, the critical success factors, become a part of the understanding about the major value drivers. Not all activity is equal. Some represent investment with annuity stream payoffs; others may have one-time effects only.

The importance of context—of value—is critical. An objective of "reduce operating costs" is a poorly formed objective. It does not consider the impact on value (and far too often is addressed, at least in some aspects, in a way that causes value destruction). An alternative value objective would be "reduce operational wastes." In this context, we have a clear objective, the outcome of which *must* be measured in a value context. Waste means value-destroying activity. To fulfill this objective *is* more difficult than the first one. The organization must understand which activities and which expenses are wasteful because they destroy value. It requires an inquiry and a fact base. It also provides the basis for new and better questions: Can this waste become valuable? (Here the 3M Post-it notes example comes to mind.[6]) And it requires methodologies to help the organization find a better way. Continuing to follow the format of metric choices and uses (Exhibits 9.2 and 9.3), let's look at value drivers in those contexts.

Time

While value remains a constant focus over time, value drivers for an organization do change. Value drivers are the components that create the result of value. The derivation of value comes from the actions of constituents. Organizations that study their major value drivers understand more about themselves, their constituents, and their peers. Because the value drivers of an organization do change and the relative importance of any given value driver changes, it is important to make sure that value drivers or metrics that are purported to be major value drivers really are. Organizations have stumbled when they did not recognize their own unique value proposition or combination of value drivers. It is for this reason that value drivers must be studied in the context of overall value creation. Failure to do so can actually destroy a well-run company. Understanding the answer to the evaluative questions of value and utilizing the techniques we have discussed can create the basis for informed hypothesis about what, in fact, the major value drivers are. For example, the ValueMap™ technique, which provides an understanding from the perspective of all constituents, is very helpful in discerning the major value drivers.

Value drivers for the organization will change due to strategic changes and changes that occur within the constituent base. This is another reason a tool like the ValueMap™ can be useful. The ValueMap™ can help the organization to clearly define what it does and does not know from a constituent perspective. This also helps the organization to better understand when a suggested value driver is merely hypothesized and when there is a fact base to support the view that it is major.

"Dunken Financial" developed strategies for a product that created a *higher touch* customer experience. (They did not use overall value, the left side on Exhibit 9.13, or the ValueMap™ technique in their strategy development process.) Without the fact base to support this new approach (this, in fact, was a product where the customer valued efficiency, speed, and commodity pricing), the organization developed a strategy that did not relate to customer values and beliefs. Without the discipline of a fact base, Dunken Financial, like other organizations, can head in the wrong direction by incorrectly intuiting what is or could drive value.

As another example, employee values can and do change, and these changes do influence an organization's creation of value. A typical scorecard for an organization may monitor overall employee satisfaction or number of training courses attended per year. A ValueMap™ would include information for the employee similar to that shown in Exhibit 9.7 for the customer. This kind of information is important because in many organizations the values of employees on the front line, dealing with the customers each day, may be very different from those in the back office or in executive management. Understanding changes that occur as well as doing employee segmentation can help organizations get behind the satisfaction scores to the real drivers for employees that ultimately will impact the customer's experience and the creation of value. (See also Exhibit 10.7 for an employee example.)

Understanding the linkages to value creation helps organizations choose the most important drivers and those that from a cost perspective make sense to monitor. Unfortunately, often in building scorecards, organizations fail to address this critical point. Additionally, scorecards that encompass conflicting unreconciled goals pose other challenges as well (see Exhibit 3.7, for example).

The linkage to value can help organizations avoid what happened to "Baldwig Corp," where the customer satisfaction rating was a very important measure of success. Sales and operating managers were rewarded based on the outcome of this measure. The customer satisfaction metric was so important that these managers did anything and everything possible to raise the customer satisfaction statistic, no matter what the cost. When problems related to delivery occurred, top sales managers booked last minute flights, flew to the customers' sites, apologized in person, offered the customers rebates, and literally negotiated with the customers to get a high customer satisfaction rating on the survey form. While everyone agreed customer satisfaction was important, the measure was not weighed relative to the cost.[7]

Types of Capital

Value drivers, viewed in isolation, can also impact the ways in which organizations view their need for capital. Some organizations build inventory (because there is no charge on the income statement for doing so), and they believe it will keep their customer service levels high. Some organizations hold far more capital in reserves than they need for risk purposes because they are trying to maintain high reserve ratios, although this simply represents a shift from one account to another. Other organizations that wish to show higher equity may use off-balance sheet schemes or other mechanisms. In all these cases, a focus on the component rather than on value creation has proved to be a distraction at best and value destroying or misleading at worst.

To avoid the myopia, it is helpful to view the activities of the organization as investments. Ultimately, does this activity add to the value creation of the organization? Is it something that will translate into value for the customers and for which they are willing to pay enough to ensure a fair return to capital providers over the long term?

The organization must decide its course, weighing what it is and wants to become, its purpose and mission, to choose among that which is valued and ultimately make its decisions based on its fiduciary obligations to its capital providers. For governments, those are its citizens and taxpayers; for social organizations, its members. For for-profit entities, its creditors and shareholders.

Without this holistic view, chaos and lack of direction emerges. One example occurred in "MasonsBank" as it began to reassess its risk capital. While the level of risk capital required is an important driver in understanding value creation, it is dangerous when it becomes *the* focus. Ralph, the CFO of this well-respected institution, however, became so mesmerized with the risk capital numbers that a mental association formed. (This may seem unusual, but it happens in many organizations where there is instituted a component focus.)

To not put too fine a point on it, the association became the same as that shown in Exhibit 9.14. Once this association began, it was very hard to crack it. (This association is similar to the customer satisfaction example earlier. *Nothing* else mattered except high customer satisfaction.)

The issue with becoming mesmerized is that it invites all kinds of band-aid traps. Individuals anxious to take directed action now jump up and say: "We now have the solution." In the case of customer satisfaction, do whatever it takes: plane, train, or automobile. Rather than an examination of the

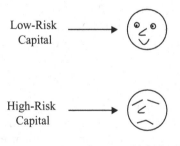

Low-Risk Capital

High-Risk Capital

EXHIBIT 9.14 Reactions to Risk Capital

process issues and making the best cost/benefit, value creating choices, the band-aid of fixing the component is employed.

Similarly, related to the risk capital fixation, the organization moves to eliminate high-risk capital products, even if on a risk-adjusted basis they provide superior returns, creating more value for the organization and its capital providers.

In the example of Ralph, the CFO, something fortunate happened during this period when a whistling consultant stopped by one day. The consultant said: "Hey listen, you have this risk capital business all wrong. The businesses need different capital amounts than you imagine. In fact, your higher-return businesses need less capital than your low-return businesses."

"How can that be?" Ralph pondered. "How is it that the high-return business has low risk and the low-return business has high risk?" With a background in investments, Ralph knew that, at least generally speaking, higher return is associated with higher risk. Ralph, fortunately, rejected the consultant's premise—but the event had done its good, because the spell of the risk capital association was broken. (No longer was high-risk capital necessarily bad.) And everyone lived happily ever after—for a year or so.

Form of Metric

It is important that the value driver's form of metric is suitable to the analysis. In Chapters 6 through 8, this book has emphasized the importance of the standard deviation form. TQM uses the standard deviation form for customer and process value drivers analyses. The standard deviation form can generate useful insights (for customer satisfaction scores, for example). The ValueMap™ includes use of this form in its value drivers sections.

Types of Adjustments

Adjustments in calculating value help to eliminate the hocus-pocus. We can see the impact of actual activity rather than future estimates. We get a clearer picture of what is going on. With this clearer picture, it is much easier to connect our intuitions related to value creation with the actual facts of value creation. This helps keep the organization focused on stewardship rather than pet projects. Exhibit 9.15 explains the distinctions that occur in a value-based scorecard (as opposed to a traditional one). Exhibit 9.16 shows another way to think about the relationship between value management and scorecard processes. The second model closely parallels the problem-solving model described in books on personality type.[8] What is important is that to be successful, all functions should be used, that is, a combination of brain and personality traits, both fact-based and imaginative options, both logical approaches and their logical and human consequences. The value-based drivers scorecard model includes all of these components. Unfortunately, many traditional scorecard processes exclude all the attributes (see

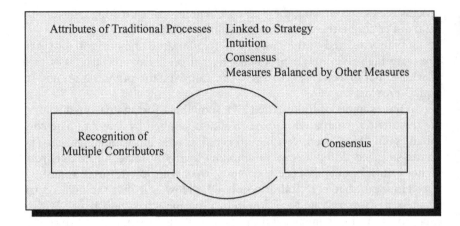

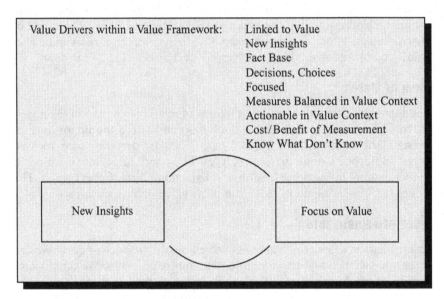

EXHIBIT 9.15   Traditional Processes and *Additional* Dimensions of the Value-Based Scorecard Process

Exhibit 9.13) that pulled together would create the desired success and focus on value.

Constituent Focus: The Alliance

In discussing customer value, the customer value driver perspective was also discussed and the fact that different customers or customer segments may have different sets of value drivers. As noted, the organization can assess

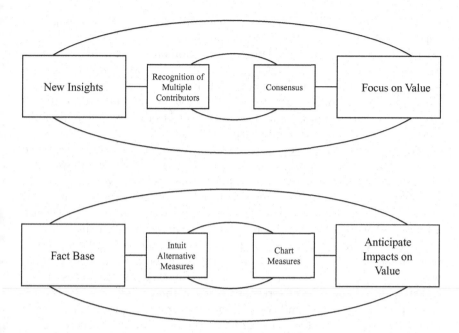

EXHIBIT 9.18 Multi-Dimensional Value-Based Scorecard (Two Views)

the impact of its products on the customer's economic value. Depending on the type of customer (individual, commercial, etc.), this impact may include cost benefits, performance benefits, advertising benefits, and so on. Organizations that do this effectively can reap two rewards: the ability to establish closer customer relationships and the ability to target product innovations that create customer value (and thus will be valued by customers). As with customers, employees may also have value drivers that differ. Because of this, a one-size-fits-all measurement scorecard based on consensus and intuition (the right side in Exhibit 9.13) and not on facts can provide false comfort.

As noted earlier, when organizations use a consensus approach to arrive at the key drivers of value, they have developed a set of metrics that will drive a consensus view, not necessarily a set of metrics that describes what really makes a difference to value creation for that organization and its constituents.

"Purpose determines process," I often say to whoever will listen.

One popular process of creating a performance driver scorecard takes possible ideas and puts them in a box that is acceptable to everyone (see top square, for example, in Exhibit 9.19). The caution here is that, instead of new thinking, thinking is moved into the box. (Now for some organizations, where people have never talked to each other before about these issues, this can be a huge leap forward and the benefits should *not* be underestimated. Small understandings can grow much larger because of the dialogue.)

See Exhibits 9.17 and 9.18 for a pictorial representation of what can happen and thus what the organization should work to prevent. Many organizations that do not calculate value creation on an evaluative basis (i.e., have we created value?), do not know whether they have or not and also do not know what the major drivers of value are. How could they? This book has demonstrated that the results, on a value basis, can differ dramatically from a standard earnings result. This is what makes the ValueMap™ and the linkage to value approach so powerful.

Many scorecards present four perspectives. These are often described as financial, customer, internal business process, and learning and growth.[9] As Exhibit 9.19 shows, one way to think of these perspectives is as follows: The work of an organization begins with its human resources, with its R&D and its intellectual capital. Those resources build a process. That process attracts customers. All of these activities have financial consequences. And even *before there is customer service, there are financial consequences*— there are salaries to be paid and raw materials to be provided. And before we pay those salaries, we must calculate the financial consequences of that investment and the fiduciary responsibility to the capital provider. Financial and economic issues and consequences occur at the very beginning and every step of the way. They are *not* just some output on the back end.

Some have suggested that the scorecard is less a "rigorous, disciplined and focused financial system" and more a "holistic, innovative, judgment-based, people intense management process built around achieving stretch

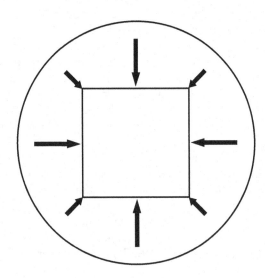

Note: Metrics limited too early by consensus, with insufficient facts.

EXHIBIT 9.17 Metrics Generated

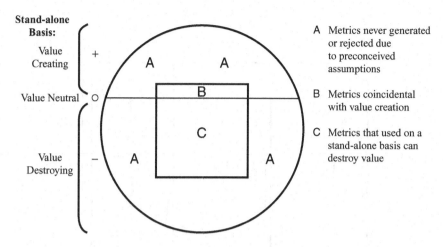

Stand-alone Basis:

Value Creating +

Value Neutral O

Value Destroying −

A Metrics never generated or rejected due to preconceived assumptions

B Metrics coincidental with value creation

C Metrics that used on a stand-alone basis can destroy value

EXHIBIT 9.18 Using Metrics on a Stand-alone Basis: Impacts on Value Creation

targets for customers, internal processes, employees and systems."[10] Every action that is an inherently financial and economic act, a disciplined and focused process, that supports the goal of stewardship is a worthwhile aim. Achieving stretch targets is a good thing—but only if they create value, not if they spend capital providers' nickels with no return. Certainly the dot.coms have proven the truth in this. Ultimately, all decisions are judgment based. However, the question to be addressed is, how equipped is the organization to make that judgment? Does the organization have the facts, the information, the insights it needs?

Integration of Metrics

The reason to measure at all is to drive a process to reach an outcome, to drive behaviors that will create value. It is important, therefore, to understand the impacts of activities on value creation: activity-based costs, activity-based revenue, and activity-based capital. TQM can help the organization fine-tune its process. Reengineering efforts can help the organization eliminate unnecessary steps. One view of the organization is this: Customers purchase a bundle of activities; which activities add value that compensate them for their payments?

In the context of activities, a constituent view can help to build out elements missing in traditional ABC/ABM (activity based costing/activity based management) models. For example, drivers of certain *overhead* activities can be regulatory based. While some practitioners may argue that drivers are only associated with the process and customer-related activities, a fuller constituent view can help the organization identify the other drivers as well. This can also broaden the framework used for drivers beyond the four perspectives often used in typical scorecards.

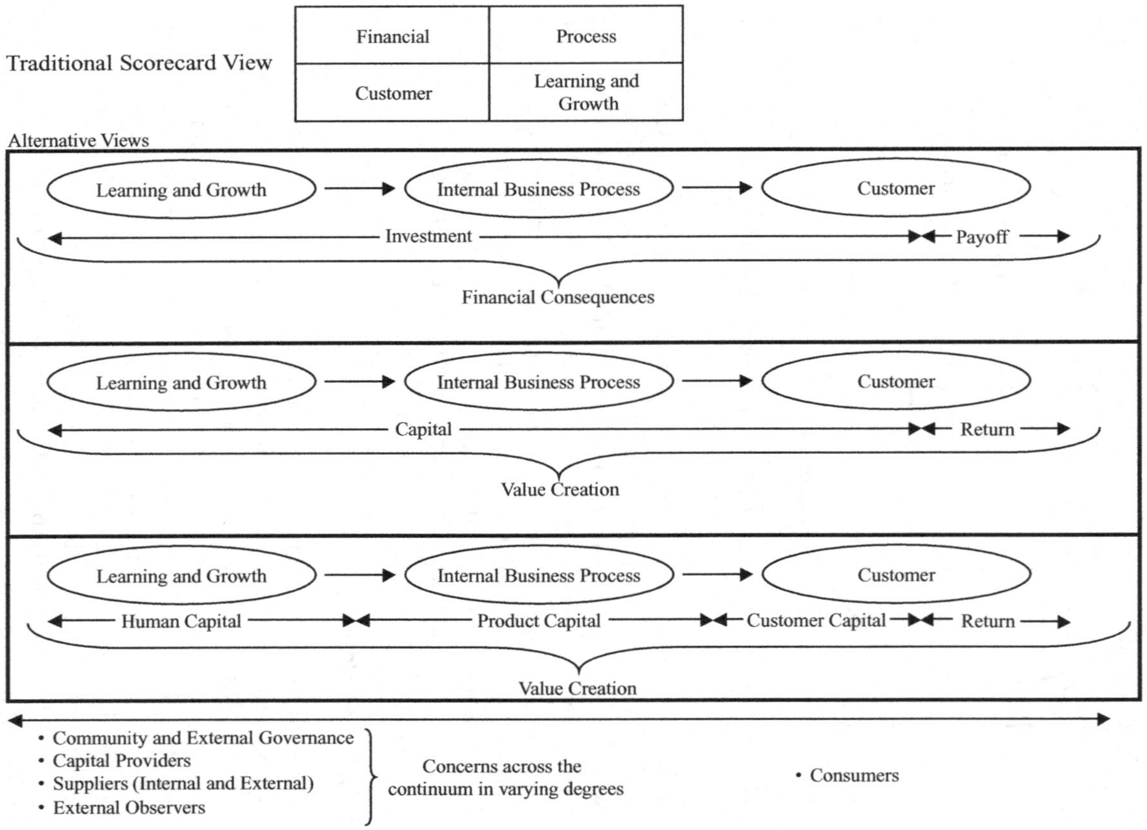
Traditional Scorecard View
Financial
Process
Customer
Learning and Growth
Alternative Views
Learning and Growth
Internal Business Process
Customer
Investment
Payoff
Financial Consequences
Learning and Growth
Internal Business Process
Customer
Capital
Return
Value Creation
Learning and Growth
Internal Business Process
Customer
Human Capital
Product Capital
Customer Capital
Return
Value Creation
• Community and External Governance
• Capital Providers
• Suppliers (Internal and External)
• External Observers
Concerns across the continuum in varying degrees
• Consumers

EXHIBIT 9.19 Business Views

Integration of Techniques

Patterns of Value Creation. Review of patterns of value driver information can provide insights into how changes in a value driver impact ultimate value creation (see Exhibit 7.9, for example). Sometimes, the benefit of a value driver is not coincident with value creation. The investment is made first, and the benefit payoff comes later. Patterns of value creation can help an organization determine the average time until benefits are received. Is it a four-year horizon? Six-year? Longer? What could impact those results into the future? (What impacts the patterns of that value driver, i.e., what drives it?) Patterns of value creation studies can help answer these questions.

Volatility Analysis. Volatility analyses of value drivers often provide great early warning signals. Volatility analyses represents one of the bases of TQM, measuring the standard deviations of certain processes. With a value framework, these measurements can now be performed in the context of value and the value impact.

Information Gap Analyses™. Information Gap Analyses™ are critical to understanding value drivers in a value context. In this process, the quality of information—its information value—is distinguished. The cost/benefit ratios are also assessed. Is it possible to achieve a similar result lightly and simply with more focus? Must the process be *people intense?* Can it be made clear and direct by understanding what is most important—and what information will create value, rather than being just nice to have?

This, in fact, is a problem that many scorecard practitioners find themselves in. A group of executives at "Basin Street Bank" used a consensus format to come up with a list of measures—there was just no way to measure them. (Which brings us back to: Do we need to measure it? How badly do we need that information?)

Certainly, when faced with a cost/benefit challenge and a desire to better understand what it should do, an organization can look at its value creation today, look at its past processes, and attempt to discern causality. Sometimes general direction with a focus on value rather than precise measures is all that is required to turn the ship—or at least provide an 80/20 solution.[11] The alternatives should be considered so that value can be optimized.

Statistical Prediction Rules. Statistical prediction rules (SPRs) represent a way to relate drivers to a broader measure, that is, value creation. (See discussion on risk capital in the section on "Types of Capital" and Exhibit 9.14.) Indicators or key performance indicators (KPIs), rather than drivers, are measures where that level of causality cannot be drawn, that is, where the relationship is less direct or the context less clear. Exhibits 9.17 and 9.18 show the danger in emphasizing these kinds of metrics on a stand-alone basis. Formulating and testing SPRs (the left side of Exhibit 9.13) can help the organization understand the nature of the measures: Is it a driver or an indicator? To do this requires action to gather the intelligence required. To take this action, it is important to gather as many preliminary facts as possible to discern that even this exercise is worth doing, that ultimately this information is useful in understanding and creating value.

The ValueMap™. The ValueMap™ provides a way to show the interrelationships among constituents and the drivers of value from each perspective.

Applications of Metrics

Performance Assessment. In the context of value, the drivers can provide additional information about how the organization has performed, how working together value has either been created or destroyed. From a performance assessment standpoint, the most important use of value drivers is to understand how the organization has performed vis-à-vis the driver over time.[12] An organization may not wish to follow the path of its peers. However, the organization will wish to understand how they are different so that they can effectively articulate to customers and other constituents the differences in their value propositions.

Strategy. To be successful, strategy processes need to be formed on the basis of new insights. The dialogue suggested in scorecard processes can be a first step for organizations that have never discussed what the organization is really about with each other. Inspiration, however, often comes from perspiration. Dig for facts—and new connections can be made, new ideas formed. It is important that strategy begin on these solid bases. Not on "as it always has been" nor in ignorance of what is. It is in this context that strategy should use value drivers—to better understand what is happening in the creation of value, of what is known, and what is unknown. The goal of an organization is not to follow a particular strategy. The goal is to act with stewardship to create value. The strategy must adapt to the goal and not be confused with it.

If a new idea is formed, it should not be judged based upon being part of a strategy (which was a group's idea at the time) but rather whether it supports more generally the vision, mission, who the organization wants to be, and the organization's goal of value creation. It is very important to avoid the trap of some traditional processes that stifle innovation by representing a reassertion rather than a true vision. The ability to create from an insight and create value in the process is after all the essence of an organization's mission.

Process and Technology. Value drivers often require additional information systems and point to the need for the addition, elimination, or modification of processes. Activity based costing (ABC) systems, for example, often call for the use of drivers and require technology support. If this work is done in the context of value, the chances improve that any investment will produce payoffs that warrant the expenditures. Fortunately, Economic Value Management also provides a means to monitor the effectiveness of technology expenditures on an ongoing basis—not simply upfront as a one-shot investment analysis (see Chapter 5). Investments of this type also benefit from the context of Information Gap Analyses™. That context also helps improve the chances for the technology solution's effectiveness.

Organizational Structure. A common issue of perspective that can influence the effectiveness of the scorecard is the process of development of the scorecard based on *existing* organizational structures. Although ultimately these structures must be taken into account, the approach, from a development standpoint, can create a number of difficulties. One difficulty arises because today in most large organizations strategic objectives create value *horizontally* across many, if not all, major organizations within the firm. (As noted in discussing sector value, this can create measurement challenges as well.) Rather than resolve this by changing the scorecard process, perhaps the difficulty is best resolved by management's consideration of an idea described in Malcolm Gladwell's *The Tipping Point: How Little Things Can Make a Big Difference.* Citing the successful example of Gore, the maker of Gore-tex and other products, and what Gladwell calls the *Rule of 150,* Gladwell argues that cells of a limited size can be much more effective than far-flung operations where people must coordinate across wide spans.[13] Gore practices this principle by creating effective, stand-alone units of size no bigger than 150 people. Such an organizational structure change creates innovative and responsive units that can clearly focus on their mission and purpose (and focus on value creation as a unit).

Rewards Process. Often, organizational structure is based on an organization's view of its value drivers. Often, rewards processes are built that mirror these views. As a result, competing objectives flourish and differing goals create impacts that must be guarded against in different organizations. As noted earlier, different measures ("value drivers") can pull the organization in different directions: sales for the sales staff, operating efficiency for the operations staff, risk assessment for the risk staff. Organizations can create unnecessary tensions when the structure and rewards processes focus on individual drivers for each unit rather than overall value creation. To play a symphony requires the musicians to play their individual parts—in the right tempo, loudness, and harmony to create the overall result.[14] That means synchronicity in terms of the individual effects on overall value. The individual efforts, in an integrated fashion, come together to make it work.

When "Mutual of Cripple Creek" embarked on Economic Value Management, it had not recognized how divisive its organizational process, structure, and objectives were. The value process allowed them to witness those tensions that created value destruction. Many organizations often act without realizing there is another way. Here again, the Rule of 150 can help organizations to create units that can focus on value—with that as the straightforward and clear objective.

Training and Communications. Value driver information is very useful for investors. Companies are now providing more of this information than ever before.[15] Just as investors appreciate sector information provided under FAS 131, value driver information is also highly prized. Some organizations have received excellent press by providing investor's information on their major value drivers, and in the case of complex industries, providing information on general industry value drivers as well. This information has been well received and, universally, external observers like analysts, and capital providers like investors, appreciate the additional information. One cautionary note: Organizations that discuss a myriad of metrics and *state* that these conflicting measures are their objectives call into question their own focus and judgment. "RiverBank" did this and, rather than create confidence, the multiple conflicting measures projected a startling lack of strategic focus (which was, in fact, the case).

However, providing the information that measures important value driver performance, is regarded very favorably. In the best cases, organizations provide information on the relative importance of the value drivers, how they have changed, and their impact on value. On that basis, investors and other constituents are better able to understand what, in that context, those value drivers mean. For more information on value drivers, see Chapter 10's section on "Integration of Metrics."

HOW HAS VALUE CREATION CHANGED OVER TIME?

This section of Chapter 9 covers the last of the evaluative questions (see Question 7, Exhibit 9.1) using the format of "Metrics Choices and Uses" outlined in Exhibits 9.2 and 9.3. The answer to this question is a critical area that we have already addressed to a great extent in the review of the evaluative questions. Understanding patterns of value creation is one component. Using the standard deviation form of the metric and understanding variability over time is another component. The analyses of volatility forms another. Options values obviously change over time, and it is these that get reflected in the market price for an organization. The answer to the question of changes in value creation helps the organization to pinpoint what may have been effective in the past and is not working now (or vice versa). This helps the organization connect value to the value drivers.

Time

From a time perspective, as always, a longer view helps the organization and its constituents to assess the nature of the changes. Are they cyclical? Are they caused by new phenomenon? Certainly, value drivers are best put in context in this way.

Types of Adjustments

Changes in accounting or the way in which data are captured or stored may create changes to calculations of value needed to provide apples-to-apples comparisons. See Chapter 6, where these issues are discussed in detail.

Constituent Focus: The Alliance

As value creation changes over time, community and external governance constituents may develop different views on the risks the organization faces and their possible response to those risks. Providers of capital often look to take advantage of market situations that may represent issues broader than the organization's. By studying these trends in changes in value creation across the industry as a whole, they are able to assess who is most impacted and which organizations will create the most value in the future. Consumers are often on the lookout as well. "McDull Savings Bank" had experienced a decline in its stock price and value creation following a merger. Consumers actively inquired of third parties the reasons for the declines and the potential impacts. Since changing suppliers can take time, consumers wanted to understand the drivers of the changes. They were concerned about disruptions to service down the road, issues that an organization might be able to paper over for a while but could adversely impact the consumers over the long run.

Integration of Metrics

For activity-based information, the changes over time can be some of the most important activity insights an organization receives. Monitoring changes is one of the primary bases for TQM and thus fully supported by its standard methodologies. As noted earlier, changes to scorecard items like customer service and efficiency can help an organization pinpoint and understand that item's impact on value creation.

Integration of Techniques

In terms of changes in value creation, use of the patterns of value creation techniques takes the benefits to the next level. This process involves developing an understanding of how the patterns themselves have changed over time. Volatility analyses are used in the context of change over time to understand how the volatility itself has changed over time. Information Gap

Analyses™ are used in this context to discern changes in information needs and changes in impacts in value creation. Improvement measures become important and being able to analyze the quality and needs for certain data come to the fore. SPRs are used to predict changes and their impacts on value. As demonstrated in Chapter 7, pictures are a useful tool to show the changes in value creation over time, and the ValueMap™ represents changes and their application for the constituent groups.

Applications of Metrics

Performance Assessment. Understanding changes in value creation is key to using value as a tool for performance assessment, strategy development, and rewards. To that end, the organization must assess how the organization has improved over time, how it has improved vis-à-vis its peers, how its component pieces have improved, and how constituents view the organization's level of improvement.

Strategy. How has the organization's strategy and value changed over time? The answer to this question provides a basis for understanding current issues impacting the organization's value and areas the organization may encounter in the future. These analyses can help the organization develop new insights related to indicators for the need for strategy shifts. This need may arise because of changes in the external reality or changes internally in terms of the organization's own ability to execute.

Process and Technology. The organization may need to change its ability to execute by leveraging its technology or implementing needed process changes. Certainly, the advent of the Internet offered many organizations the opportunity to capitalize on another outreach mechanism to customers. The customer segments attracted to organizations with this capability began to diverge from those without the capability, as this mechanism became a desirable means of interaction in certain industries.

Organizational Structure. How has the organizational structure and value changed over time? Often, the answer to this question shows the impact of organizational structure changes. When "The Sternum Group" was performing this analysis, they noted the impact of organizational changes in reviewing their numbers. These insights provided cautionary tales, Marvin, the CEO, says: "It enabled us to understand what we should guard against and plan to do, related to structure, in the future."

Rewards Process. The rewards process is centered around improvement. It is about employees and managers sharing with investors in the improvement in value creation that the organization experiences. It is about ensuring that incentives encourage that improvement. That not only is value created, but that it improves over time. That is the basis of the rewards in Economic Value Management. The key is defining *over time* over a long enough horizon to ensure that the changes and improvements are *sustainable* and the rewards are large enough to incent the behaviors that will result in maximum value creation.

Training and Communication. One of the important measures of the change in value over time is an assessment in the change in the value of human capital. Organizations need to identify what is working and what is not working related to training efforts. At times this can be difficult. It is certainly worth the effort, however. "Curbside Insurance Company" has used analyses of its training efforts to reinforce the importance of its training investment and continually improve those training programs as well.

IMPROVEMENT: WHY IMPROVEMENT MATTERS

Any discussion of change in a value context always generates discussions around the areas of improvement and continuous improvement. Before we move to the final chapter and a discussion of the predictive questions, a discussion of improvement is an excellent transition from evaluations to predictions, from what is to what could be.

The Oxford English Dictionary defines the word *improvement* as "an addition or alteration that improves something or adds to its value" and further defines the word *improve* as "to make or become better . . . more valuable . . . or to make good use of." The dictionary definitions pull together the relationship among *improvement, change* (addition or alteration), *value creation* (adds to its value), and *stewardship* (make good use of it).

The organizations that are the best at continuous improvement have a clear understanding of these relationships and use that understanding to create a focus on value and a commitment to continuous improvement. These organizations understand that as the speed of change increases, a focus on value and improvement provides a rudder to the organization's employees and customers. This focus provides a meaningful response and a way to move forward that can provide clear direction when everything appears to be changing.

Magazines such as *Fast Company* talk about the accelerating importance of meaning, not just materialism, in the work lives of new careerists. A mind-set of improvement, particularly in a value context, provides a meaningful intention to workplace actions. Since perfection is not achievable, improvement represents a worthwhile aim. For organizations that understand the significance of improvement and the choices around it, it is possible both to create meaning and improve economic results as well.

With improvement in economic value creation as the goal, one key step for any organization is to identify even more specifically what it wants to improve. One approach organizations take is to conduct benchmarking studies to identify their results on a series of measures as compared to their peers. Constructed carefully, benchmarking measurement processes help the organization to better understand the views of its actions (both customer and labor viewpoints) and its areas of efficiency (or lack thereof). This phase is one example of information gathering.

Another phase involves selection. The organization must carefully examine its strengths and weaknesses during the selection process and determine what the organization intends to become, what part of this reality it will create internally, and what part will be outsourced. Based on assessments, the organization can then construct a plan that suits the context of their organization and its capabilities and the value drivers relevant to it. Rather than simply beginning to look like their peers, the organization may choose to improve strengths rather than correct weaknesses. In so doing, the organization will continue to delineate its unique pattern of offering to customers. In recommitting to continuous improvement in costs, for example, the organization may determine that "over-spending" in certain areas compared to peer benchmarks, makes sense based on its strategic positioning. In other areas of cost, however, where the organization may already be ahead of its peers, it may continue to look for efficiencies that will provide a strategic edge.

Both a commitment to improvement and discernment about what to improve are important for the organization's ultimate success. This is why understanding employee and customer desires and shareholder requirements, among other constituents, in the selection process is so critical. Expectations of employees, customers, and shareholders are linked to their views of what improvement means. For employees, improvement relates directly to the definition. They want to be able to add value and to become more valuable. They want their voices to be heard and their talents to be used and recognized. They want to share in the value they create, and they want changes that will make their lives better. Organizational changes that limit their ability to add value, stymie their ability to become more valuable, do not use their talents, and give them a smaller share of the value they create or influence their lives for the worse will be met with resistance and not viewed as improvement.

Similarly, customers will view organizational changes as improvements if they provide better (more desirable) products and services, which provide value to them, and make good use of their time and money. What matters to each individual customer may differ. Their expectations, however, matter. All companies know to focus on these aspects, yet not all do. Without the commitment to improvement, the organization will lapse and produce inferior products, provide shoddy service, charge more, waste customer

			Present Value of		Present Value of	
Market Value (a)	=	Capital (b) +	Current Economic (c) + Value in Perpetuity		Future Improvements (d) in Economic Value	

EXHIBIT 9.20   Market Value Formula

time, and provide poor value. Understanding which changes and trade-offs are important to each customer and represent improvement to the customer is key to avoiding these errors.

Quantifiably, shareholders require improvement. The growth in capital they have committed to the organization depends on improvement, specifically, on improvement in the results of its use. Without a focus on improvement, shareholders will not be adequately rewarded. To understand their expectations, organizations must benchmark them as well. First, the organization must understand how to perform a market value analysis, that is, how to calculate shareholder expectations for value creation as represented by the formula in Exhibit 9.20.[16] Using inputs for *a, b,* and *c,* they must calculate and understand *d,* the value of improvements that shareholders require. Knowing this, they then must benchmark the results against the expectations for competitor firms. Using this information and historical information on their own organization's expectations and performance, they can then develop the improvement targets that will meet shareholder requirements. Shareholder expectations for improvement include the expectation that management will act as stewards, making the firm more valuable by putting to good use the funds they have supplied.

In the best organizations, a commitment to improvement means improvement in multiple dimensions. It is about creating value based on sustainable improvement. And it is about stewardship. It means appropriate value creation for all constituents and change with a focus on and a commitment to that which is better.

Organizations that continuously improve in this way are value led. And Economic Value Management "is an integration of a number of disciplines, all coming together to make it work."[17]

NOTES

1. Robert Blattberg, Gary Getz, and Jacquelyn Thomas, *Customer Equity: Building and Managing Relationships as Valuable Assets,* Boston: Harvard Business School Press, 2001.

2. Ordinal statistics involve data that can be ranked.

3. Robert S. Kaplan and David P. Norton, *The Balanced Scorecard: Translating Strategy Into Action,* Boston: Harvard Business School Press, 1996, pp. 164–165.

4. Data can also be gathered in other forms to drill down and answer additional questions including:

- Average value per customer in each segment, by year
- Customer segment value, by year of customer acquisition
- Average value per customer in each segment, by year of customer acquisition

Bucketed segment data by year of customer acquisition can be very helpful in understanding the shape of the life cycle value curve for customers of different segments.

5. Both of the following books provide useful examples of these processes: Tom Copeland, Tim Koller, and Jack Murrin, *Valuation: Measuring and Managing the Value of Companies,* New York: John Wiley and Sons, 1995; and S. David Young and Stephen F. O'Byrne, *EVA® and Value Based Management: A Practical Guide to Implementation.* New York: McGraw-Hill, 2001.

6. Dr. Spence Silver, a research scientist at 3M, was trying to make a very strong adhesive. His efforts failed. Instead, he created a glue that had the property that it could stick and be unstuck very easily. Rather than throw it away, "the waste" came to be used on one of the fastest growing products at the end of the last century. The product, invented at 3M by Art Fry, was named Post-it Notes.

7. Eleanor Bloxham, "Finding Value Solutions: Resolving Cost and Performance Conflicts," *The Journal of Cost Management,* March/April 2001.

8. Paul D. Tieger and Barbara Barron-Tieger, *Do What You Are: Discover the Perfect Career for You Through the Secrets of Personality Type, Second Edition,* Boston: Little, Brown & Company, 1995. Per Tieger, the problem-solving model was adapted by Eleanor Corlett from *People Types and Tiger Stripes* by Gordon Lawrence.

9. Kaplan and Norton's, *The Balanced Scorecard: Translating Strategy Into Action* provides a detailed description of these perspectives and other relevant issues.

10. Kaplan and Norton, pg. 290.

11. An 80/20 solution is one in which 20% of the efforts yields 80% of the beneficial impact. (To achieve the remaining 20% may require four times the original effort.)

12. G. Bennett Stewart III, *The Quest For Value,* New York: Harper Business, 1991, pp. 108–109.

13. Malcolm Gladwell, *The Tipping Point: How Little Things Can Make a Big Difference.* Back Bay Books, Boston: Little, Brown & Company, 2002, p. 182.

14. Bennett Stewart uses a similar analogy in *The Quest For Value,* p. 108.

15. Eleanor Bloxham, *Value-led Organizations,* Oxford: Capstone Publishing (Wiley & Sons), 2002, p. 61, "A Tale of Four Disclosures."

16. S. David Young and Stephen F. O'Byrne, *EVA® and Value Based Management: A Practical Guide to Implementation.* New York: McGraw Hill, 2001.

17. The author while being interviewed by William Mahoney in *Shareholder Value* magazine.

CHAPTER 10

Creating Value in the Future

O ne of the payoffs for the digging comes in being able to generate bet-ter answers to the predictive questions.[1] (See Exhibit 10.1, Questions 8 through 14.) We have, in fact, covered these questions in some detail as we have discussed the evaluative questions.

Evaluative

1. Has the organization added value? How much?
2. How does this compare to the organization's peers and competitors?
3. Has the organization been managed such that each sector has added value?
4. Has the organization been managed such that each product, service, distribution channel, or process added value?
5. Has the organization been managed such that each custo-mer relationship added value?
6. What are the major drivers of value creation for the orga-nization?
7. For all of the above, how has this changed over time?

You Are Here > **Predictive**

8. How much value does the organization expect to create?
9. How much value do capital providers (shareholders, if pub-licly traded) expect the organization to create?
10. How much value does the organization expect to create by sector, product, service, distribution channel, process, and customer?
11. What are the expectations related to the major drivers of value creation over time?

EXHIBIT 10.1 The Questions

(continued)

EXHIBIT 10.1   The Questions *(Continued)*

12. What are the capital provider's expectations for the organization's peers? What are the peer's expectations for itself
by sector, product, service, distribution channel, process,
customer, and major drivers of value creation?

13. How do internal, peer, and capital provider expectations
differ from current steady-state value creations?

14. For all of the above, how will this change over time?

We refer back to Chapter 4 (in the section "Different Measures of Value
for Different Purposes: The Predictive Metrics") and we recognize that to
date we have discussed many of the issues in predictive measurement associated with fixed versus changing boundaries. In Chapter 6, as we laid out
the framework of metrics, techniques, and applications for evaluative questions, we set the stage for answering questions of value creation in the
future. In fact, it was this context that shaped our discussions and insights
in Chapters 6 through 9. Nevertheless, we have several issues to make clear
before we are ready to release the genie from the bottle.

EXPECTATIONS OF FUTURE VALUE: THE FIRST PREDICTIVE QUESTIONS

How much value does the organization expect to create (Exhibit 10.2,
Question 8), and how much value does the organization expect to create by
sector, product, service, distribution channel, process, and customer (Exhibit
10.2, Question 10)? What are the expectations related to the major value
drivers over time (Exhibit 10.2, Question 11), and what are the peer's
expectations related to its organization, sector, product, service, distribution
channel, process, and customer (Exhibit 10.2, second half of Question 12)?
All require similar techniques and approaches. While the organization may
have more information to answer questions about itself than about its peers,
the groundwork laid in Chapters 6 and 7 provide the necessary background
for addressing the issues of peer information. For other constituents, the
task is the same. For this reason, in this chapter we will address these questions as a unit.

The Benefits of Multiple Approaches and Techniques

The answer to this and the related questions is often the outcome of an
organization's strategy process. The digging that has already been performed
in answering the evaluative questions helps make the answers to the predictive questions stronger, more realistic, and fact based. The extra measure
of information about *what is* will help the organization to reject the typical

Evaluative

1. Has the organization added value? How much?
2. How does this compare to the organization's peers and competitors?
3. Has the organization been managed such that each sector has added value?
4. Has the organization been managed such that each product, service, distribution channel, or process added value?
5. Has the organization been managed such that each customer relationship added value?
6. What are the major drivers of value creation for the organization?
7. For all of the above, how has this changed over time?

Predictive

> You Are Here

8. How much value does the organization expect to create?
9. How much value do capital providers (shareholders, if publicly traded) expect the organization to create?

> And Here

10. How much value does the organization expect to create by sector, product, service, distribution channel, process, and customer?

> And Here

11. What are the expectations related to the major drivers of value creation over time?

> And Here

12. What are the capital provider's expectations for the organization's peers? What are the peer's expectations for itself by sector, product, service, distribution channel, process, customer, and major drivers of value creation?
13. How do internal, peer, and capital provider expectations differ from current steady-state value creations?
14. For all of the above, how will this change over time?

EXHIBIT 10.2 The Questions

hockey-stick projections found in many strategic plans (see Exhibit 10.3).[2] The examples of value creation did not show any hockey sticks, did they? And one is not likely to find them. Because hockey sticks are what earnings may look like—but not value. Earnings may look like that when a new CEO comes on board, cleans house, incurs one-time charges, and then produces earnings increases year after year. Value creation is generally not like that—it's messier. There are bumps along the way, as the charts in Chapter 7 demonstrated.

Of course, to each constituent, in answer to this question, the meaning of value will differ. Many constituents will use their understanding of value

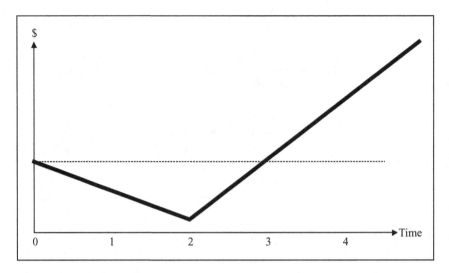

EXHIBIT 10.3 Typical Hockey Stick Forecast

drivers and of expected changes to help them predict the organization's value creation and what the organization will become in relation to them. The techniques we have discussed will also help the organization to develop the answers to this question.

The connection from the past to the future is change and improvement (see Chapter 9's "Improvement: Why Improvement Matters" section). To anticipate and develop more useful predictions can occur by using just one or two of the techniques we have discussed. Multiple approaches can make the predictions even more robust.

Even outside the world of Economic Value Management, organizations have known this. In the early 1980s, the "Magnolia Corporation" was installing a rigorous planning and budgeting discipline. As the structure for the process was being developed, the organization recognized the need for checks and balances on the numbers submitted. Sylvia, the head of budgeting, explains: "To set up the checks and balances we needed, we developed a series of schedules for the business units to complete. Generally, around June, we began the process with a schedule that asked the business units to project their staffing estimates for the remainder of the year and the next year on a month-by-month basis. We then checked these schedules against the unit's current staffing levels.

"Invariably," she smiled, "several business units planned to hire large numbers of staff, at unprecedented levels, over the next few months. Coincidentally, these large staffing increases would make the next year's request look comparatively small."

"As each month of the process went forward," she continued, "we would monitor the real staffing. Of course, they were never able to hire all the staff anticipated. Shortly after the staffing schedules were received, we would mail out a request for line item budgets. My unit would then take the salary and budget costs that were submitted and divide them by the staffing figures originally submitted. We actually found that, without saying no to the budgeting requests, by asking multiple questions and taking multiple approaches to the process, it was much easier for us to have conversations about what was reasonably likely to occur and to structure budgets without the fat or padding."

Similarly, in an October 9, 2000, article in the *New Yorker*, James Surowiecki discusses experiments that show that the more approaches to a problem, the better the final outcome would be.[3] He cites a common business school experiment where the professor asks each student to guess the number of jelly beans in a jar. While their individual guesses are highly inaccurate, the class average guess is, Surowiecki says, within 3% of the correct number.

In discussing the development of risk capital, we discussed how multiple approaches, working together, can help the organization arrive at a better answer. In predictions or forecasts of expectation, the same is true. The techniques outlined in the "Time" through "Applications of Metrics" sections that follow can be used by all constituents to understand the organization better and to understand value from their vantage point.

From a forecasting standpoint, there are many applications of these techniques. Mergers are an example where the business community has traditionally been a relatively poor judge of outcome. The use of these techniques can yield very positive results in providing the organization with better information for decisions—from merge, build, buy, acquire—down to day-to-day operational activities.

To answer these questions, the following is a review of some of the Metrics choices and uses we have discussed, following the format outlined on Exhibits 10.4 and 10.5.

Time

In making forecasts, one of the issues involved is determining the *forecast time horizon*, the period of time that can be forecast explicitly. In valuing into the future, the forecast beyond the explicit forecast horizon requires broad assumptions, including assumptions about whether value creation will remain steady, decline, and so on, and for how long. The longer the explicit forecast, the less important these assumptions are (since the further out in time they are, the less impact on present value they will have). Detailed discussions of typical assumptions used after the explicit forecast horizon can be found in other texts.[4]

Metric Characteristics:	From (Traditional Implementation)	To (Economic Value Management)
Time	Evaluative, Primarily Annual	Evaluative and Predictive, Variable Time Periods
Type of Capital	Debt and Equity	Multiple Types of Capital
Form of Metric	Dollars or Percents	Dollars, Percents, Standard Deviation, i.e., Multiple Forms
Types of Adjustments	Simple	Simple and Complex
Measurement and Management Perspectives:		
Constituent Focus	Shareholder	Alliance of Constituents
Integrating Metrics	None or Few	Multiple—Optimal Number
Integrating Techniques	None	Multiple
Applications of Metrics	Strategic, Valuation	Broad Applications

EXHIBIT 10.4 How Economic Value Management Differs: Evolution of Value Practices

"TexaTrust" was constructing incentive plans on a value basis and reviewing the market value analyses for a number of peers (see Market Value formula in Exhibit 9.20). "We found that time horizon issues did impact our results," said David, the project manager. "However, when we looked at it in total, with all the other information we had, we were able to choose time horizon assumptions that worked with the other data we had. It really is more art than science. Before just choosing the assumption, it is best to look at all the information you have. We have several industries we operate in. For each, there were different time horizon assumptions that made sense. The review itself sure helped us understand the industries better. My suggestion? Run the numbers using a variety of assumptions. With your past data in hand, you'll be able to tell when the assumption *fits* and what assumption to use."

Types of Capital

Multiple Forms of Capital. One way to better forecast an organization's future value is to carefully examine its capital. To what extent has the organization invested in human capital, for instance? What are the organization's investments in training? In R&D and innovation? What is the organization's risk profile?

All these questions related to capital provide vital insights into the organization's ability to create future value. They also provide the organization

Metric Characteristics:

Time	Types of Capital	Form of Metric	Types of Adjustments

※ Evaluative and/or predictive
※ Time horizon
	※ Debt or equity
	※ Equity
	※ Special case equity equivalents
	  – Human
	  – Customer
	  – Product
	※ Regulatory
	※ Risk
	※ Cost of capital
	※ Market value/ purchase price
	※ Taxes, dues
		※ Dollar
		※ Percentage
		※ Standard deviation
			※ Availability
			※ Complexity
			※ Fixed/changed boundaries
			※ Options value

Measurement and Management Perspectives:

Constituent Focus	Integration of Metrics	Integration of Techniques	Applications of Metrics

※ Community and external governance
※ Providers of capital
※ Suppliers
※ Consumers
※ Observers/ critics (see Exhibit 6.3)
	※ Value drivers (the value-based balanced scorecard)
	  – Relationship
	  – Process
	  – Choices
	※ Activity-based information
	  – Cost, revenue, capital
	※ TQM process measures
		※ Patterns of value creation
		  – Trend and regression analysis
		※ Volatility analyses
		※ Information Gap Analyses™
		※ Statistical prediction rules
		※ Market value analysis
		※ Pictures
		※ Scenario planning
		※ Monte Carlo simulations
		※ ValueMap™
			The Wheel™:
			※ Performance assessment
			※ Strategy
			※ Process and technology
			※ Organizational structure
			※ Rewards process
			※ Training and communication (see Exhibit 6.4)

EXHIBIT 10.5 Economic Value Management: Metric Choices and Uses

with better information about the impacts of actions like layoffs, for example, over time.

Constituent Focus: The Alliance

Constituent value and the ValueMap™ technique provide good information that help organizations and constituents to answer the question of how much value the organization expects to create. The organization's ability to hire top talent will be based on its ability to generate employee value. Similarly, customer value analyses—understanding how the organization is or is not creating value for the customer—and understanding the drivers of value from the customer's perspective contribute to better understanding the organization's ability to create value in the future.

Not only has this information been used to better forecast, organizations have also used it to create value in the future by developing a solid understanding of their customers and the products that they need.

Integration of Metrics

Understanding value drivers is another useful approach. One of the easiest and best ways to get started is to first develop a value driver tree. To do this, begin with the value calculation. Using value makes the technique much more robust than using traditional net income as the basis. Breaking the starting numbers into their financial components provides a useful picture as the organization begins to map the relationship between financial and activity drivers (see also Chapter 9's "Value Drivers" section). Next, it is important to gather the quantitative detail available to flesh out the value driver tree with quantitative detail for the past and the current state. Doing trees from both the past and the present allows the organization to witness what has changed, from a value standpoint, over time. The drivers that are used may include external drivers like the level of interest rates or consumer spending and internal drivers like prospects contacted. By breaking the numbers down for the past and current states, it is easier to understand what inputs matter most in the forecast. This allows those making the calculation of expected value to focus their efforts on the most important assumptions. (These activities are even more robust when performed in conjunction with patterns of value analyses and SPRs. See the following section on "Integration of Techniques," as well as Chapters 6 through 9.)

The next step is to forecast the impact of any changes on elements of the value driver tree due to a new initiative (or any anticipated external changes). (This is often performed by organizations in the context of a strategy change.) And finally, then, develop a value driver tree and calculate a value amount for the potential future state (see Exhibits 10.6 and 9.12).

"Complicorp" had just started its work in the area of economic value and had developed a calculation of value for its business when it began

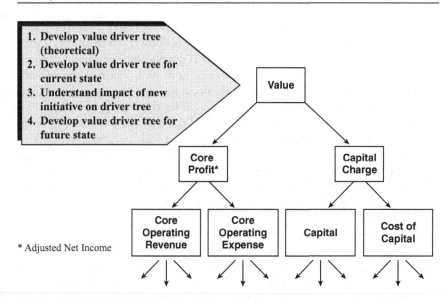

EXHIBIT 10.6 Value Driver Analysis: Getting Started Step by Step

contemplating a strategic change. Complicorp wanted to expand its business model to include a new product offering that was somewhat similar but not exactly like its current products. One of the major concerns that Harrison, the CFO, had about the new product offering was that it would require more capital than the existing products. Before deciding whether the new product would be a go or no go, Complicorp constructed a value driver tree for its current state. Next, the organization began to contemplate the changes that the new initiative would bring, including the additional capital, the sales level that would be required at breakeven value, and so on. As the discussion grew louder related to the expense base required to make the sales happen, Tom, the operations manager, spoke up. "What about pricing?" he asked. "By changing pricing in a minor way—and this product has additional features created for a select audience—we can do more to make this product viable than 50 changes to lower capital or pushing the sales force too hard on the front end." Using the value drivers tree with the quantitative components helped the organization to *see* the drivers or factors that were most important. While the organization had been spending a lot of focus and energy concerned about appropriate capital levels, they discovered (via hypothesis and testing) that pricing was fairly elastic, especially in their new product set, and that it was more important for them to focus on the additional value the new products provided, that warranted the price differential, than on expenses, or capital, or a given kind of sales effort. The organization test marketed the product. It was highly successful and created significant value in the first year alone.

The value driver technique helps an organizations better understand the value the organization expects to create in the future, given on-the-table initiatives (see Exhibit 10.2, Question 8). This same technique can be applied to the organization's thinking about the value it will create at the sector, product, service, distribution-channel, process, and customer level (see Exhibit 10.2, Question 10). The approach causes the organization to think thoughtfully about its value drivers and their relative importance over time (see Exhibit 10.2, Question 11). It also provides a way to develop an understanding of peer expectations related to value creation for its organization, sector, product, service, distribution channel, process, customer, and major value drivers and to put those understandings into a broader context. The answers to these questions help provide partial answers to Questions 13 and 14 as well (see Exhibit 10.2).

Value drivers are an important tool from a constituent perspective as well, both for understanding the organization and understanding value creation at the constituent level. (See Chapter 9's section on "Value Drivers" "Application of Metrics," subsection "Training and Communications.") For constituents, an ordered, prioritized set of value drivers may form the basis for the calculation of value, with importance levels assigned to each driver. Constituents can thus use the techniques to predict changes in the organization's value creation and in the organization's creation of value for them. For employees, for example, this can mean using the process to evaluate their current interaction and what they expect it to be in the future. (For example, see Exhibit 10.7.) From the employee's perspective, they may structure their calculation with a floor and a cap (0.7 to 1.3 in this case) that outline the most likely outcomes (80% to 90% likely). The employee can then compare the current state and expectations with alternative situations.

From the organization's perspective, the information helps them to quantify the benefits and trade-offs of items like training and learning, or span of control and work environment, from the employee's perspective.

Investors can also use value drivers to help create an expectation of where the value the organization will create in the future may come from. Their overall expectation, in terms of value creation, is observable in market prices, which will be discussed in "The Remaining Predictive Questions" section in this chapter. (See also Chapter 9's "Why Improvement Matters" section and Exhibit 9.20.)

Integration of Techniques

Multiple techniques help answer the first set of predictive questions: How much value does the organization expect to create (Exhibit 10.2, Question 8), and how much value does the organization expect to create by sector, product, service, distribution channel, process, and customer (Exhibit 10.2, Question 10)? What are the expectations related to the major value drivers

Organization

Evaluation of value drivers—expected changes:

    Cutbacks on training and travel costs

    Division shutdown and layoff in part of company

    One-year salary freeze

Develop expected impacts on organization's value creation including morale and short-term disruption impacts.

Develop proforma expected value creation for the organization.

Employee   1 = par   range = .7–1.3

	Relative Weights	Now	One Year	Five Years	Range 0.7	Range 1.3
Training and Learning/Growth	0.2	1.1	0.7	0.9		
Pay/Compensation and Benefits	0.6	1	0.9	1		
Span of Control	0.1	0.8	1.1	1.2		
General Work Environment	0.1	$\dfrac{1.1}{1.01}$	$\dfrac{1}{0.89}$	$\dfrac{1}{1}$		
Value Neutral at Par in Dollar Terms (1,000s)	$ 40	$ 44	$ 28	$ 36	$ 28	$ 52
	$120	$120	$108	$120	$ 84	$156
	$ 20	$ 16	$ 22	$ 24	$ 14	$ 26
	$\dfrac{\$\ 20}{\$200}$	$\dfrac{\$\ 22}{\$202}$	$\dfrac{\$\ 20}{\$178}$	$\dfrac{\$\ 20}{\$200}$	$\dfrac{\$\ 14}{\$140}$	$\dfrac{\$\ 26}{\$260}$

EXHIBIT 10-7   Employee Perspective

over time (Exhibit 10.2, Question 11), and what are the peer's expectations related to its organization, sector, product, service, distribution channel, process, and customer (Exhibit 10.2, second half of Question 12)?

Patterns of Value Creation. In using patterns of value creation to forecast expectations for the future, it is useful to study the mathematical components of the patterns. One way to do this is to decompose the information. "It is generally believed that time series data are composed of four elements: Trend (T), Cyclicality (C), Seasonality (S) and Irregularity (I) . . . [and] that the four elements yield time series data through a multiplicative model T X C X S X I . . . [where] trend is the long run general direction of the business climate over periods of several years . . . Cycles are patterns of highs and lows through which data flow over time periods of more than one year. Seasonal effects are the shorter cycles which occur in time periods of less than one year. Other rapid changes or 'bleeps' in the data . . . , referred to as irregular fluctuations, can occur in even shorter time frames than seasonal effects."[5] With this information, the organization can decompose and better understand the past patterns for value creation. This understanding can help inform the true nature of value drivers that in turn can be used to provide useful expectations for the future. Regression models can also be used to discern trends in the patterns of value creation and the relevant value drivers.

As discussed related to risk capital, understanding the patterns of value creation and causality can be important in discerning risk and potential outcomes as well. Clearly, value numbers have the information content to provide useful information that the gently sloping, ever increasing earnings numbers do not. (See Exhibits 7.7 and 7.17, which demonstrate this.)

"ConsumersBank" applied the patterns of value creation technique to its credit card unit. Before developing economic profit and studying the patterns of value creation, ConsumersBank had believed that their credit card unit was becoming more and more profitable and was rewarding its managers as such. Maxwell, the CEO, said: "We had built forecasts into our planning processes based on these assumptions. After developing value numbers, we had a much better handle on the true patterns of value creation and what the drivers of the business were. These analyses gave us a better way to forecast the realistic outcomes for the business going forward."

"It also gave us ideas concerning the strategies that would most improve the performance of the credit card area," said Ben, head of the credit card unit. "This included a reassessment of acquisition strategies, geographic valuations, and credit policies. The patterns of value creation analyses impacted not only our ability to forecast but also to optimize our future."

"Mortgage World" used the patterns of value creation to better understand and forecast the impacts of economic scenarios (among other factors) on their servicing and origination businesses. Again, the outcome was two pronged: a better assessment in terms of expected value creation *and* the ability to develop well informed strategies and tactics.

When pattern of value creation analyses are combined with peer reviews (second half of Question 12 in Exhibit 10.2), they are extremely powerful tools in improving forecast quality.

Volatility Analyses. Volatility analyses can be used stand-alone or even more effectively in combination with the value drivers and patterns of value creation analyses to answer the first set of predictive questions. To do this, the value that has been created is studied in as much detail as possible over as long a time horizon as possible. Detailed line items are studied as well. Standard deviations are calculated over different time horizons—annually; rolling two-, four-, and six- year; and entire history, for example. Analyses of the standard deviations themselves provide very useful perspectives about the organization; sector, product, and the like; the context of value creation; and their interactions.

"Whirledwide Industries" used the techniques of patterns along with volatility studies. They calculated value for their sectors and plotted their results. In addition, they calculated the volatilities for the sectors and line items within the sectors over a long time horizon. (To gain perspective, they made the calculations over one-year, rolling two-year, and the entire history.) As a result, Jorge, the CEO, said: "We were alerted to a major downturn in one of our sectors long before the results began to develop in the financials. What appeared as ripples in the value numbers, placed in context, was quite dramatic and signaled a shift in industry dynamics, barely noticeable by any other means. This information allowed us to better forecast our future prospects in this sector (Question 10, Exhibit 10.1) and reassess our previous risk analyses. While long-range trends showed the business as low risk, the information contained in the volatility analyses, showed different behaviors. Upon closer examination, it revealed industry changes that were not going to go away and would impact the value of this sector into the future. The volatility analysis helped us assess the relative value of this sector going forward, its riskiness and informed our choices related to resource allocations in the future as well."

"Tricolor Automobile Association" used the same technique, slicing its business by geography as well. These analyses revealed concerns in Japan, although according to all accounting reports at the time, Japan appeared to be a healthy growth area. The risk/reward relationship was reassessed using value calculations in conjunction with volatility analyses. The analyses suggested caution in extrapolations before the accounting results showed any negative trends. "As a result," Alicia, the project manager said: "We were better able to understand value creation for this sector into the future. Because Japan is such an important area for us, it impacted our projections for the entire firm as well. Without the volatility analyses, there would have been blind spots in our understanding of future value creation. Potential weaknesses in our earlier forecasts were clear when we saw the value and volatility analyses."

Information Gap Analyses™. Information Gap Analyses™ can also be used to understand more about the predictive value of a forecast. One technique, obviously, is to examine forecasting error itself (that is, the differences between forecasts and the actual values for a similar time period). Another is to use Information Gap Analyses™ to help quantify the impact of lack of good information—whether caused by no data, poor quality of data, lack of availability of data, timeliness of data, inconsistency of data, or inconsistent or invalid manipulation of data. These analyses can be done in conjunction with the ValueMap™ by identifying the areas of value drivers for which the organization has little or no information and estimating the impact of no, poor quality, lack of availability, and so on.

"Fawlty Pharmaceuticals" reviewed the information gaps for those required to forecast financial results. They discovered issues in terms of quality and availability which, when addressed, would make Fawlty's forecasting process not only more efficient but also more accurate.

Some organizations have used these techniques to forecast the benefits of technology projects. "Studley Stewright & Sons" used Information Gap Analyses™ to not only forecast the benefits but also to create momentum behind the project itself. As Melvin, the project manager explained: "Some of the quantification was straightforward, such as the impacts of duplicative staff or multiple systems. Others were part art, such as quantifying the decision impacts."[6] Organizations that use these processes help inform their future expectations of value for their own organization, its sector, and so on, and maximize the benefits of their technology investments and thus influence future value as well.

Statistical Prediction Rules. One common form of SPR used in forecasting is regression analysis, where past data are used to predict future outcomes.[7] These math algorithms can be used to understand the relative importance of value drivers and to obtain an assessment of risk in the future, for example. As with the jelly bean exercise, using multiple tests can often improve the quality of the results obtained. It is also important to assess the accuracy of the tests. To this end it is recommended that the probability of true positives be plotted against false positives: The objective with any test is to have as many true positives compared to false positives as possible.[8] These studies of diagnostic accuracy can be used not only in reviewing one diagnostic, but multiple diagnostics as well. These studies can help the organization to develop useful information about the predictive validity of certain criteria and the benefits of multiple diagnoses, particularly where the prediction really matters. In our context, when value creation is at stake.

The steps for using SPRs are shown on Exhibit 10.8. One way organizations have made effective use of SPRs is in the arena of marketing and the prediction of customer behavior, which ultimately is reflected in any estimate of future value. Another has been in the area of risk capital.[9]

"Scotty Transportation" used SPRs to forecast sales pipeline size and content using economic indicators (themselves the result of SPRs), marketing campaign, and demographic information. These SPRs were used to both forecast future business and plan staffing needs to maximize value.

Pictures. Pictures provide information that can be processed by the human brain in ways that the output from other techniques cannot. All of the techniques discussed can benefit from the use of pictures. In addition, raw data placed in pictorial form can often yield significant informational benefits.[10]

Scenario Planning. Rather than simply use forecast techniques that extrapolate from the past, scenario planning is an approach to envision possible futures. Economic Value Management helps organizations to broaden the context of their thinking to include scenarios and big picture changes they might otherwise not be aware of. This is critical to the success of effective scenario planning (see Exhibit 2.2). With Economic Value Management, the de Mello bus shades (referred to in Chapter 1) are pulled up. Awareness is expanded. Better forecasts and, thus decisions, are the result.

Monte Carlo Simulations. Mathematical techniques like Monte Carlo Simulations can also be used to model potential futures. Incorporating volatility analyses, these financial models are particularly useful in understanding ranges

1. Select areas of interest where robust tool set is value added
2. Develop a series of diagnoses
3. Develop assessment of joint probabilities or probable interactions
4. Evaluate predictive power of rules over time: Develop true positive versus false positive graphs and other measures of accuracy
5. Update rules with changes and information based on testing and new information from other techniques

EXHIBIT 10.8 Statistical Prediction Rules: Getting Started Step by Step

of potential outcomes critical to value-based rewards processes. Rewards processes represent a unique interaction between the organization and internal suppliers. As discussed in earlier chapters, the risk appetite of internal suppliers may be very different from other constituents and their ability to diversify may be limited as well. Value information does not follow a smooth, manipulated path. To pay internal suppliers based on a quite variable reality when their ability to diversify is limited could cause serious problems were it not for the careful structuring of value-based reward plans. Economic Value Management reward processes that use this technique help to ensure more accurate forecasts *and* better compensation plan structures that take potential volatility into consideration. (See "Comparing Expectations: The Market's Expectations and The Remaining Predictive Questions" for additional discussion.)

The ValueMap™. Since the ValueMap™ includes information on all constituents, it also helps to broaden scenario plans and to promote consideration of possibilities that may not currently represent a strong concern but could be of critical importance in the future.

Applications of Metrics

All the techniques outlined help organizations answer the questions of future value creation for themselves and their peers. They also help an organization to make better decisions in terms of fixed and changing boundary analyses such as those listed in Exhibit 10.9. They help organizations to

---

Fixed Boundary Analyses (Examples)

► What distribution channels to use?

► What organizations structure is best?

► What work environment to have?

► How to price products?

► What marketing efforts to use?

► Where to allocate resources (within current operation)?

► How to operate?

► What risks to mitigate?

► What work to outsource (on a specific basis)?

(continued)

EXHIBIT 10.9   Boundary Analyses

EXHIBIT 10.9　　Boundary Analyses *(Continued)*

Changing Boundary Analyses (Examples)
▶ What activities represent core work of the organization and, on the broadest level, what work should be done elsewhere? ▶ The impact on current operations of expansion or exit, purchase or sale.

structure their work environments, marketing efforts, and operations. They help them to decide where to allocate resources. The answers to the questions provide insights into tactics and strategies, processes and technologies.

"MorningLight Inc." used the answers to these questions to clearly understand the impact of their strategies on future value creation. Using value calculations for their strategies allowed MorningLight to understand the potential market value of their efforts and to discern, therefore, if a bidder were suggesting a fair price.

The techniques are also critically important in structuring rewards processes and communicating the impact of future activities both internally and externally. "Sunrise Bank of Michigan" used the answers to these questions to frame their rewards process, in a way that is similar to that shown in Exhibit 7.22. These analyses of both peer and the Sunrise Bank's own value creation became essential inputs to the reward plan they developed.

COMPARING EXPECTATIONS: THE MARKET'S EXPECTATIONS AND THE REMAINING PREDICTIVE QUESTIONS

How much value do capital providers expect the organization to create? (Exhibit 10.10, Question 9)? What are the capital provider's expectations for the organization's peers (first half of Question 12)? How do internal, peer, and capital provider expectations differ from current steady-state value creation (Question 13)? For all of the above, how will this change over time (Question 14)?

Market prices help provide the answers to these questions (see Exhibit 10.11). *Market value analyses,* the last of the techniques to be discussed (see Exhibit 10.4), answer these questions and provide a way for the organization and its constituents to understand expectations for future economic values. For a given market value for the organization and its peers, the expectations in terms of future improvements built into the stock price can be quantified.

Evaluative

1. Has the organization added value? How much?
2. How does this compare to the organization's peers and competitors?
3. Has the organization been managed such that each sector has added value?
4. Has the organization been managed such that each product, service, distribution channel, or process added value?
5. Has the organization been managed such that each customer relationship added value?
6. What are the major drivers of value creation for the organization?
7. For all of the above, how has this changed over time?

Predictive

8. How much value does the organization expect to create?

> You Are Here

9. How much value do capital providers (shareholders, if publicly traded) expect the organization to create?
10. How much value does the organization expect to create by sector, product, service, distribution channel, process, and customer?
11. What are the expectations related to the major drivers of value creation over time?

> And Here

12. What are the capital provider's expectations for the organization's peers? What are the peer's expectations for itself by sector, product, service, distribution channel, process, customer, and major drivers of value creation?

> And Here

13. How do internal, peer, and capital provider expectations differ from current steady-state value creations?

> And Here

14. For all of the above, how will this change over time?

EXHIBIT 10.10 The Questions

While this yields a great deal of information, *market value analyses are too little used.*

Obviously, investors will want to assess the extent to which the market price in their judgment will yield an adequate return. Understanding the market's price, what it means in terms of expected value creation, and how that compares to their own estimations of the organization's future value creation should be reviewed before making *any* buy or sell decisions. If an investor's estimates differ from the market's, this may represent a buy or sell signal to the investor (a buy if they anticipate more value creation than the market; a sell, if they forecast less value creation).

			Present Value of		Present Value of	
Market Value (a)	=	Capital (b) +	Current Economic (c) +		Future Improvements (d)	
			Value in Perpetuity		in Economic Value	

EXHIBIT 10.11   Market Value Formula

Because, as with any time series, there can be blips in the data, it is important to choose the time frame over which to review market value and the present value of economic profit in the equation. (See the formula in Exhibit 10.11.) Some organizations decide to use information that involves averages over a time period, rather than using points in time, to eliminate the irregularities in the data. Organizations may use the most recent market value or an average over the last year, for example. Rather than performing one calculation for the current period, taking snapshots over the past can be quite illuminating in understanding not only what capital providers currently expect, but also what they expected in the past, and the patterns, if any, of those expectations and how they have changed over time.

"Coughee Inc." performed this analysis for itself and its peers. Whether it used a 5-, 10-, or 20-year or perpetuity assumptions for future improvements in value creation (item d in Exhibit 10.11), Coughee could not understand how the market could be holding such large expectations for value improvement. "As it turned out," said John, the CEO, "We were right to be alarmed. In fact, our firm and our competitors did face market declines. None of us were able to maintain the improvements embedded in the market's forecasts. At Coughee, we were just happy to have some advance warning. Because of the analysis, it did not catch us by surprise, as it did some of our competitors."

While current market prices represent investors' current expectations of value creation in the future, to continue to hold a stock, investors expect even more! They expect a cost of capital return on their investment. To do that means that organizations must do more than maintain the current stock price (i.e., meet current market value requirements). They must measure investor's future requirements as well, calculated as a cost of capital return on market value.[11] Here, finally, we have the use of market value capital. These future market value requirements can be plugged into market value (a) in the formula on Exhibit 10.11 to understand the implications in the future for (d) improvements in economic value.

The answer to the question of what capital providers expect currently, and in the future, can be informative to everyone. Organizations can understand the "gap" between current strategies and market expectations for value improvements. They can also perform Information Gap Analyses™ to understand the impact of lack of disclosure on market value. As an example of this impact, on November 12, 2001, Bethany McLean wrote an article in

Fortune, "Ken, Lay Your Cards on the Table." While Enron had other issues that we now know about, here were the perceptions driving stock price at the time. "In the past two months, Enron's stock has sunk another 60% to $16 amid concern that the company's murky disclosure may be a sign of deeper business problems. A conference call that Lay held on October 23, ostensibly to reassure skittish investors, was widely regarded as a disaster. Enron 'wiggled, squirmed and gave a bunch of no answers,' as one listener put it. Even formerly docile sell side analysts are turning hostile. After the call, Prudential's Carol Coale downgraded Enron to a sell 'not because of things that we know, but because of things we potentially don't know.'"[12] The impacts of lack of disclosure on market value represent a diminution of expectation because, as McLean states, "The company's murky disclosure may be a sign of deeper business problems."

Suppliers can use market value analyses to discern customer "gap," the difference between current value creation by the customer organization and future expectation for value creation. And then target their products to help close the "gap."

From a community and external governance standpoint, understanding market views of a given industry can be very helpful. For example, what do declines in the market values of the automobile, housing, or banking industries mean from a public policy standpoint? The author was asked to speak at an FDIC conference to address just this point for the financial services industry: "Incorporating Market Information into Financial Supervision."

Exhibits 10.12 through 10.19 show examples of market value analyses performed by different organizations. Exhibit 10.12 shows the calculated market value breakdown (see Exhibit 10.11 for the formula) of three organizations, "UniversalTin," "MegaGold," and "SilverGalaxy."[13] All three are in the same industry and of similar size. The line on the graph represents the market value for each of the organizations. The bars represent the three components of market value: capital, the present value of current economic value in perpetuity, and the present value of future improvements in economic value. As Exhibit 10.12 shows, UniversalTin and MegaGold both have positive values for all three components. Because SilverGalaxy's current economic value is negative, the present value of current economic value in perpetuity is also negative.

Marie, the project manager for the market value analysis, said: "One of the first things we observed when we reviewed UniversalTin, MegaGold, and SilverGalaxy was that while the market values for UniversalTin and MegaGold are fairly similar, UniversalTin uses much less capital, generates more economic value, and is expected by the market to improve its economic value even more than its peers in the future. We dug further to look at UniversalTin's strategies because they must be doing something right!"

Exhibit 10.13 represents a market value analysis for "Tinitin," "Minygold," "Silverspot," and "Microsteel." Marie explains: "All four are in the

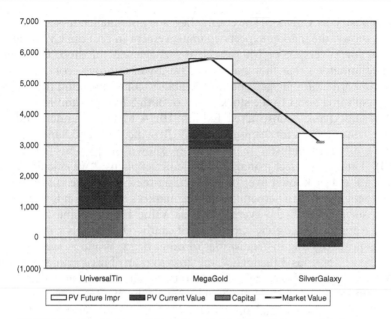

EXHIBIT 10.12 UniversalTin, MegaGold, SilverGalaxy—Market Value Breakdown

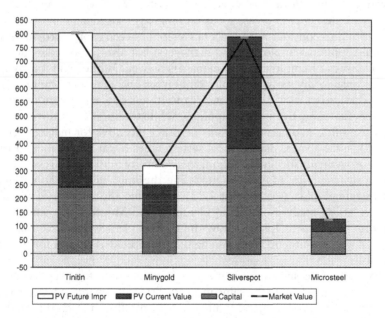

EXHIBIT 10.13 Tinitin, Minygold, Silverspot, Microsteel—Breakdown of Market Value

same industry as UniversalTin et al.; they are just smaller in size." As the exhibit shows, the market expects *no* improvement in economic value going forward for Silverspot or Microsteel. If management of those firms have strategic initiatives that they can execute and will improve economic value going forward *and* management has credibility, communicating those plans could result in a boost to the stock prices of both Silverspot and Microsteel.

"BenedictBank" constructed Exhibit 10.14 to better understand the market value analysis for "SunsetSavings." (BenedictBank and SunsetSavings are in a different industry than the firms shown on Exhibits 10.12 and 10.13). Tim, the project manager at Benedict explains: "We calculated the market value breakdown over time including the capital, the current value of economic profit into perpetuity, and the market's expectation for improvement associated with the average market value for that time period. As shown, SunsetSavings grew capital significantly. During this time period, this was primarily due to acquisitions of other firms. While Sunset's market value grew in periods 3 through 5, the growth is attributed primarily to the growth in the size of the organization, rather than increasing expectations for the future. Exhibit 10.15 shows a review of the market expectations for improvement versus actual improvement that we did on a year-by-year basis. As shown, the market's expectation for improvement each year was relatively stable compared to the actual results of the firm."

This has implications, of course, for reward systems. Year over year, true operating results *will* vary considerably. Economic Value Management reward systems are designed to create focus on long-term sustainable improvement in value and to consider not only a fair share between capital providers and internal suppliers (employees and managers) but also to consider the constituent issues of employees and managers as well. While capital providers may be able to diversify, generally employees and managers cannot. This means that the true volatility of an organization's operations cannot be easily diversified away by internal suppliers. While traditional incentive systems might use smoothed earnings results (another incentive for management to smooth), since a value management system bases rewards on value creation and improvements in value creation, this volatility must be addressed in the reward structure. In addition to modeling the impacts under an organization's strategic plan (see Exhibit 7.22), modeling the impacts of the plan using volatility analyses, scenario planning, and Monte Carlo simulations help organizations to forecast how the reward plans will impact employee and manager constituents. Establishing the appropriate risk level for the plan is critical.

Exhibit 10.16 shows the market value breakdown for "PridefillBank," a more successful firm in the same industry. Pridefill generates positive value in all years and grows capital gradually over the five-year time period. As Exhibit 10.17 shows, they also improved each year. Again, notice how the

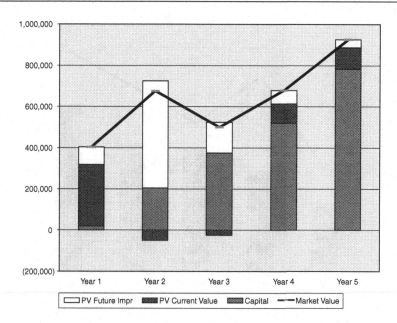

EXHIBIT 10.14   SunsetSavings: 5-Year Review of Market Value

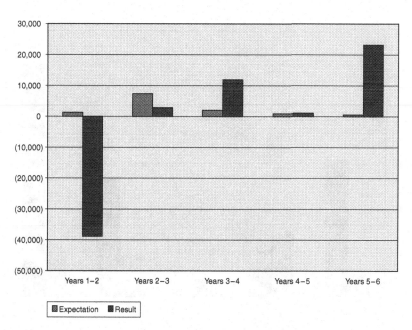

EXHIBIT 10.15   SunsetSavings: 5-Year Improvement Comparison: Expectation versus Result

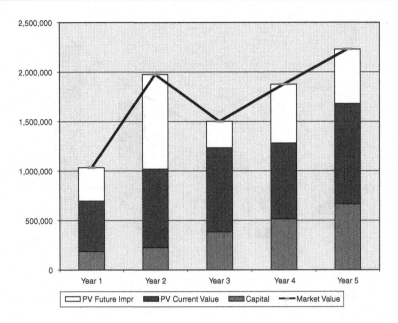

EXHIBIT 10.16 PridefillBank: 5-Year Market Value Breakdown

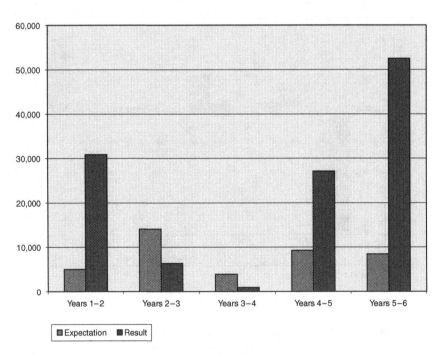

EXHIBIT 10.17 PridefillBank's Expected Improvement versus Result

pattern of actual improvement is much more volatile than the expectation built into the different market values for each period.

To contrast, in Exhibit 10.18 "TreatlessSavings" shows another firm in the same industry that consistently destroys value. (In year 4, the market even had a negative future improvement expectation.) Exhibit 10.19 shows this organization's improvement pattern vis-à-vis expectation.

How do nontraded firms or sectors put expected value creation in context? One way is to benchmark against peers (see Exhibit 10.20). Many organizations find ways to develop reasonable data sources and come to new insights in the process. In addition, organizations can use reasonable approximations, which they can test and feed back into the system over time.

As noted in Chapter 7's "Peers and Competitors" section, whatever is done will represent a group of information for the survivors. For some industries, on a relative basis, survival is a tough standard. "Marchment Papers" had this issue as it developed market expectations for one of its sectors. Each year the pool of stand-alone traded entities, from which market information could be gleaned, shrank. As it did, the prospects for the remaining players improved, increasing expectations for the future.

"Endersons" was in a very cyclical business. When organizations in that business improved their value creation during peaks in the cycle, market

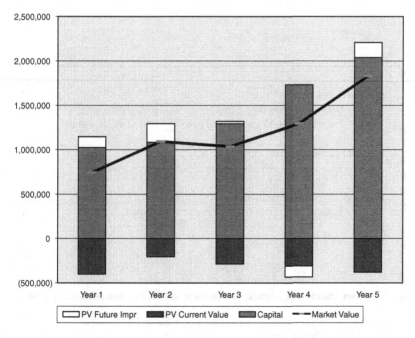

EXHIBIT 10.18 Treatless Saving's 5-Year Market Value Breakdown

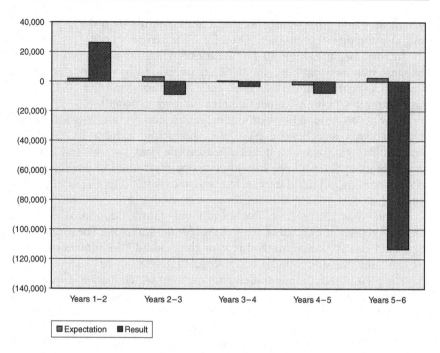

EXHIBIT 10.19 Treatless Saving's Expected Improvement versus Result

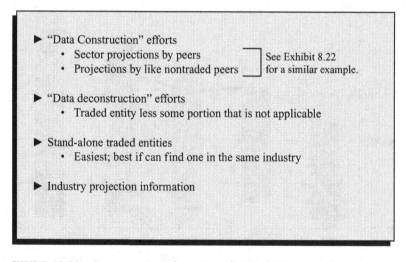

EXHIBIT 10.20 Expectation Information for Both Nontraded
Organizations or Sectors of Organizations

values did not shift upward. Rather the market expected the troughs to come. And when the troughs hit and value creation was low or negative, the market anticipated the turnaround in the cycle as well.

Understanding the organization's expectations, those of its peers and of capital providers, gives organizations and everyone better information to make decisions and to create better budgets and plans, grounded in reality and the potential for what can be.

Drivers, start your engines!

NOTES

1. As Chapters 6 through 9 showed, understanding the past can provide important insights for better understanding the future, which in turn produces better decisions. And better decisions produce superior, value-creating results. All decisions are based on forecasts, on estimations of how changes may impact the future, on cause and effect. Better answers to the predictive questions, then, are directly linked to better results, which create value for the organization and its constituents.

2. Hockey stick projections are popular. Promise low for now, then it is easier to overdeliver later. (Get paid well as a result!) And promise that the far-off future will be glorious.

3. James Surowiecki, "Markets Always Outsmart Mavens," *New Yorker,* October 9, 2000.

4. See David S. Young and Stephen F. O'Byrne, *EVA® and Value Based Management: A Practical Guide to Implementation,* New York: McGraw-Hill, 2001; and Tom Copeland, Tim Koller, and Jack Murrin, *Valuation: Measuring and Managing the Value of Companies,* New York: John Wiley and Sons, 1995.

5. Ken Black, *Business Statistics: Contemporary Decision Making,* St. Paul, MN: West Publishing Company, 1997, p. 738. Not only is this text written clearly, throughout the book there are breakout boxes that describe ethical uses of statistics, important in stewardship and clearly understanding the results.

6. *Made to Measure,* Fall 2001, pp. 29–36. eCFO provides some interesting perspectives on quantifying technology investments.

7. John Smets, Robyn Dames, and John Monahan, "Better Decisions through Science," *Scientific American,* October 2000, pp. 82–87. This article discusses the use of SPRs to make decisions and to determine "whether or not a certain condition exists or will occur."

8. Ibid., pp. 84–86.

9. For example, Dr. Eric Falkenstein's private company risk models developed for Moodys.

10. For more information, the following books are recommended: William S. Cleveland, *The Elements of Graphing Data* (1993) and *Visualizing Data* (1994), both from Hobart Press, Summit, NJ; and Edward R. Tufte, *The Visual Display*

of *Quantitative Information* (2001) and *Envisioning Information* (1990), both from Graphics Press.

11. For further information on this topic, see also: David S. Young and Stephen F. O'Byrne, *EVA® and Value Based Management: A Practical Guide to Implementation.* New York: McGraw-Hill, 2001; Tom Copeland, Tim Koller, and Jack Murrin, *Valuation: Measuring and Managing the Value of Companies,* New York: John Wiley and Sons, 1995; G. Bennett Stewart, III, *The Quest For Value,* New York: Harper Business, 1991; and Bartley J. Madden, *CFROI Valuation: A Total System Approach to Valuing the Firm,* Oxford, UK: Butterworth Heinemann, 1999.

12. Bethany McLean, "Ken, Lay Your Cards on the Table," *Fortune,* November 12, 2001, pp. 37–38.

13. These calculations were made using equity capital. To see the derivations of the formulas in detail, see *EVA® and Value Based Management* (note 4) pp. 308–318.

afterword

This book provides a look at some of the issues, applications, and techniques in Economic Value Management. It encourages the reader to remove unnecessary constraints that do not serve the decision-making process by eliminating the status quo of conflicting measures. It encourages the reader to dig. You may not know what you will find, but Economic Value Management is antithetical to avoidance. It is a way of intent and awareness. And it recognizes that everyone has a role to play.

This book touches briefly on what those roles are and recognizes the joint effort it can take to lift the shades of the de Mello bus and to see something very different for the very first time. With the bus shades lifted, there is no longer the illusion of neat, tidy, upwardly sloping earnings. With the bus shades pulled up, the scenery is always changing. Economic Value Management asks that, for the sake of stewardship, we confront this reality and, by doing that, reinvent who we are and move closer to our vision of what we want to be.

In another bus story in the same book, de Mello discusses teaching and learning: "Imagine a group of tourists in a bus. The shades of the bus are down and they don't see or hear or touch or smell a single thing from the strange exotic country that they are passing through, while all the while their guide chatters away, giving them what he thinks is a vivid description of the smells, sounds and sights of the world outside. The only things they will experience are the images that his words create in their heads."[1]

It is my fervent hope that rather than a bus tour guide, this book is the brochure that will cause you to buy a bus ticket, pull up the shades, and look outside for yourself, experience the digging and the discovery, and really see.

---

1. Anthony de Mello, *The Way to Love: The Last Meditations of Anthony de Mello*, New York: Doubleday, 1992.

index